垣野内成美 &ことりくらぶ
原案/アルゴ・ピクチャーズ

DALLIA THE VAMPIRE
ダリア ザ ヴァンパイア

DAHLIA
THE VAMPIRE
ダリア ザ ヴァンパイア

Contents

act.1
レ イ ニ イ　ブ ラ ッ ド
RAINY BLOOD
3

act.2
サロメは霧の中に
SALOME *into the mist*
33

act.3
チ ャ イ ナ　ブ ル ー
CHINA BLUE
131

- - - - - - - - - - - - - - -

ダ リ ア　ク ラ ブ
DAHLIA CLUB
189

第1幕 act.1 RAINY BLOOD

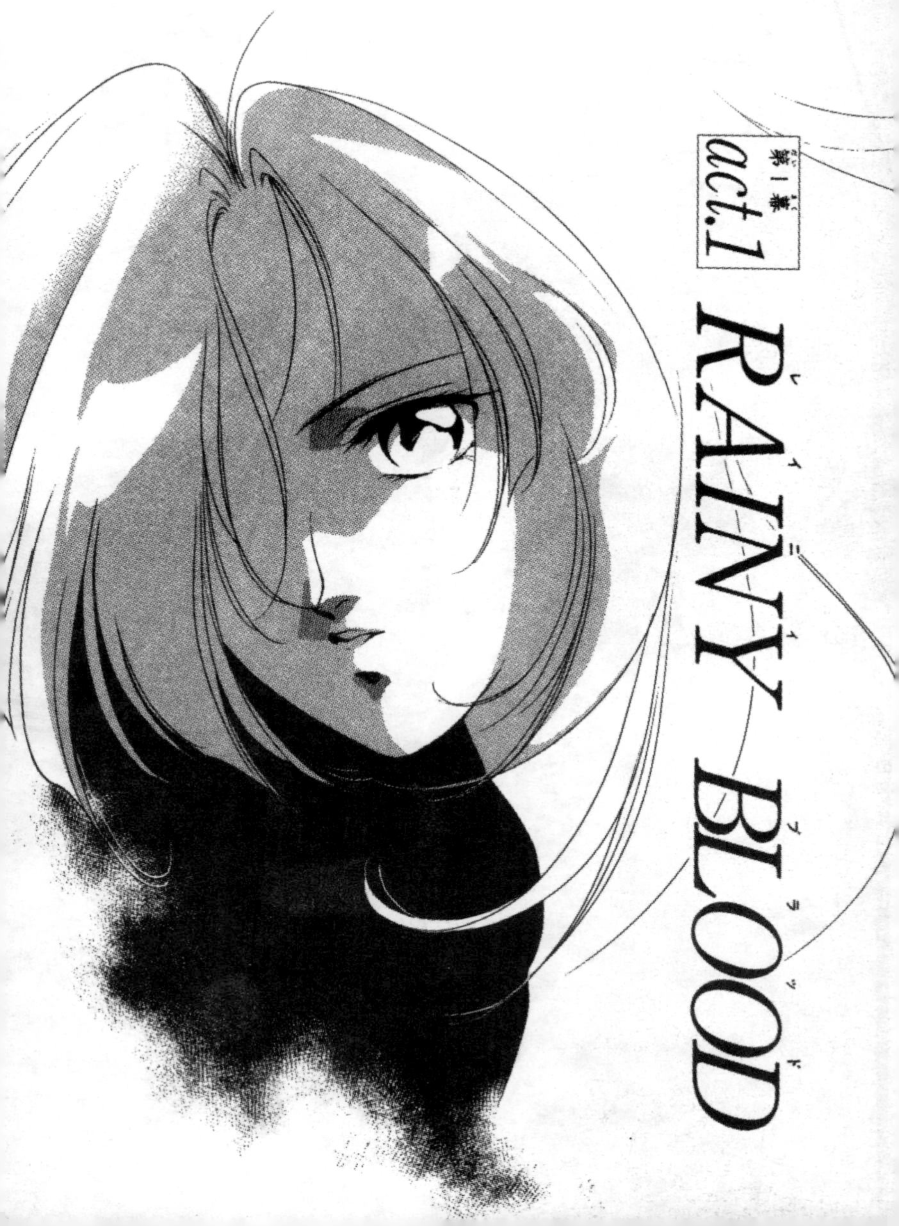

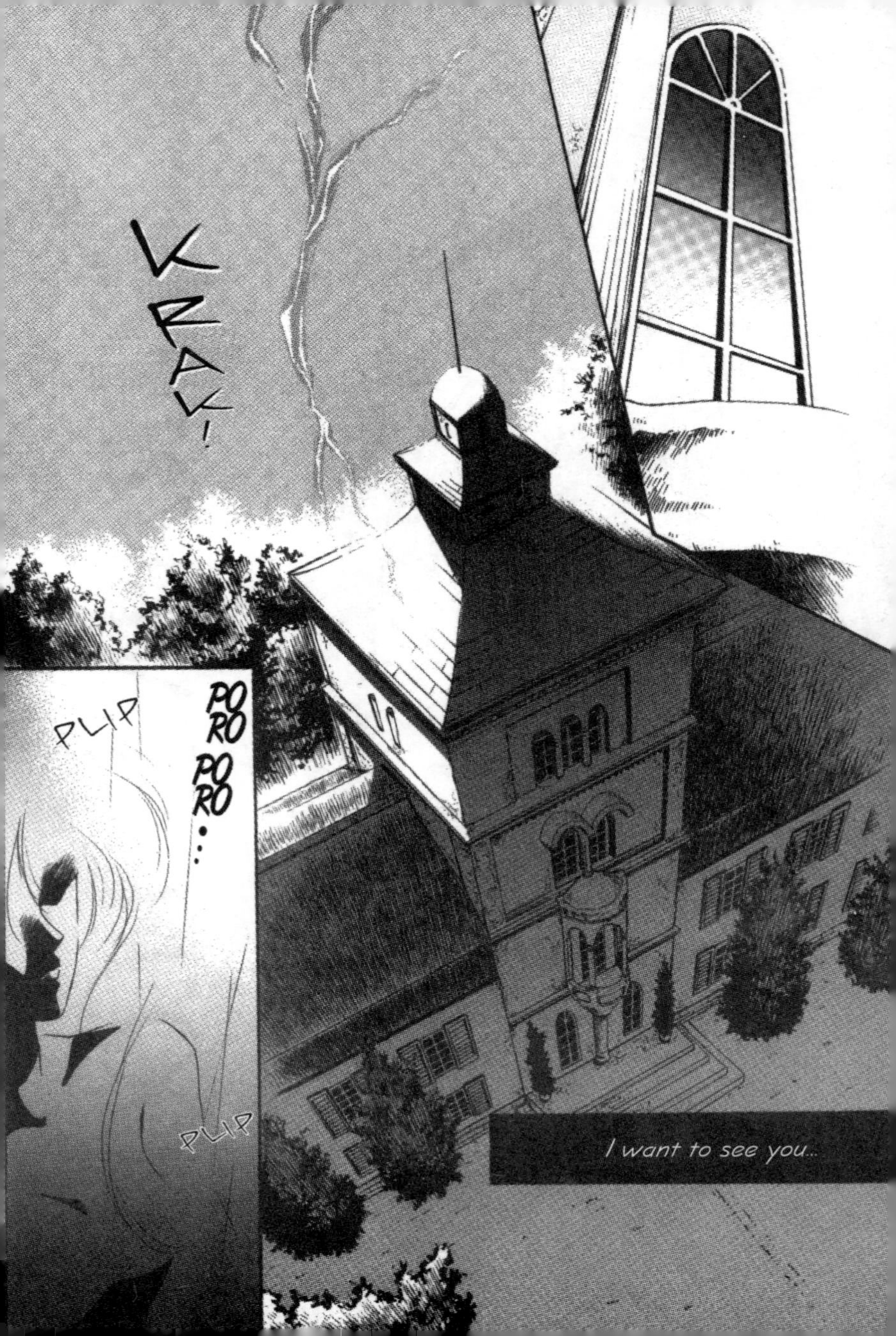
KRAK!
PORO PORO...
PLIP
PLIP
I want to see you...

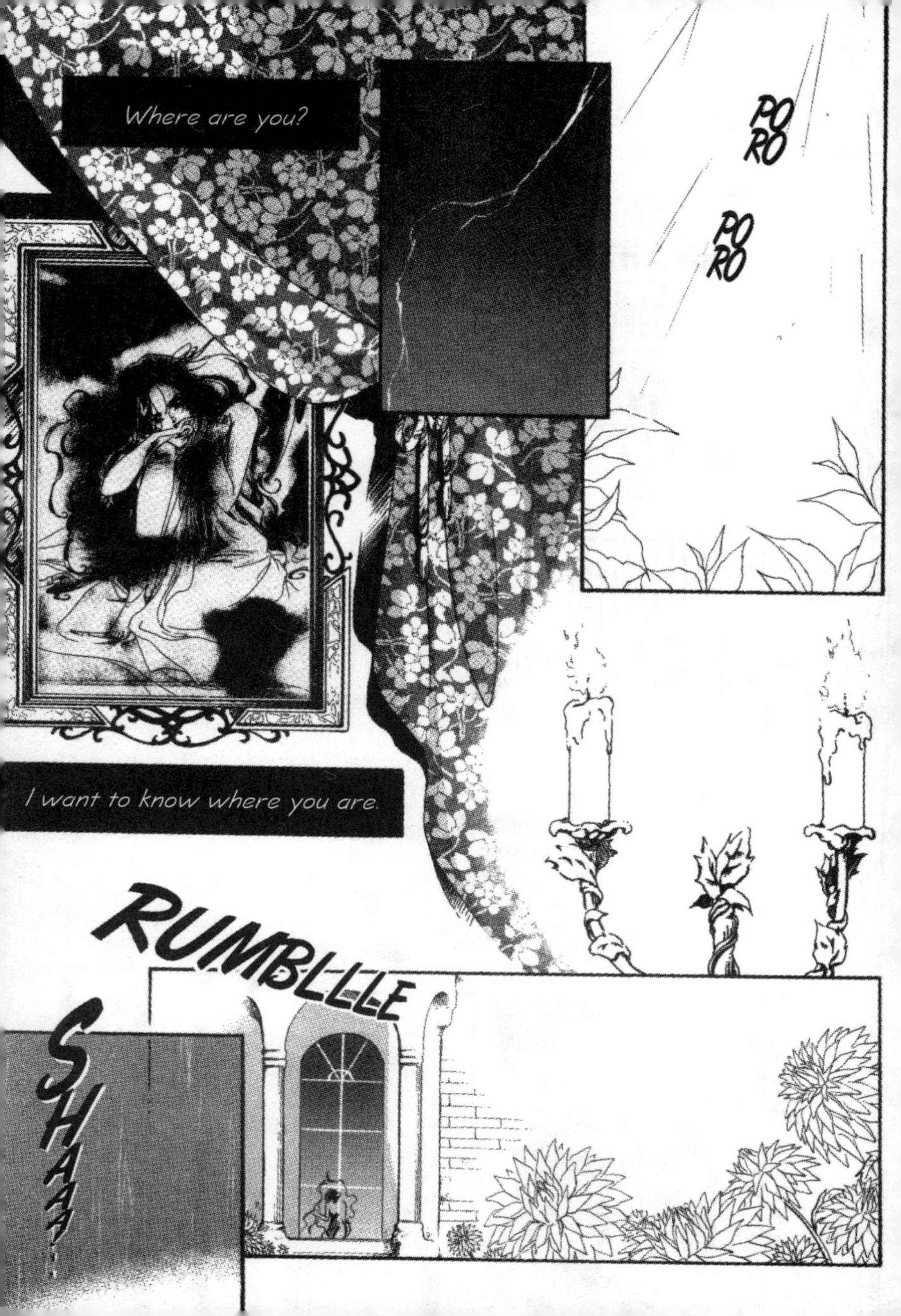

Where are you?
PORO
PORO
I want to know where you are.
RUMBLLLE
SHAAA...

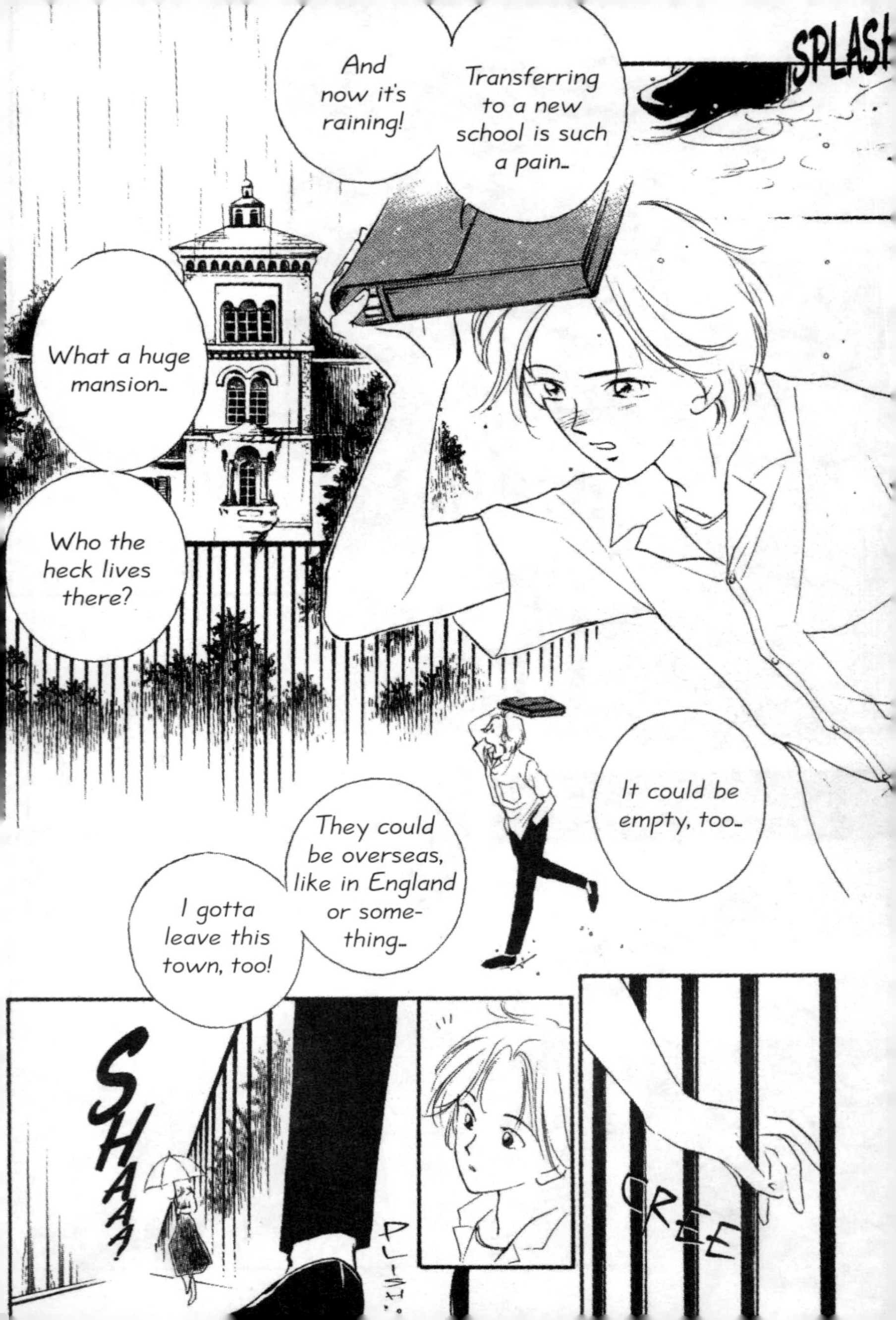
SPLASH
Transferring to a new school is such a pain...
And now it's raining!
What a huge mansion...
Who the heck lives there?
It could be empty, too...
They could be overseas, like in England or something...
I gotta leave this town, too!
SHAAA
PUSH
CREE

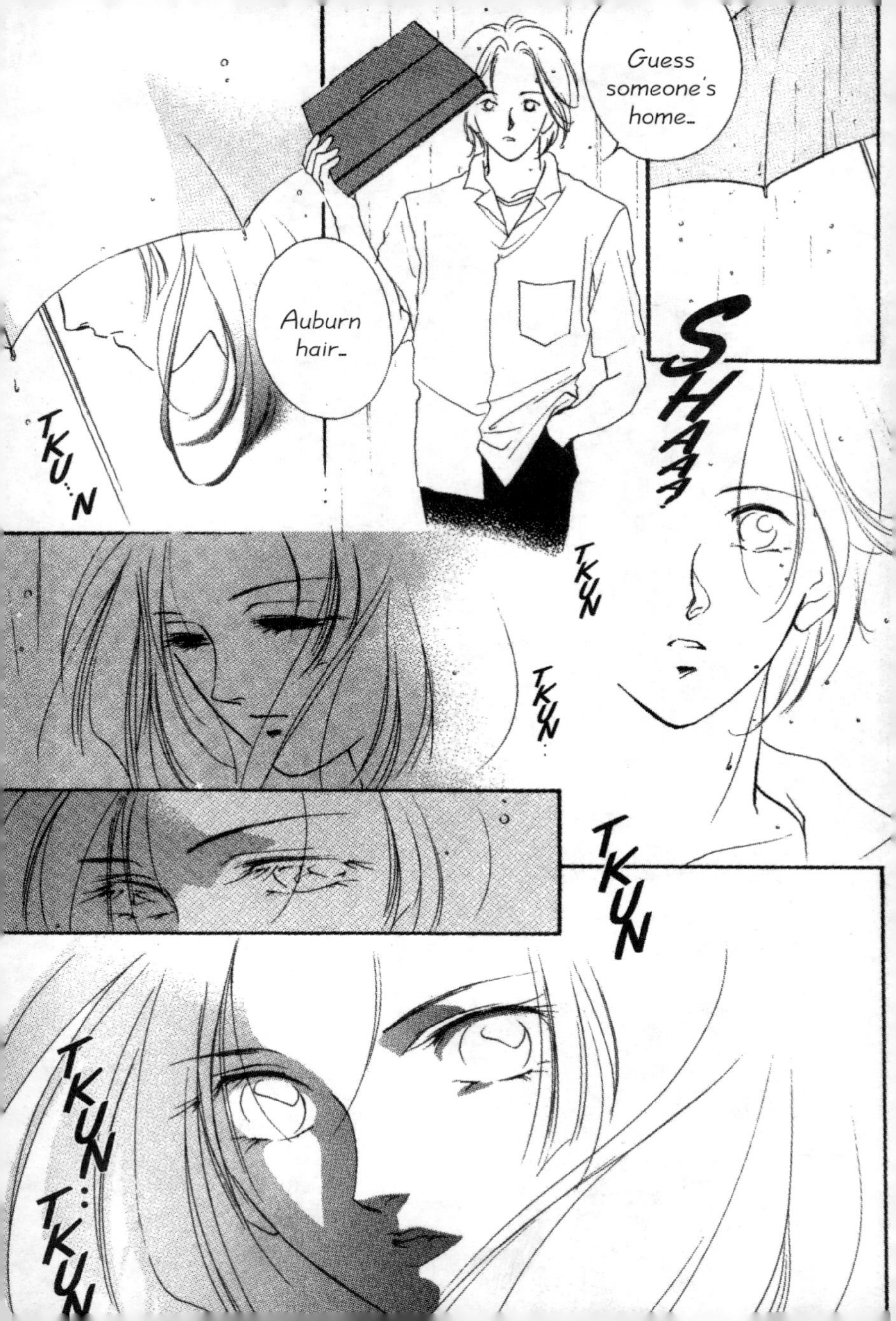

Guess someone's home..
Auburn hair..
TKU...N
SHAAA
TKUN
TKUN
TKUN
TKUN...TKUN

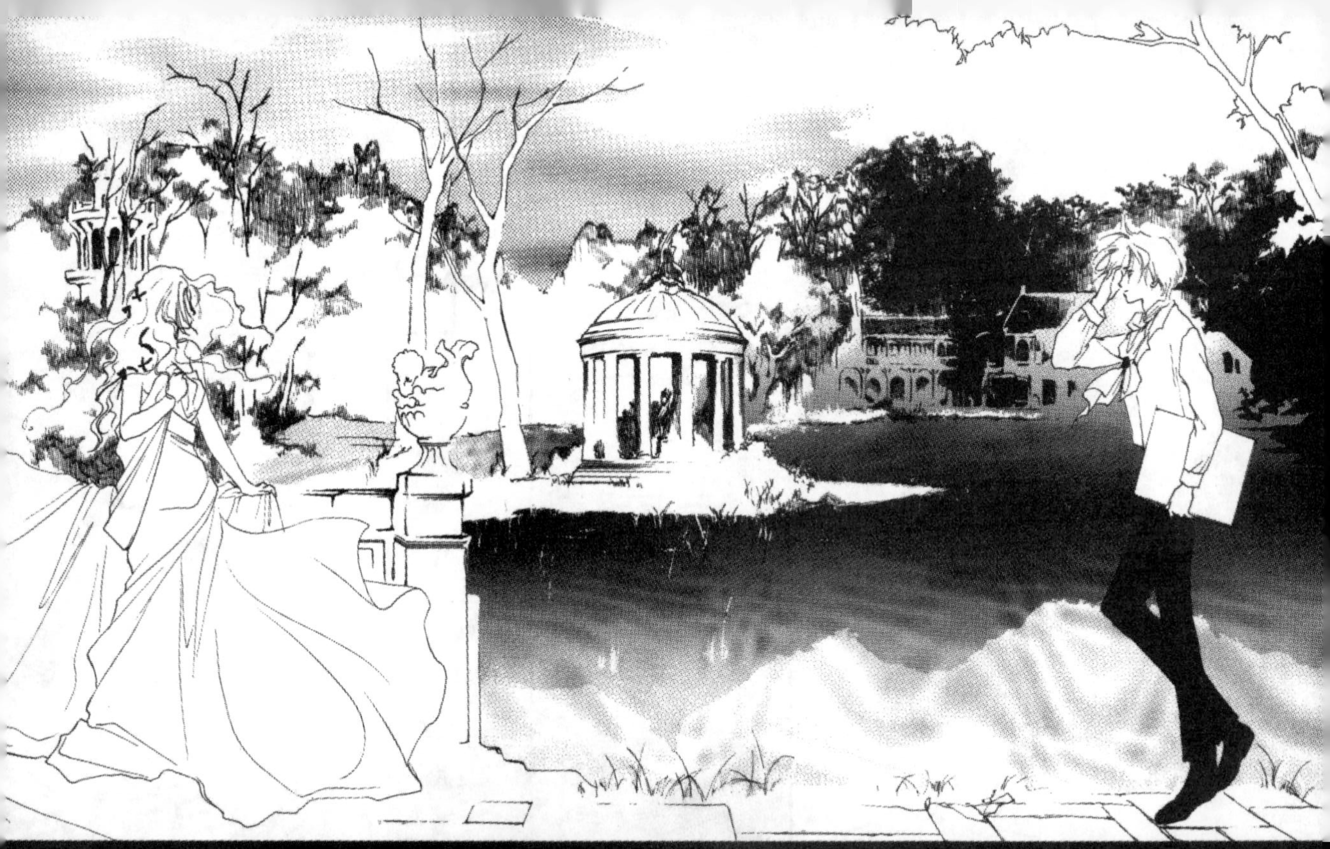

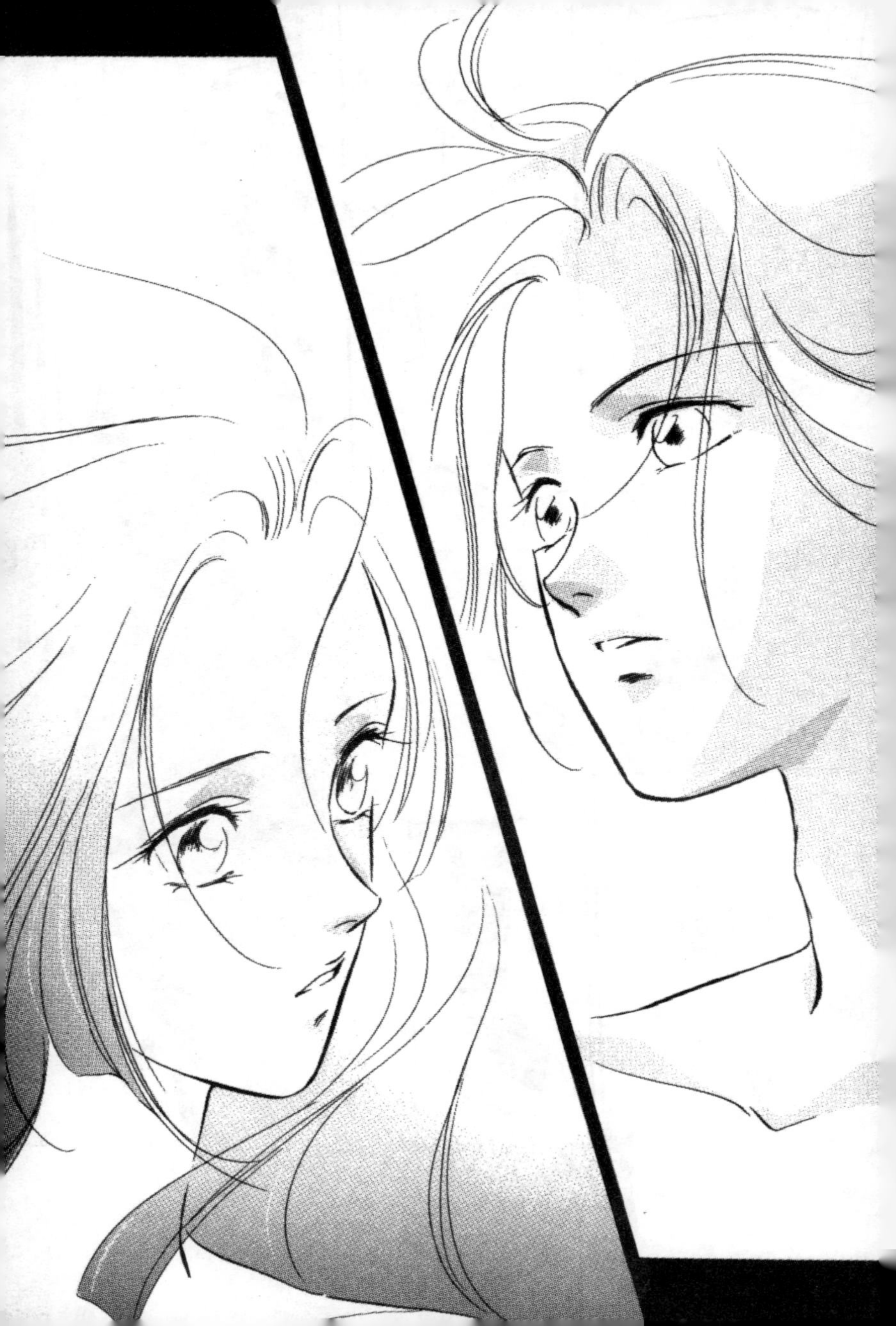

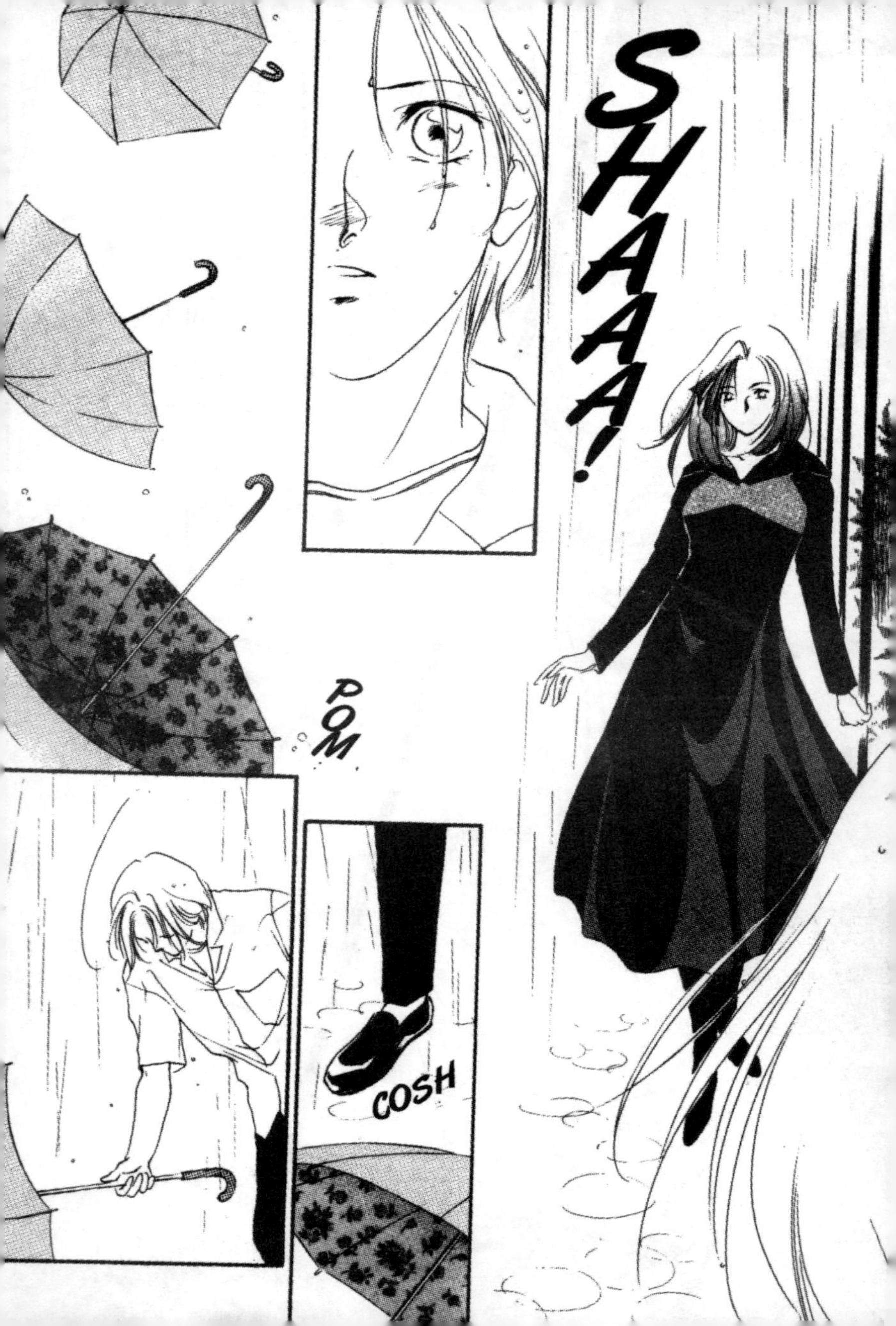
SHAAAA!
POM
COSH

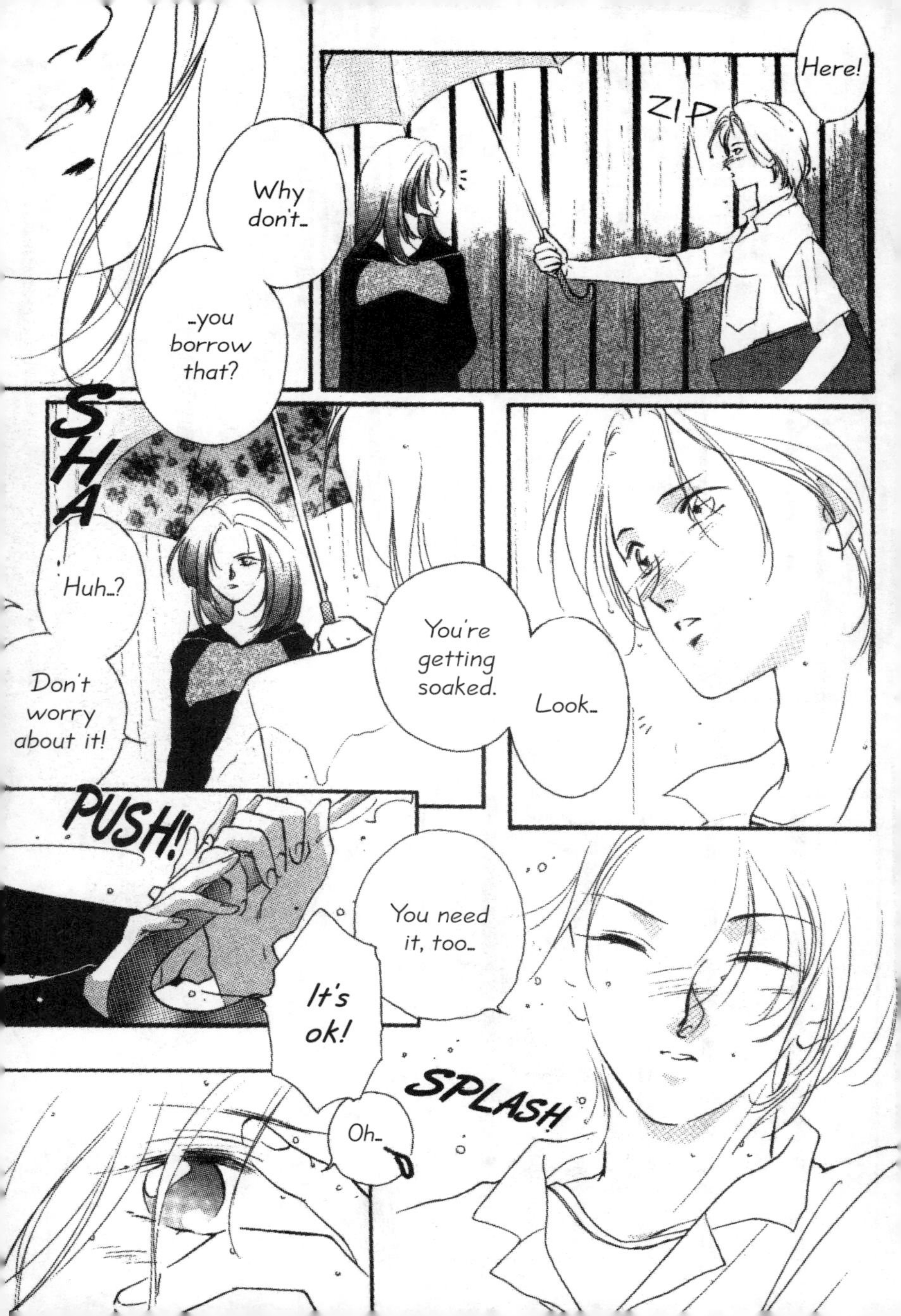
Why don't…
…you borrow that?
ZIP
Here!
SHA
Huh…?
Don't worry about it!
You're getting soaked.
Look…
PUSH!
You need it, too…
It's ok!
SPLASH
Oh…

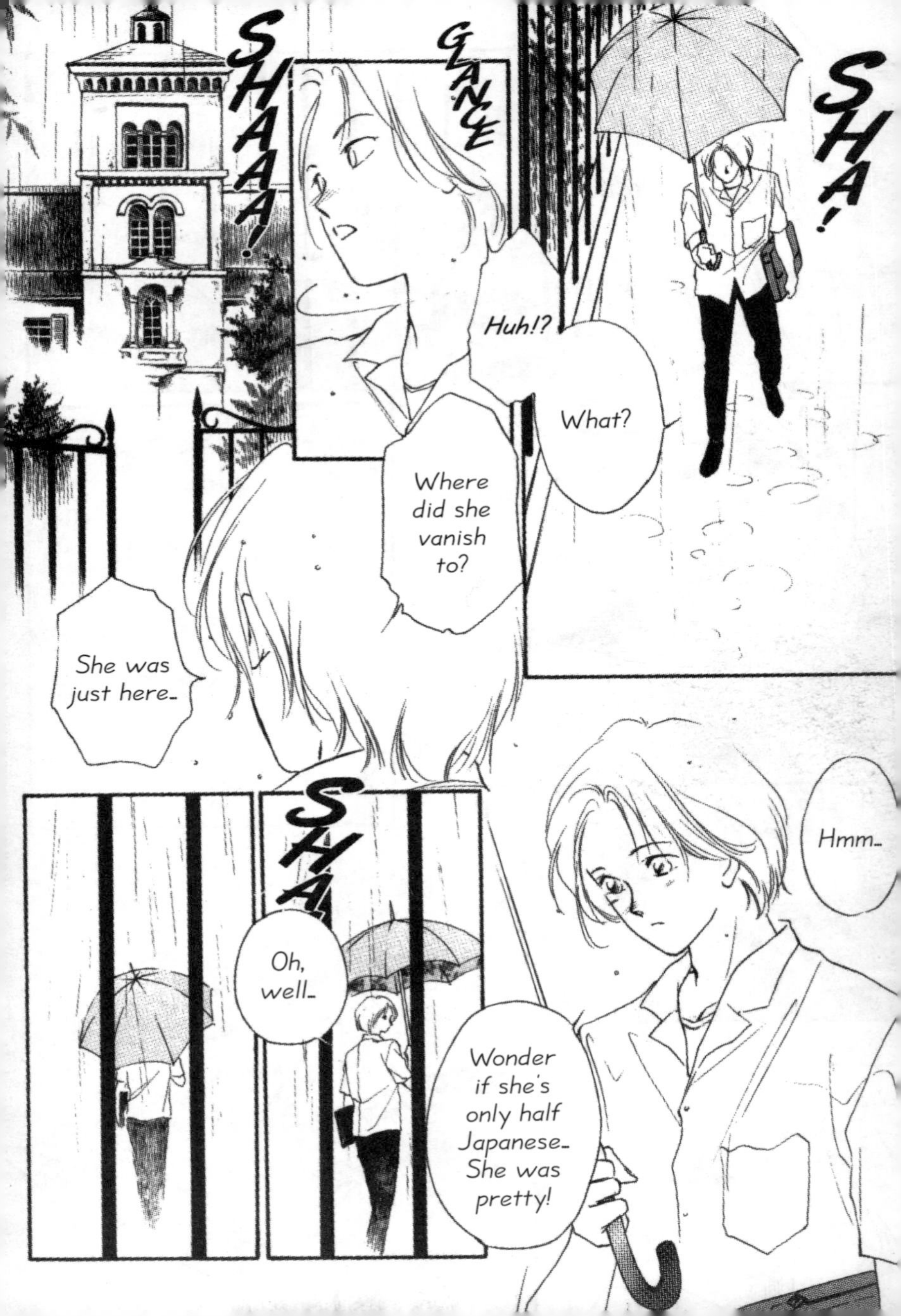
SHA!
SHAAA!
GLANCE
Huh!?
What?
Where did she vanish to?
She was just here...
Hmm...
SHA!
Oh, well...
Wonder if she's only half Japanese... She was pretty!

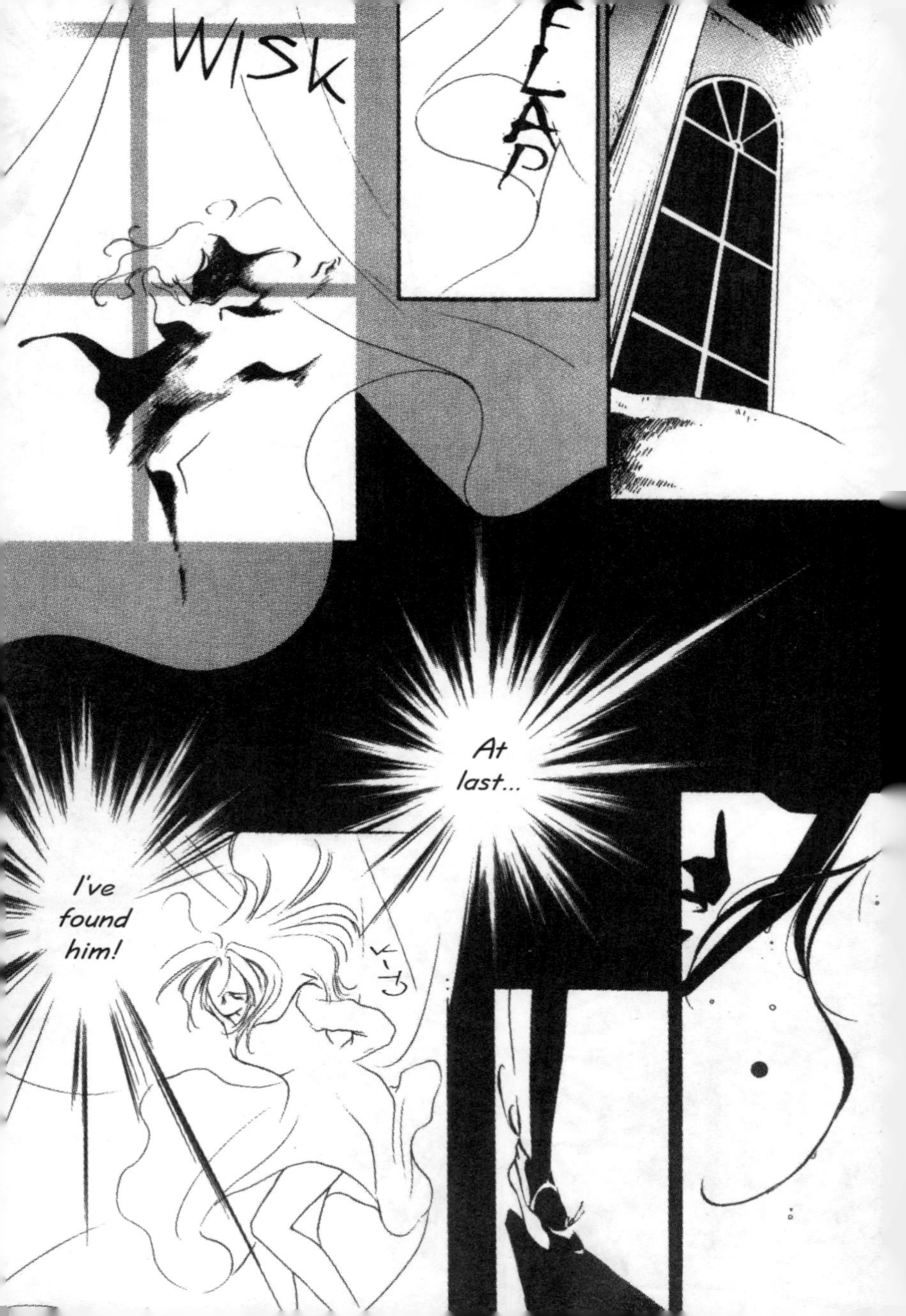
FLAP
WISK
At last...
I've found him!

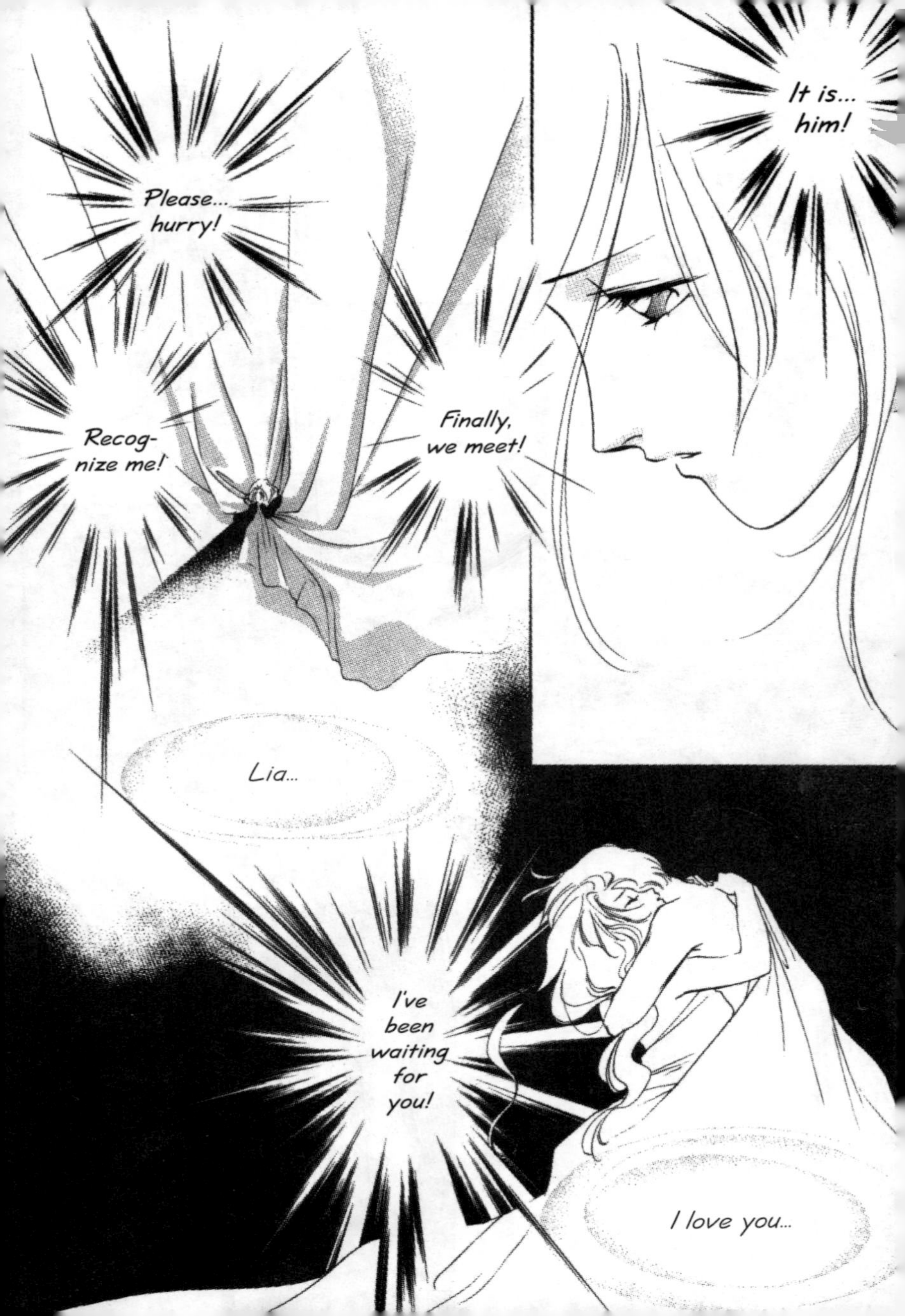
Please... hurry!
Recog-nize me!
Finally, we meet!
It is... him!
Lia...
I've been waiting for you!
I love you...

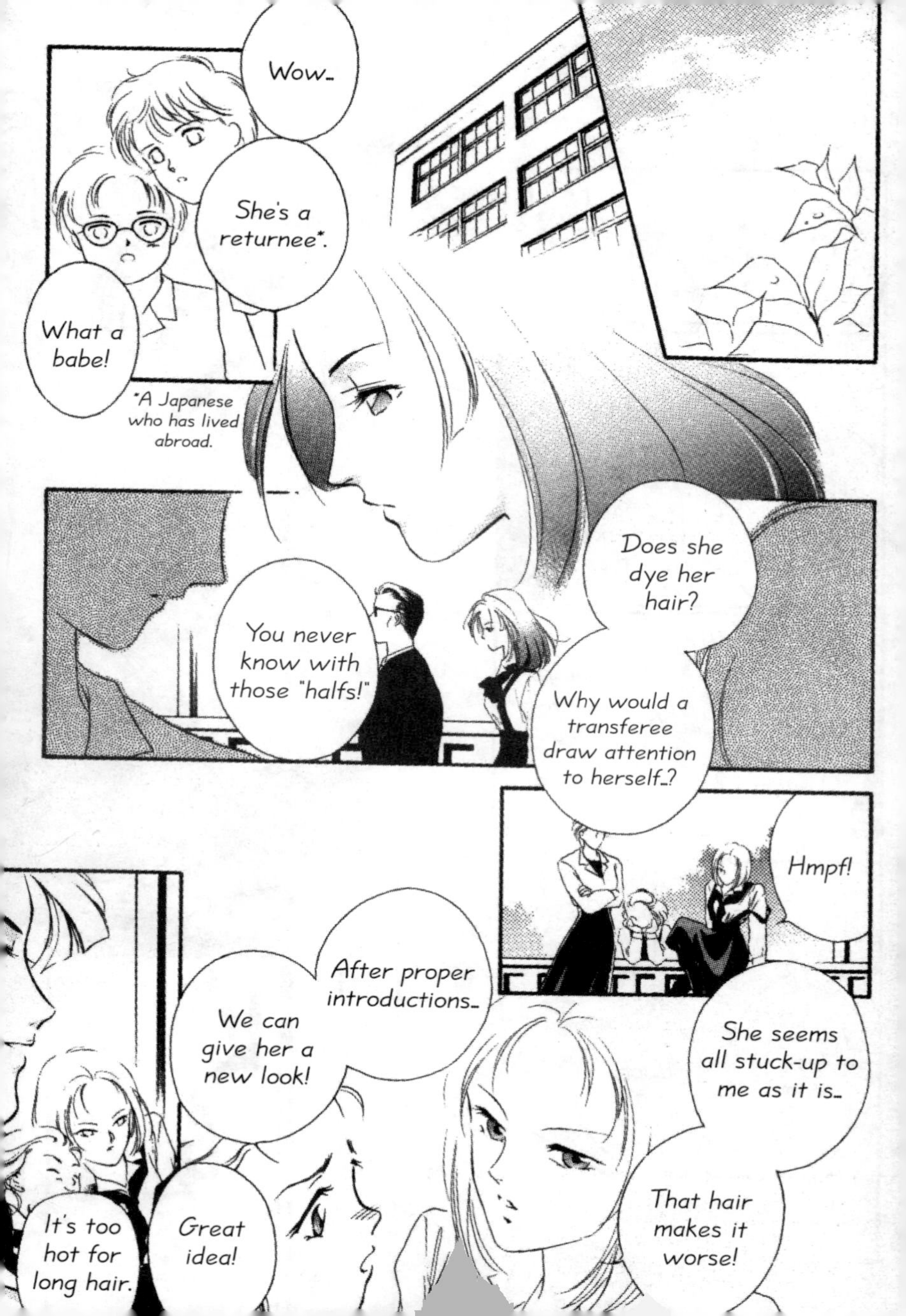
Wow…
She's a returnee*.
What a babe!
*A Japanese who has lived abroad.
Does she dye her hair?
You never know with those "halfs!"
Why would a transferee draw attention to herself…?
Hmpf!
She seems all stuck-up to me as it is…
That hair makes it worse!
After proper introductions…
We can give her a new look!
Great idea!
It's too hot for long hair.

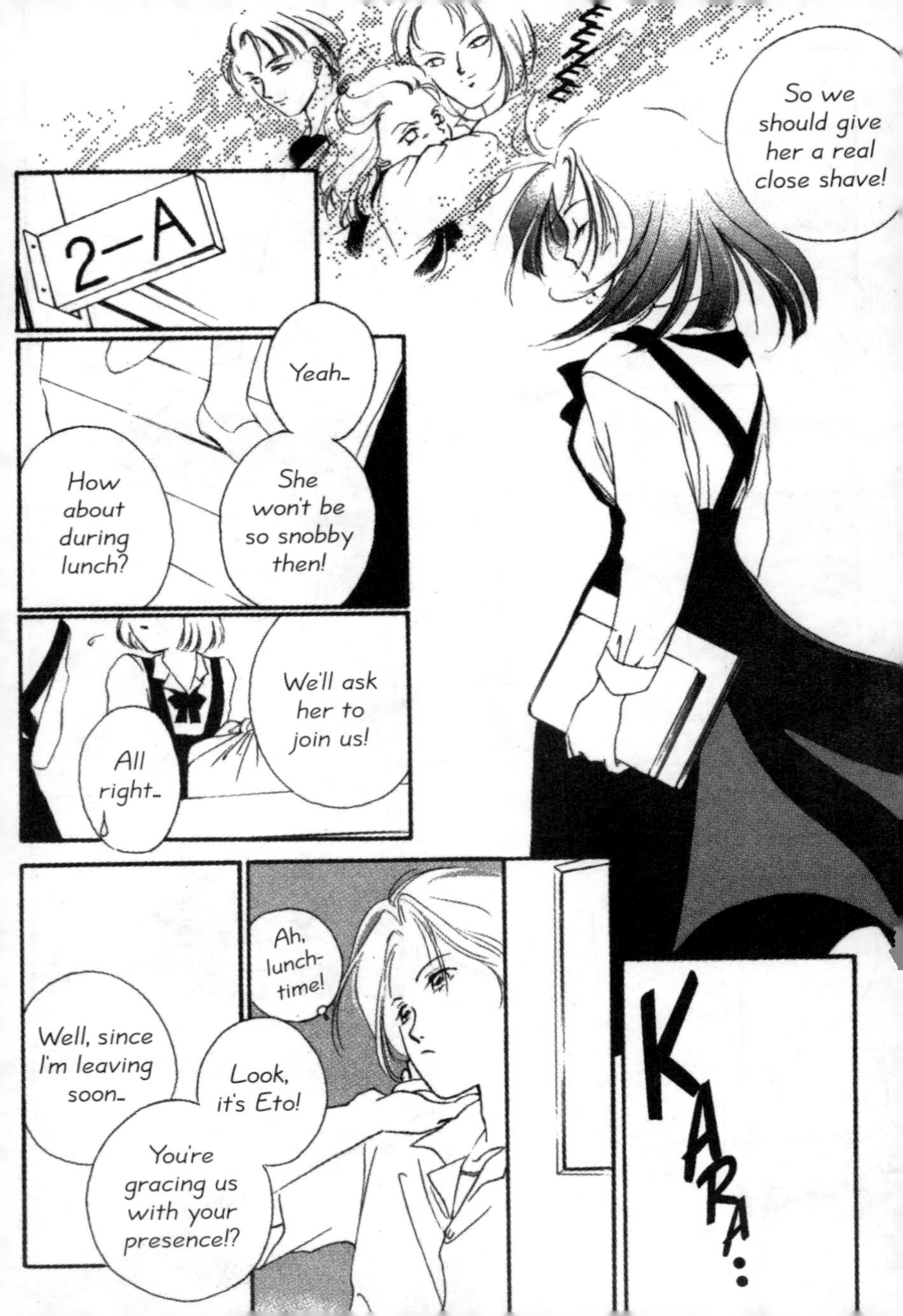
So we should give her a real close shave!
2-A
Yeah...
She won't be so snobby then!
How about during lunch?
We'll ask her to join us!
All right...
KARA..
Ah, lunch-time!
Look, it's Eto!
Well, since I'm leaving soon...
You're gracing us with your presence!?

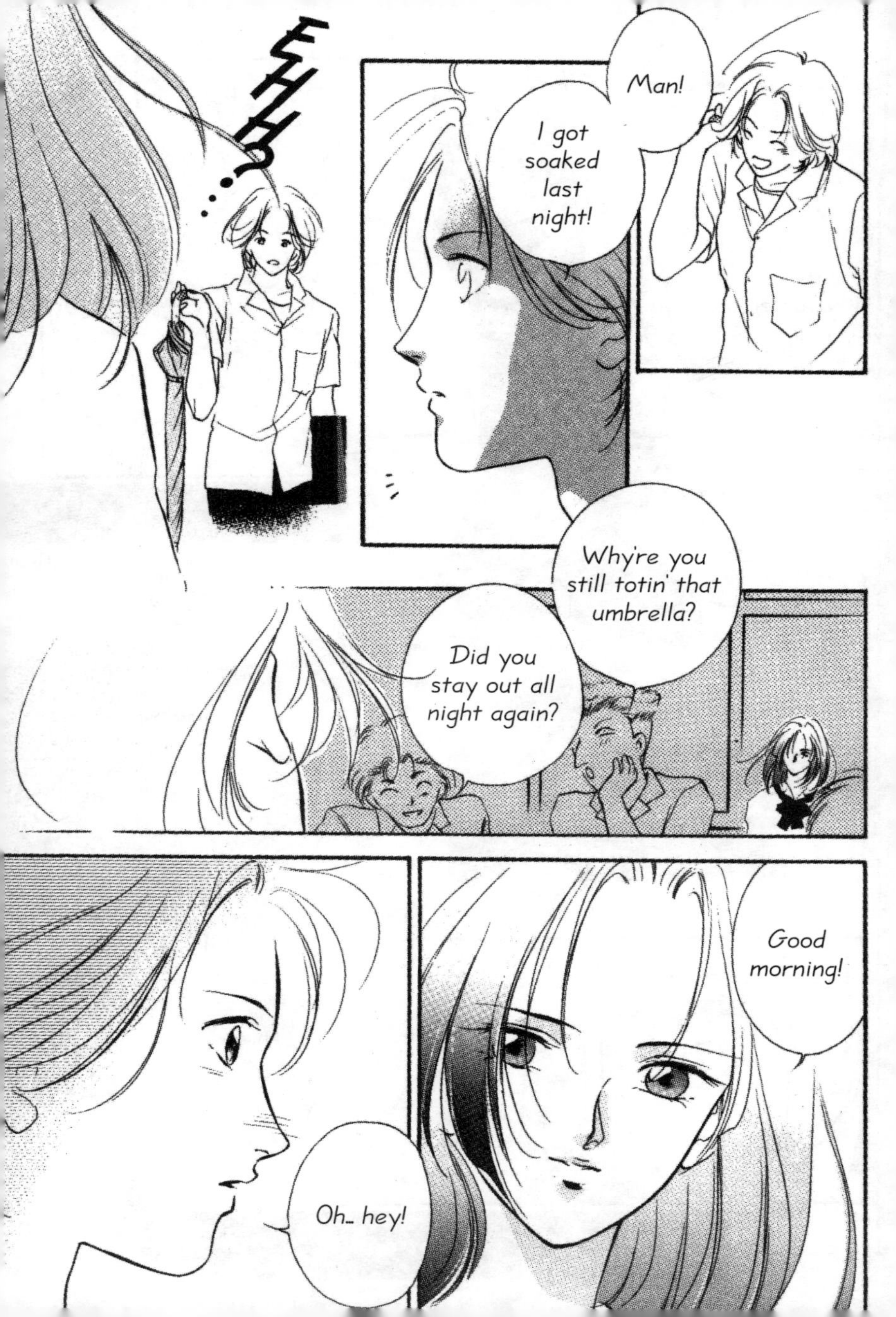

Man!
I got soaked last night!
EHH?...
Why're you still totin' that umbrella?
Did you stay out all night again?
Good morning!
Oh... hey!

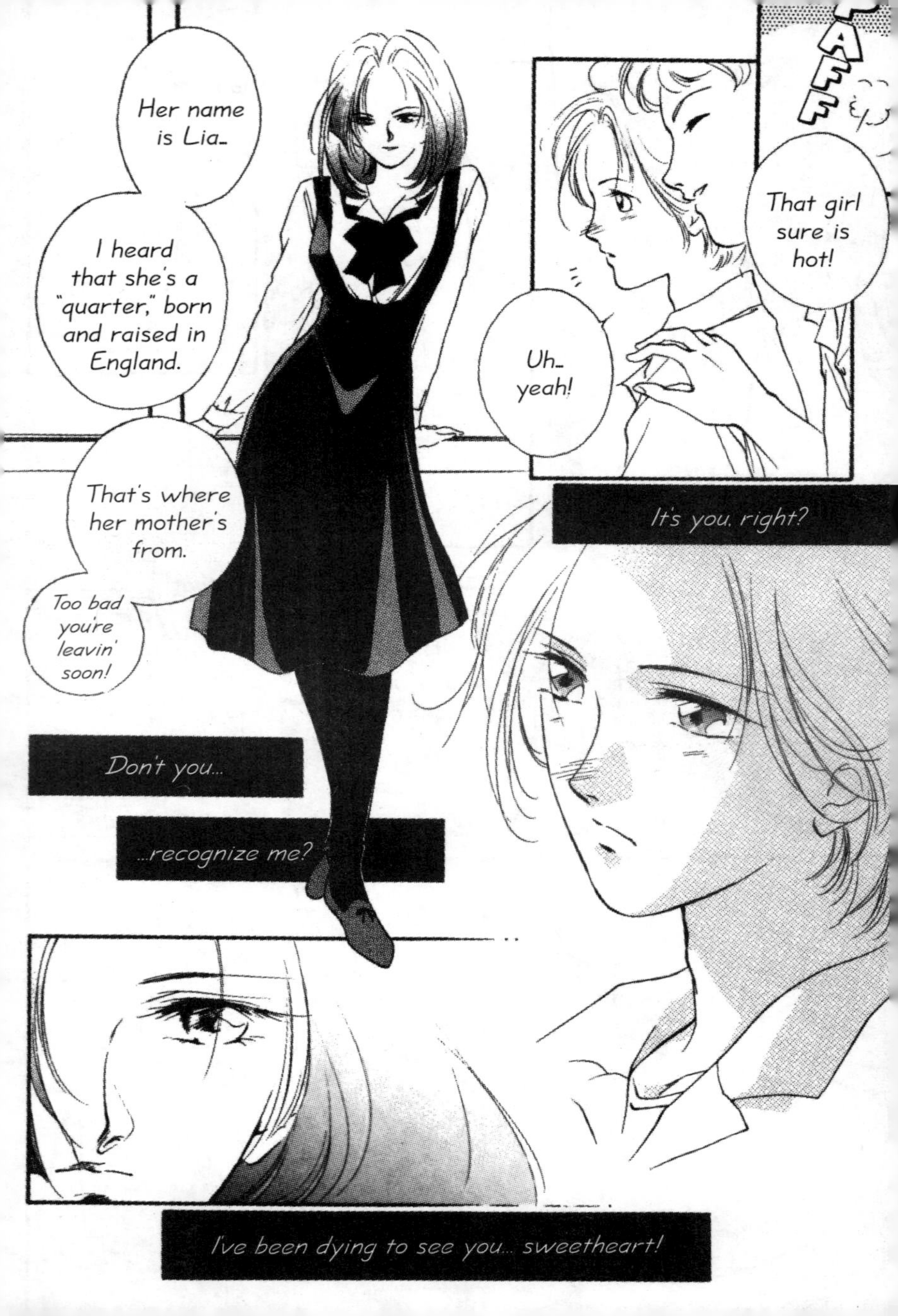
PAFF
That girl sure is hot!
Uh... yeah!
Her name is Lia...
I heard that she's a "quarter," born and raised in England.
That's where her mother's from.
Too bad you're leavin' soon!
It's you, right?
Don't you...
...recognize me?
I've been dying to see you... sweetheart!

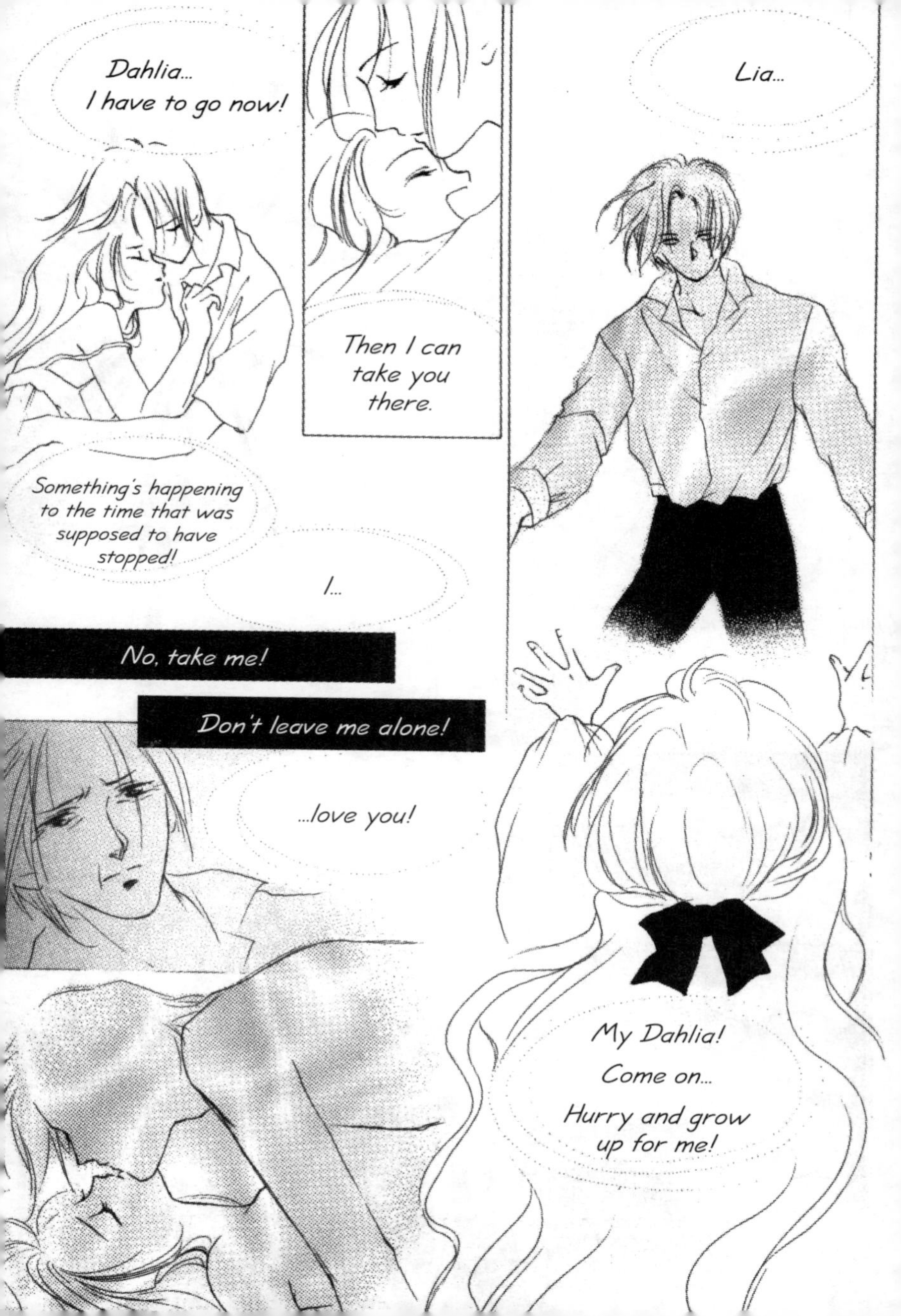
Dahlia... I have to go now!
Then I can take you there.
Lia...
Something's happening to the time that was supposed to have stopped!
I...
No, take me!
Don't leave me alone!
...love you!
My Dahlia!
Come on...
Hurry and grow up for me!

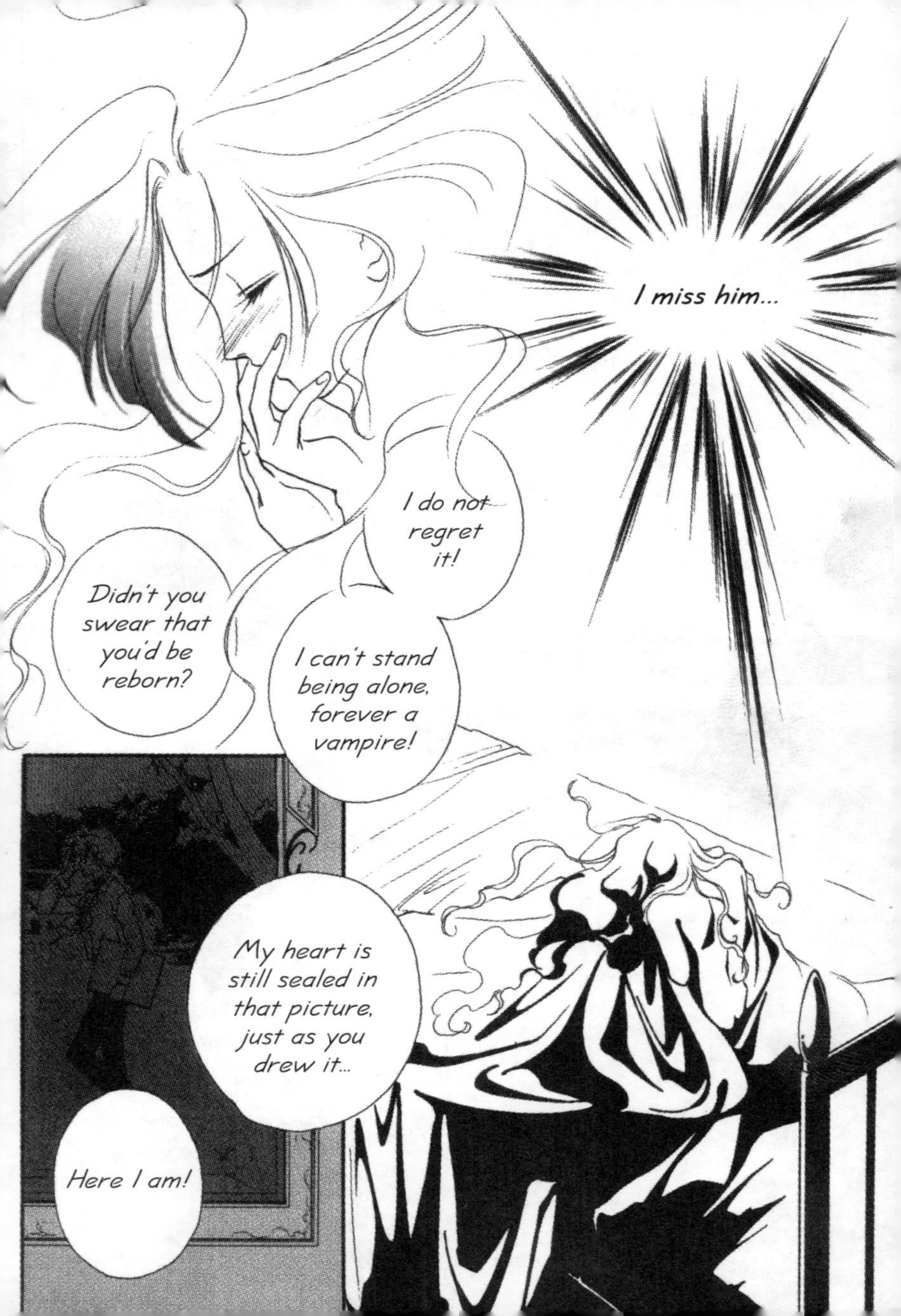
I miss him...
I do not regret it!
I can't stand being alone, forever a vampire!
Didn't you swear that you'd be reborn?
My heart is still sealed in that picture, just as you drew it...
Here I am!

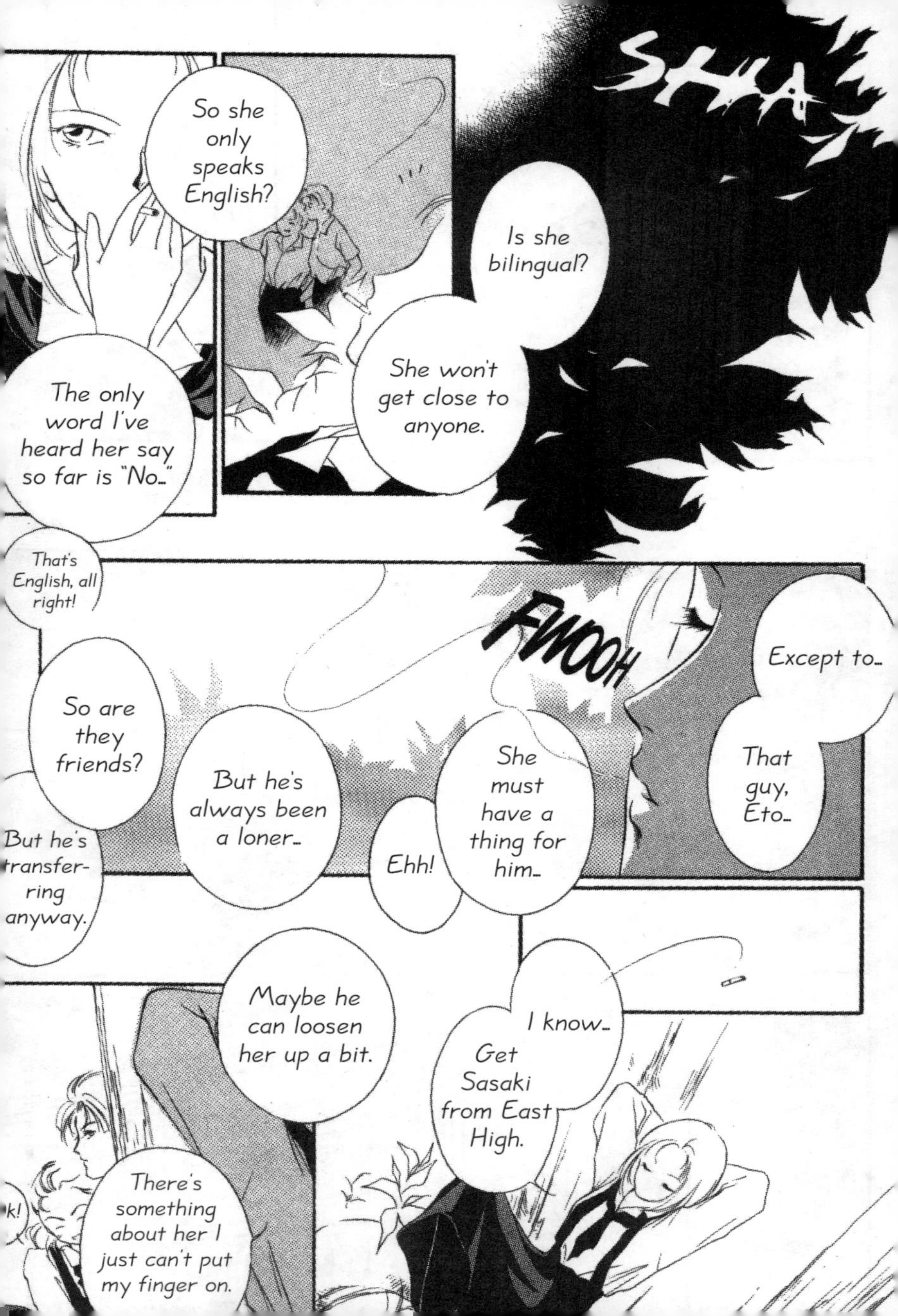
SHA
Is she bilingual?
She won't get close to anyone.
So she only speaks English?
The only word I've heard her say so far is "No..."
That's English, all right!
Except to...
That guy, Eto...
FWOOH
She must have a thing for him...
Ehh!
But he's always been a loner...
So are they friends?
But he's transferring anyway.
I know...
Get Sasaki from East High.
Maybe he can loosen her up a bit.
There's something about her I just can't put my finger on.

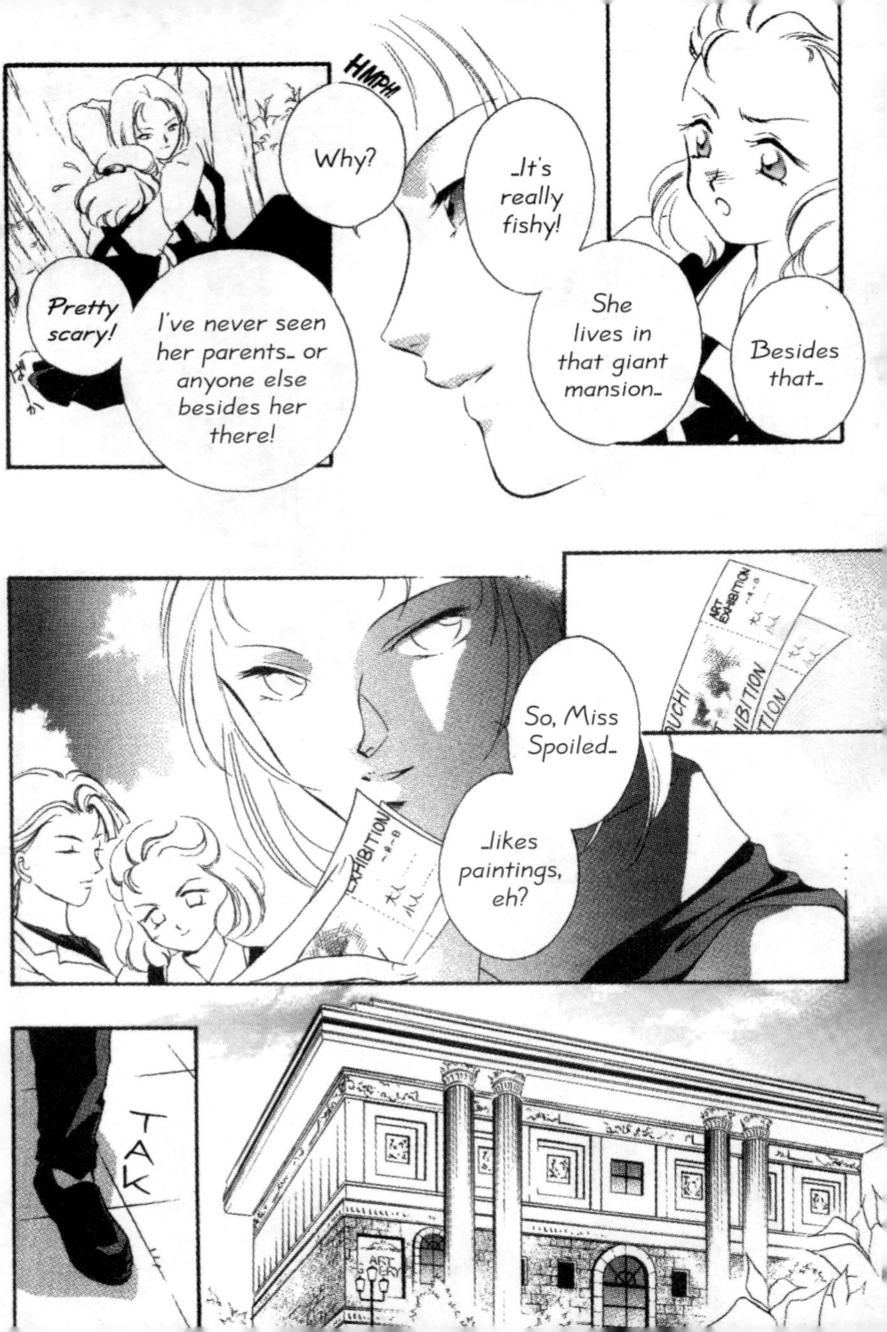
Besides that...
She lives in that giant mansion...
...It's really fishy!
HMPH!
Why?
I've never seen her parents... or anyone else besides her there!
Pretty scary!
ART EXHIBITION
So, Miss Spoiled...
...likes paintings, eh?
EXHIBITION
TAK

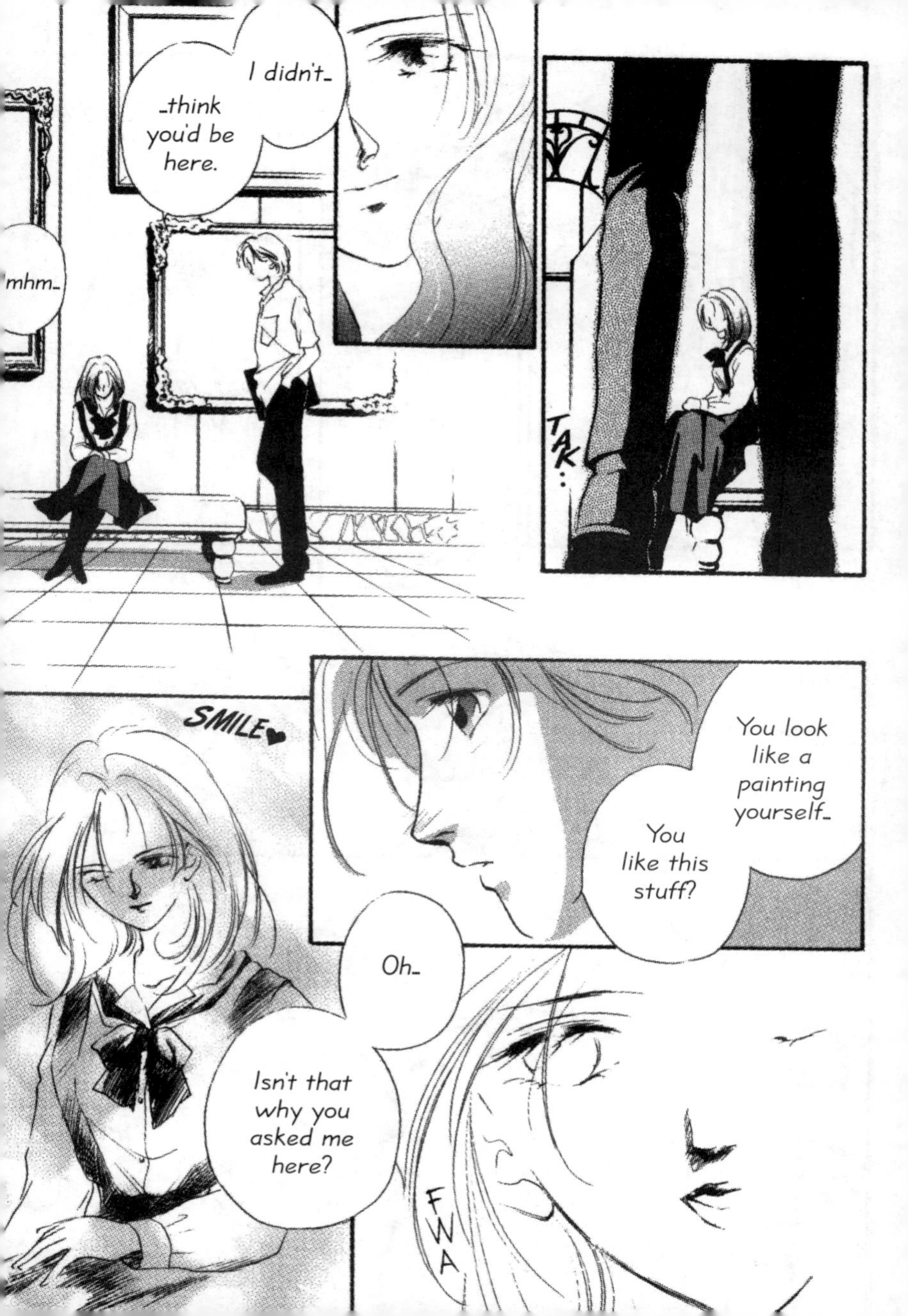

I didn't-
-think you'd be here.
mhm-
TAK..
You like this stuff?
You look like a painting yourself-
Oh-
SMILE
Isn't that why you asked me here?
FWA

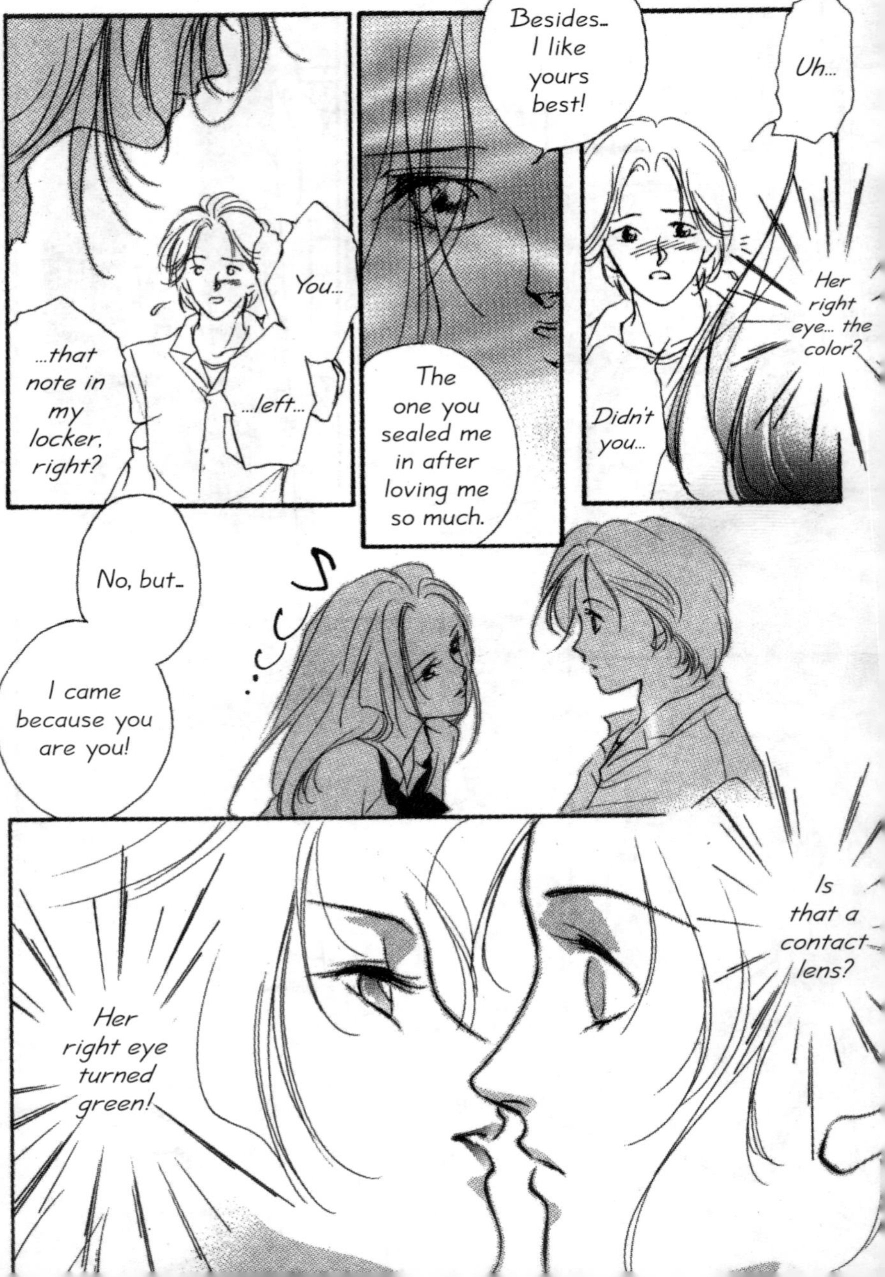
You...
...left...
...that note in my locker, right?
Besides.. I like yours best!
The one you sealed me in after loving me so much.
Uh...
Didn't you...
Her right eye... the color?
No, but-
I came because you are you!
Her right eye turned green!
Is that a contact lens?

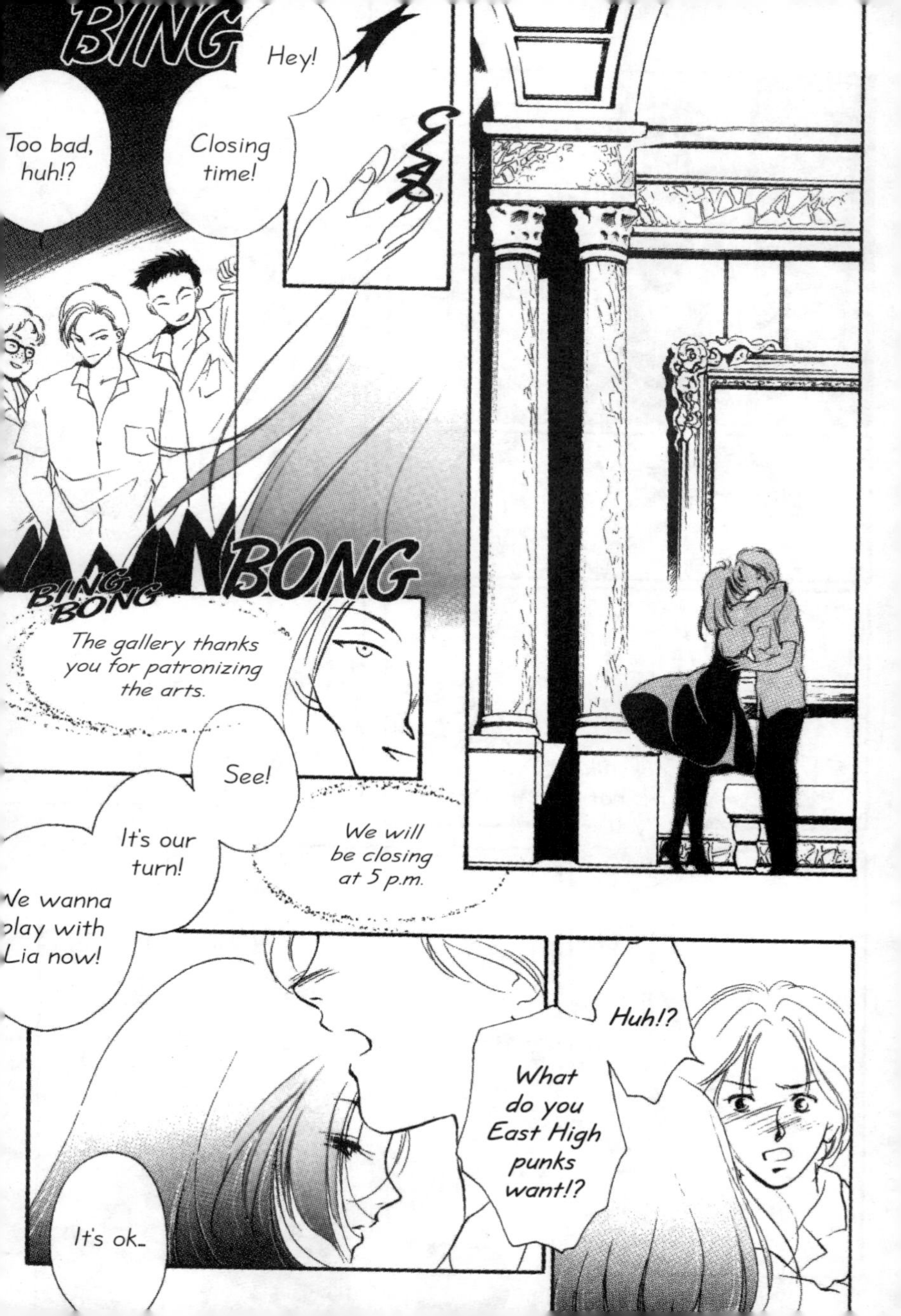
BING
Hey!
Closing time!
Too bad, huh!?
BONG
BING BONG
The gallery thanks you for patronizing the arts.
See!
We will be closing at 5 p.m.
It's our turn!
We wanna play with Lia now!
Huh!?
What do you East High punks want!?
It's ok..

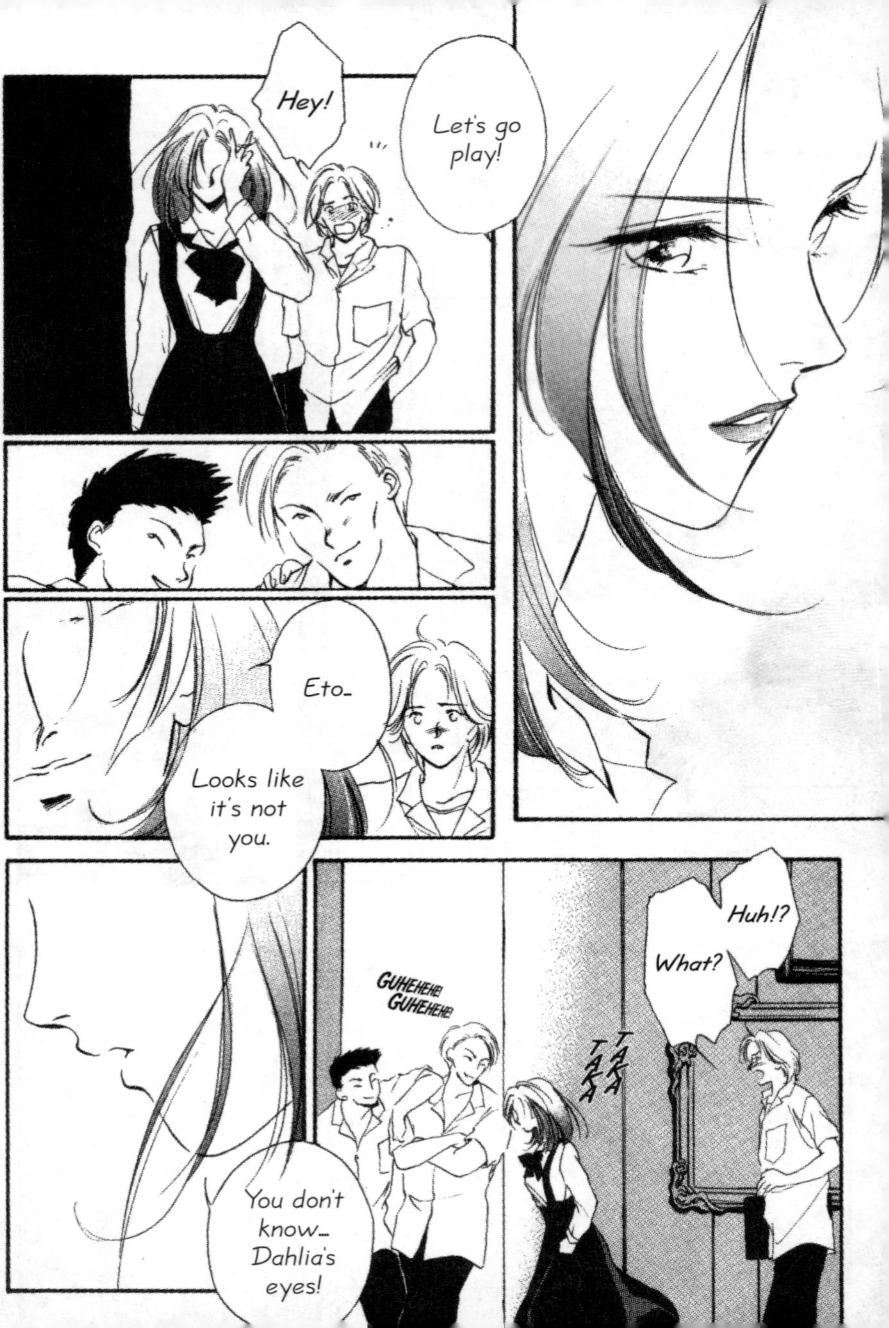
Hey!
Let's go play!
Eto...
Looks like it's not you.
Huh!?
What?
GUHEHEHE! GUHEHEHE!
TATATA
TATATA
You don't know... Dahlia's eyes!

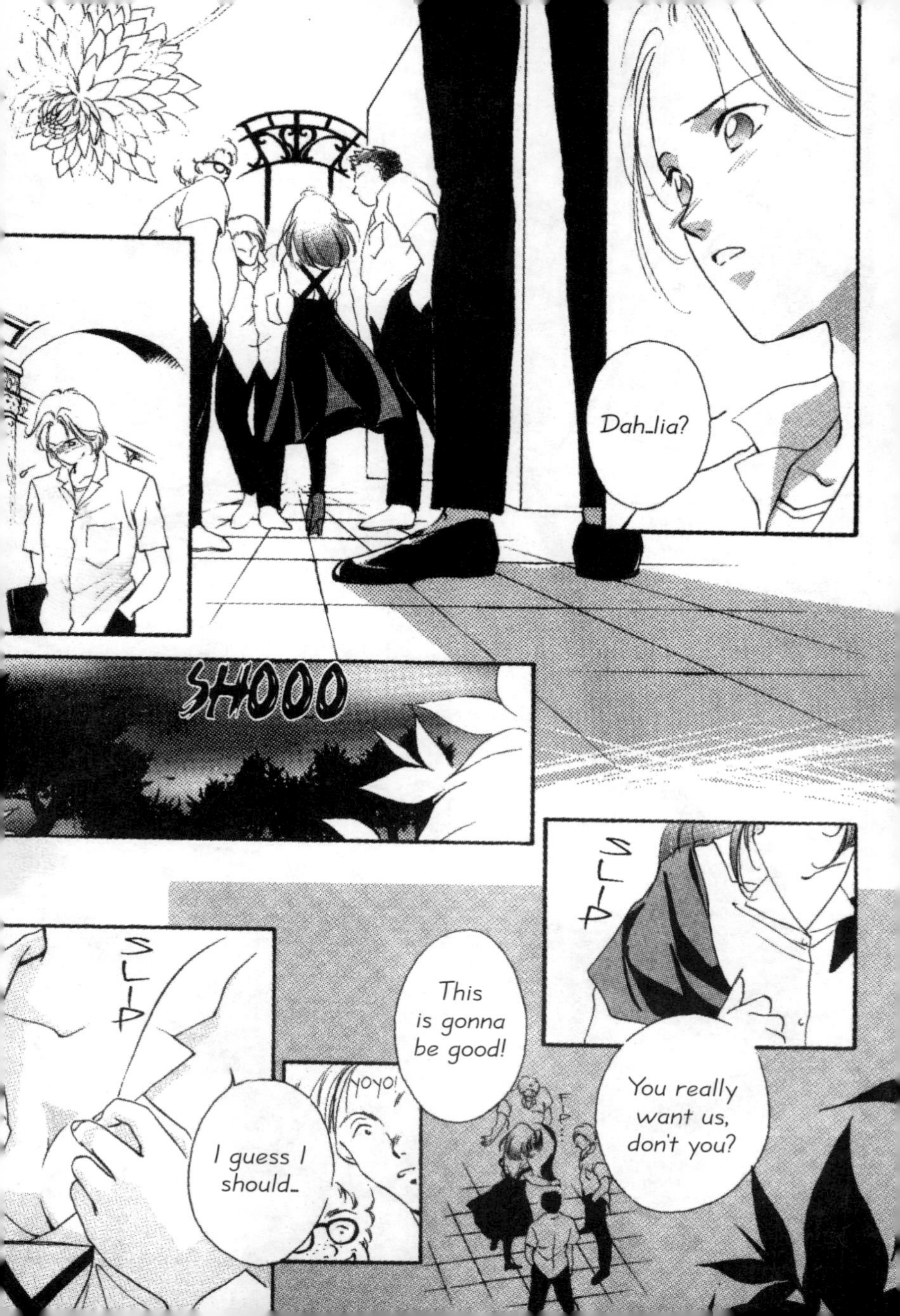
Dah..lia?
SHOOO
SLIP
You really want us, don't you?
This is gonna be good!
YOYO!
I guess I should..
SLIP

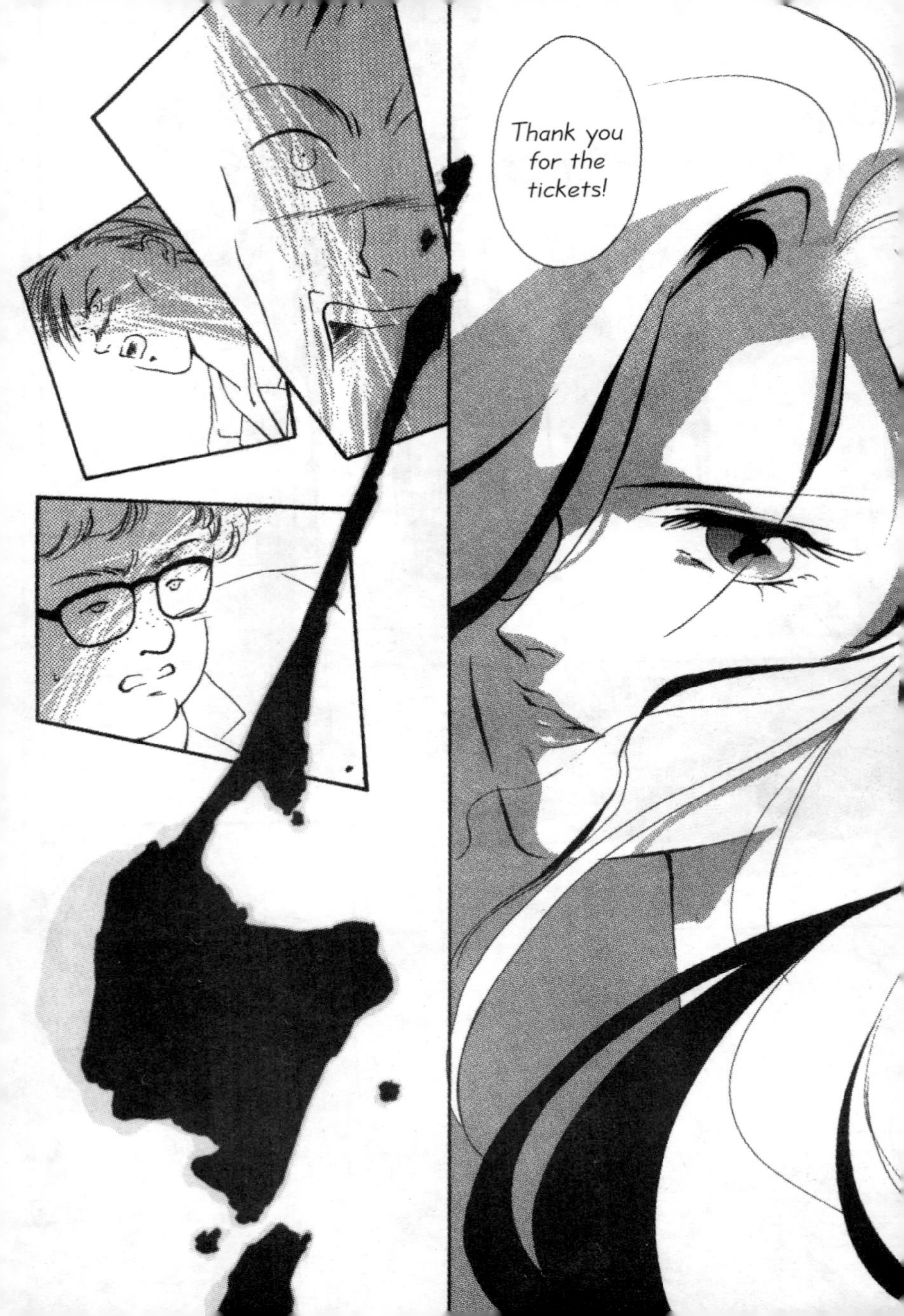
Thank you for the tickets!

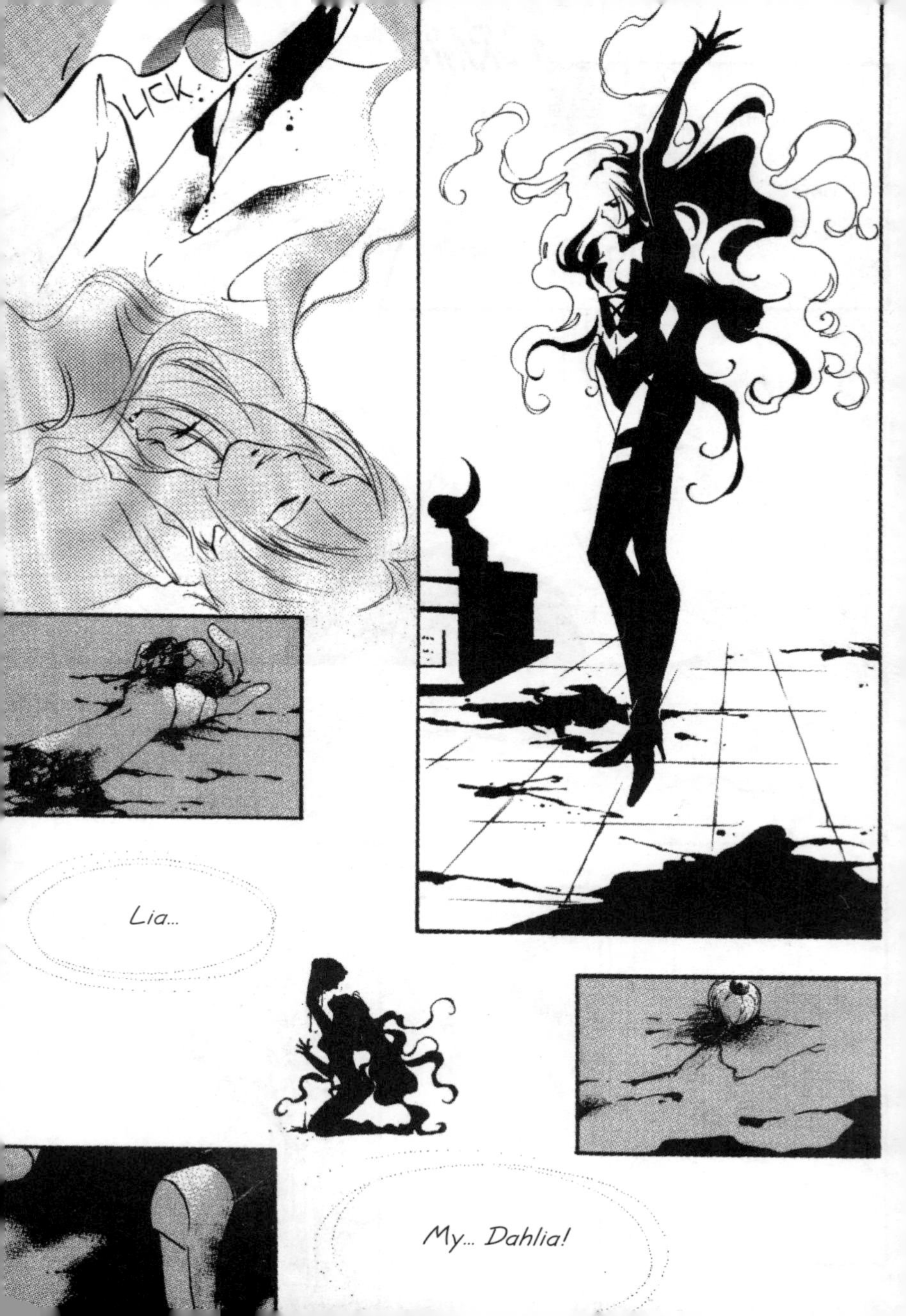
LICK
Lia...
My... Dahlia!

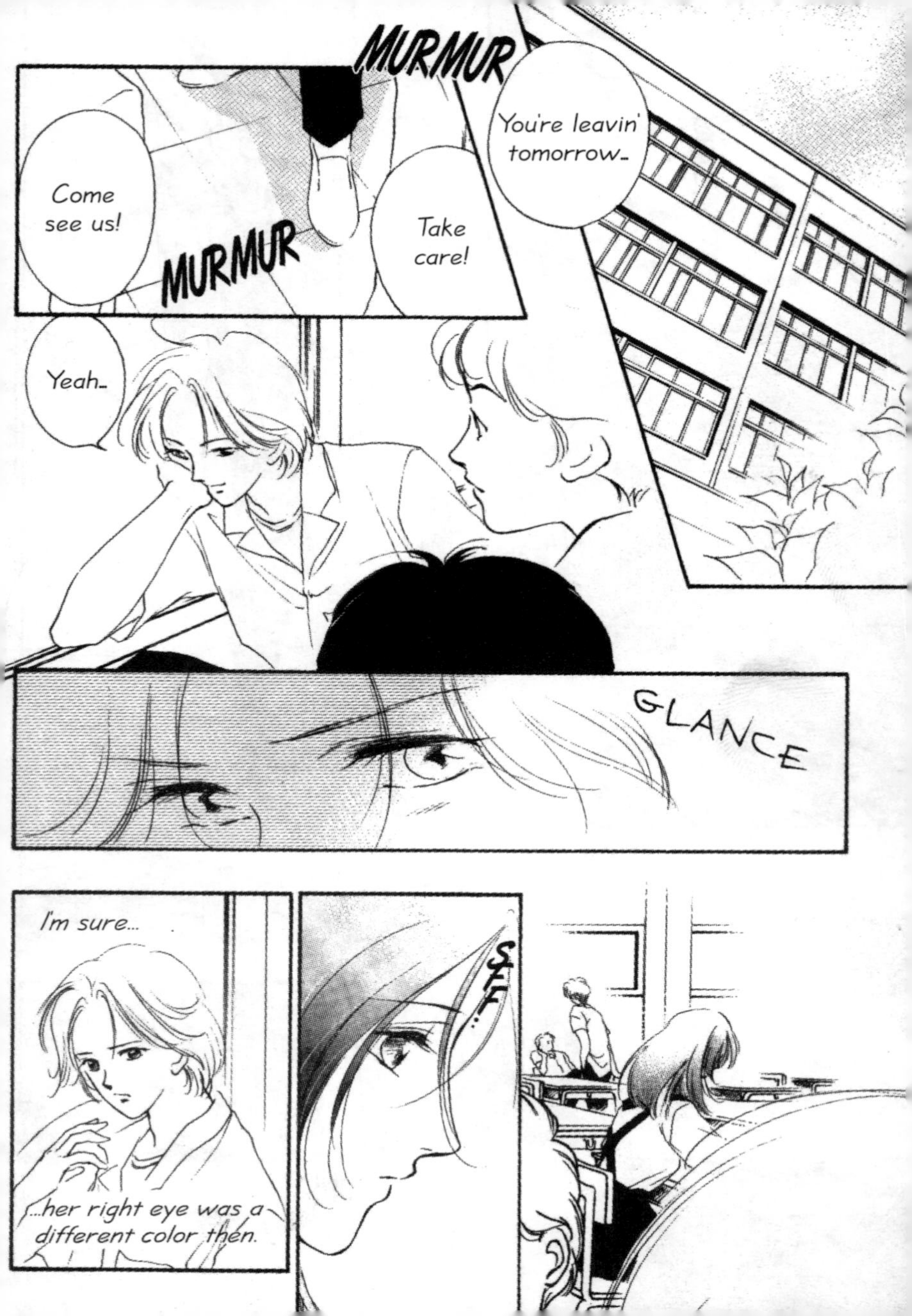
MURMUR
You're leavin' tomorrow...
Take care!
Come see us!
MURMUR
Yeah...
GLANCE
I'm sure...
...her right eye was a different color then.

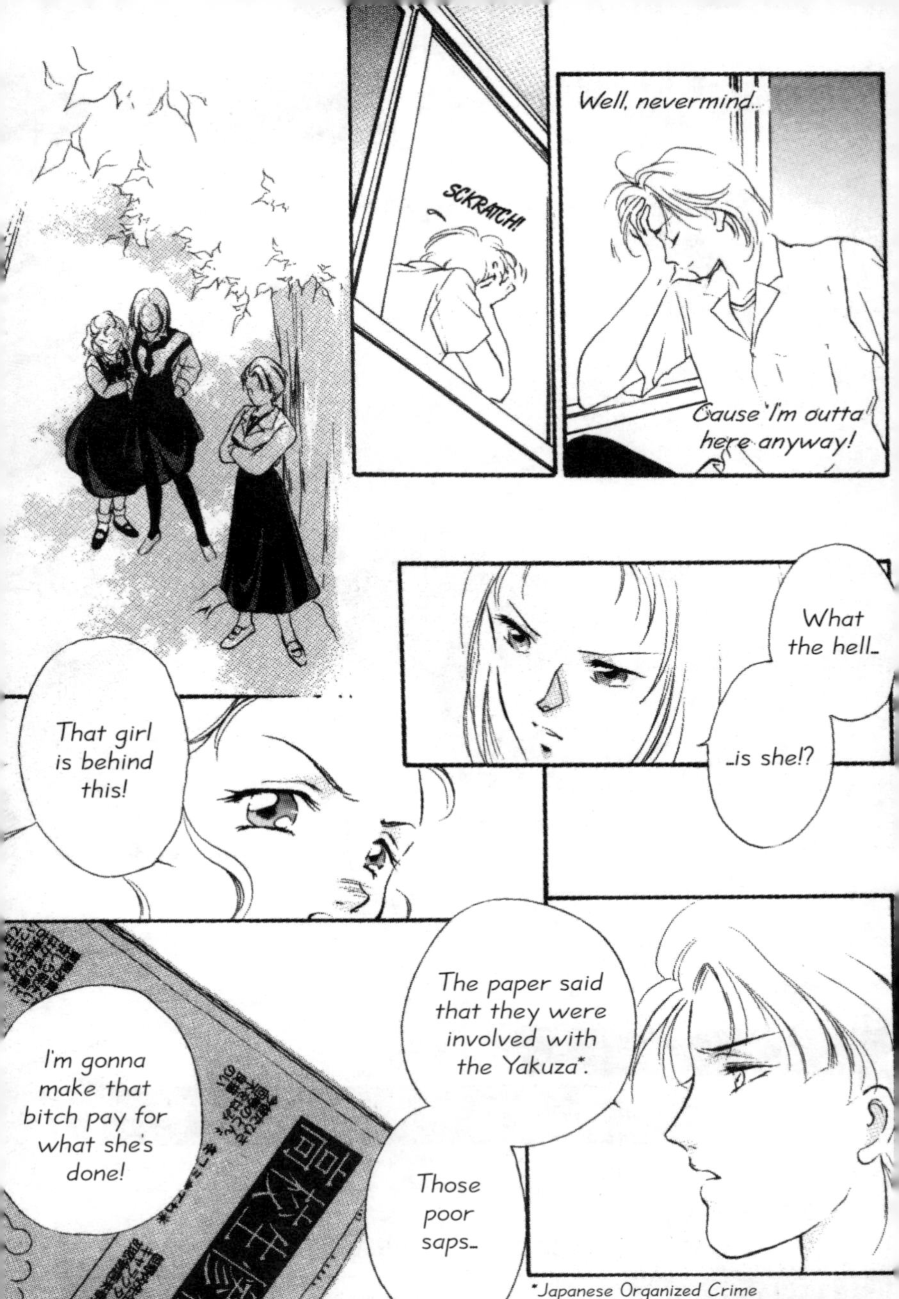
SCKRATCH!
Well, nevermind...
'Cause I'm outta here anyway!
What the hell...
...is she!?
That girl is behind this!
The paper said that they were involved with the Yakuza*.
Those poor saps...
I'm gonna make that bitch pay for what she's done!

*Japanese Organized Crime
Headline: High School Students Murdered!

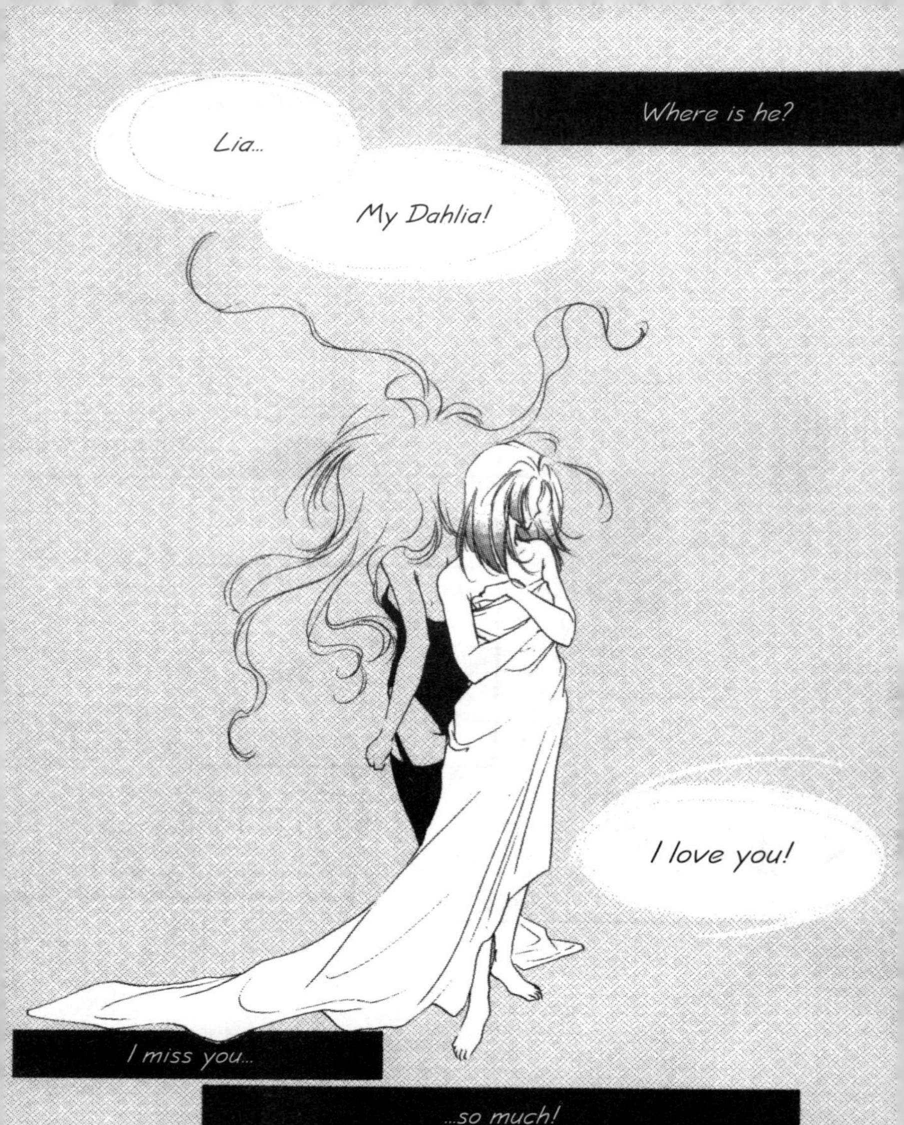
Where is he?
Lia...
My Dahlia!
I love you!
I miss you...
...so much!

STAFF(KOTORI CLUB)

Akiko H　Hitomi T　Haruna T

Thanks

RAINY BLOOD＊END

第2幕

act.2

SALOME

サロメは霧の中に

into the mist

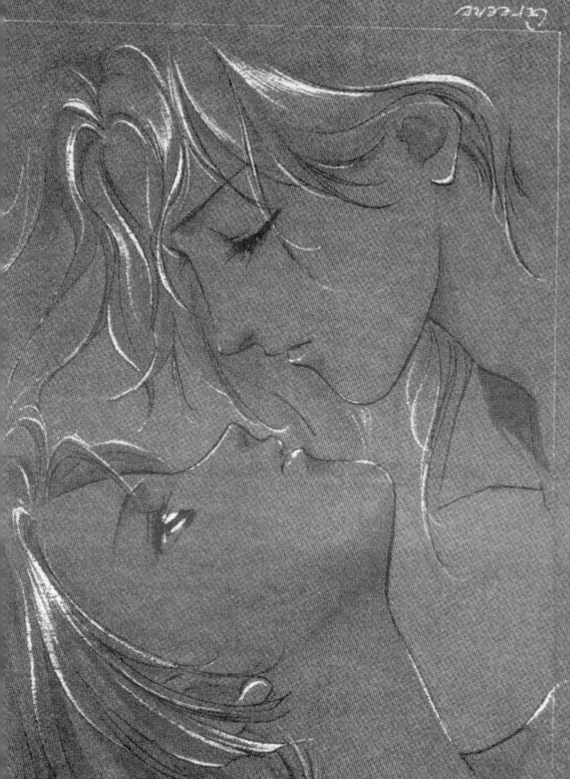
Dahlia

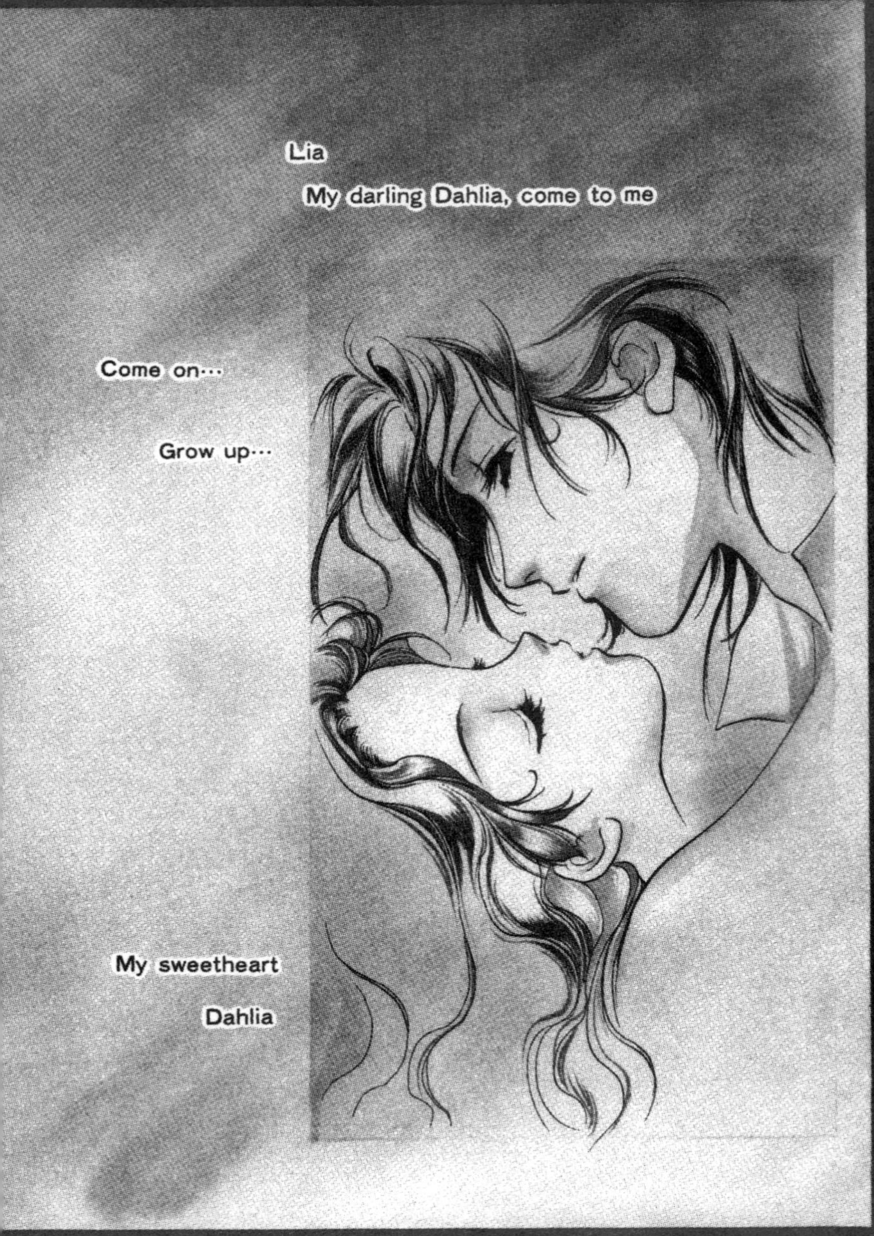
Lia
My darling Dahlia, come to me
Come on…
Grow up…
My sweetheart
Dahlia

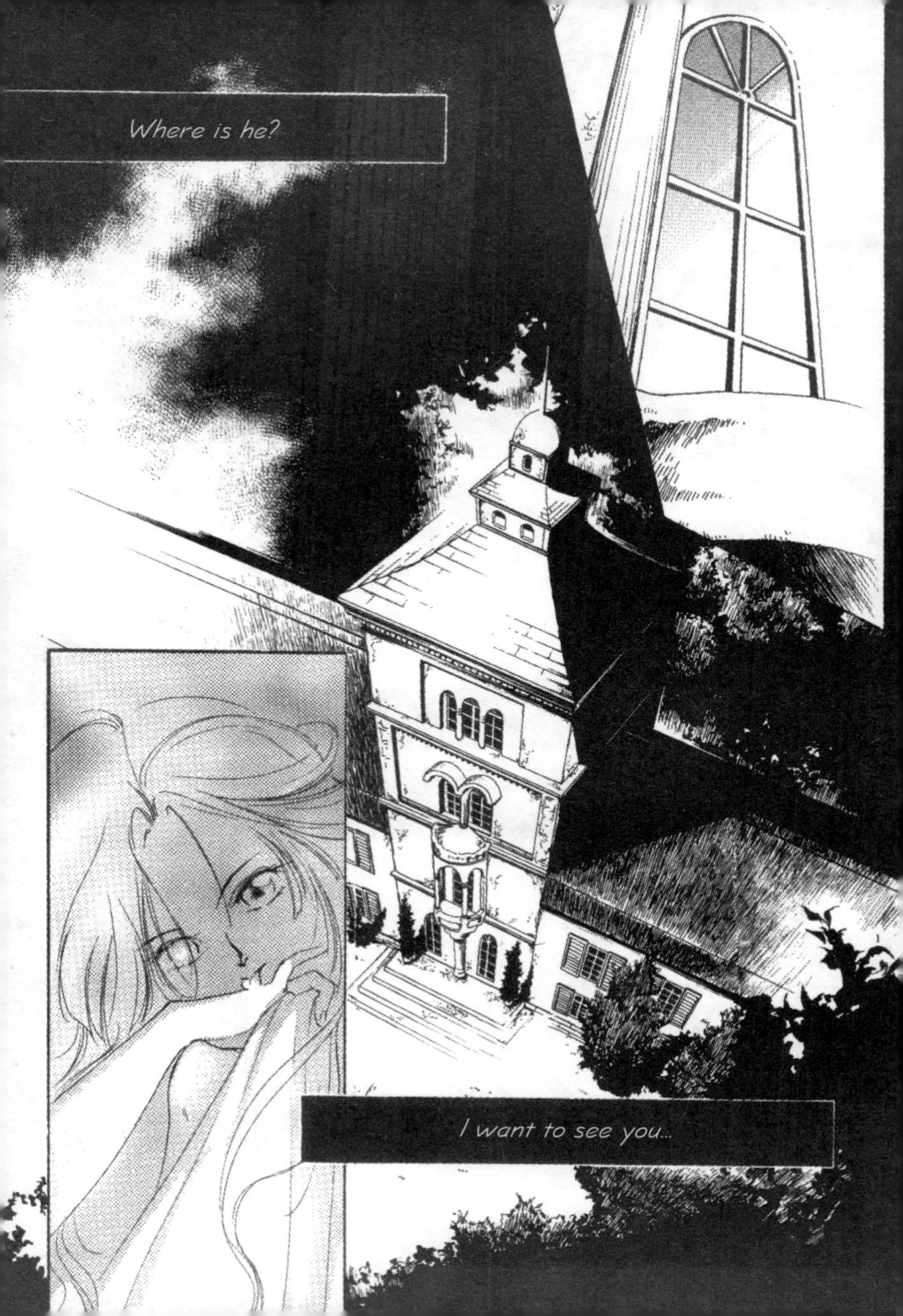
Where is he?
I want to see you...

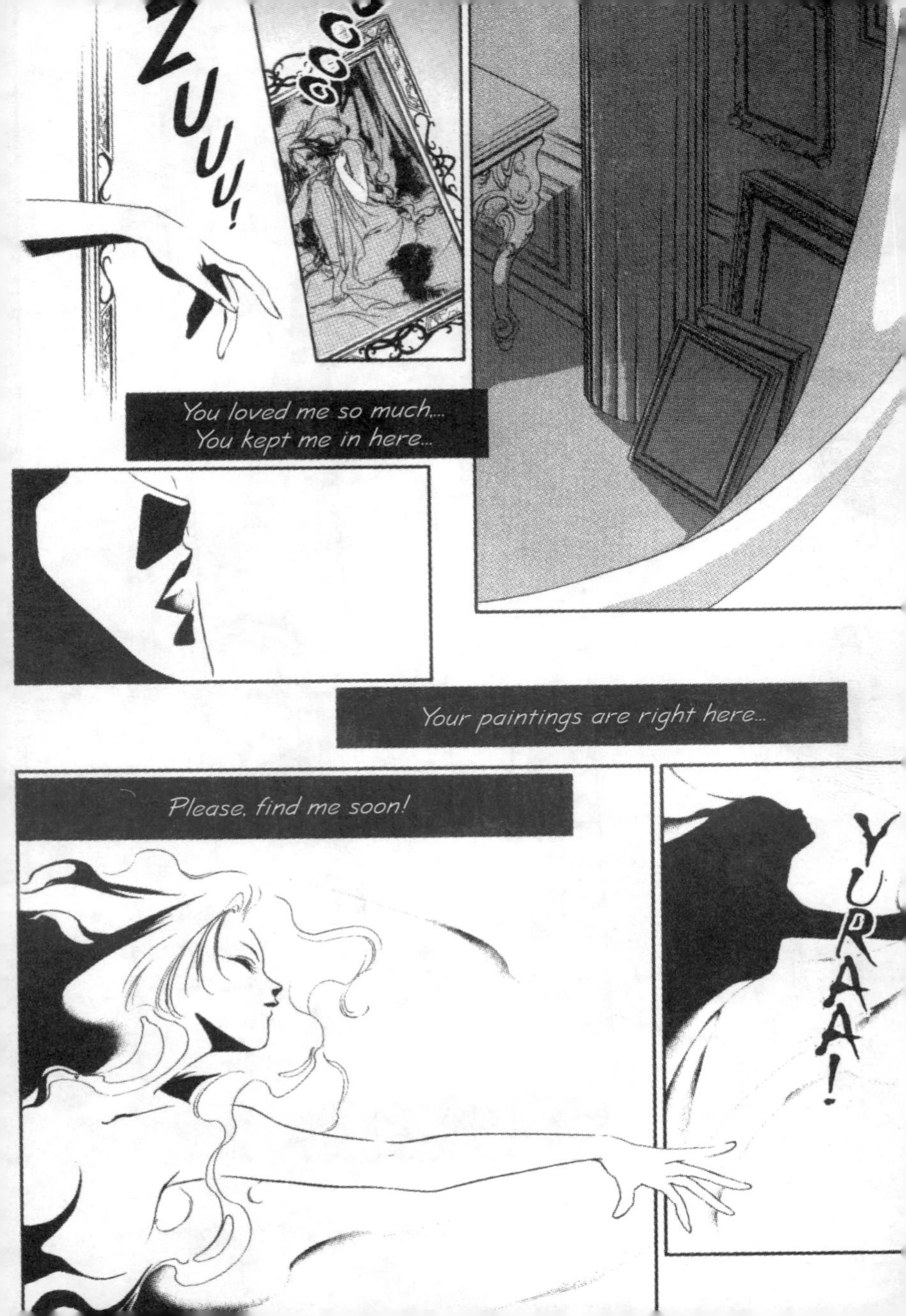
ZUUUU!
You loved me so much...
You kept me in here...
Your paintings are right here...
Please, find me soon!
YURAA!

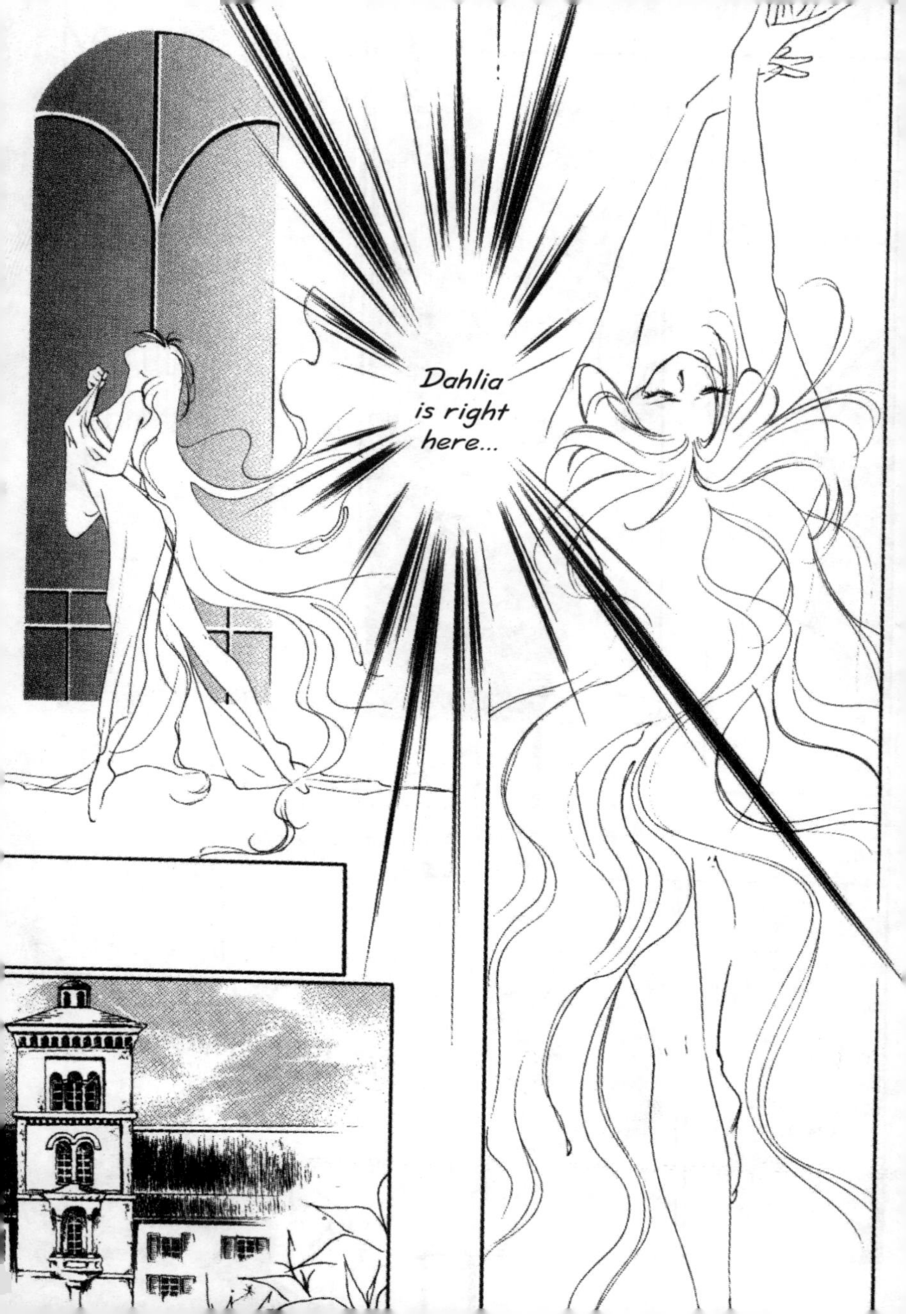
Dahlia is right here...

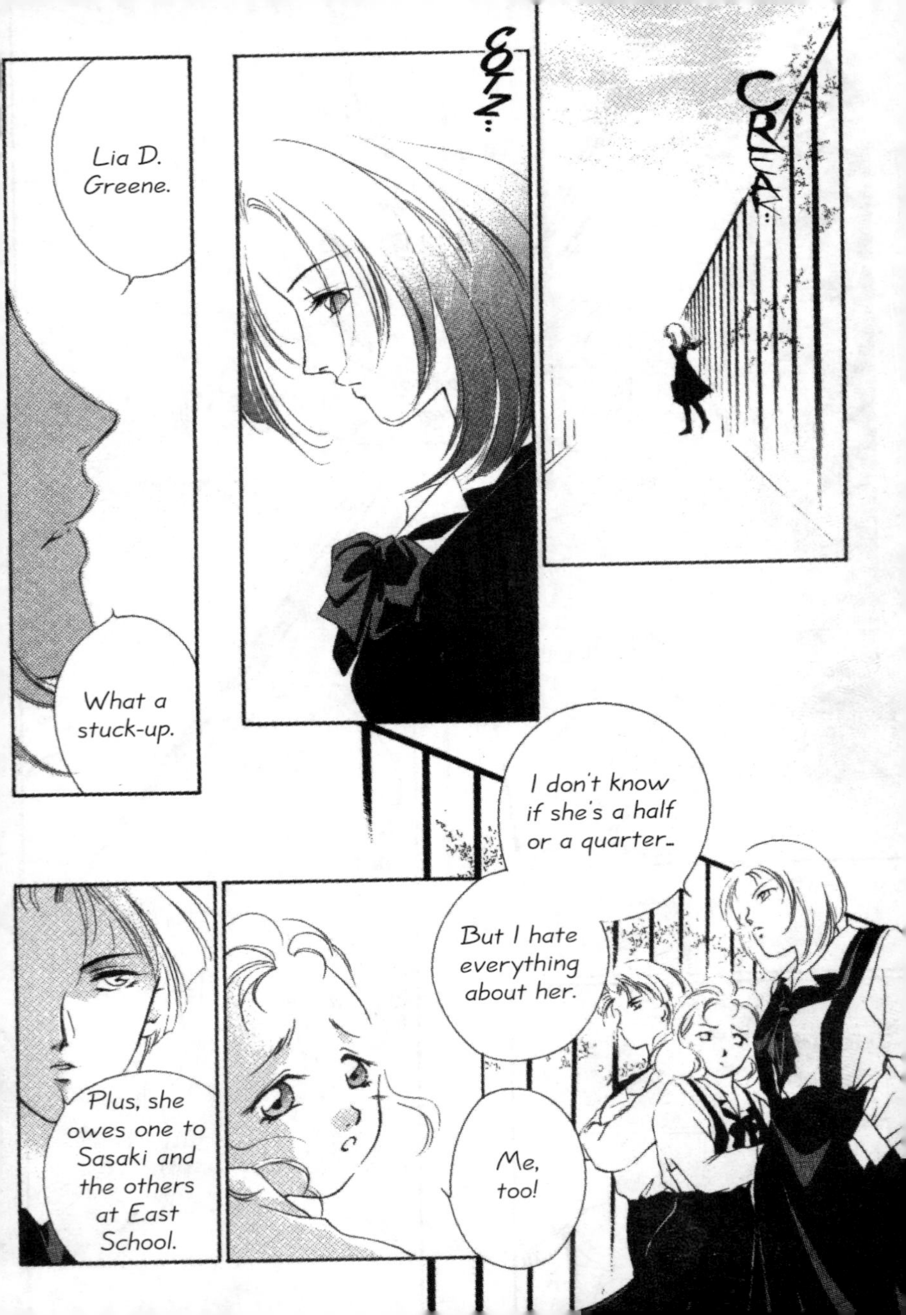
CREAK..
COTZ..
Lia D. Greene.
What a stuck-up.
I don't know if she's a half or a quarter..
But I hate everything about her.
Me, too!
Plus, she owes one to Sasaki and the others at East School.

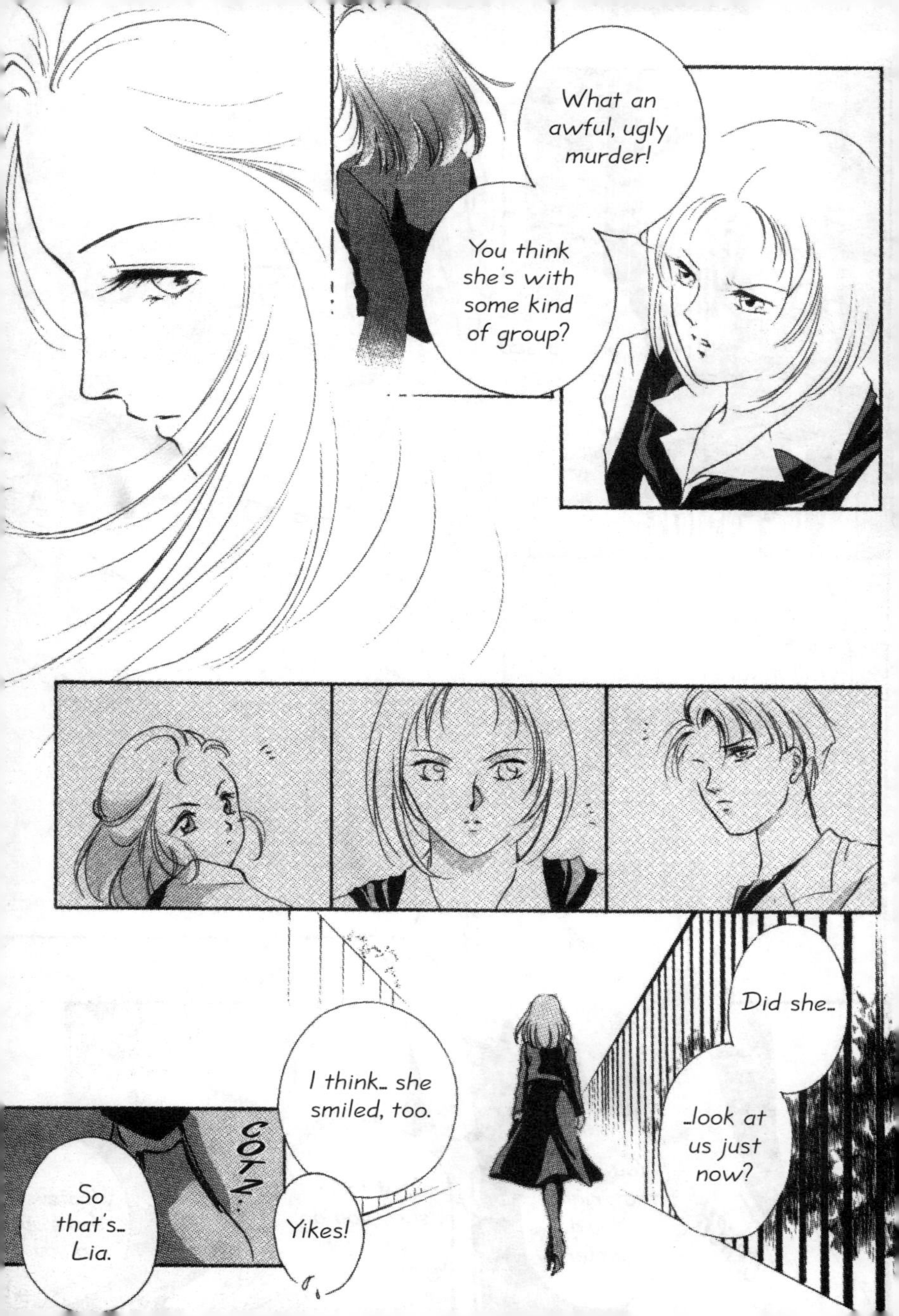
What an awful, ugly murder!
You think she's with some kind of group?
Did she...
...look at us just now?
I think... she smiled, too.
Yikes!
So that's... Lia.

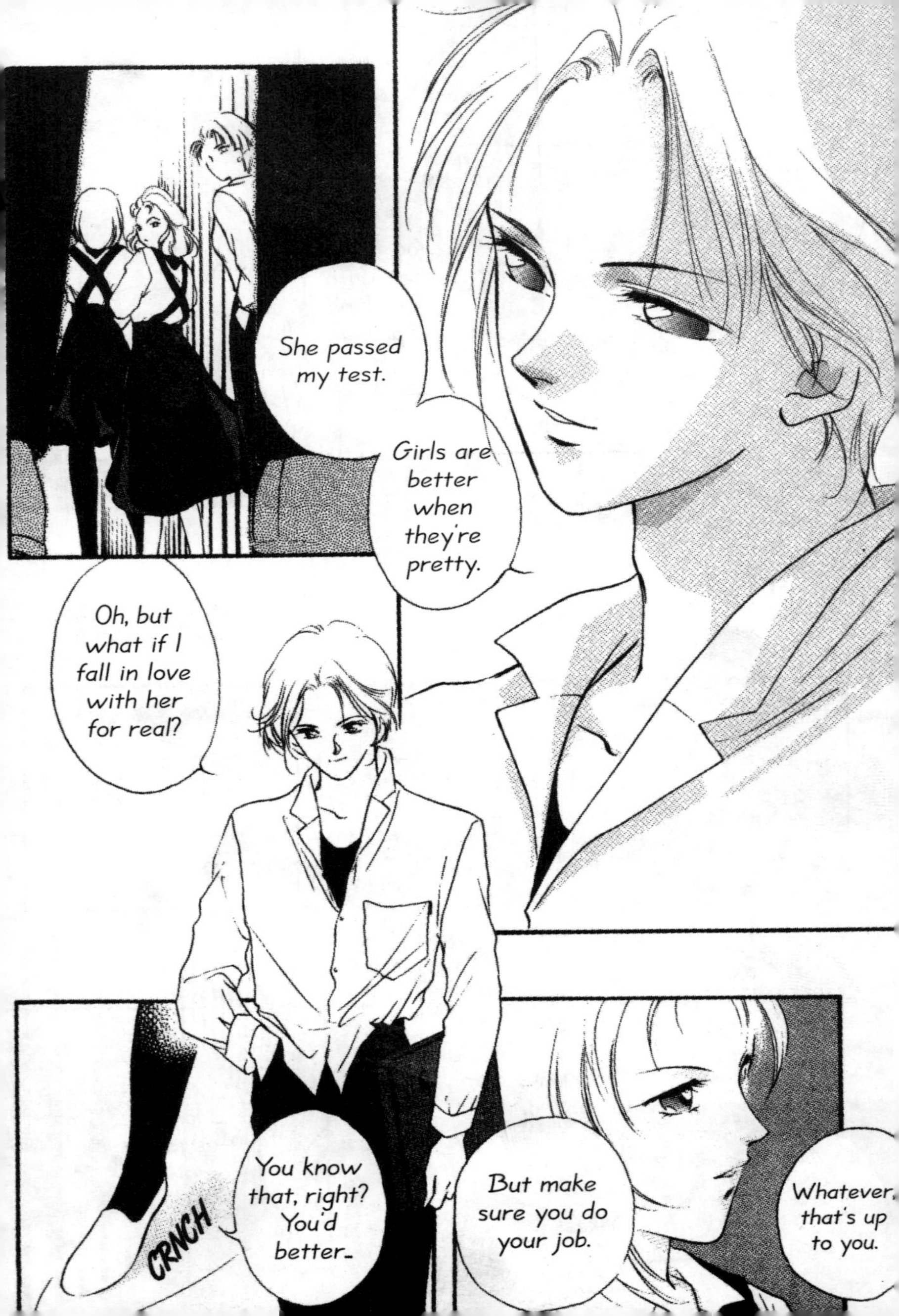
She passed my test.
Girls are better when they're pretty.
Oh, but what if I fall in love with her for real?
Whatever, that's up to you.
But make sure you do your job.
You know that, right? You'd better...
CRNCH

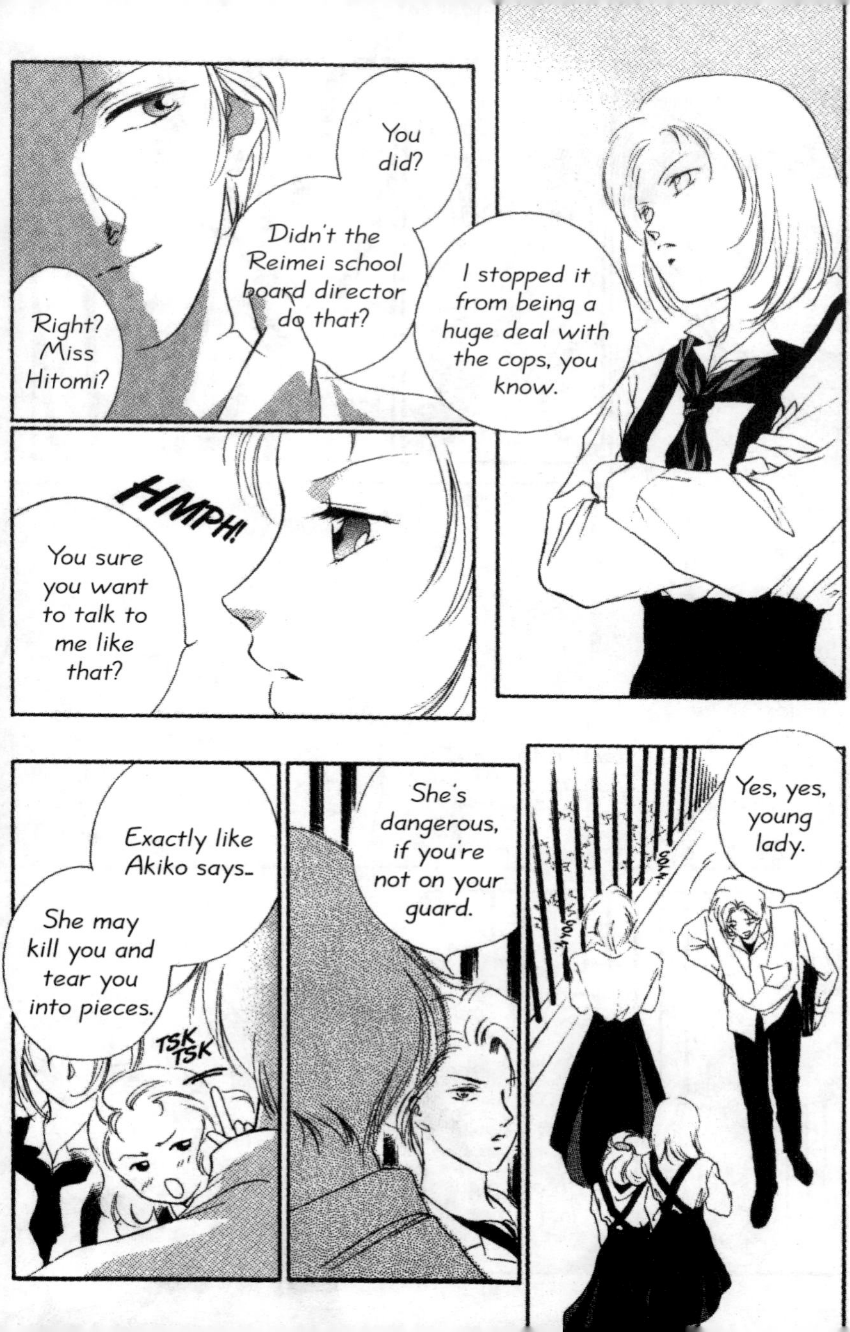
I stopped it from being a huge deal with the cops, you know.
You did?
Didn't the Reimei school board director do that?
Right? Miss Hitomi?
HMPH!
You sure you want to talk to me like that?
Yes, yes, young lady.
She's dangerous, if you're not on your guard.
Exactly like Akiko says...
She may kill you and tear you into pieces.
TSK TSK

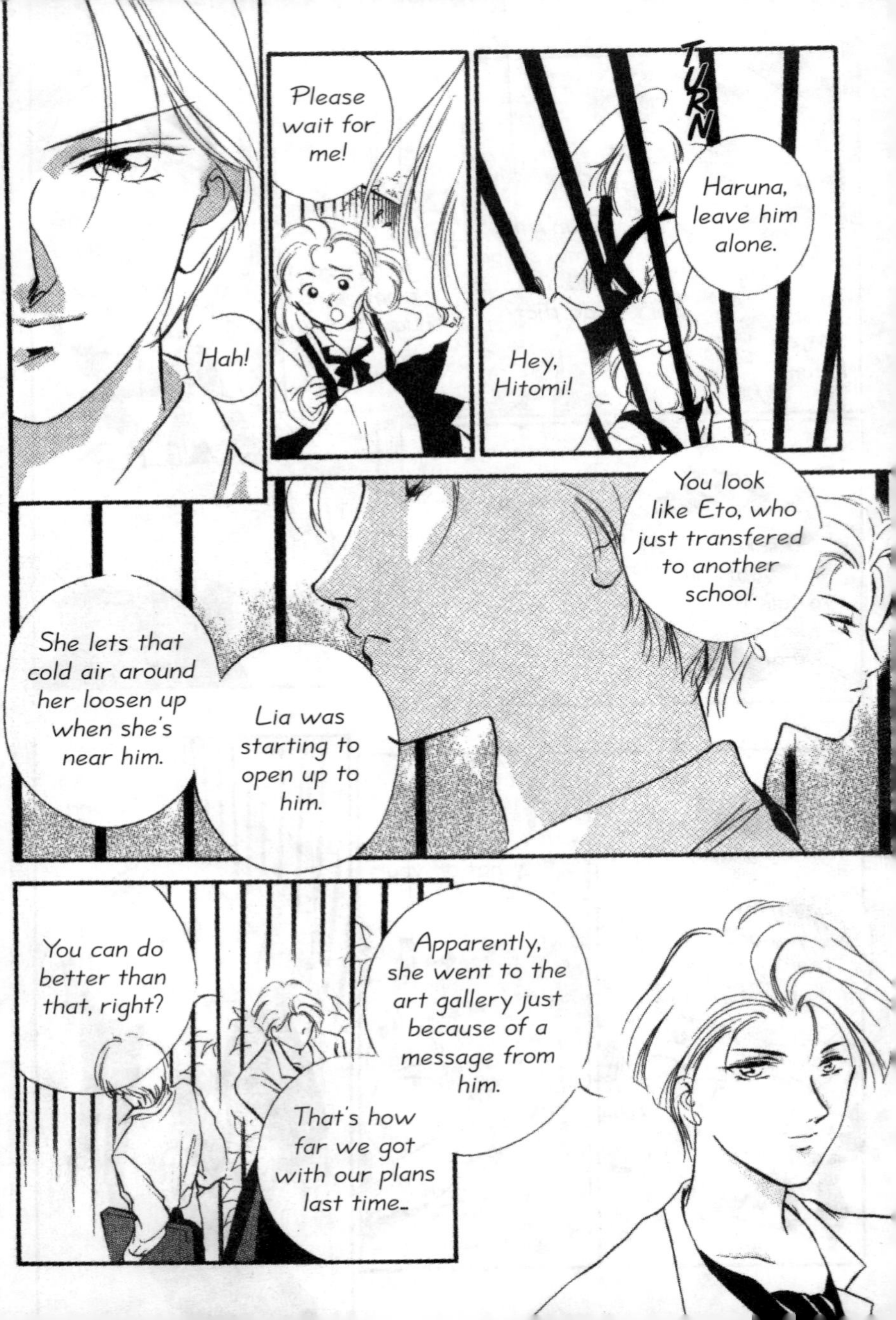
Hah!
Please wait for me!
TURN
Haruna, leave him alone.
Hey, Hitomi!
You look like Eto, who just transfered to another school.
Lia was starting to open up to him.
She lets that cold air around her loosen up when she's near him.
Apparently, she went to the art gallery just because of a message from him.
That's how far we got with our plans last time..
You can do better than that, right?

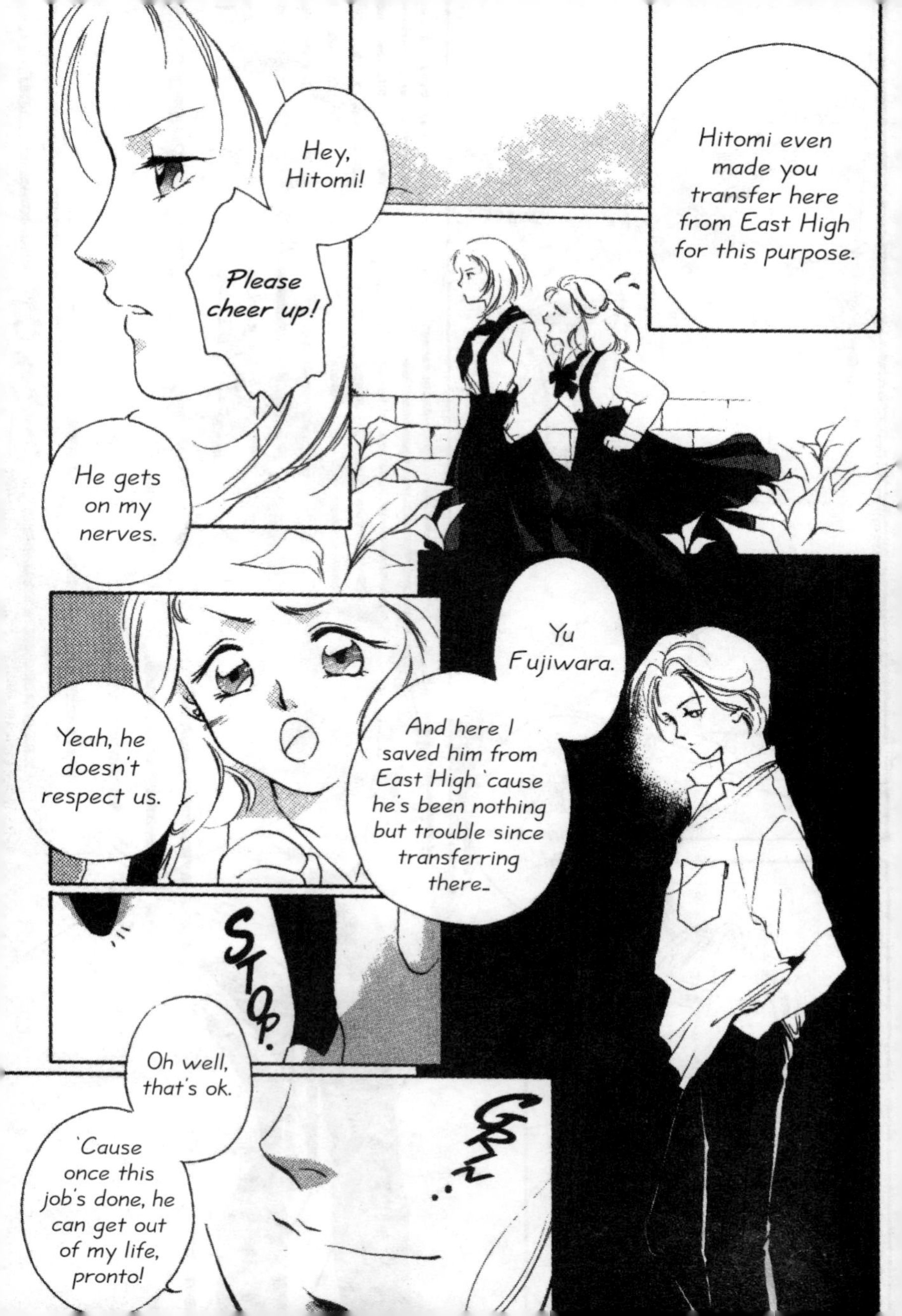
Hitomi even made you transfer here from East High for this purpose.
Hey, Hitomi!
Please cheer up!
He gets on my nerves.
Yu Fujiwara.
And here I saved him from East High 'cause he's been nothing but trouble since transferring there..
Yeah, he doesn't respect us.
STOP.
Oh well, that's ok.
'Cause once this job's done, he can get out of my life, pronto!
GRIN..

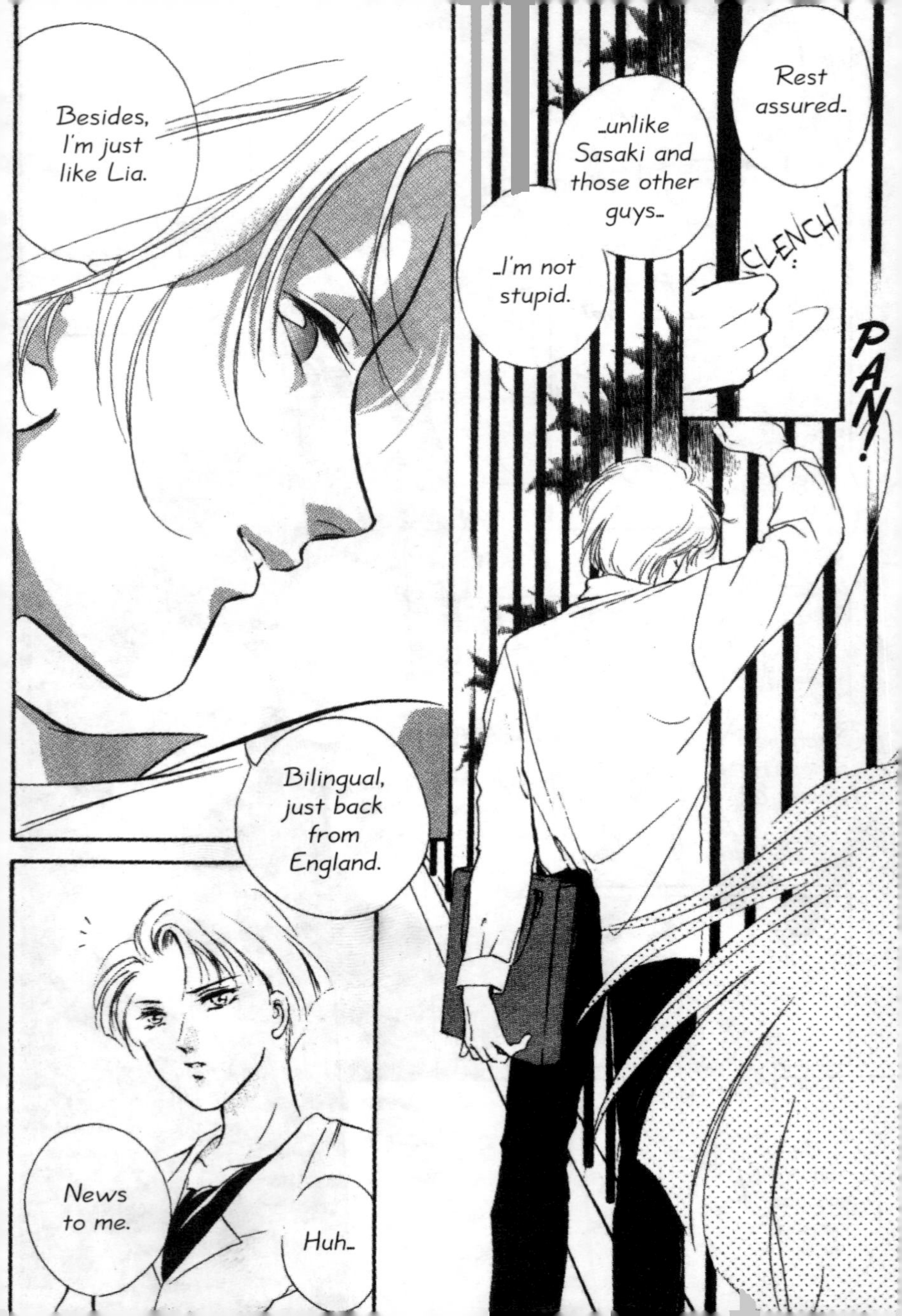

Rest assured…
…unlike Sasaki and those other guys…
…I'm not stupid.
CLENCH
PAN!
Besides, I'm just like Lia.
Bilingual, just back from England.
Huh…
News to me.

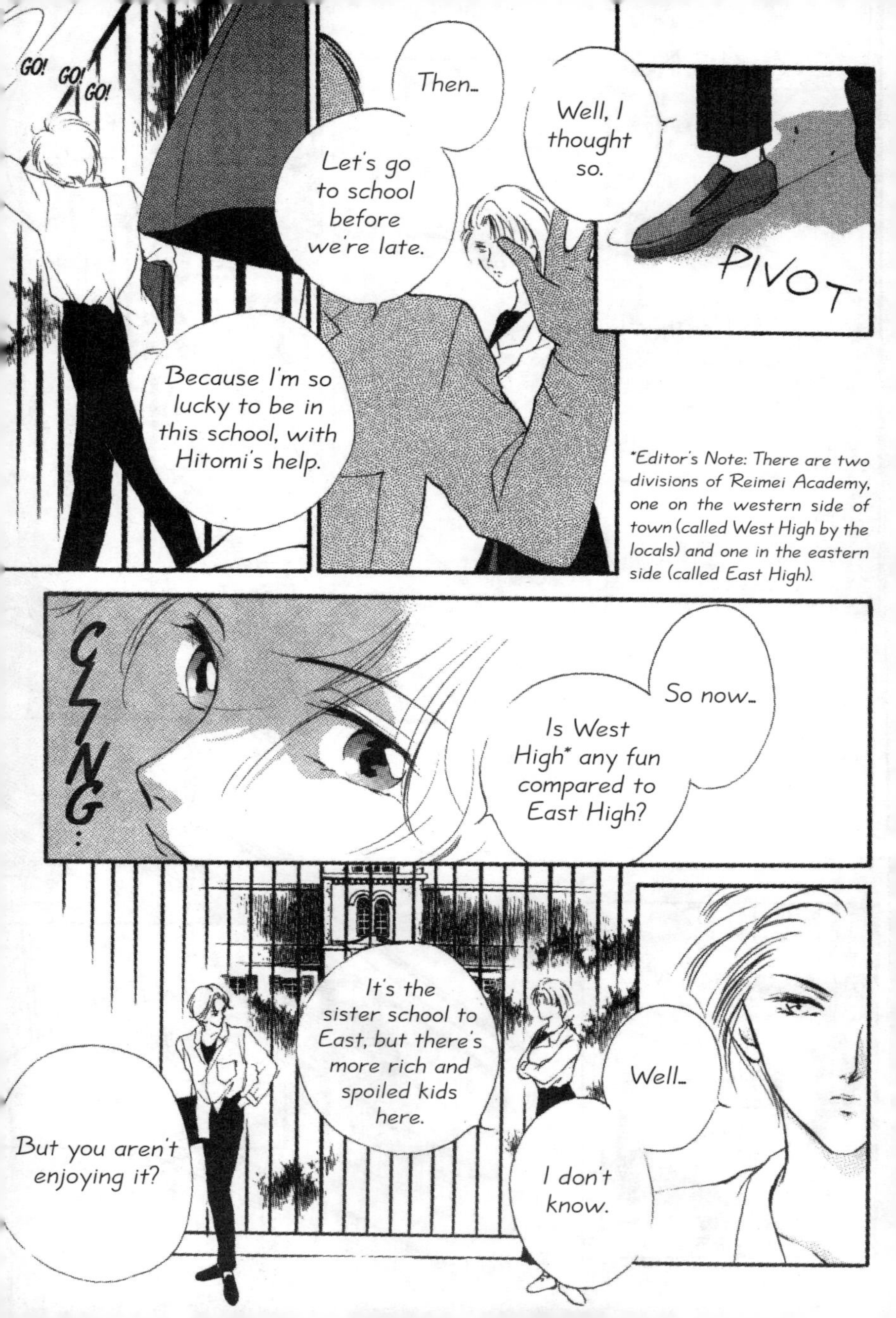
GO! GO! GO!
Because I'm so lucky to be in this school, with Hitomi's help.
Then..
Let's go to school before we're late.
Well, I thought so.
PIVOT
CLING..
So now..
Is West High* any fun compared to East High?
It's the sister school to East, but there's more rich and spoiled kids here.
But you aren't enjoying it?
Well..
I don't know.

*Editor's Note: There are two divisions of Reimei Academy, one on the western side of town (called West High by the locals) and one in the eastern side (called East High).

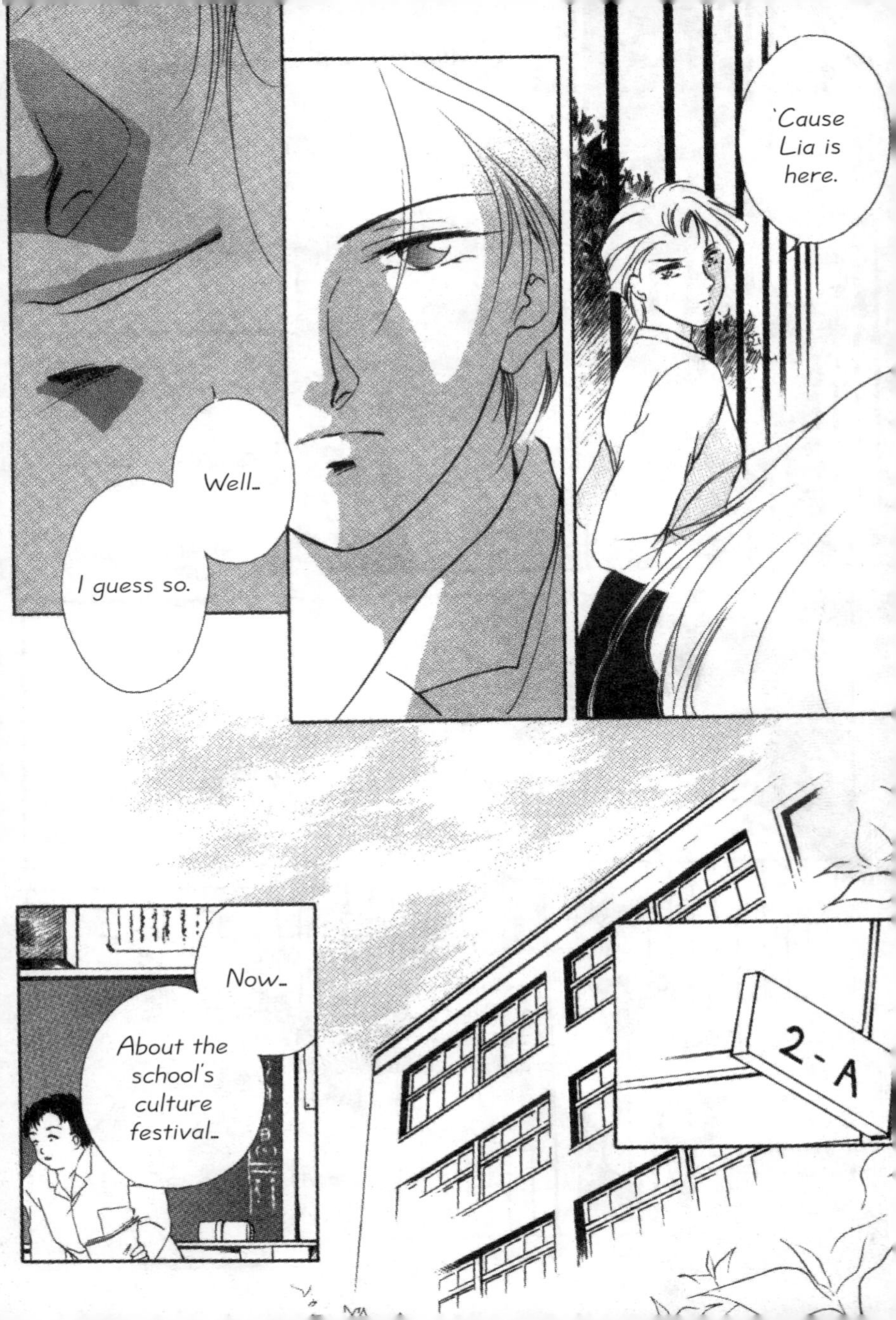
'Cause Lia is here.
Well…
I guess so.
2-A
Now…
About the school's culture festival…

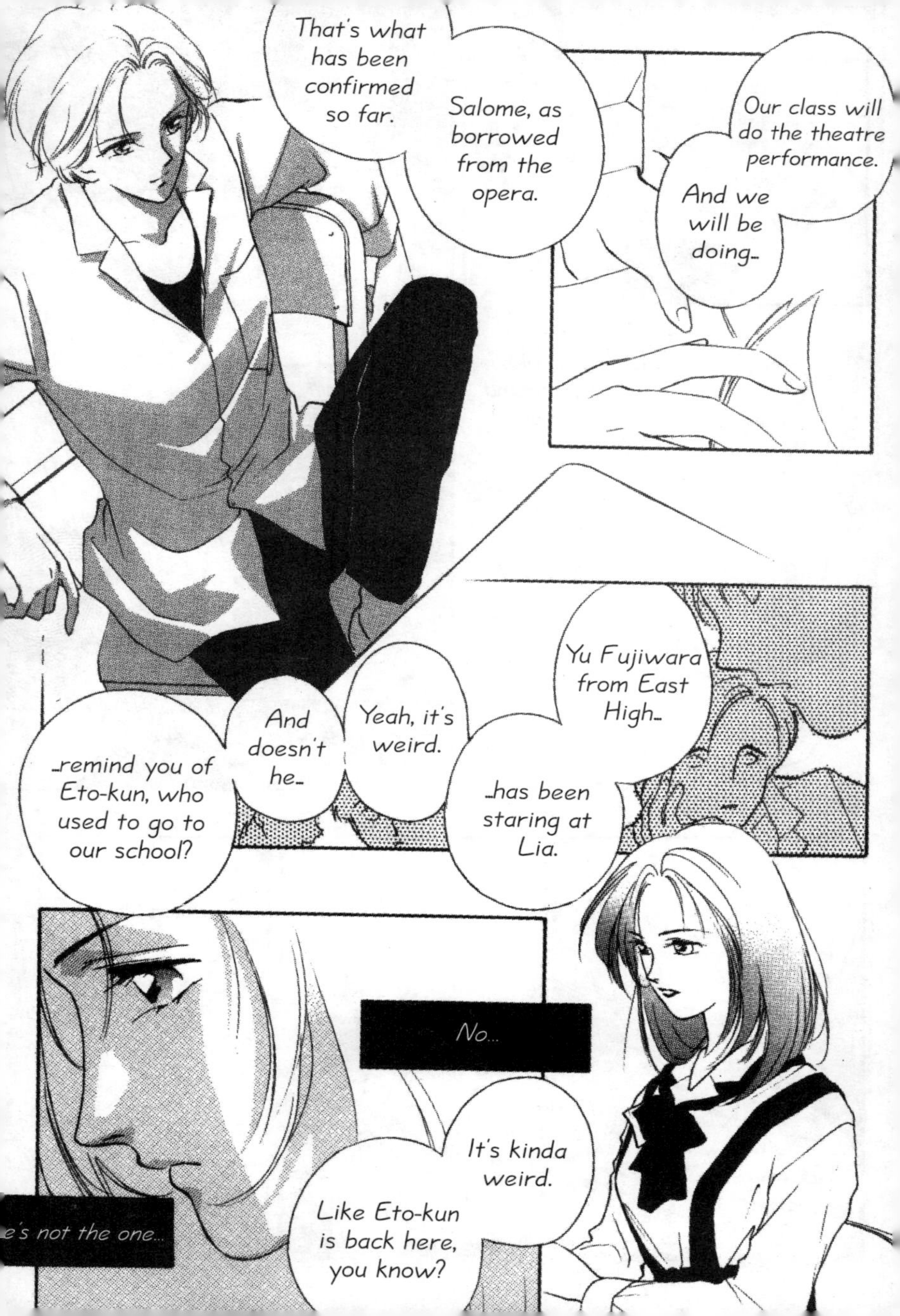
Our class will do the theatre performance.
And we will be doing...
Salome, as borrowed from the opera.
That's what has been confirmed so far.
Yu Fujiwara from East High...
...has been staring at Lia.
Yeah, it's weird.
And doesn't he...
...remind you of Eto-kun, who used to go to our school?
It's kinda weird.
Like Eto-kun is back here, you know?
No...
e's not the one...

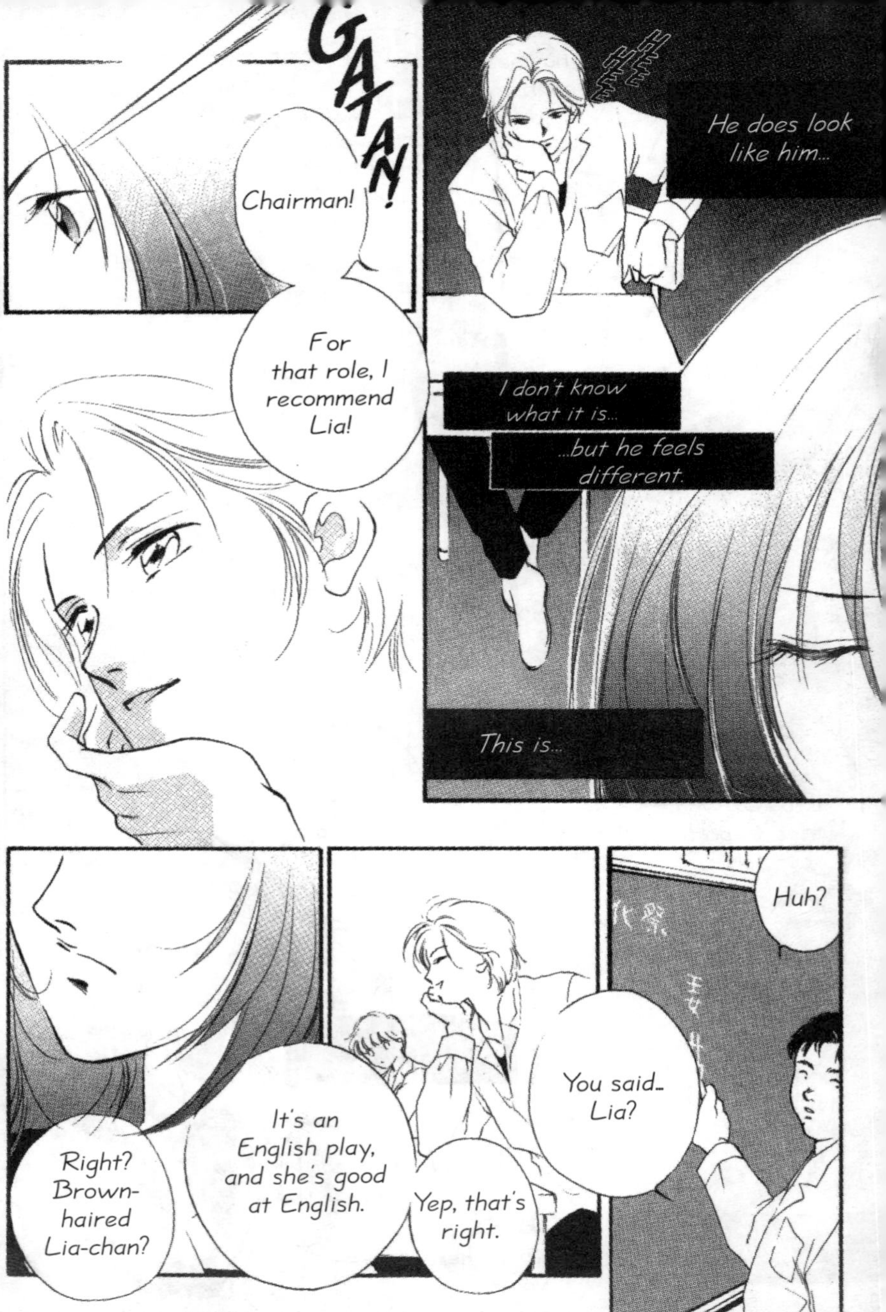
HEE HEE
He does look like him...
I don't know what it is...
...but he feels different.
This is...
GATAN!
Chairman!
For that role, I recommend Lia!
Huh?
You said... Lia?
Yep, that's right.
It's an English play, and she's good at English.
Right? Brown-haired Lia-chan?

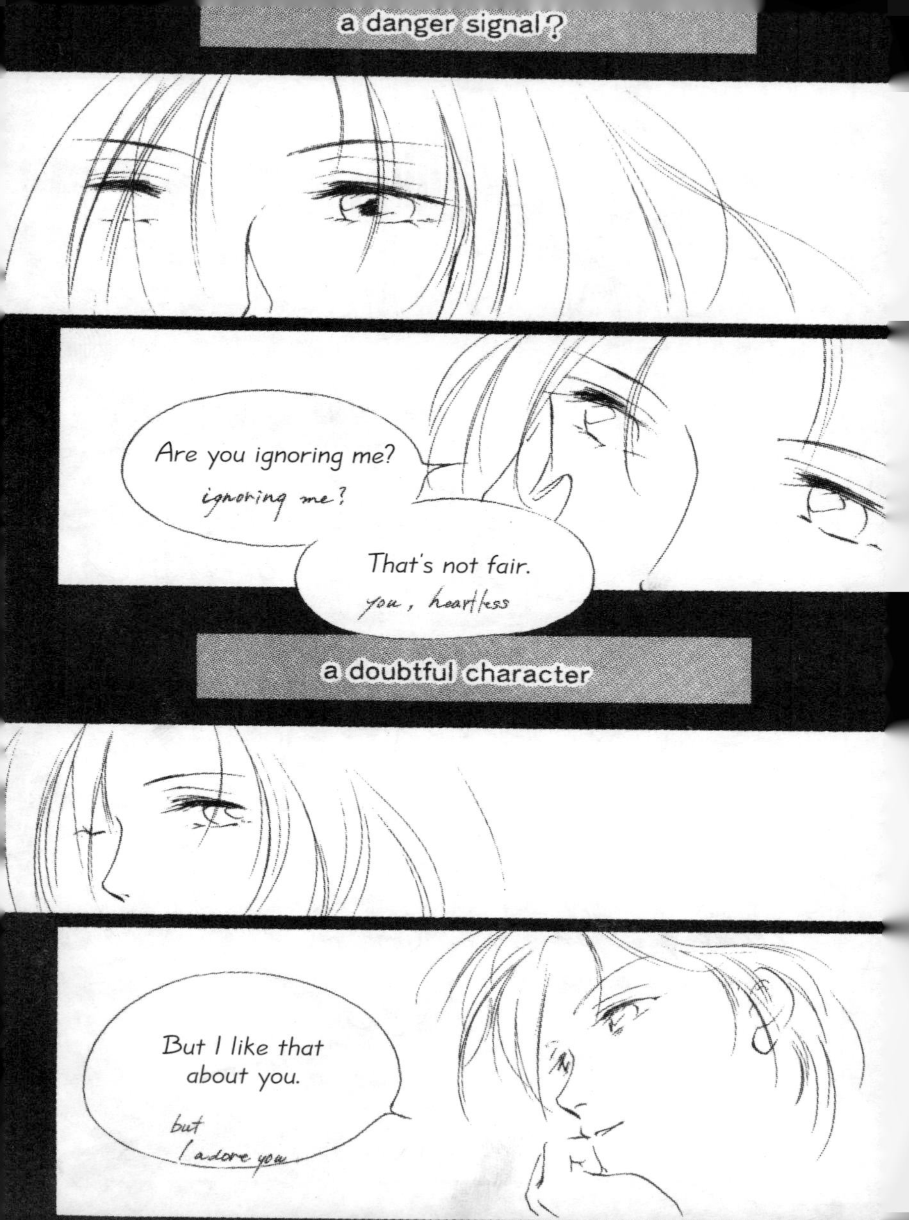
a danger signal?
Are you ignoring me?
ignoring me?
That's not fair.
you, heartless
a doubtful character
But I like that about you.
but I adore you

Editor's Note: The fancy script text is part of the original artwork. Yu is speaking in English instead of Japanese, when he speaks in the script font.

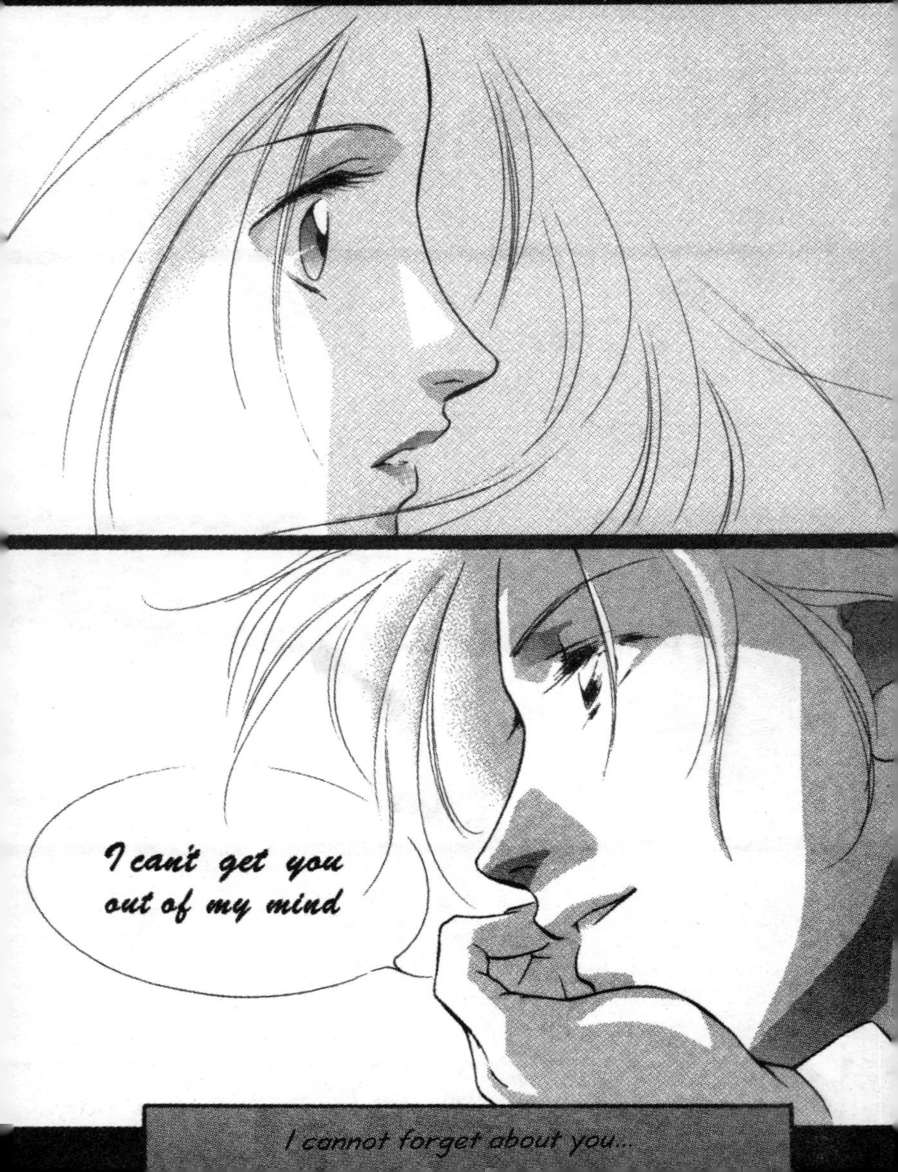
I can't get you out of my mind
I cannot forget about you...

Lia
リア

My darling Dahlia
ぼくのダリア

come to me...
おいで…

Come on...grow up
早く大人になっておくれ

I want to take you with me,
連れて行きたい

with my eternal love...
永遠を君に捧げ…

we pass the time together.
時間という空間を漂う

Lia...
リア

My sweetheart
私のダリア

I love you.
愛してる

SHHHHH...

...KOTZ ...KOTZ
...KOTZ

I'm not sure exactly, but_

Man

...KOTZ

_kinda horny-looking.

You're the right size and_

Huh? Me?

King Herod suits you, chairman.

文化

ヨカナーン（予言者）

王女サロメ・里亜 Green

Are there any more casting ideas?

Ah, excuse me!

Talk about daring.

Did you just ask her out or something?

Board list: Princess Salome (Lia Greene)
Jokanaan (Prophet)

Board top: "School Fest—"

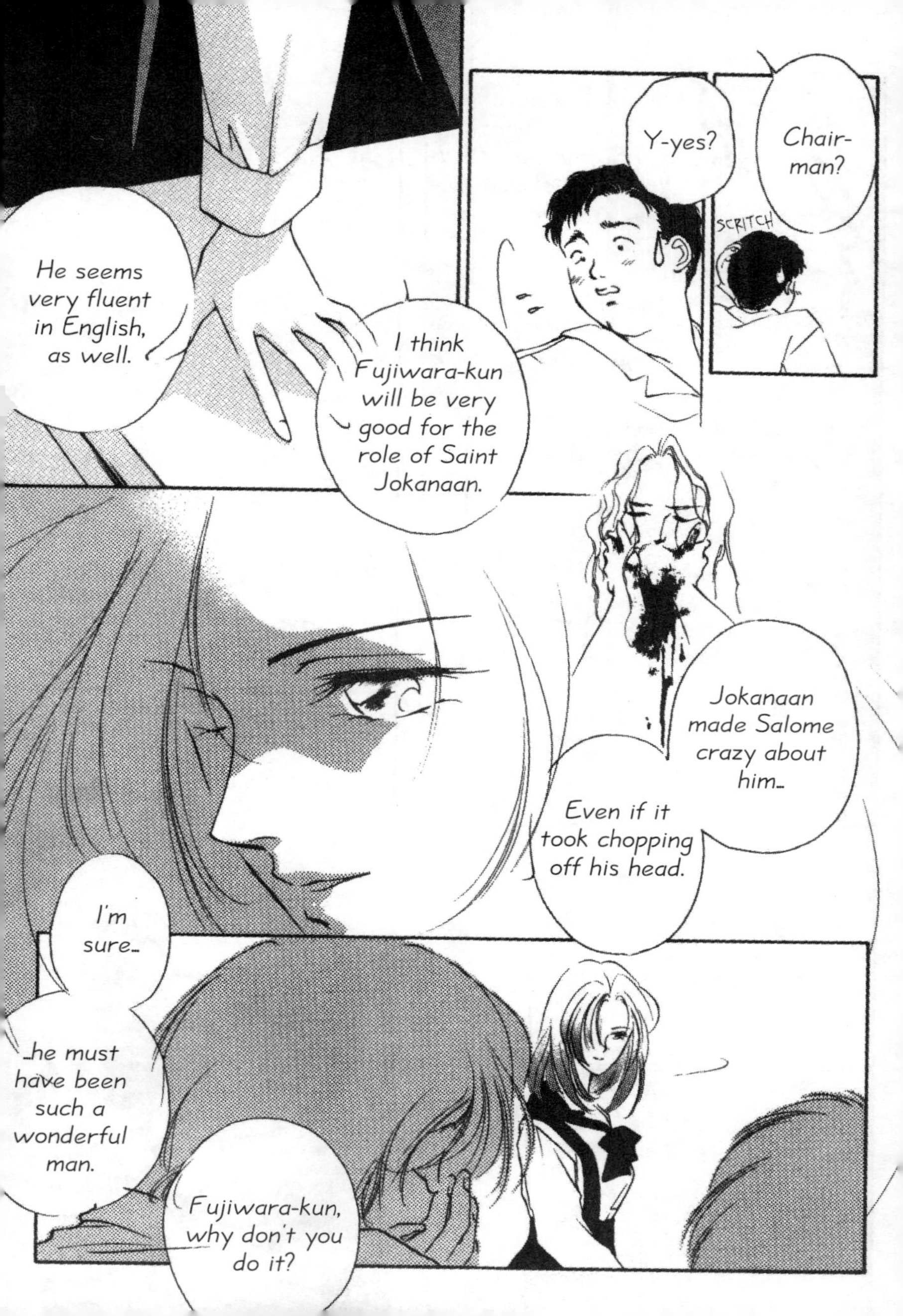
Chair-man?
Y-yes?
SCRITCH
I think Fujiwara-kun will be very good for the role of Saint Jokanaan.
He seems very fluent in English, as well.
Jokanaan made Salome crazy about him...
Even if it took chopping off his head.
I'm sure...
...he must have been such a wonderful man.
Fujiwara-kun, why don't you do it?

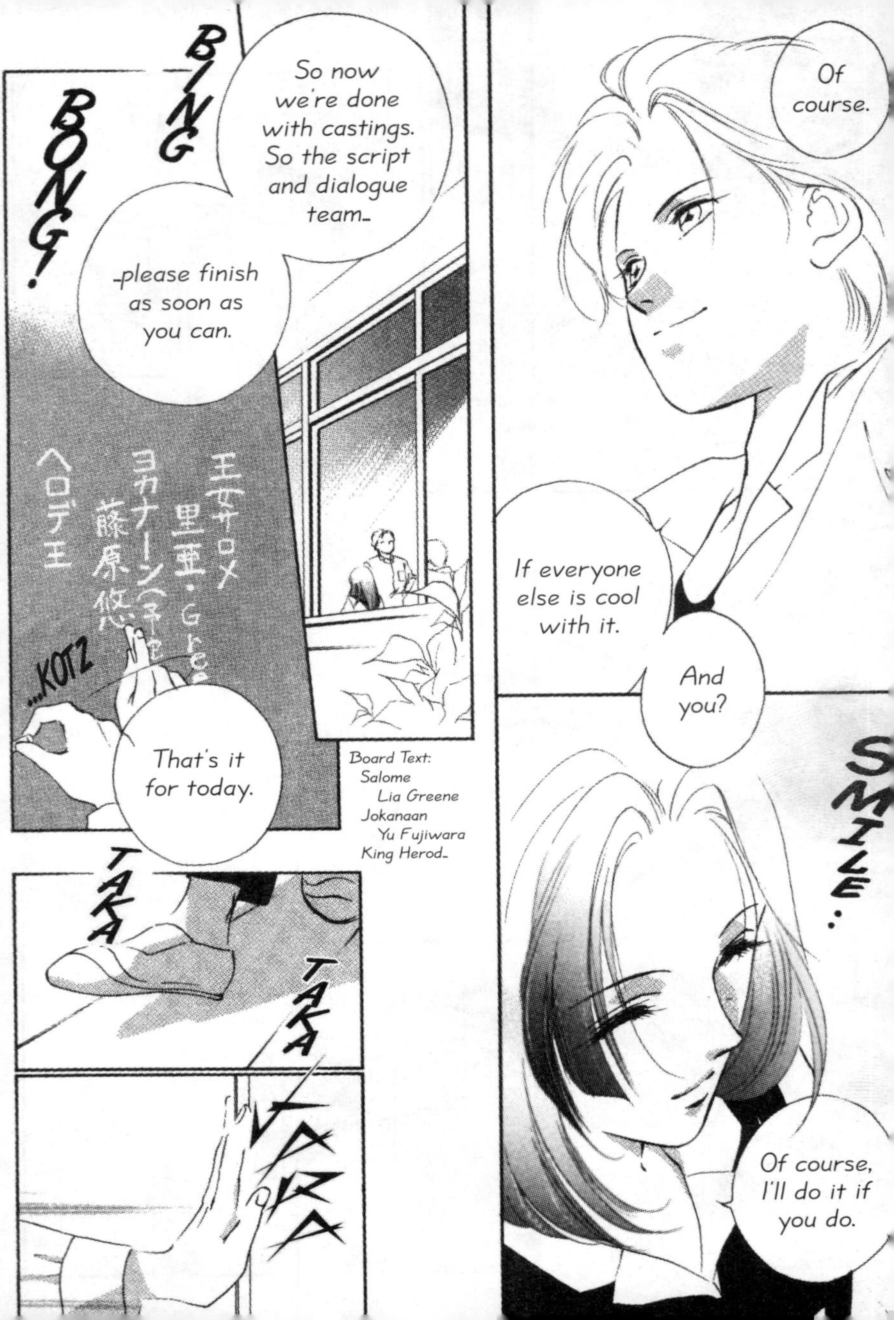
BING BONG!
So now we're done with castings. So the script and dialogue team...
...please finish as soon as you can.
Of course.
If everyone else is cool with it.
And you?
SMILE..
Of course, I'll do it if you do.
王女サロメ 里亜・Gree
ヨカナーン（予定）藤原悠
ヘロデ王
...KOTZ
That's it for today.
Board Text:
Salome
Lia Greene
Jokanaan
Yu Fujiwara
King Herod...
TAKA TAKA
TAKA TAKA
GARA

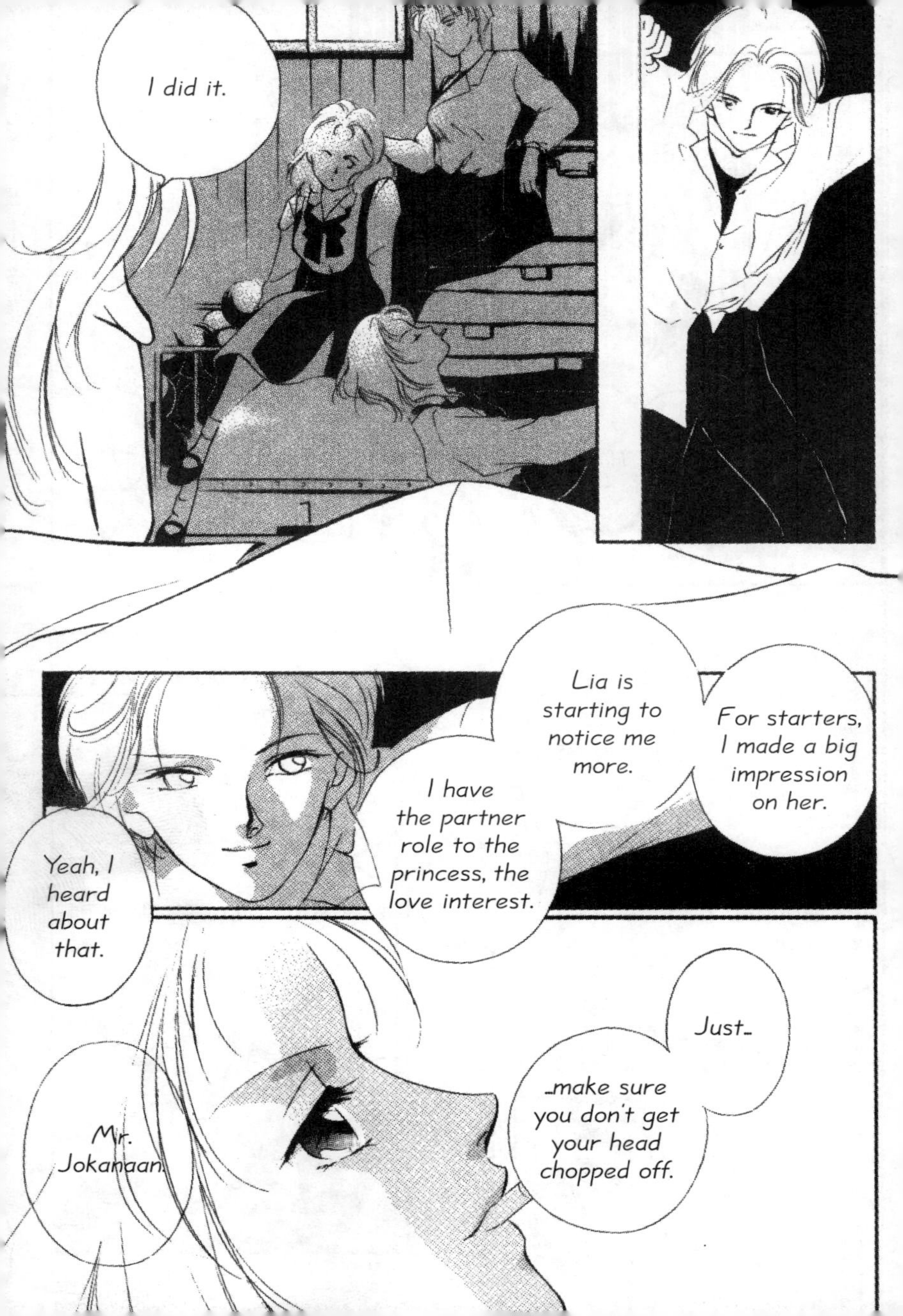
I did it.
For starters, I made a big impression on her.
Lia is starting to notice me more.
I have the partner role to the princess, the love interest.
Yeah, I heard about that.
Just...
...make sure you don't get your head chopped off.
Mr. Jokanaan.

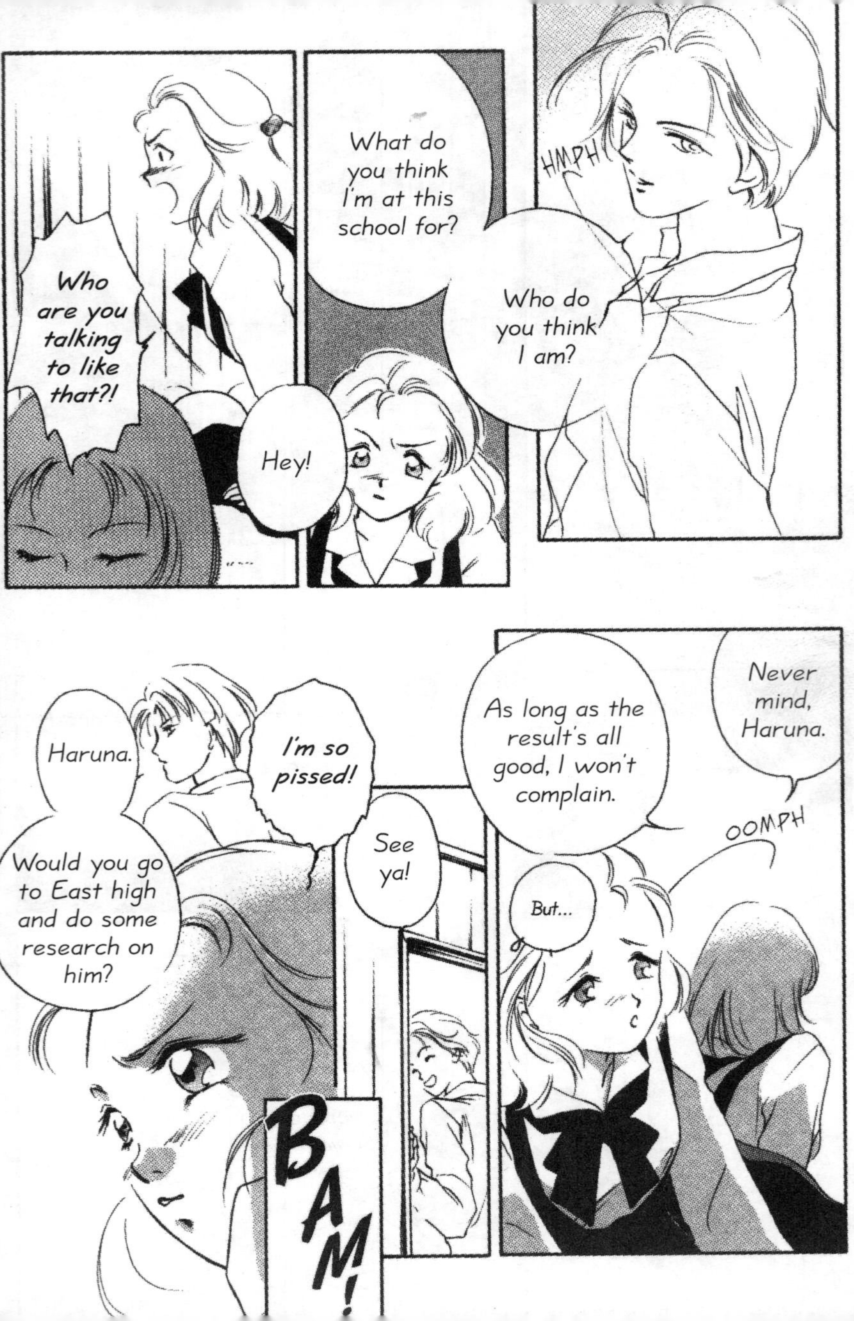
Who are you talking to like that?!
Hey!
What do you think I'm at this school for?
HMPH
Who do you think I am?
Haruna.
Would you go to East high and do some research on him?
I'm so pissed!
See ya!
BAM!
As long as the result's all good, I won't complain.
Never mind, Haruna.
OOMPH
But...

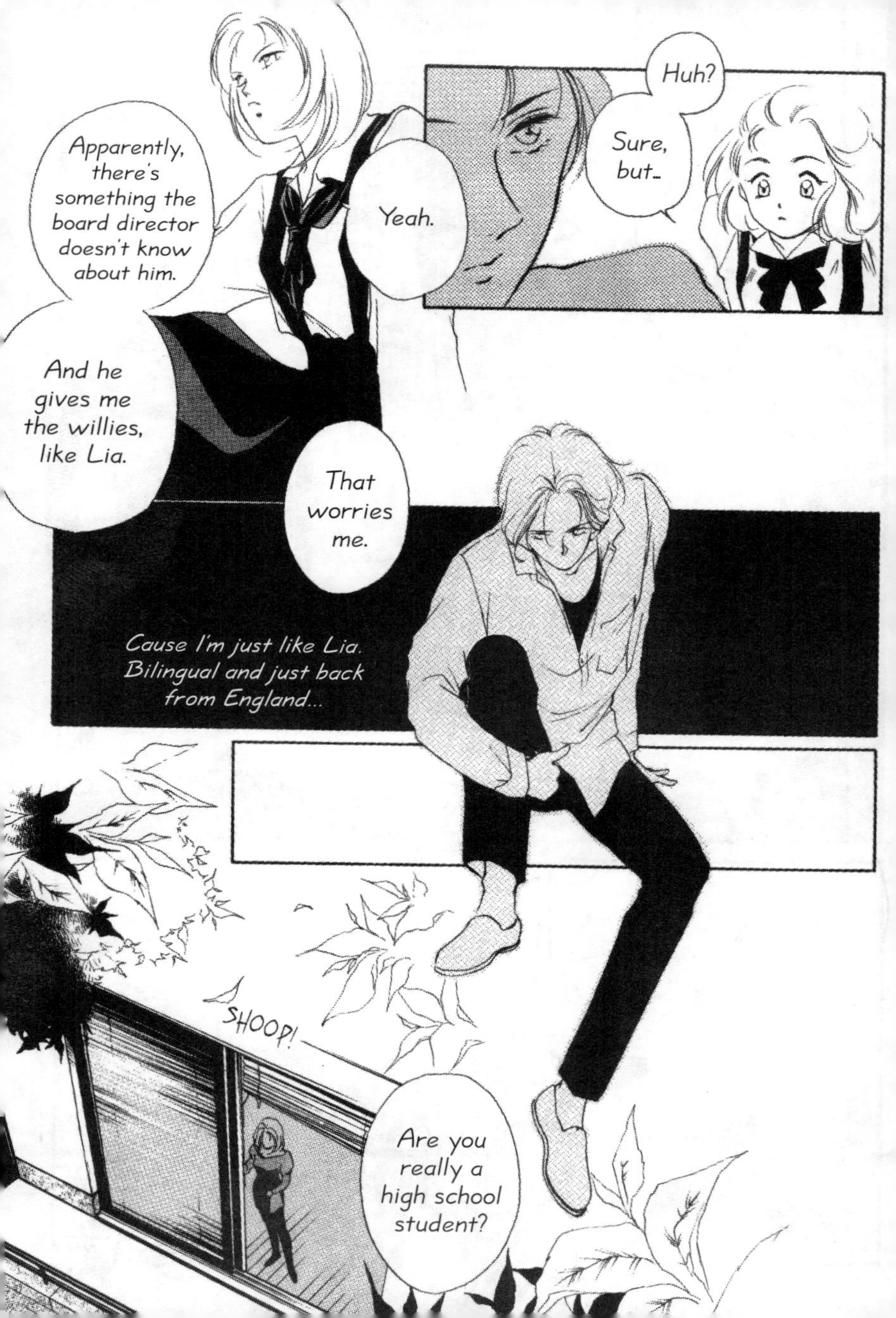
Huh?
Sure, but..
Yeah.
Apparently, there's something the board director doesn't know about him.
And he gives me the willies, like Lia.
That worries me.
Cause I'm just like Lia. Bilingual and just back from England...
SHOOP!
Are you really a high school student?

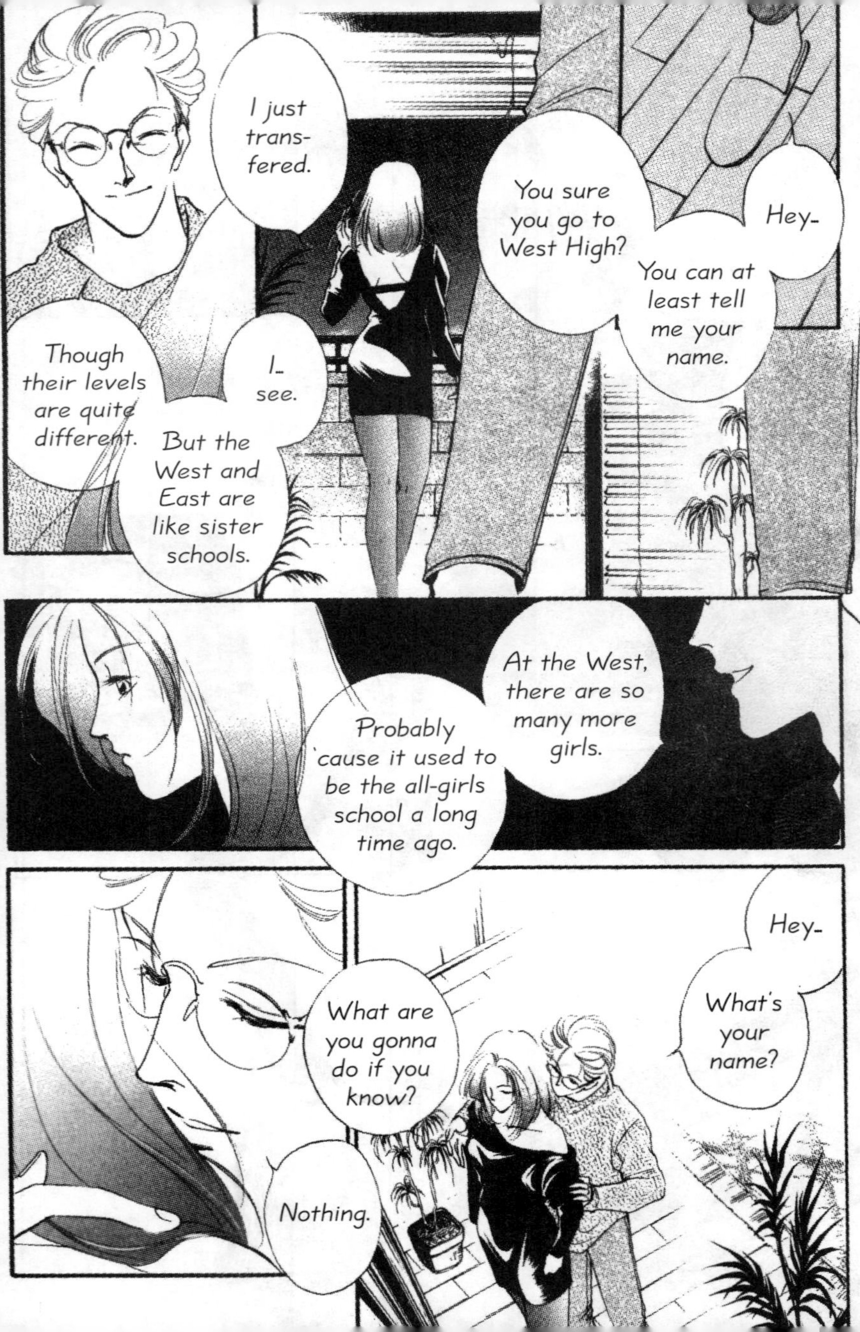
Hey-
You can at least tell me your name.
You sure you go to West High?
I just trans-fered.
I- see.
But the West and East are like sister schools.
Though their levels are quite different.
At the West, there are so many more girls.
Probably 'cause it used to be the all-girls school a long time ago.
Hey-
What's your name?
What are you gonna do if you know?
Nothing.

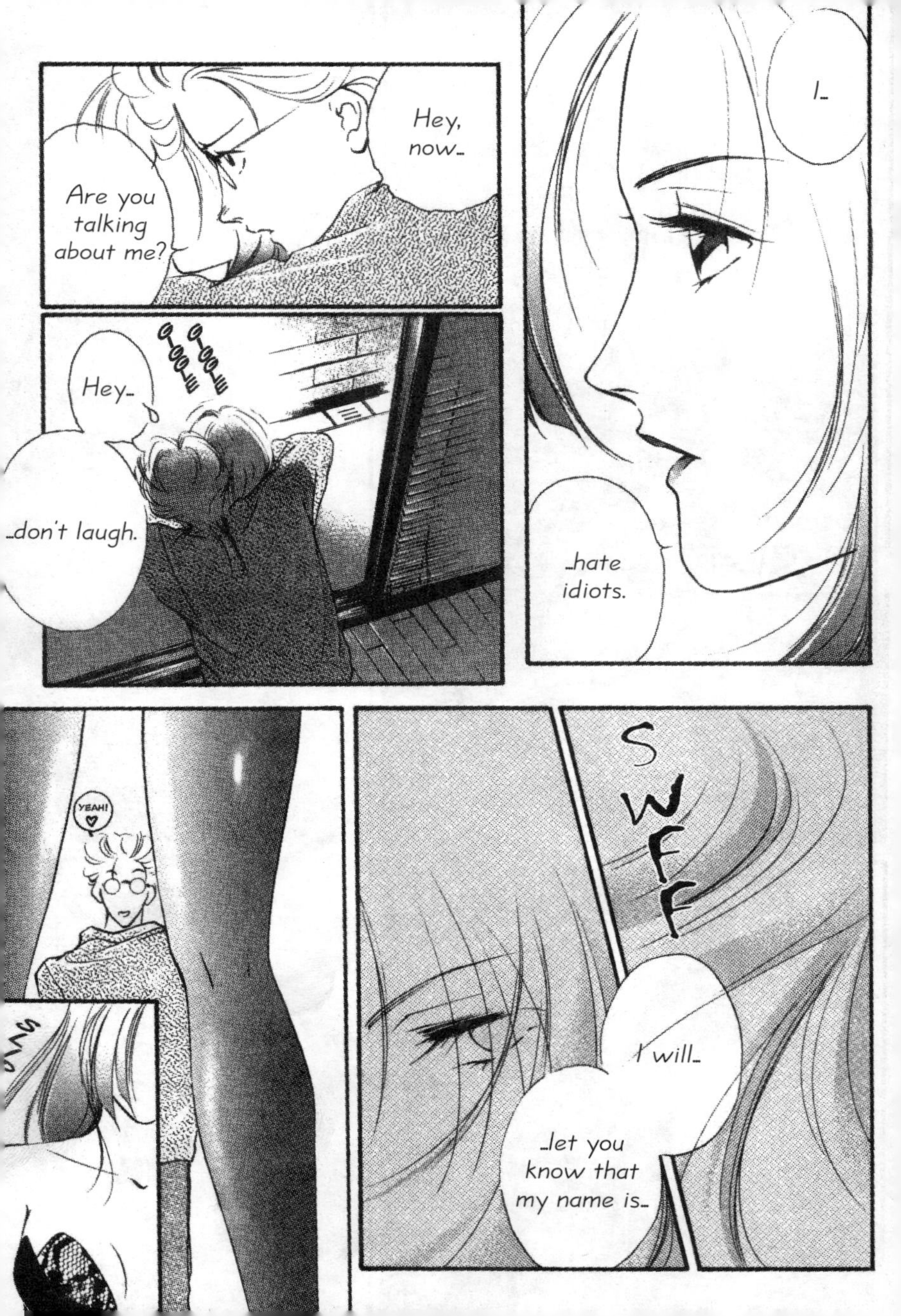
I...
...hate idiots.
Hey, now...
Are you talking about me?
Hey...
...don't laugh.
SWFF
I will...
...let you know that my name is...
YEAH!

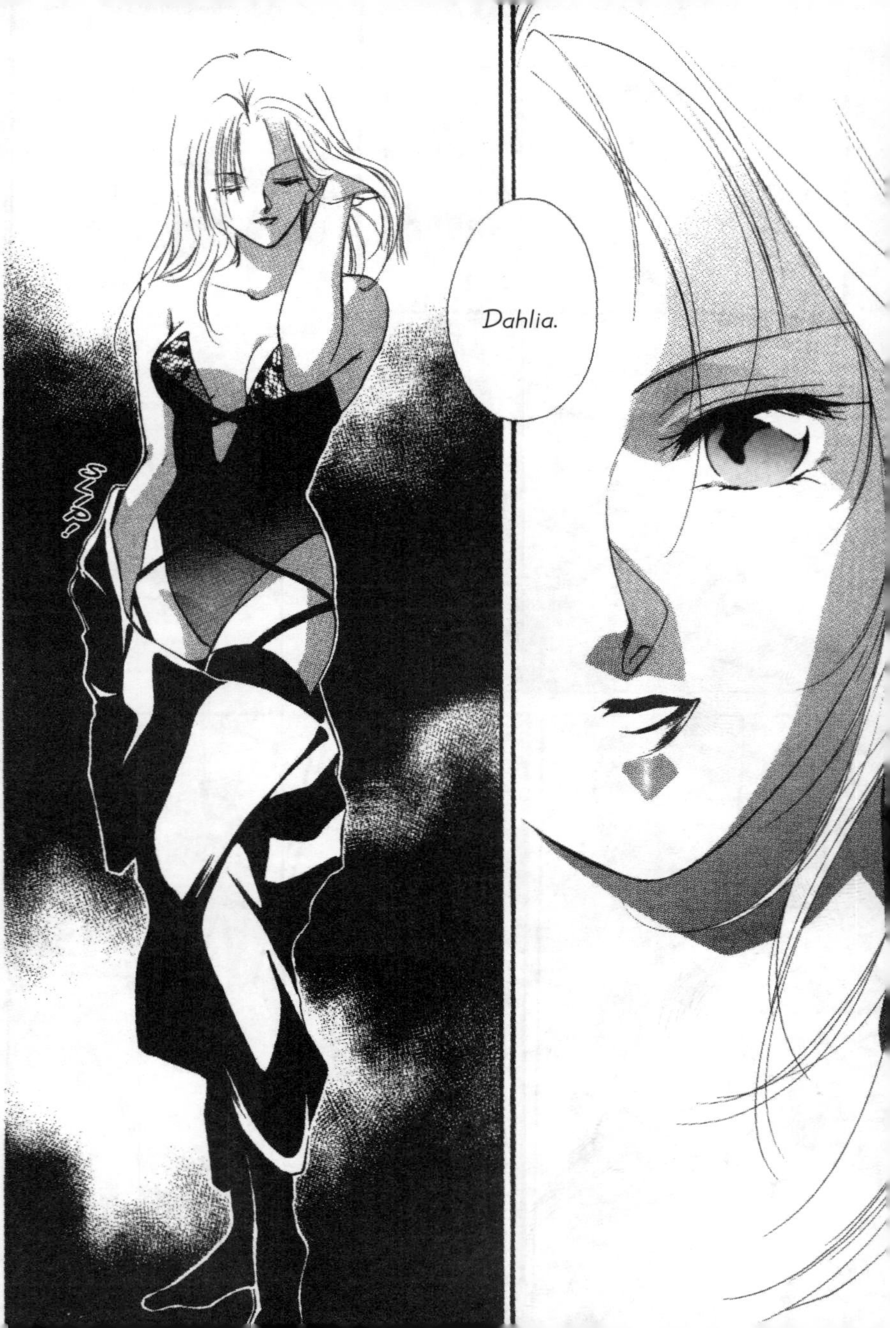
Dahlia.

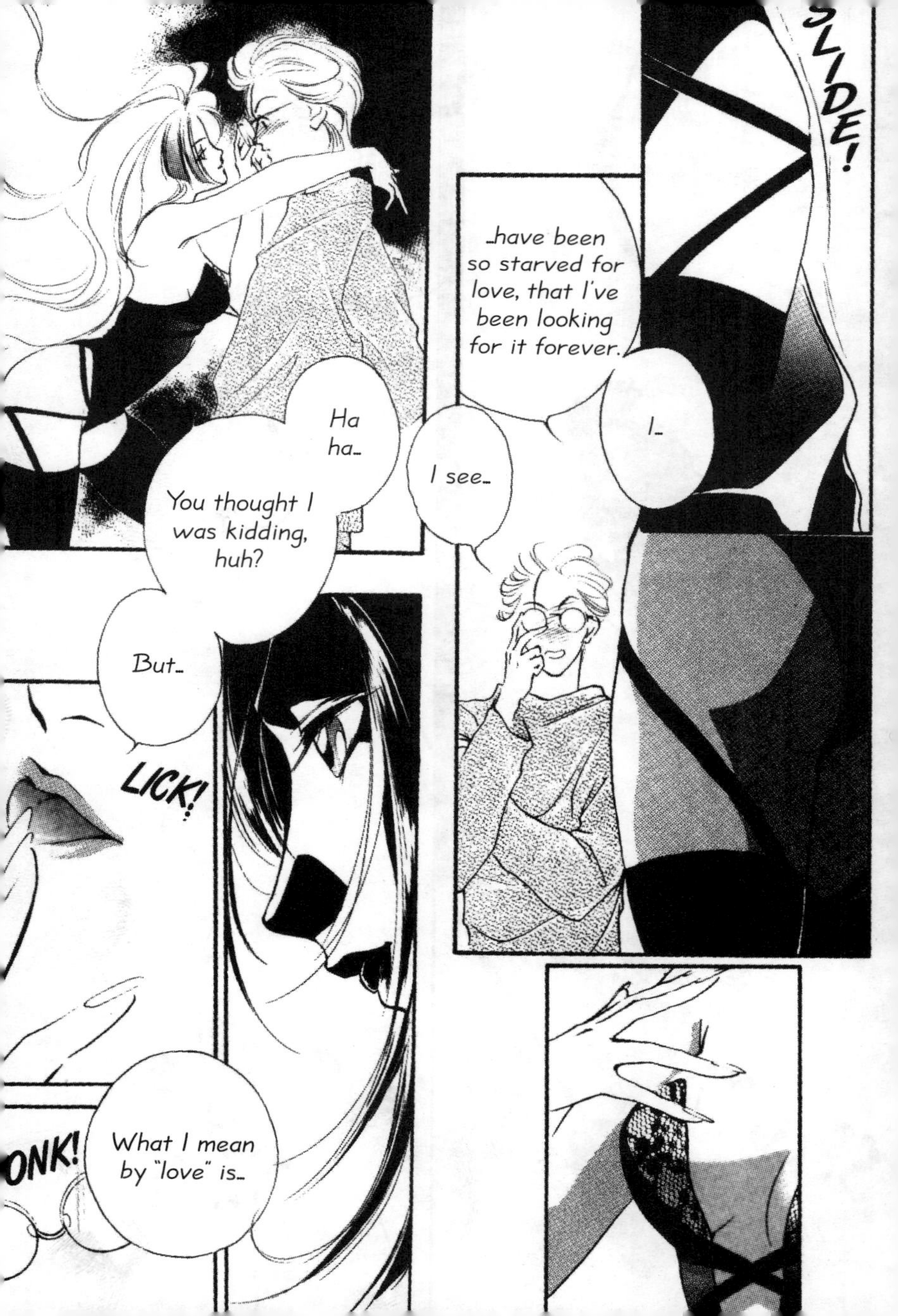
SLIDE!
I...
...have been so starved for love, that I've been looking for it forever.
I see...
Ha ha...
You thought I was kidding, huh?
But...
LICK!
What I mean by "love" is...
ONK!

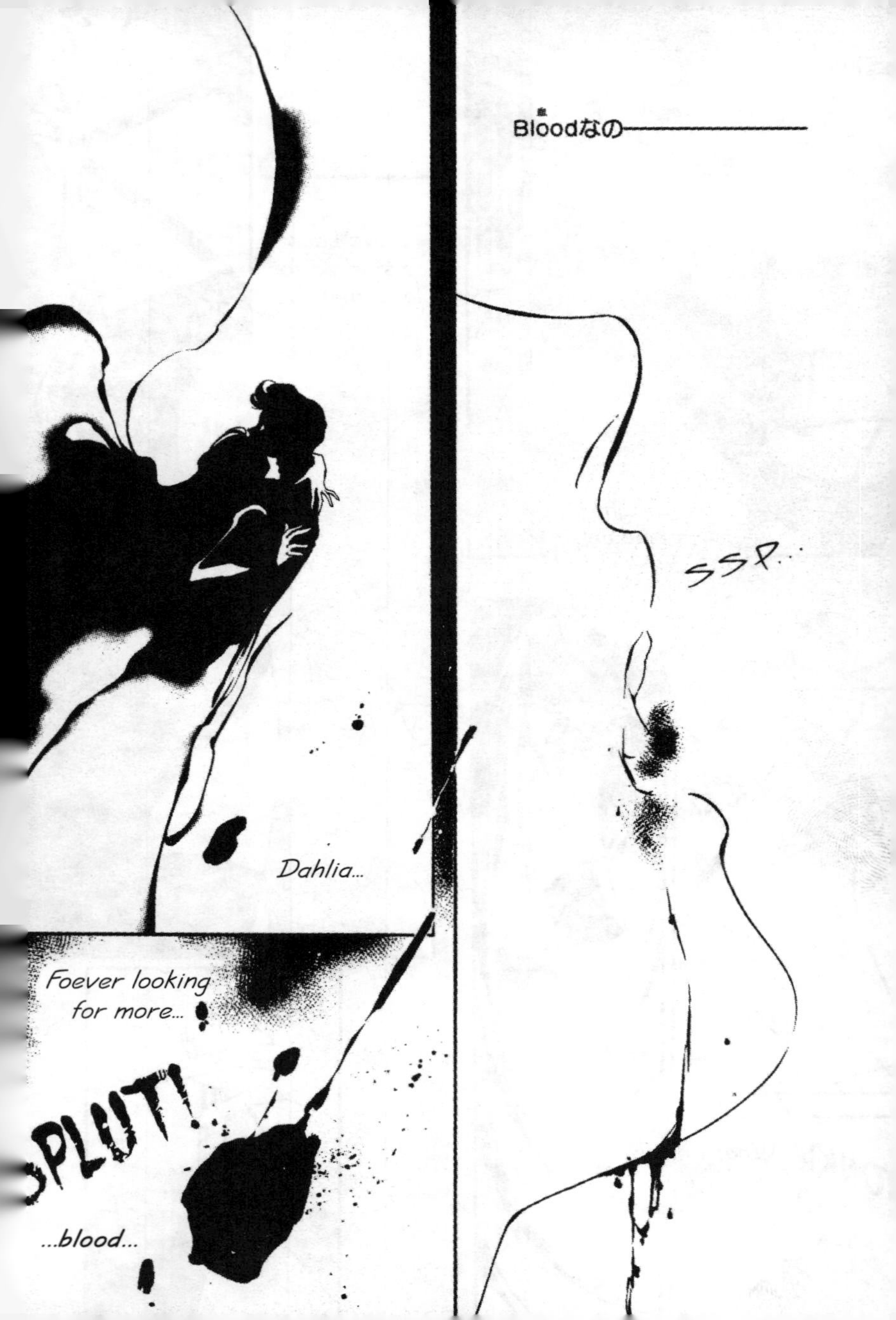

血
Bloodなの———
SSP...
Dahlia...
Foever looking for more...
SPLUT!
...blood...

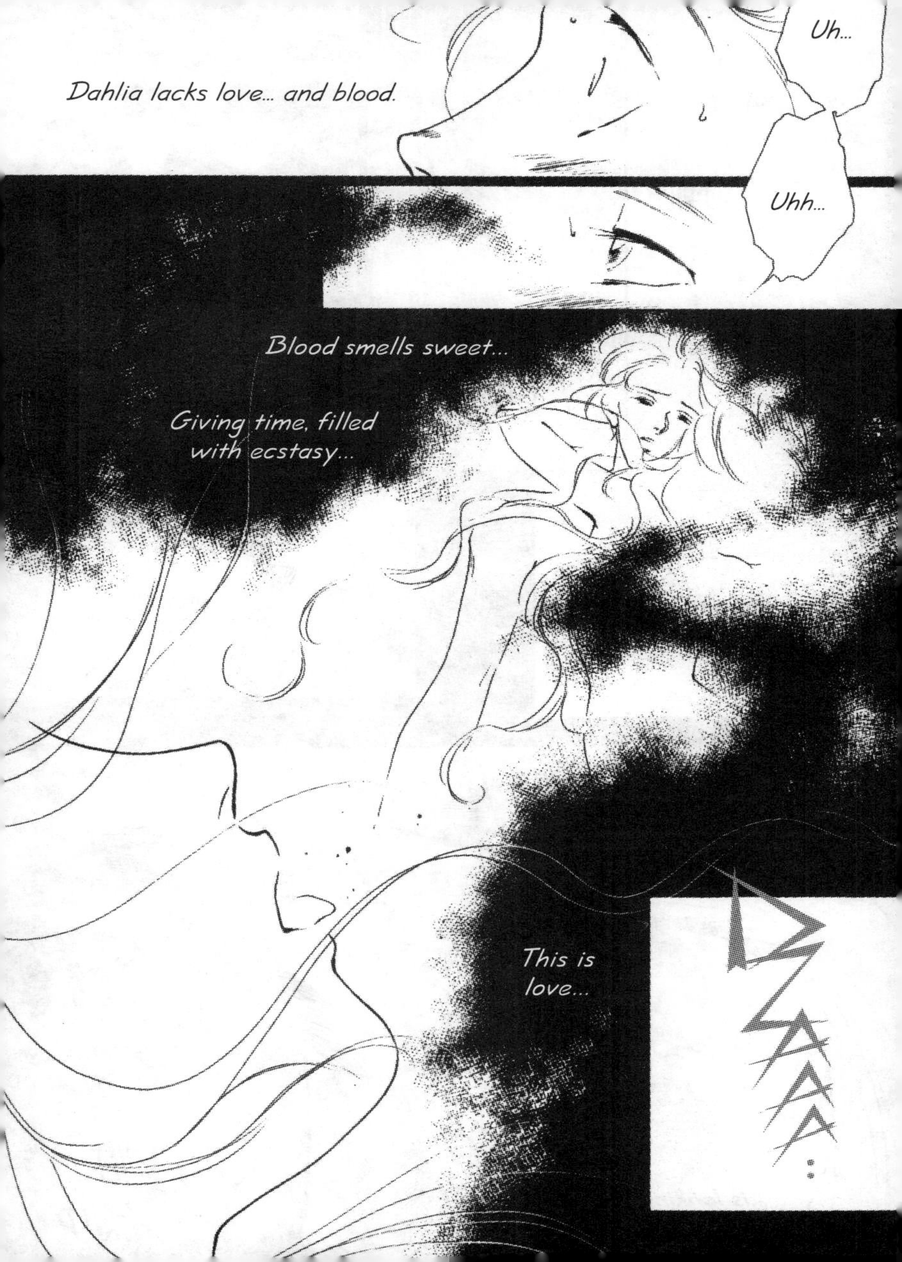
Uh...
Dahlia lacks love... and blood.
Uhh...
Blood smells sweet...
Giving time, filled with ecstasy...
This is love...

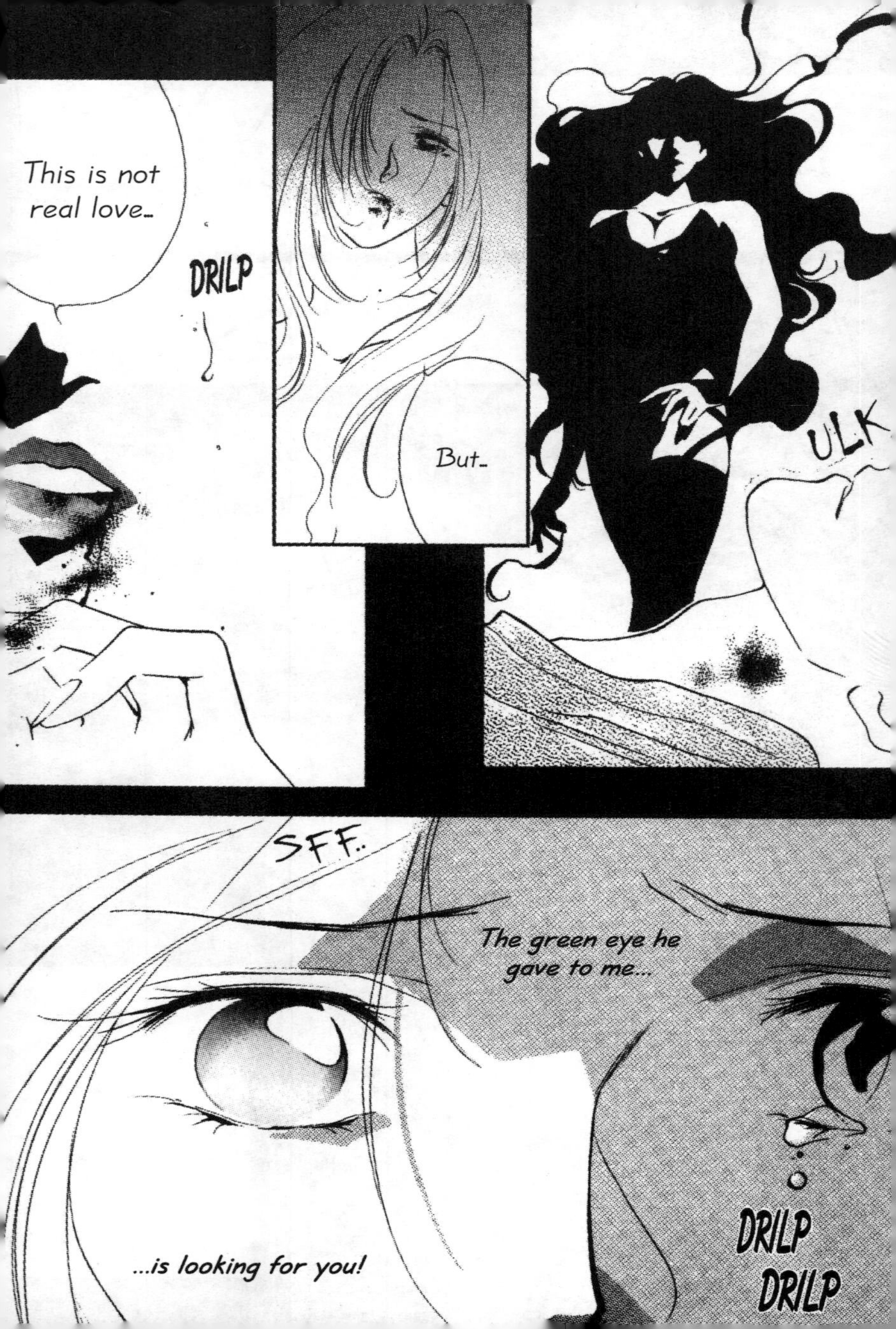

This is not real love...
DRILP
But...
ULK
SFF..
The green eye he gave to me...
...is looking for you!
DRILP
DRILP

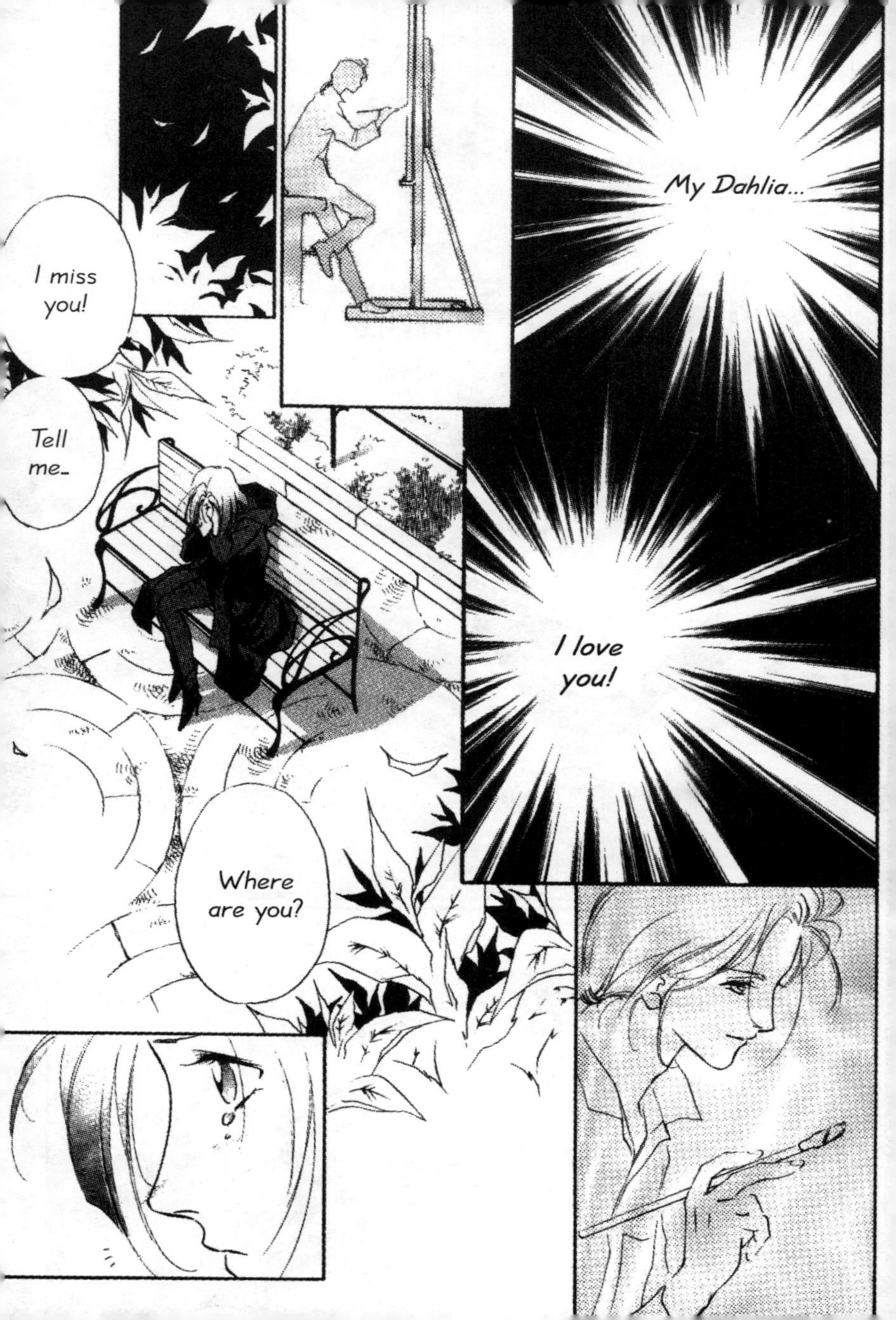
My Dahlia...
I love you!
I miss you!
Tell me_
Where are you?

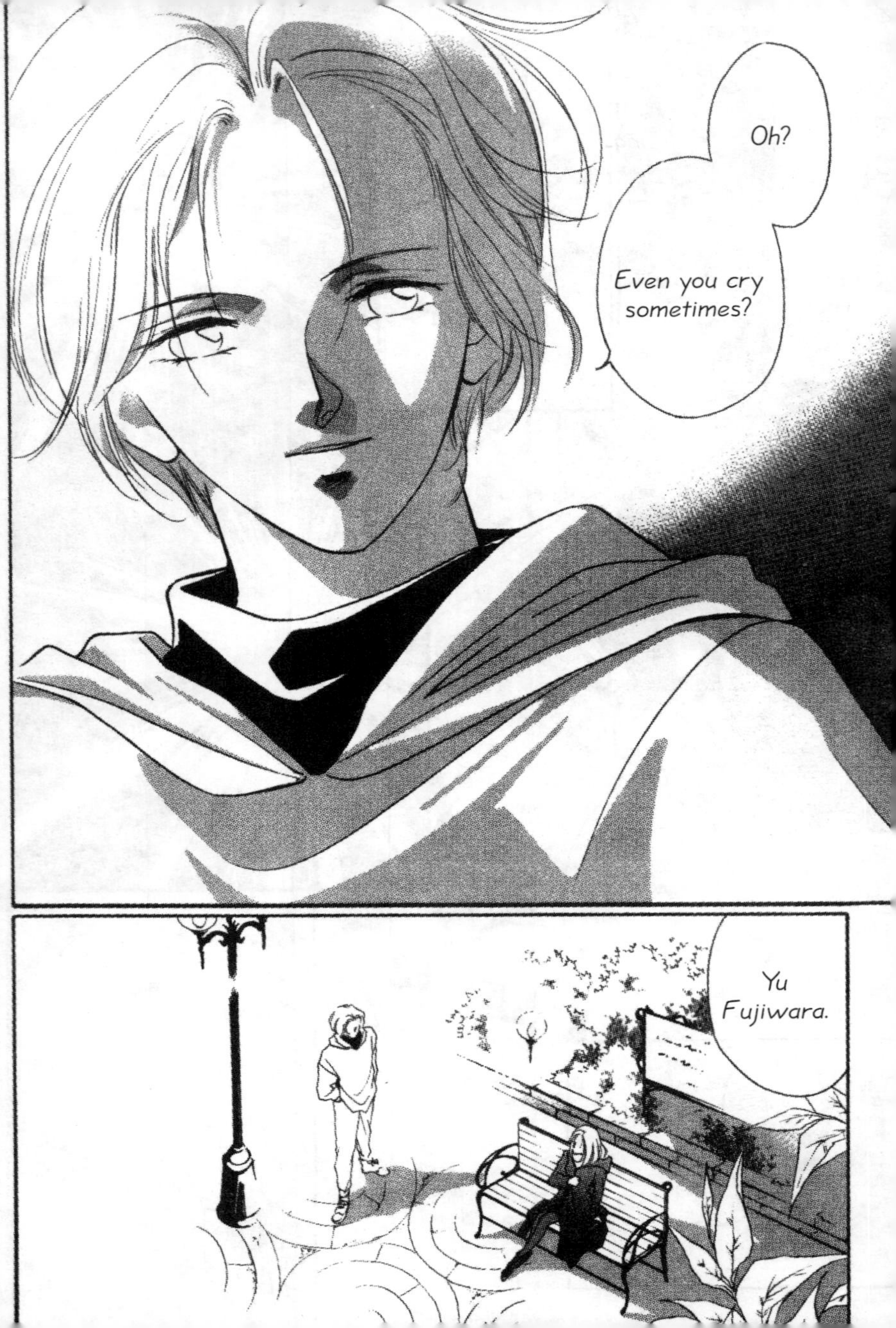
Oh?
Even you cry sometimes?
Yu Fujiwara.

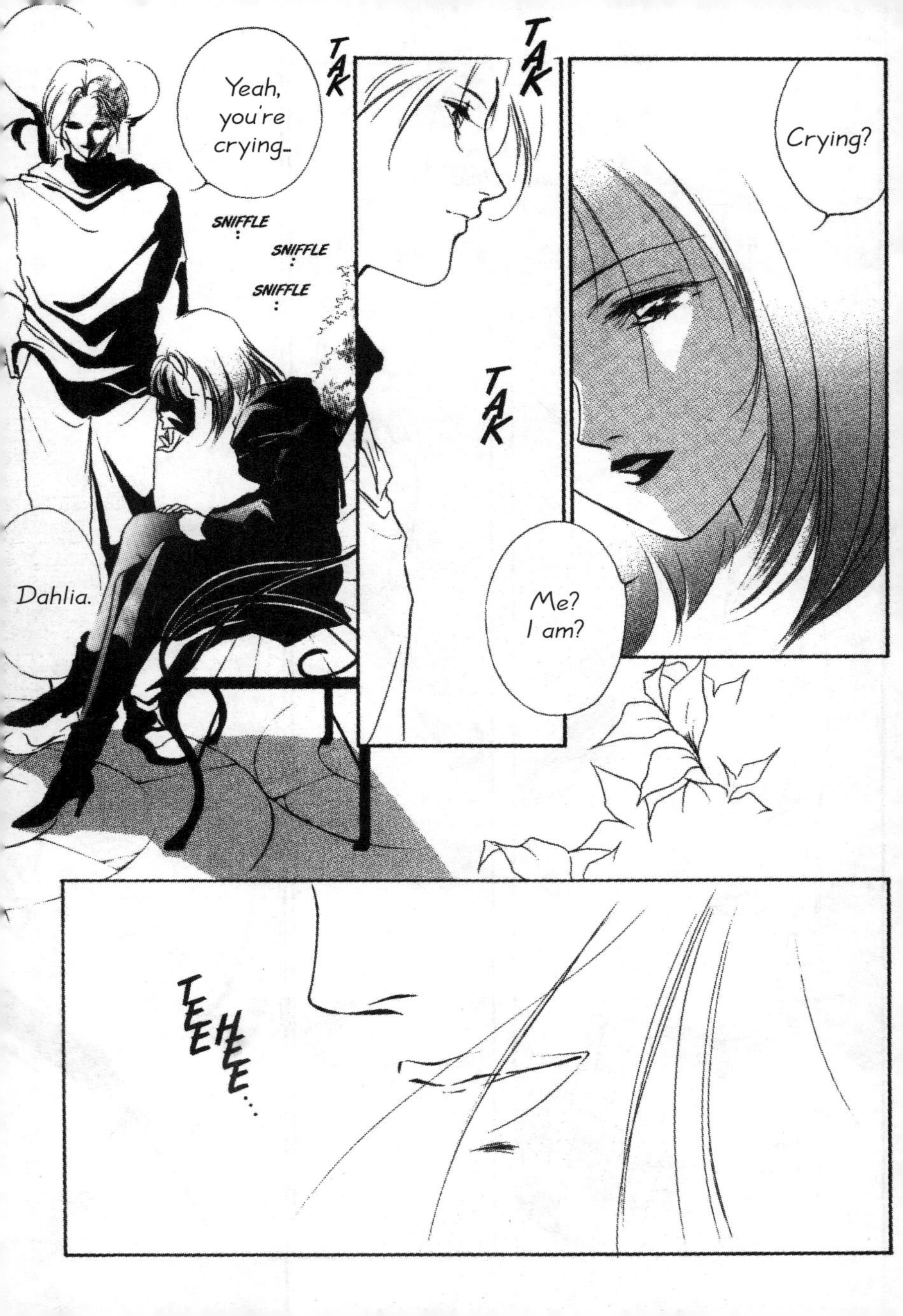
Yeah, you're crying...
SNIFFLE
SNIFFLE
SNIFFLE
Dahlia.
TAK
TAK
TAK
Crying?
Me? I am?
TEEHEE...

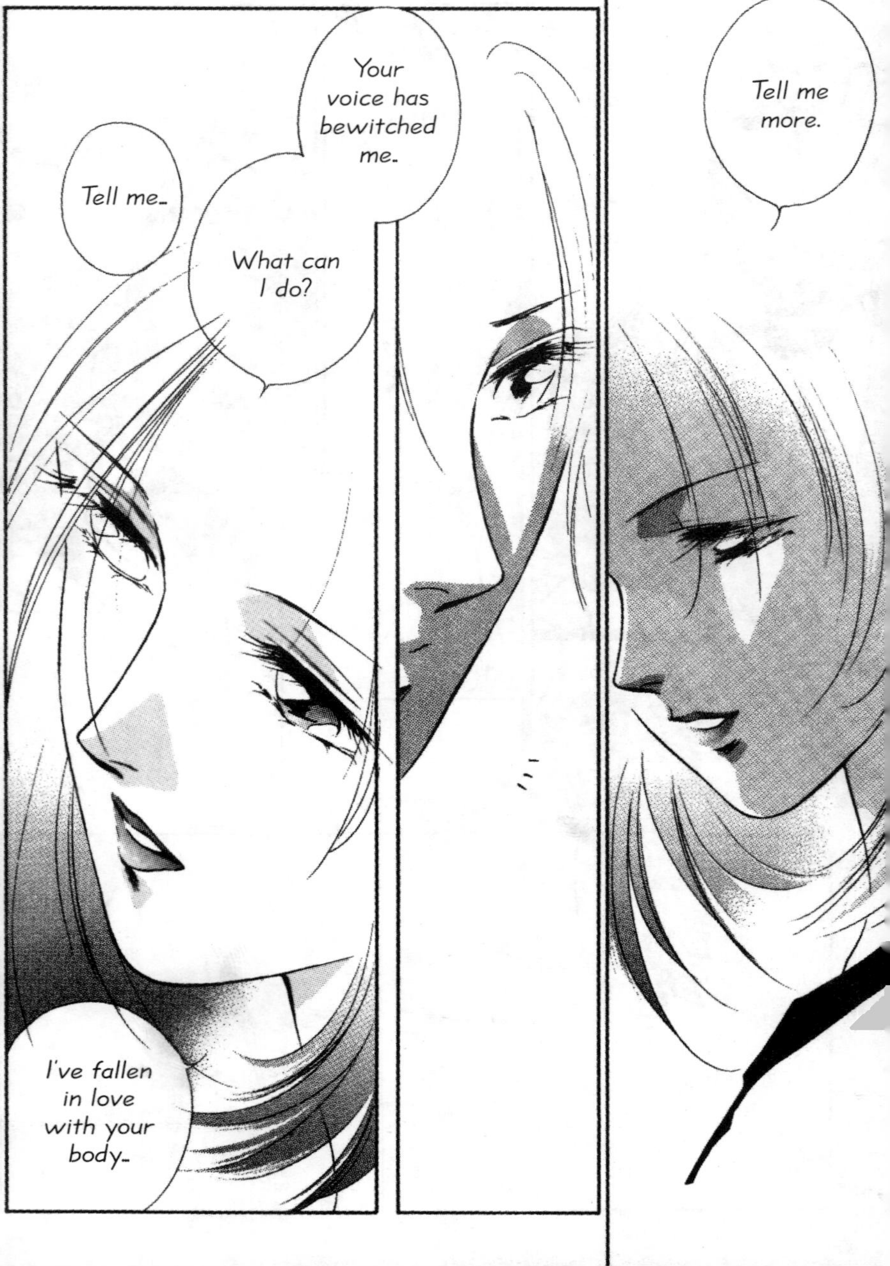
Tell me..
Your voice has bewitched me..
What can I do?
I've fallen in love with your body..
Tell me more.

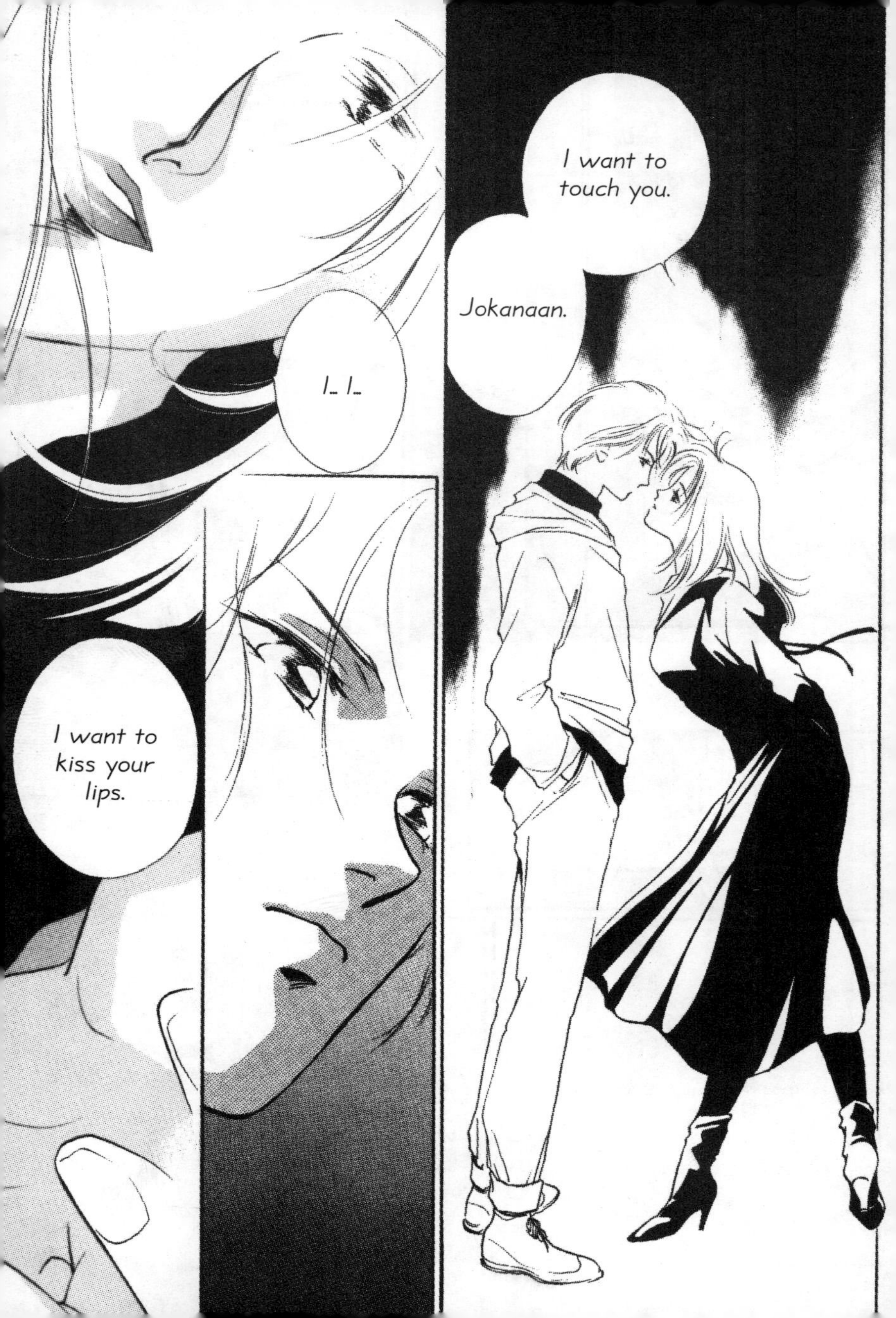
I want to touch you.
Jokanaan.
I... I...
I want to kiss your lips.

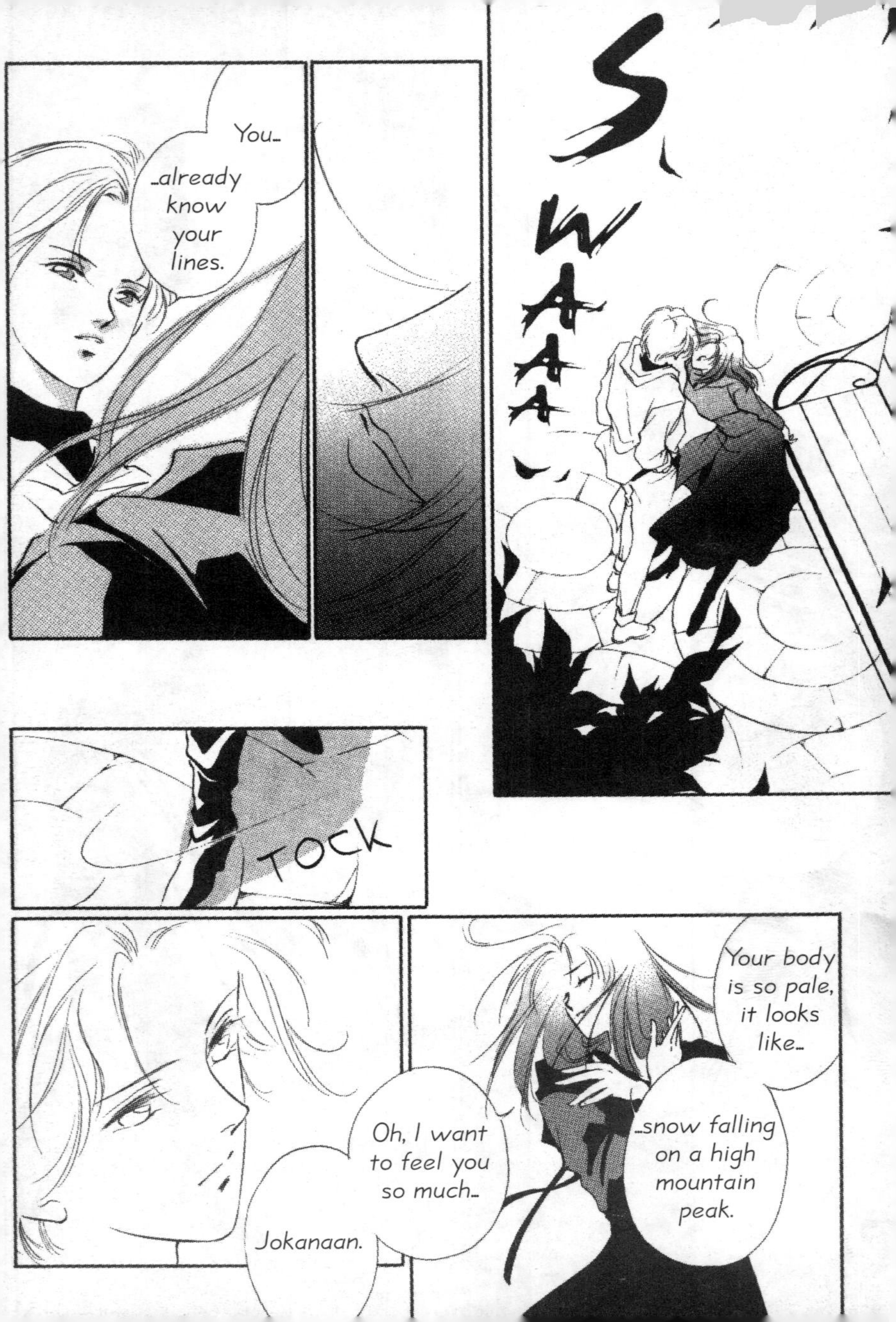

You...
...already know your lines.
SWAAAA
TOCK
Your body is so pale, it looks like...
...snow falling on a high mountain peak.
Oh, I want to feel you so much...
Jokanaan.

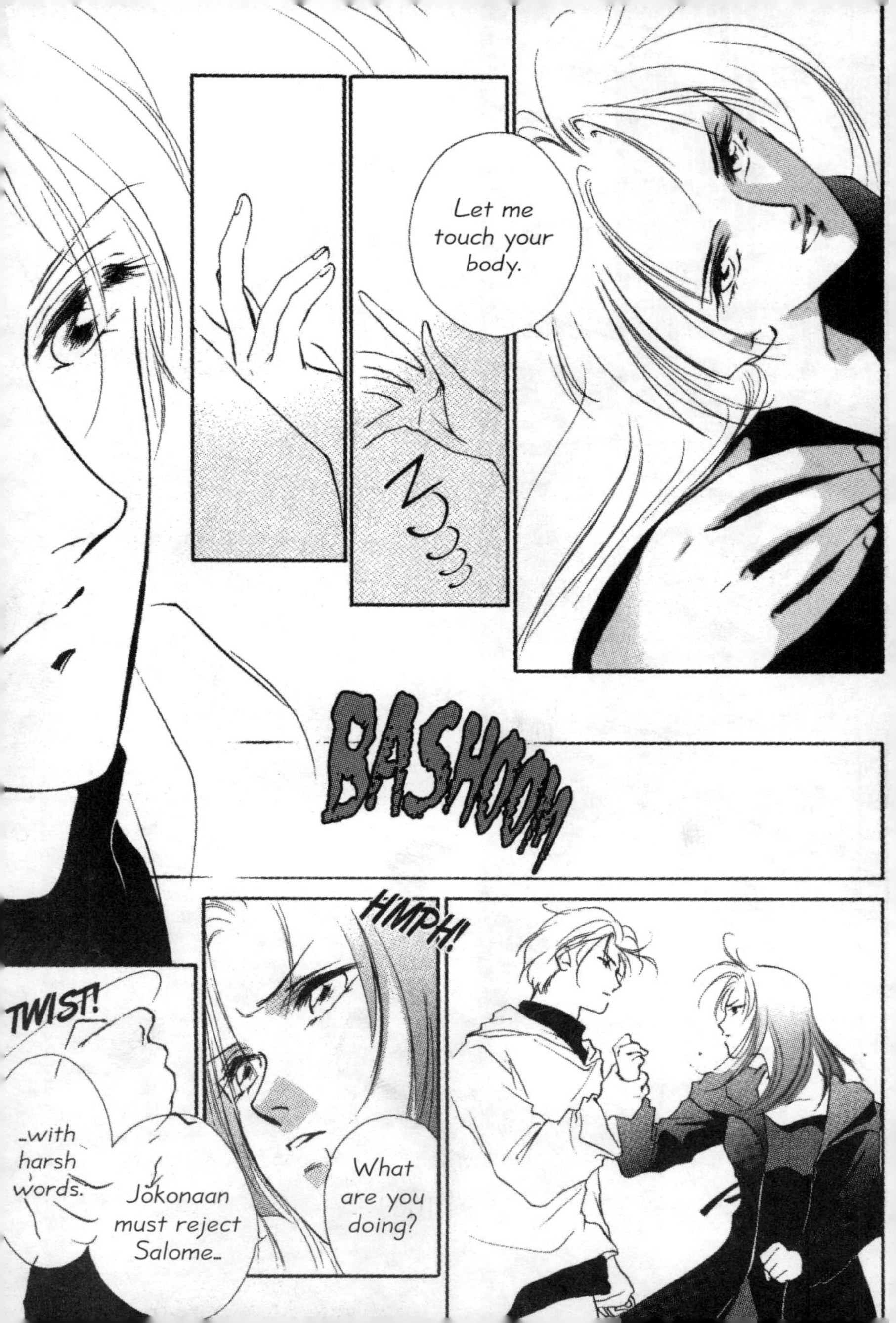
Let me touch your body.
BASHOOM
HMPH!
What are you doing?
Jokonaan must reject Salome...
...with harsh words.
TWIST!

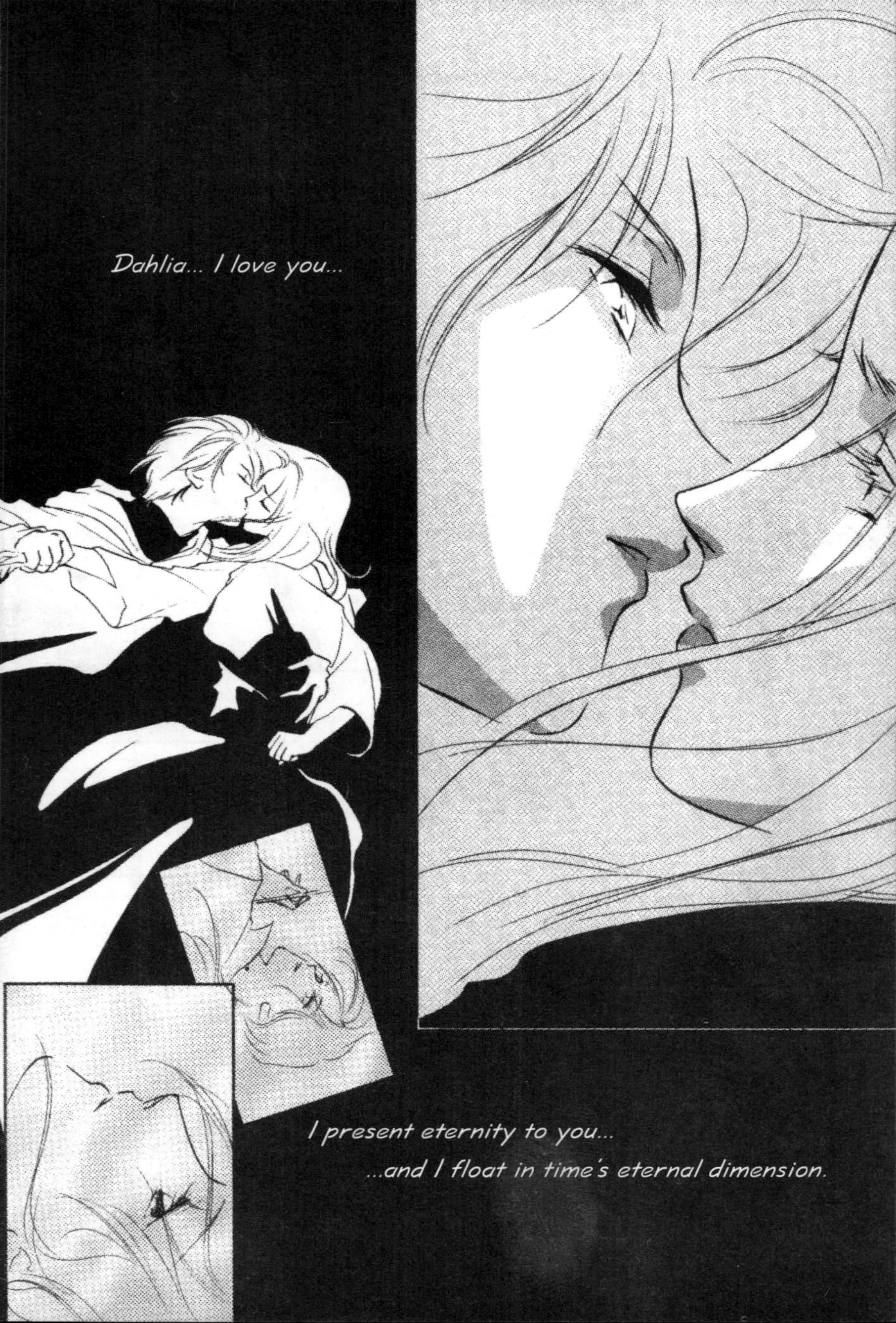
Dahlia... I love you...
I present eternity to you...
...and I float in time's eternal dimension.

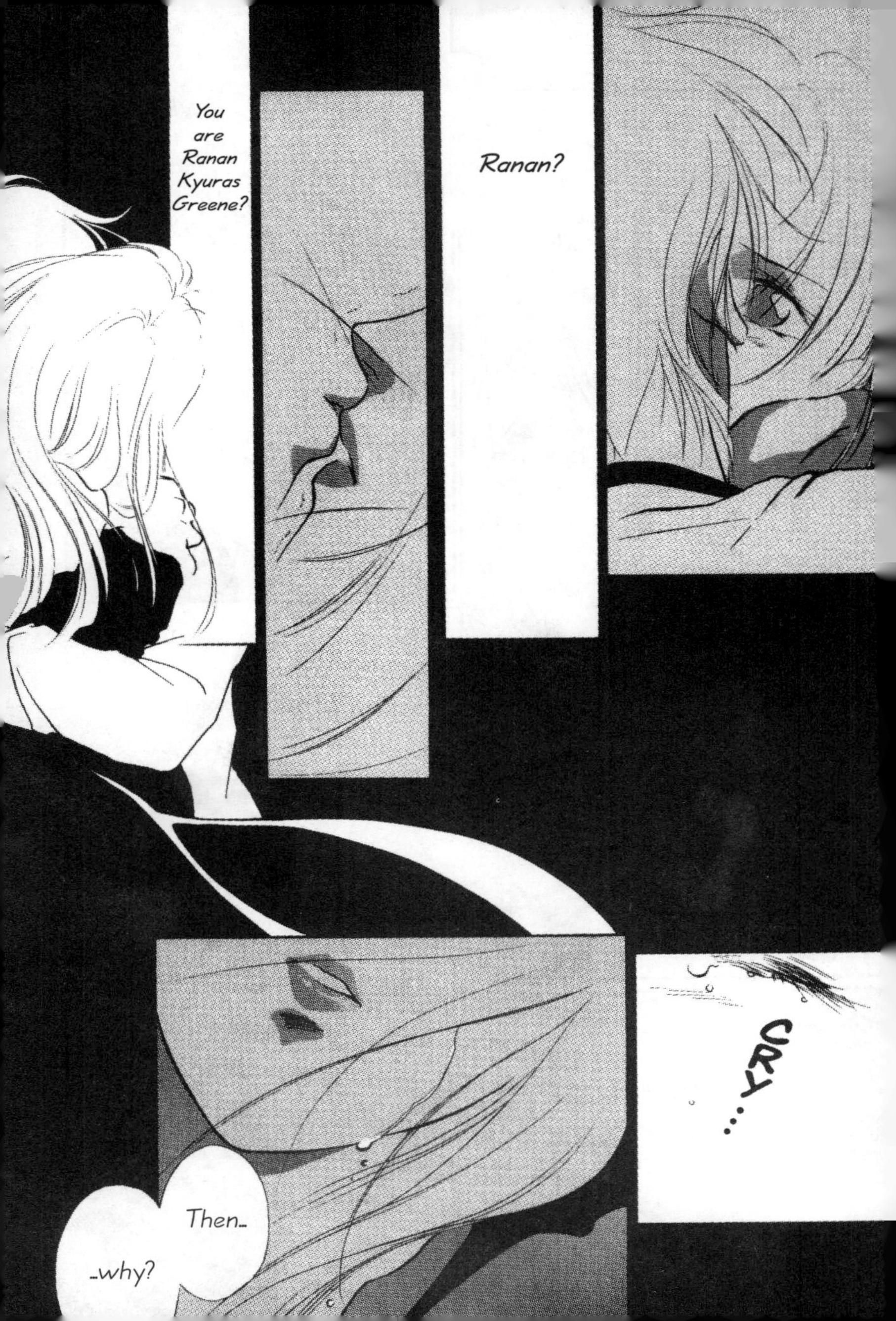
Ranan?
You are Ranan Kyuras Greene?
CRY...
Then...
...why?

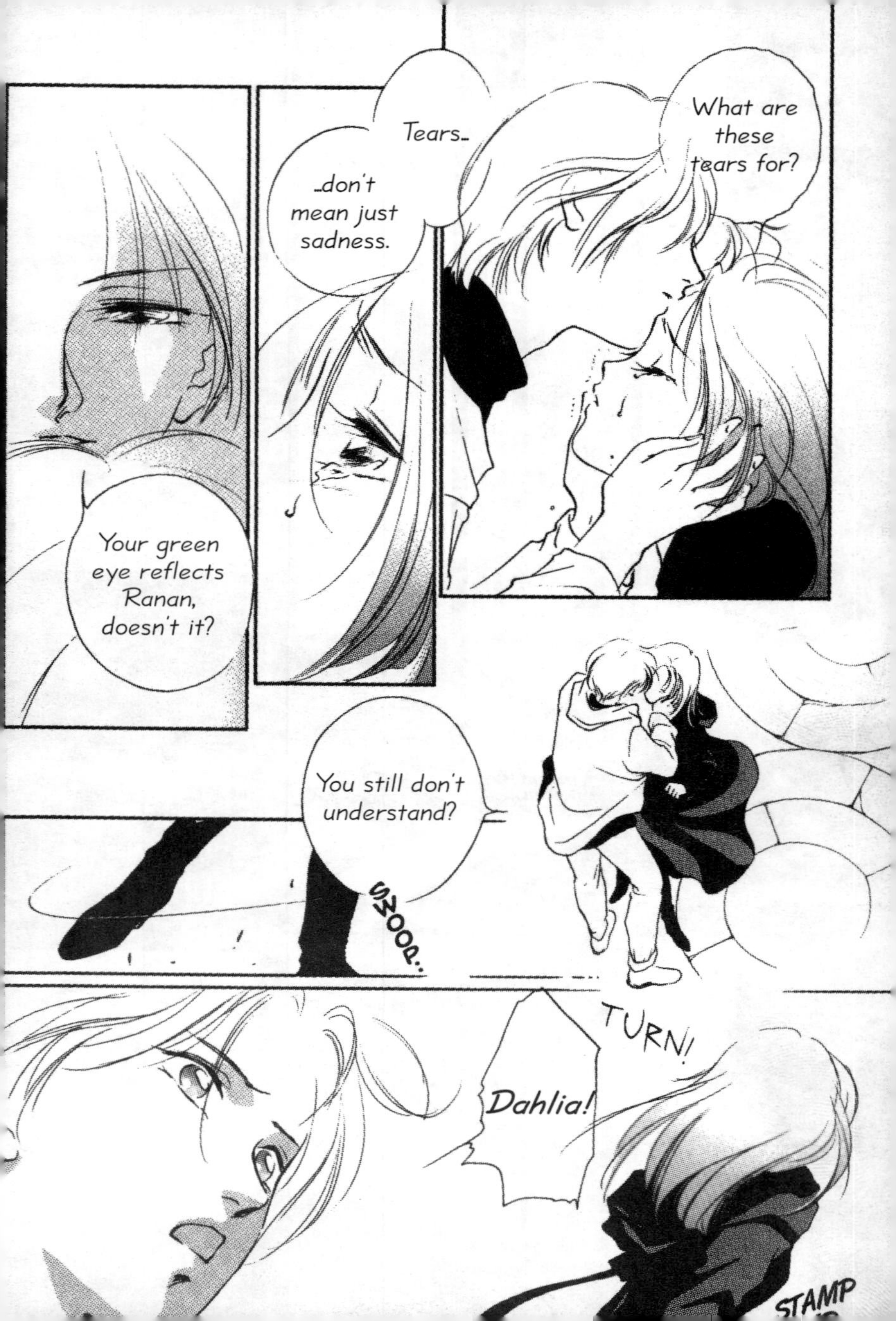
What are these tears for?
Tears…
…don't mean just sadness.
Your green eye reflects Ranan, doesn't it?
You still don't understand?
SWOOP…
TURN!
Dahlia!
STAMP

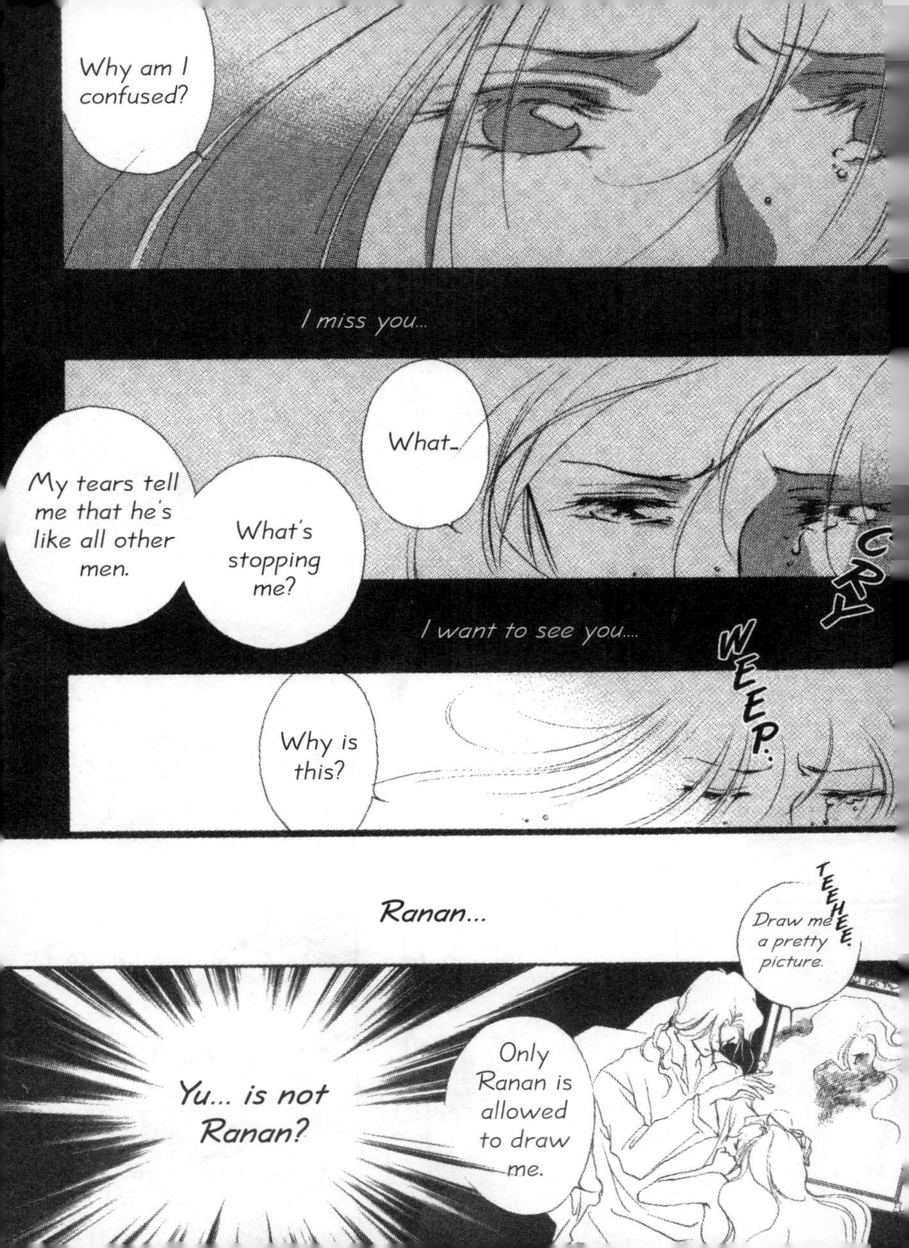
Why am I confused?
I miss you...
What...
What's stopping me?
My tears tell me that he's like all other men.
CRY
I want to see you....
WEEP.
Why is this?
Ranan...
TEEHEE.
Draw me a pretty picture.
Only Ranan is allowed to draw me.
Yu... is not Ranan?

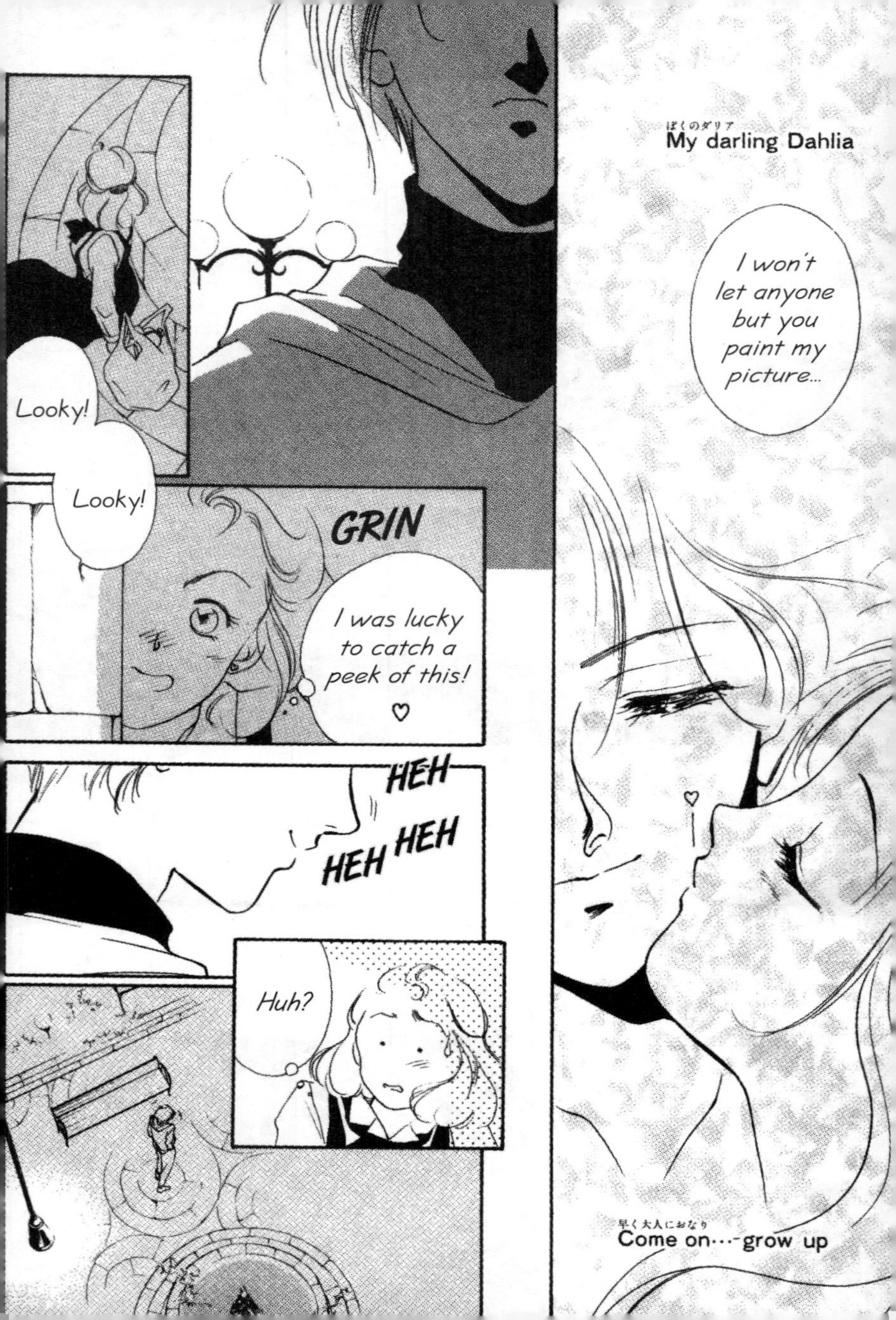
ぼくのダリア
My darling Dahlia
I won't let anyone but you paint my picture...
早く大人におなり
Come on...grow up
Looky!
Looky!
GRIN
I was lucky to catch a peek of this! ♡
HEH HEH HEH
Huh?

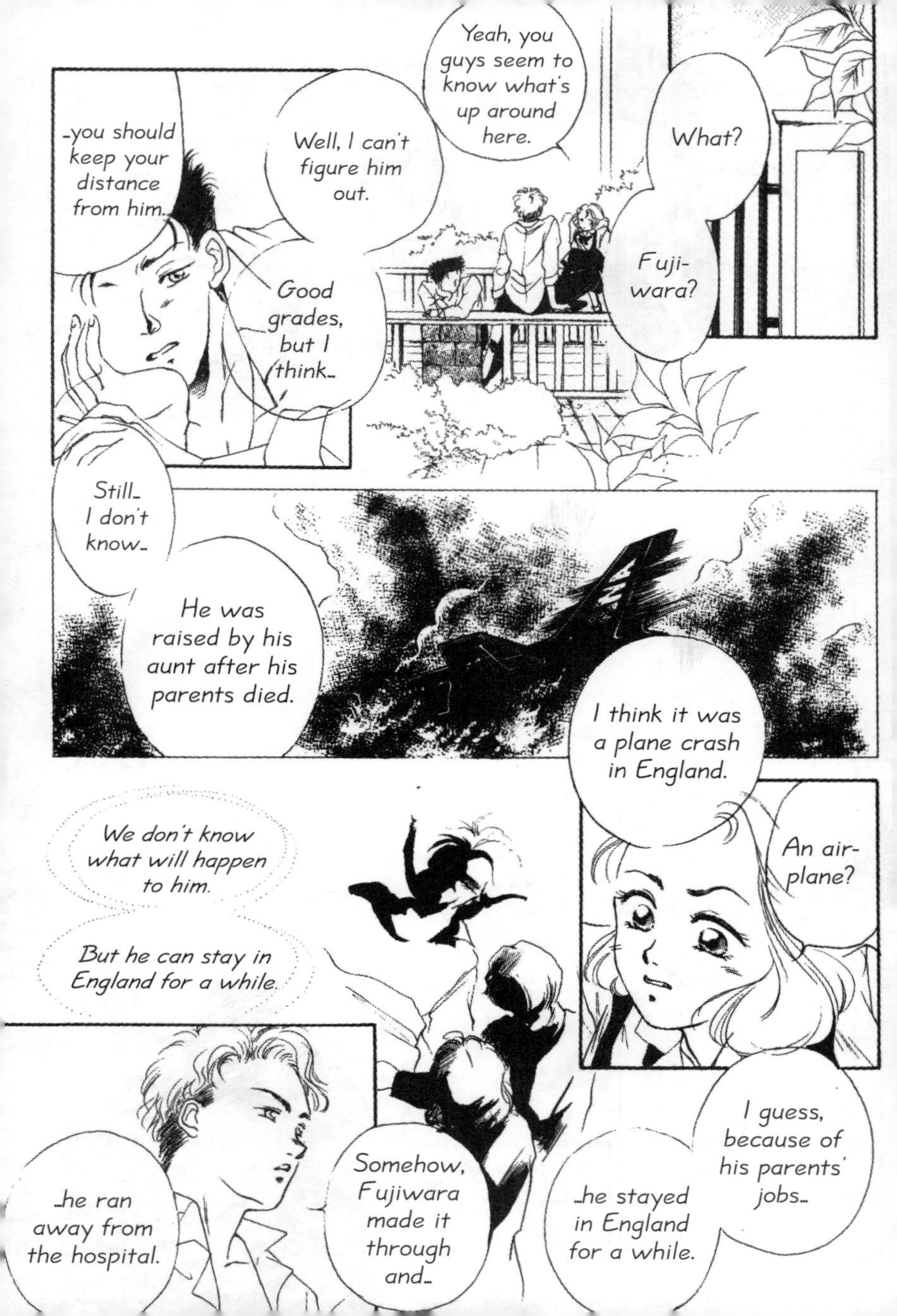
Yeah, you guys seem to know what's up around here.
Well, I can't figure him out.
..you should keep your distance from him..
Good grades, but I think..
What?
Fuji-wara?
Still.. I don't know..
He was raised by his aunt after his parents died.
I think it was a plane crash in England.
An air-plane?
We don't know what will happen to him.
But he can stay in England for a while.
I guess, because of his parents' jobs..
..he stayed in England for a while.
Somehow, Fujiwara made it through and..
..he ran away from the hospital.

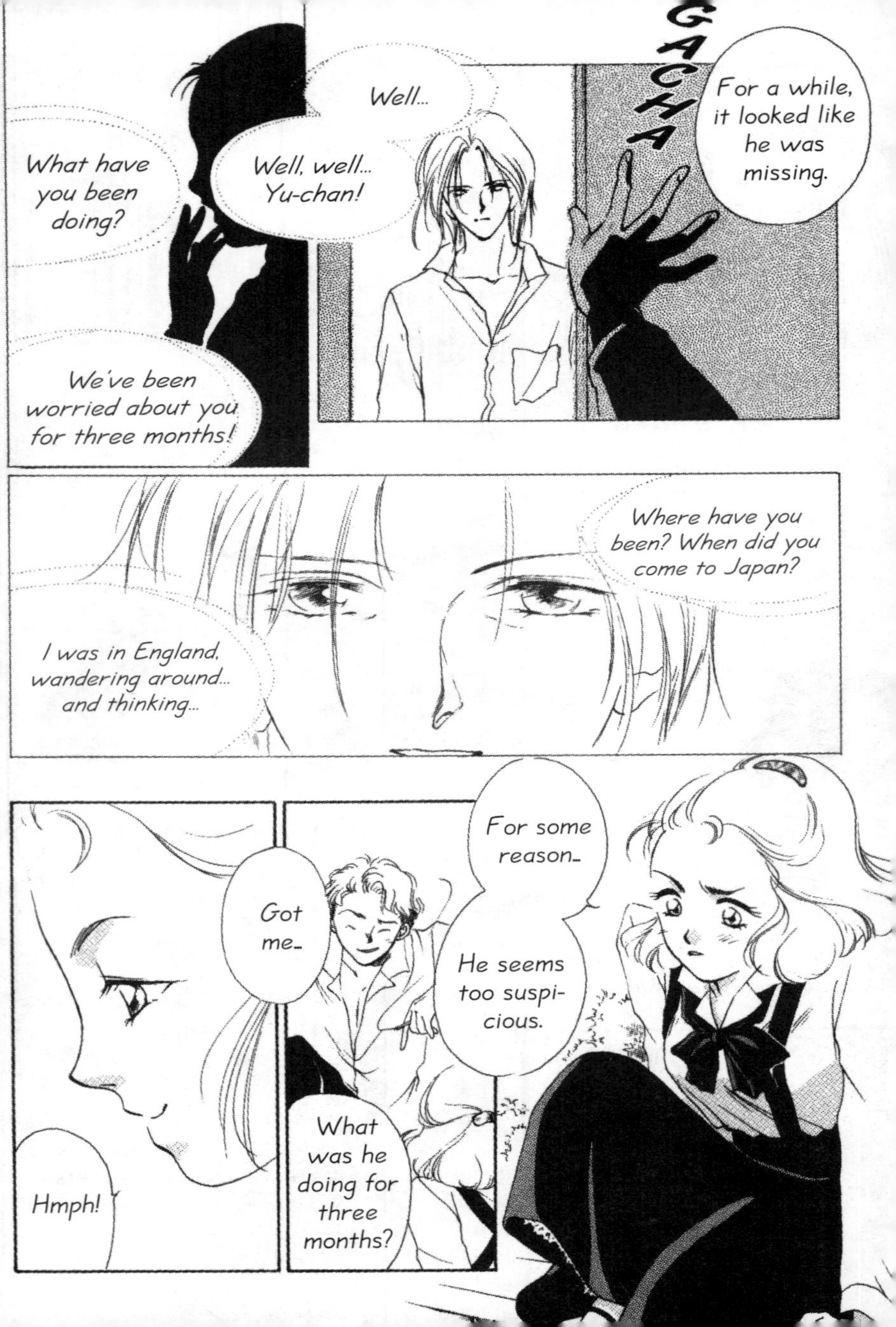
GACHA
For a while, it looked like he was missing.
Well...
Well, well... Yu-chan!
What have you been doing?
We've been worried about you for three months!
Where have you been? When did you come to Japan?
I was in England, wandering around... and thinking...
For some reason...
He seems too suspicious.
What was he doing for three months?
Got me...
Hmph!

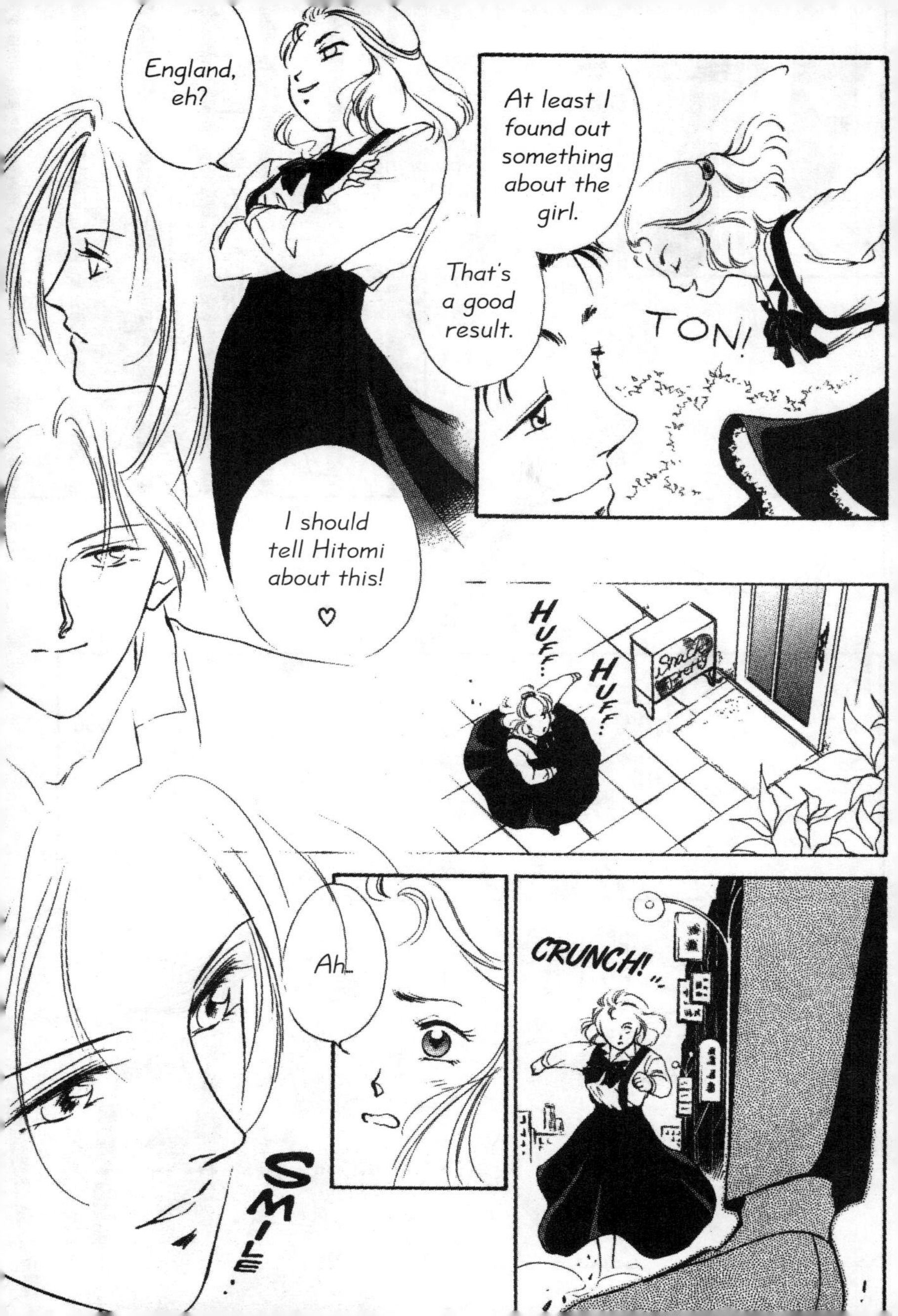

At least I found out something about the girl.
TON!
England, eh?
That's a good result.
I should tell Hitomi about this! ♡
HUFF...
HUFF...
CRUNCH!
Ah...
SMILE...

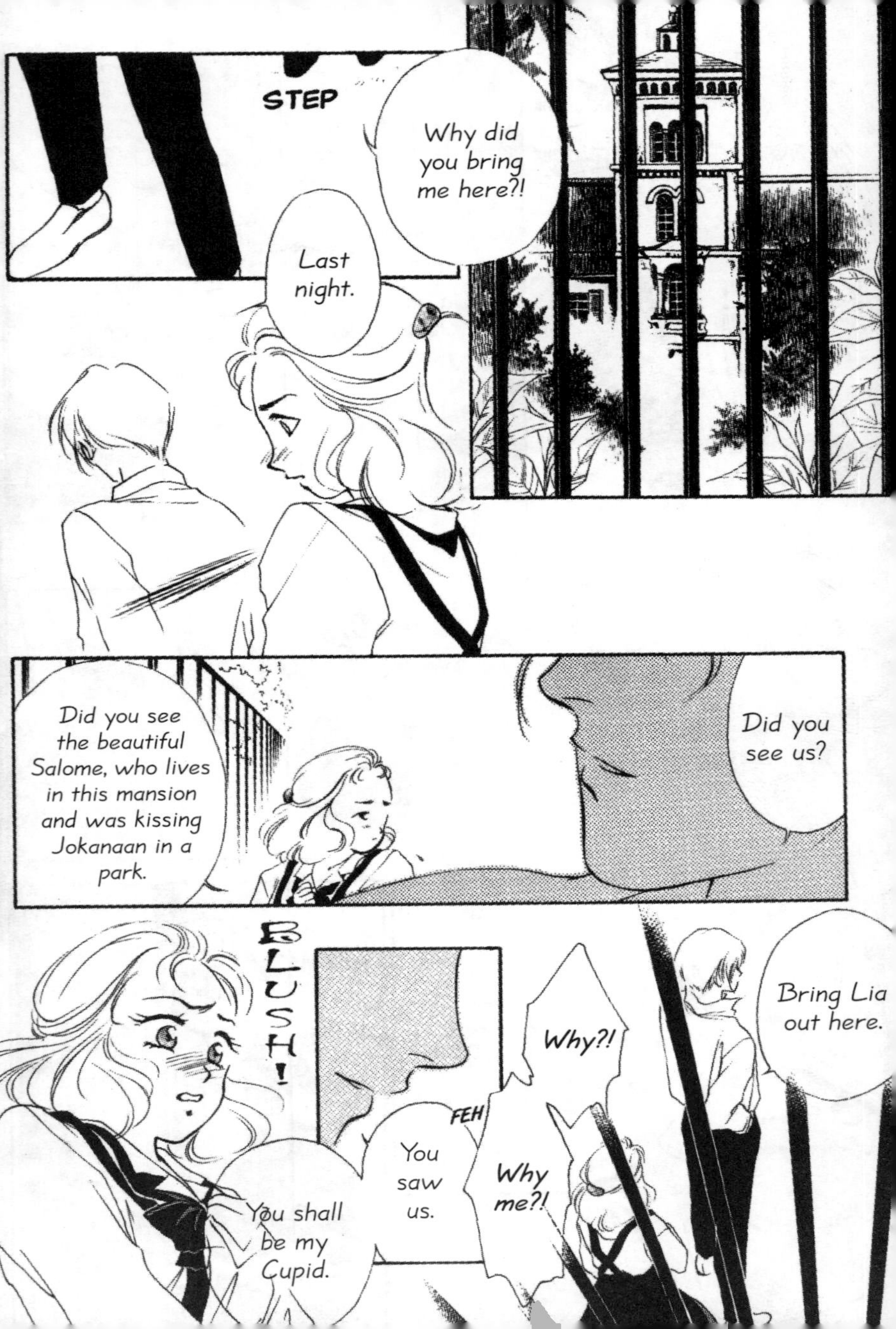
STEP
Why did you bring me here?!
Last night.
Did you see the beautiful Salome, who lives in this mansion and was kissing Jokanaan in a park.
Did you see us?
BLUSH!
You saw us.
FEH
You shall be my Cupid.
Why?!
Why me?!
Bring Lia out here.

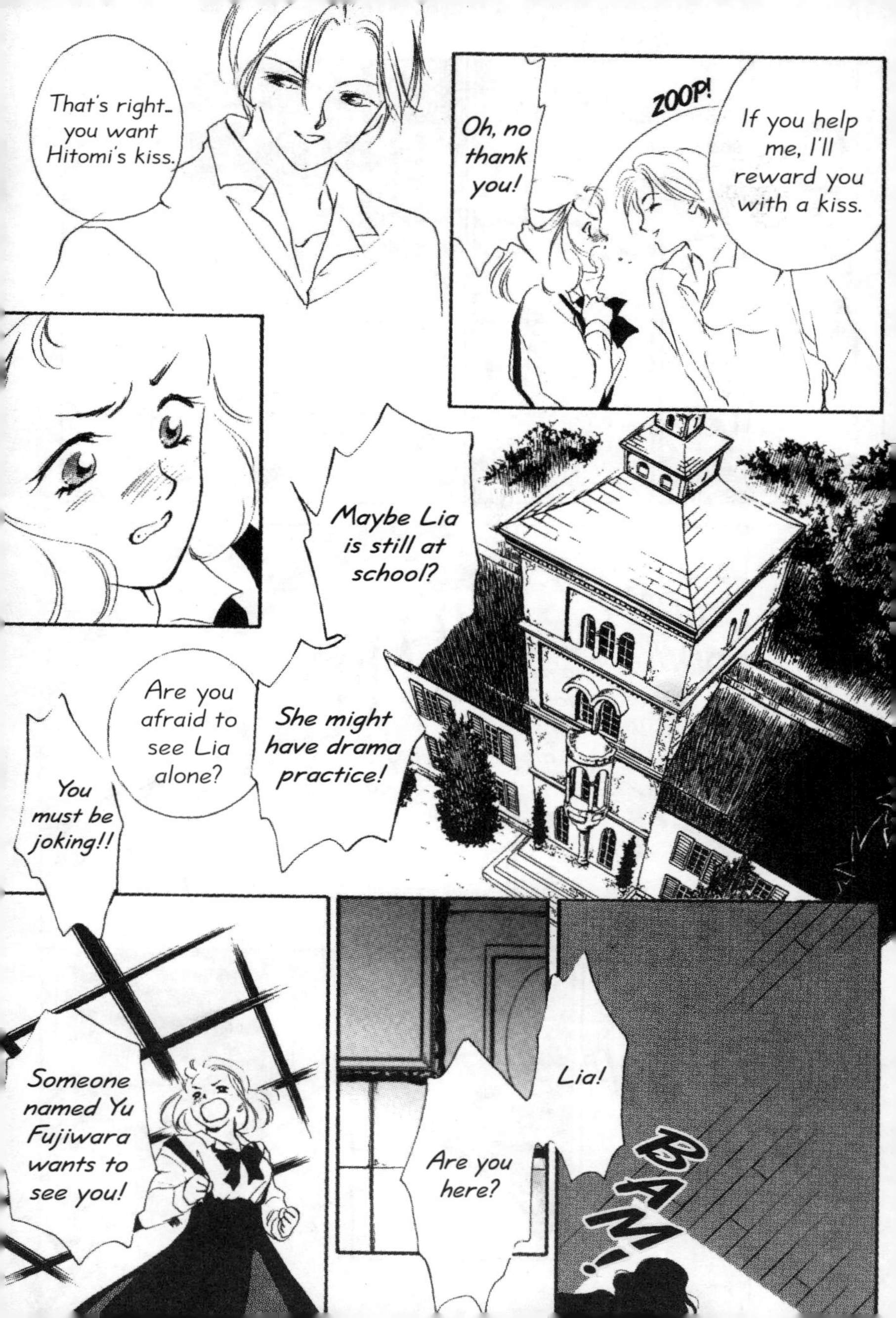

That's right- you want Hitomi's kiss.
If you help me, I'll reward you with a kiss.
ZOOP!
Oh, no thank you!
Are you afraid to see Lia alone?
You must be joking!!
Maybe Lia is still at school?
She might have drama practice!
Someone named Yu Fujiwara wants to see you!
Lia!
Are you here?
BAM!

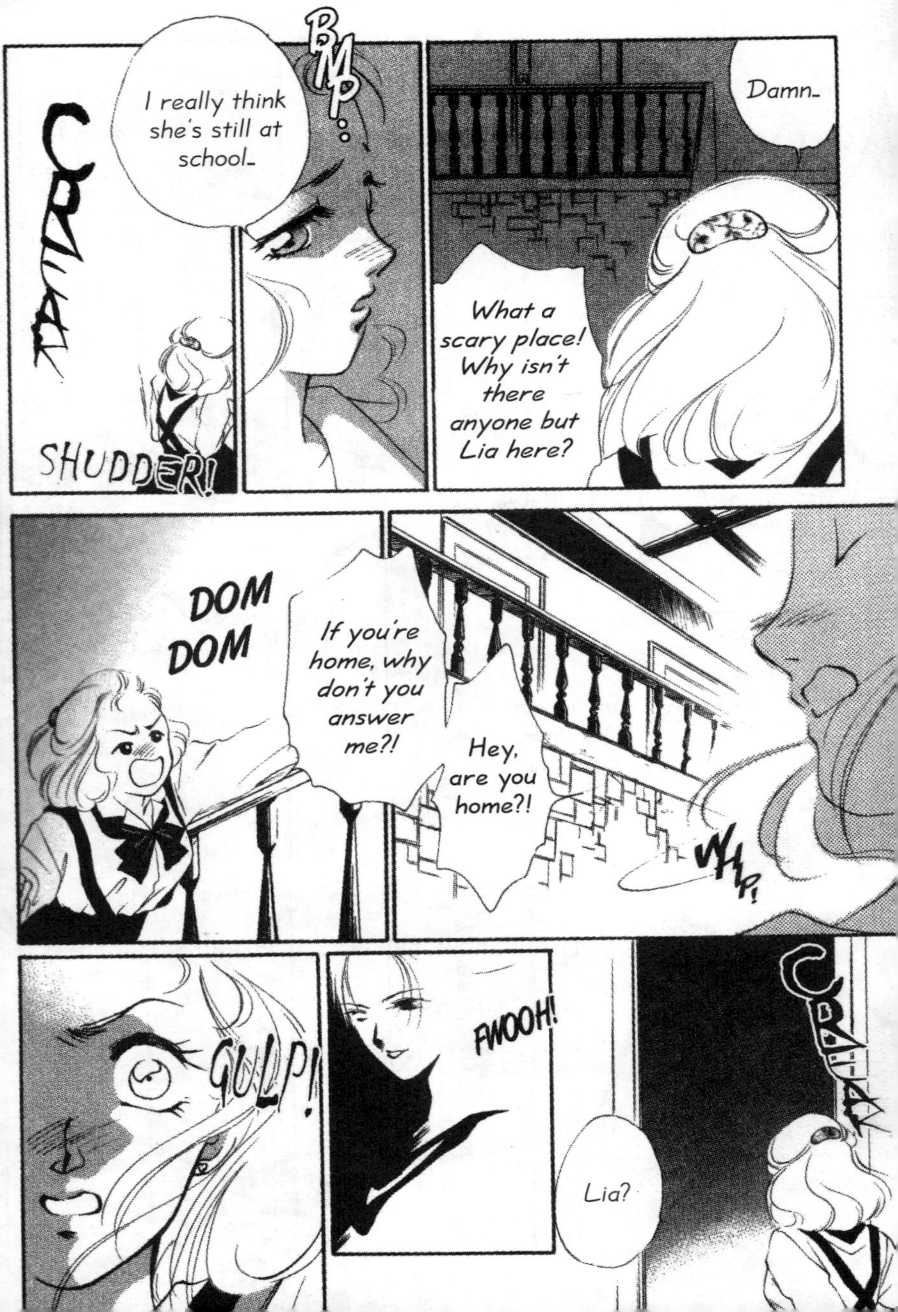
I really think she's still at school..
SHUDDER!
BMP
Damn..
What a scary place! Why isn't there anyone but Lia here?
DOM DOM
If you're home, why don't you answer me?!
Hey, are you home?!
WHIP!
GULP!
FWOOH!
Lia?

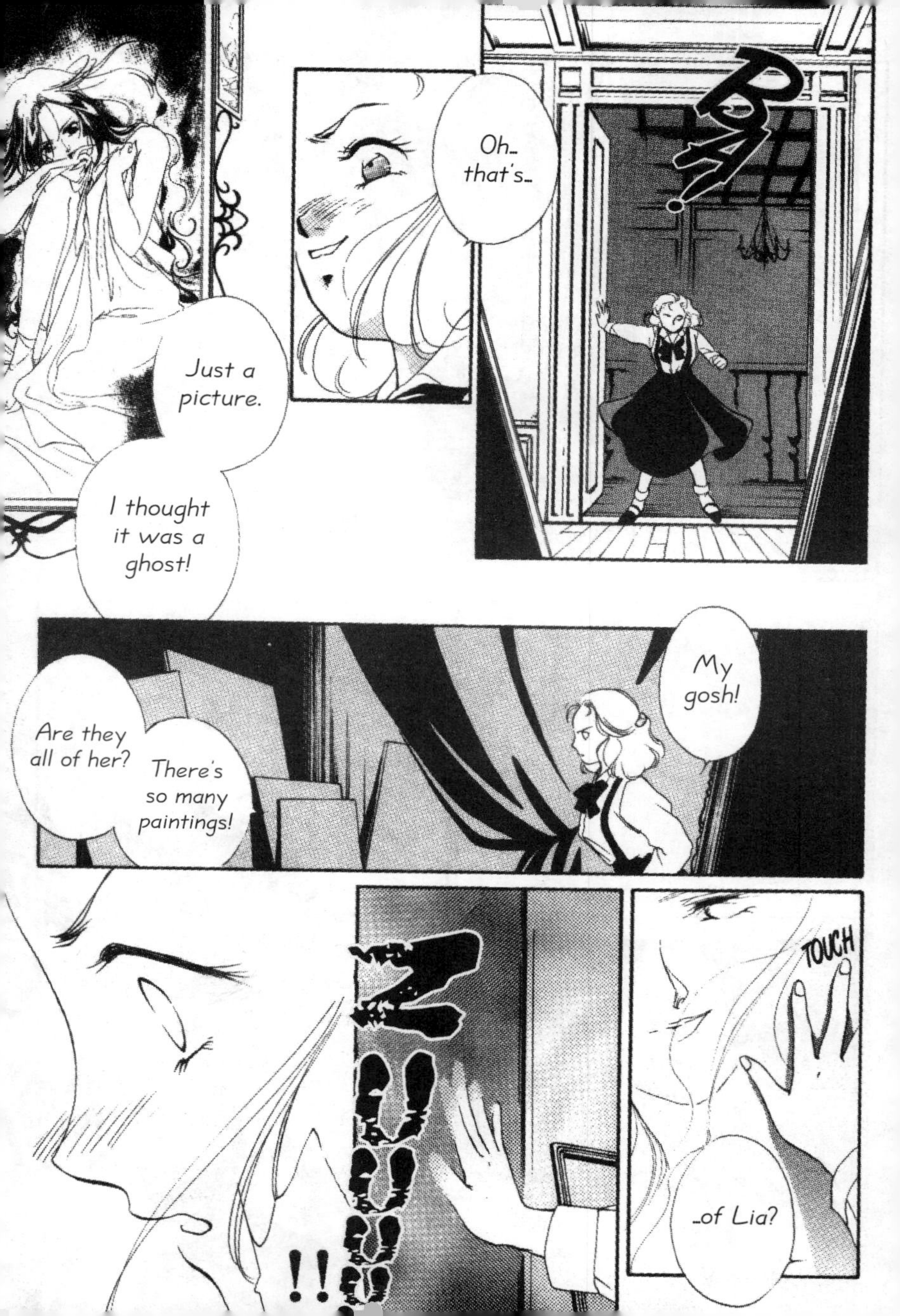
BAM!
Oh... that's...
Just a picture.
I thought it was a ghost!
My gosh!
There's so many paintings!
Are they all of her?
TOUCH
...of Lia?

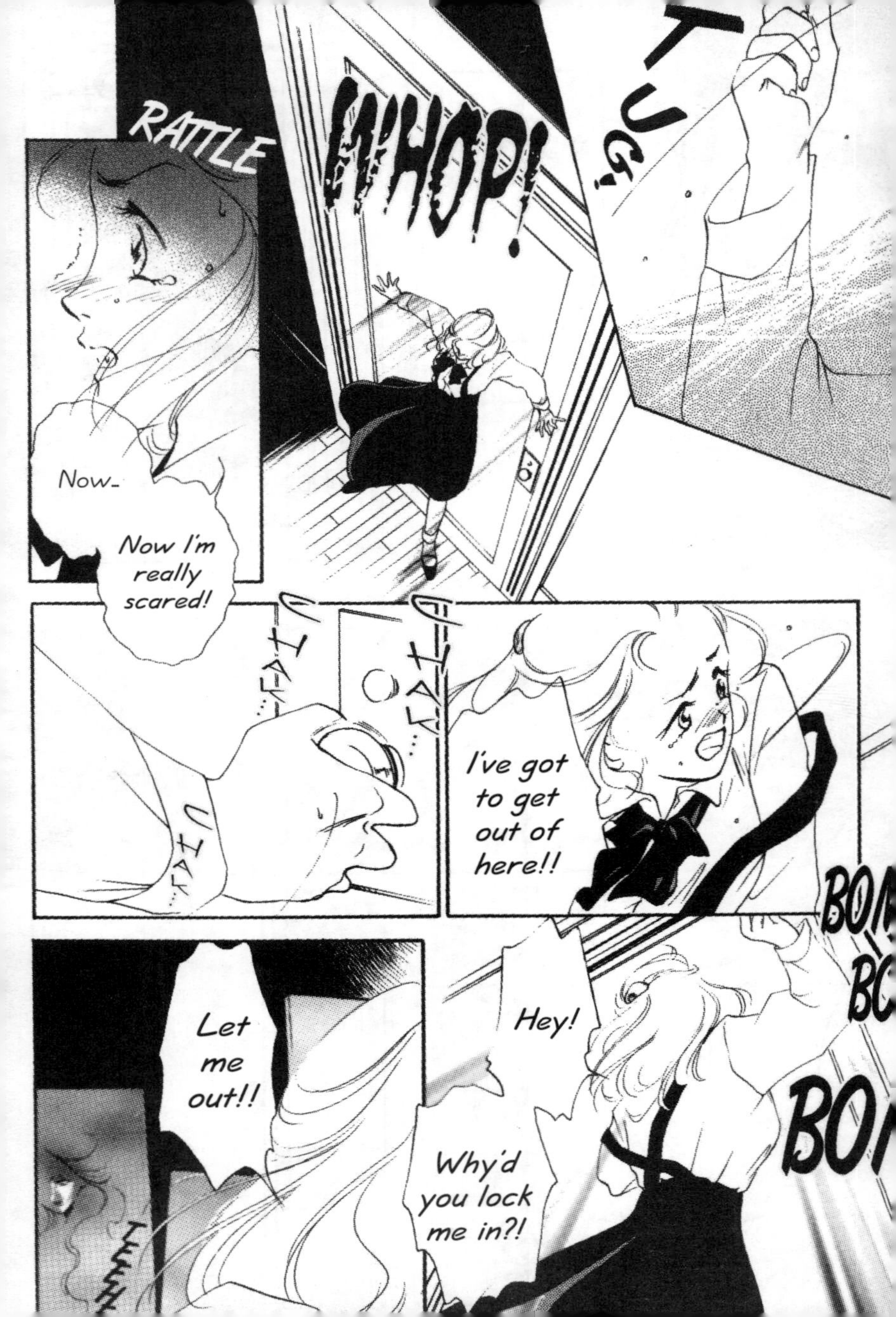
TUG!
WHOP!
RATTLE
Now-
Now I'm really scared!
I've got to get out of here!!
Hey!
Why'd you lock me in?!
Let me out!!

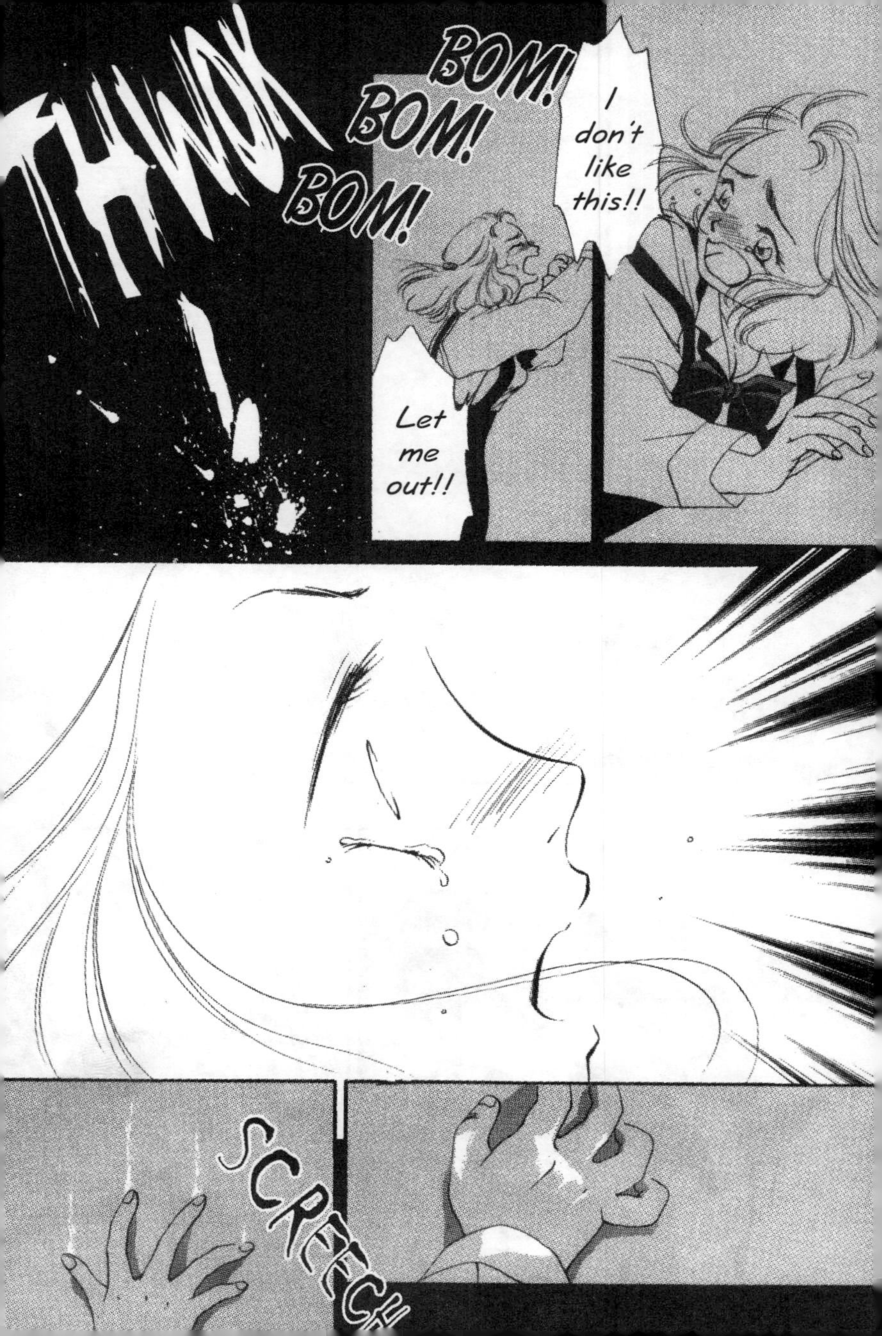
I don't like this!!
Let me out!!
BOM! BOM! BOM!
THWOK
SCREECH

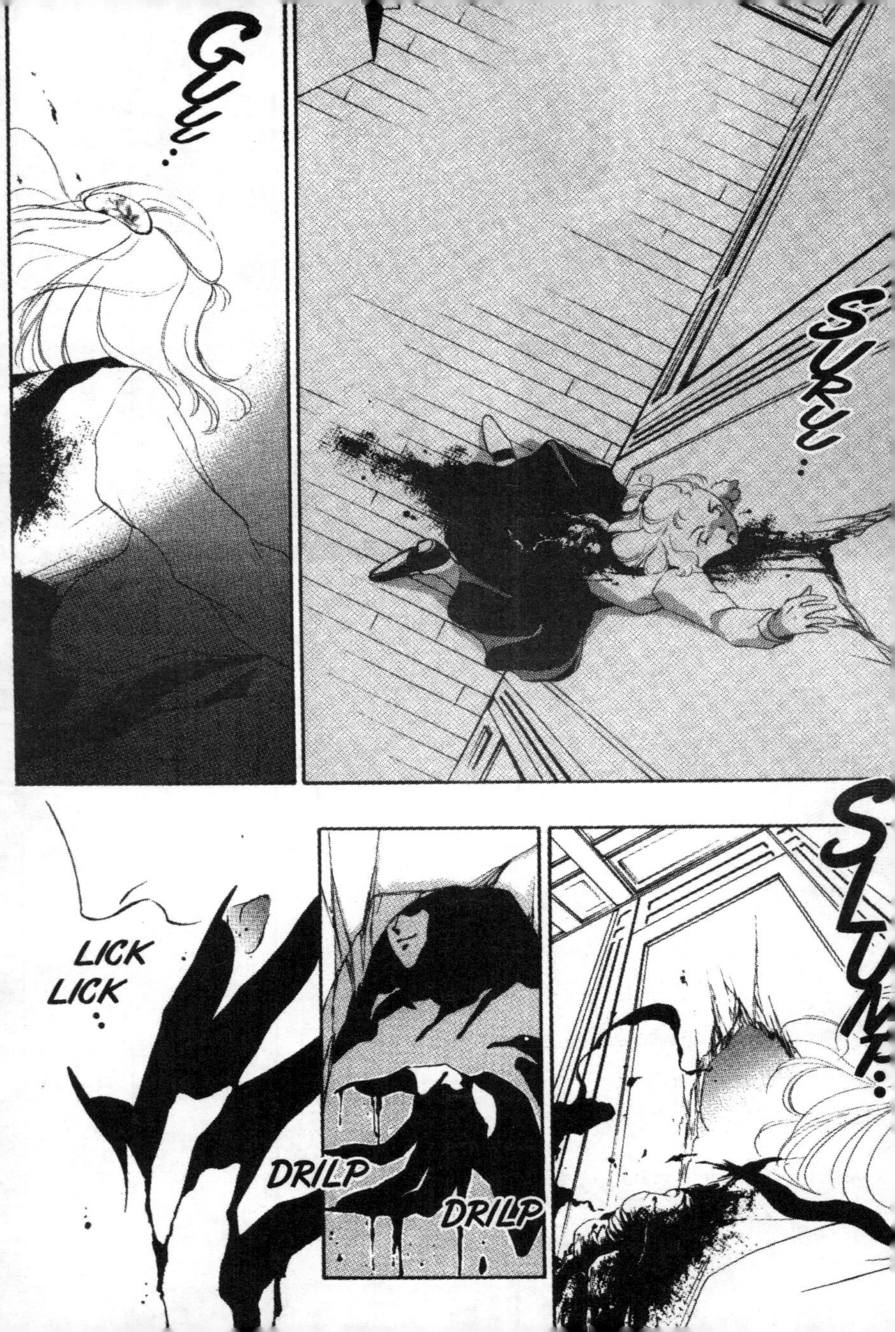
SURUU...
GUU...
SLUMP...
DRILP
DRILP
LICK
LICK...

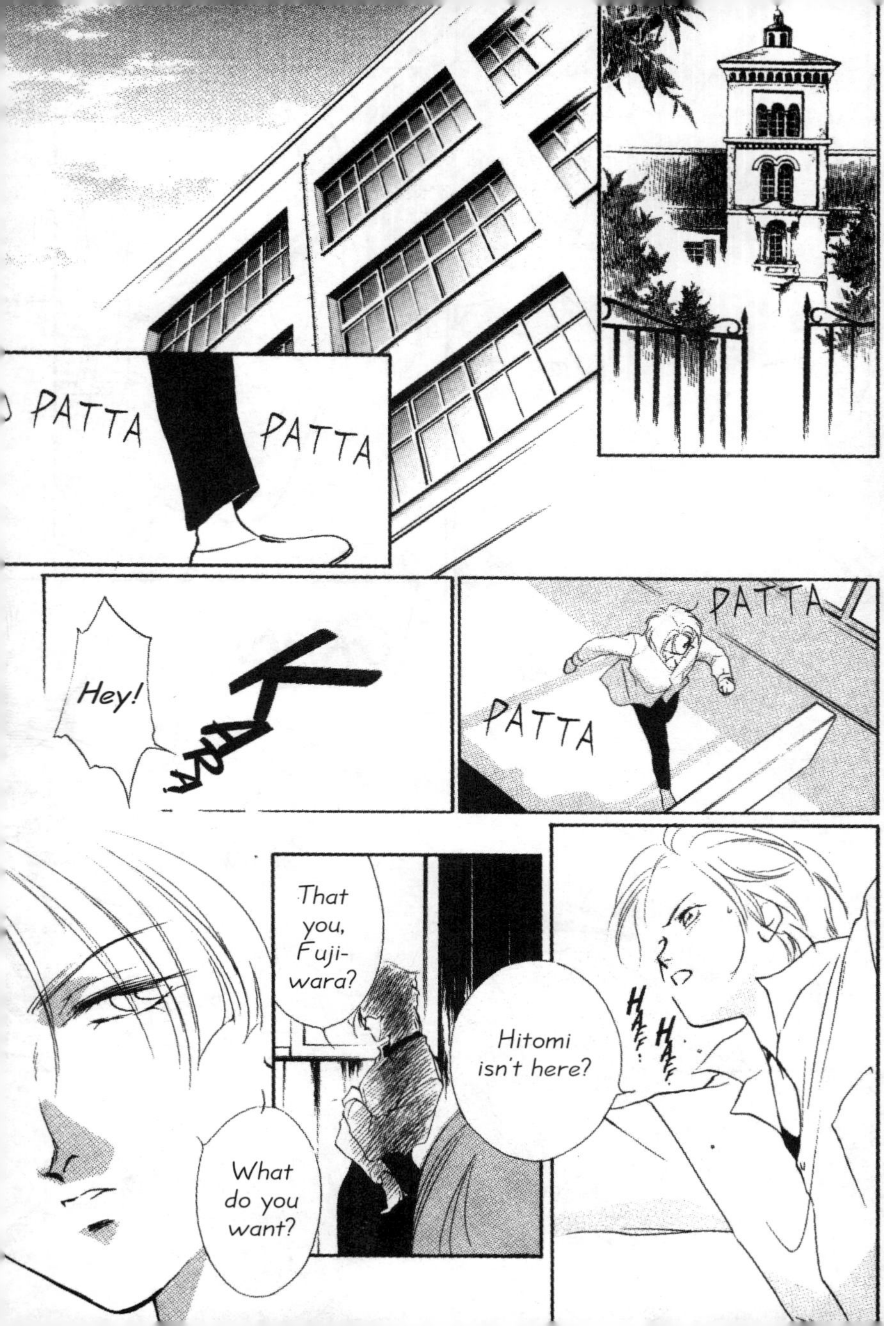

PATTA
PATTA
Hey!
KARA
PATTA
PATTA
That you, Fuji-wara?
What do you want?
Hitomi isn't here?
HAFF HAFF

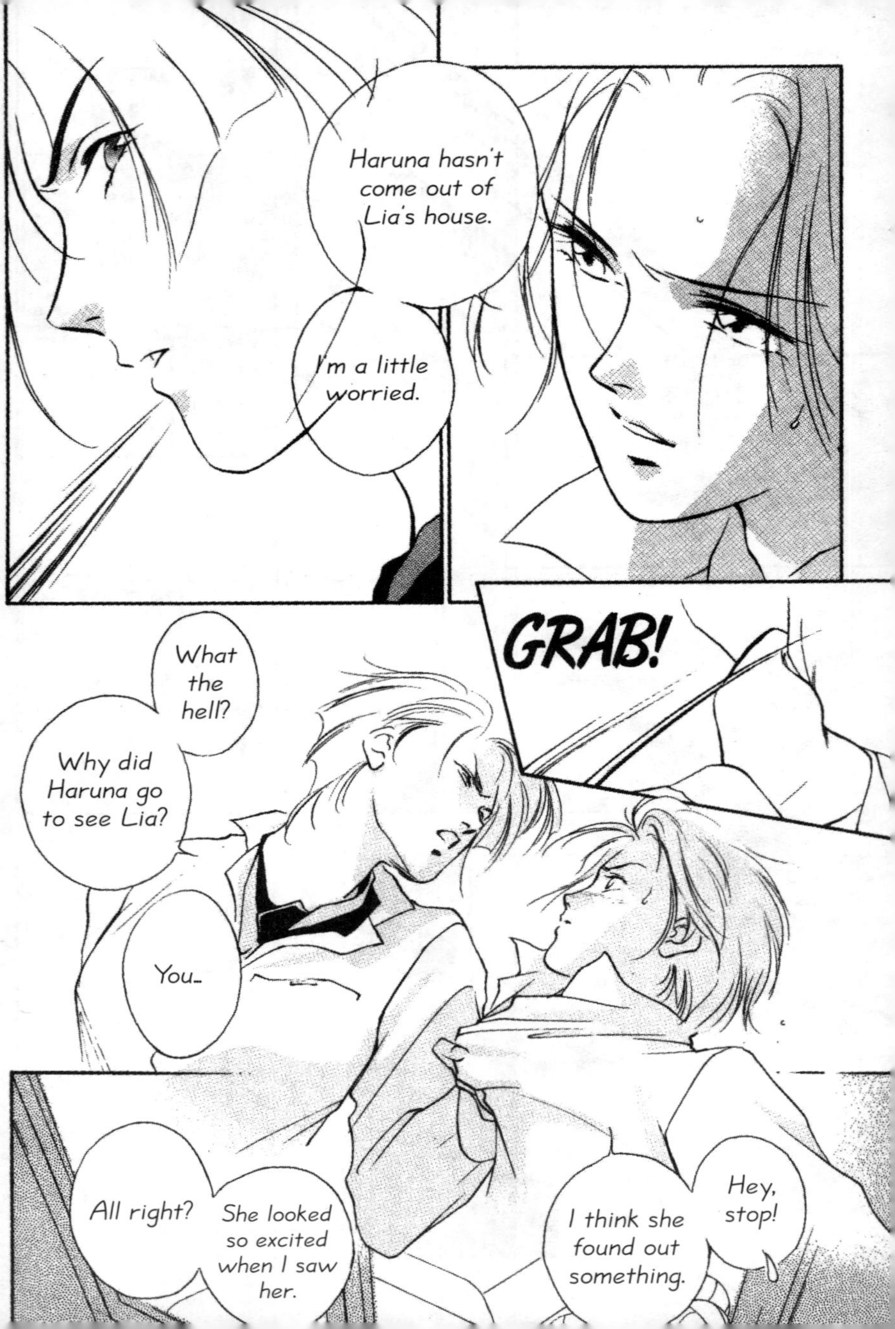
Haruna hasn't come out of Lia's house.
I'm a little worried.
GRAB!
What the hell?
Why did Haruna go to see Lia?
You...
Hey, stop!
I think she found out something.
She looked so excited when I saw her.
All right?

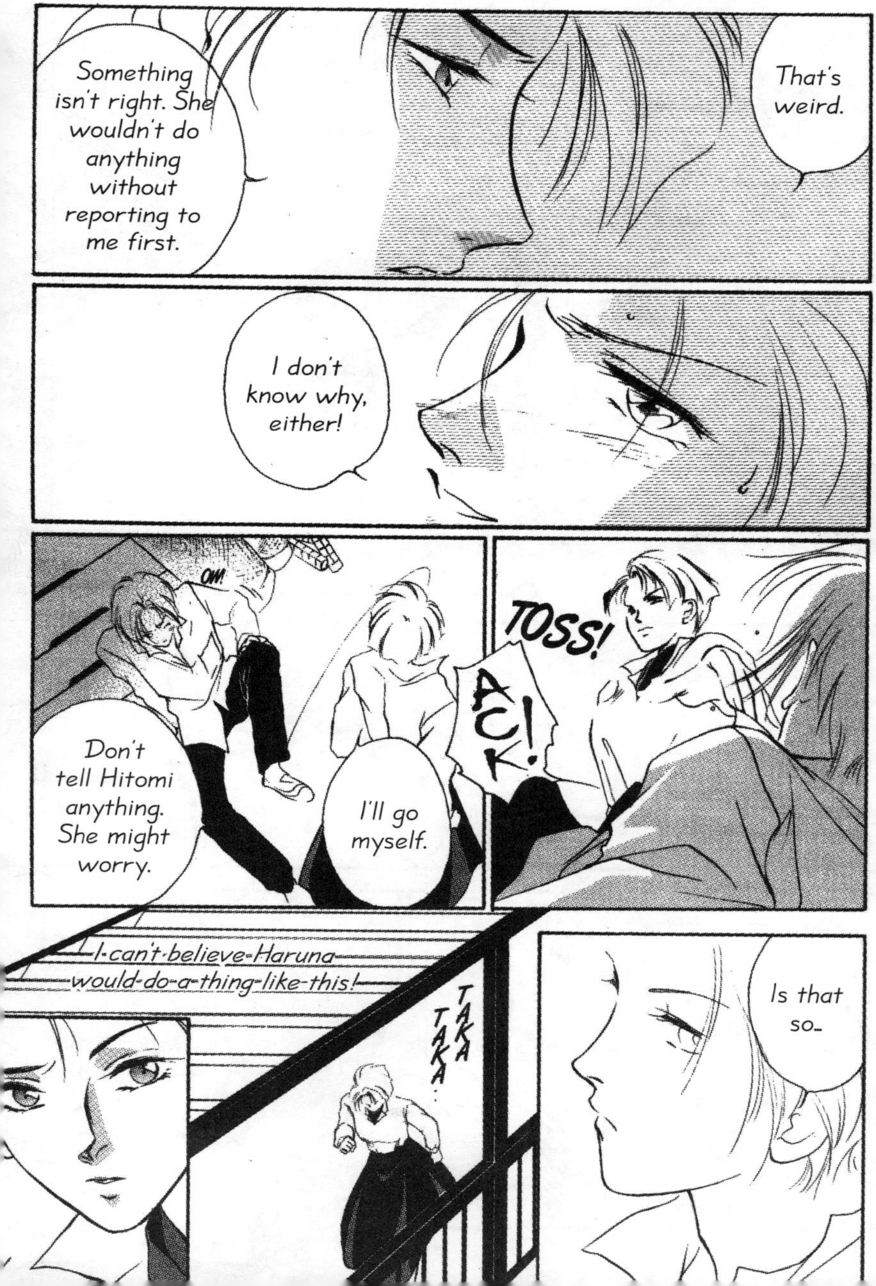
That's weird.
Something isn't right. She wouldn't do anything without reporting to me first.
I don't know why, either!
TOSS!
ACK!
I'll go myself.
Don't tell Hitomi anything. She might worry.
Is that so...
I can't believe Haruna would do a thing like this!
TAKA TAKA
TAKA

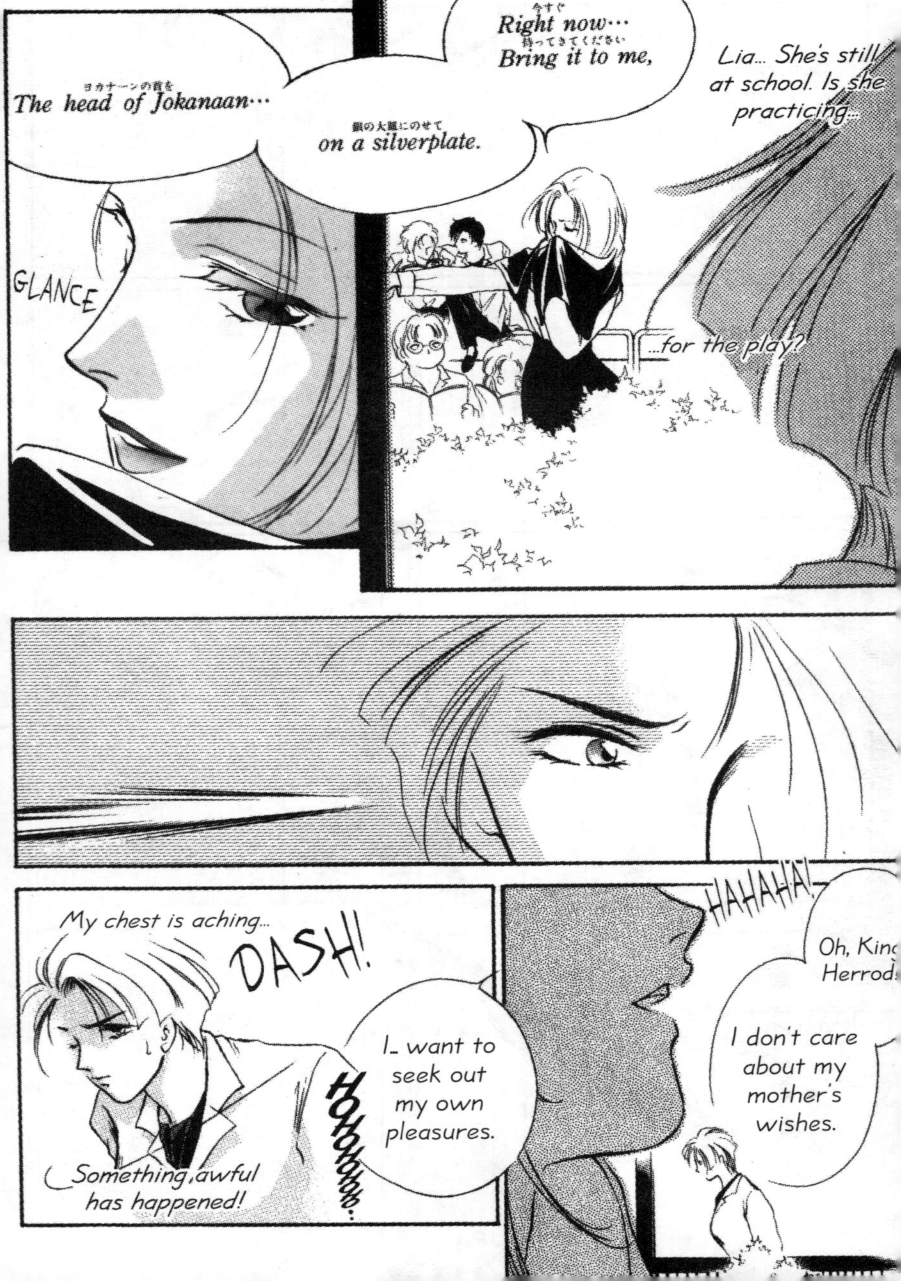
ヨカナーンの首を
The head of Jokanaan…
今すぐ
Right now…
持ってきてください
Bring it to me,
銀の大皿にのせて
on a silverplate.
Lia… She's still at school. Is she practicing…
…for the play?
GLANCE
HAHAHA!
Oh, King Herrod!
I don't care about my mother's wishes.
My chest is aching…
DASH!
I… want to seek out my own pleasures.
Something awful has happened!
HOHOHOHO…

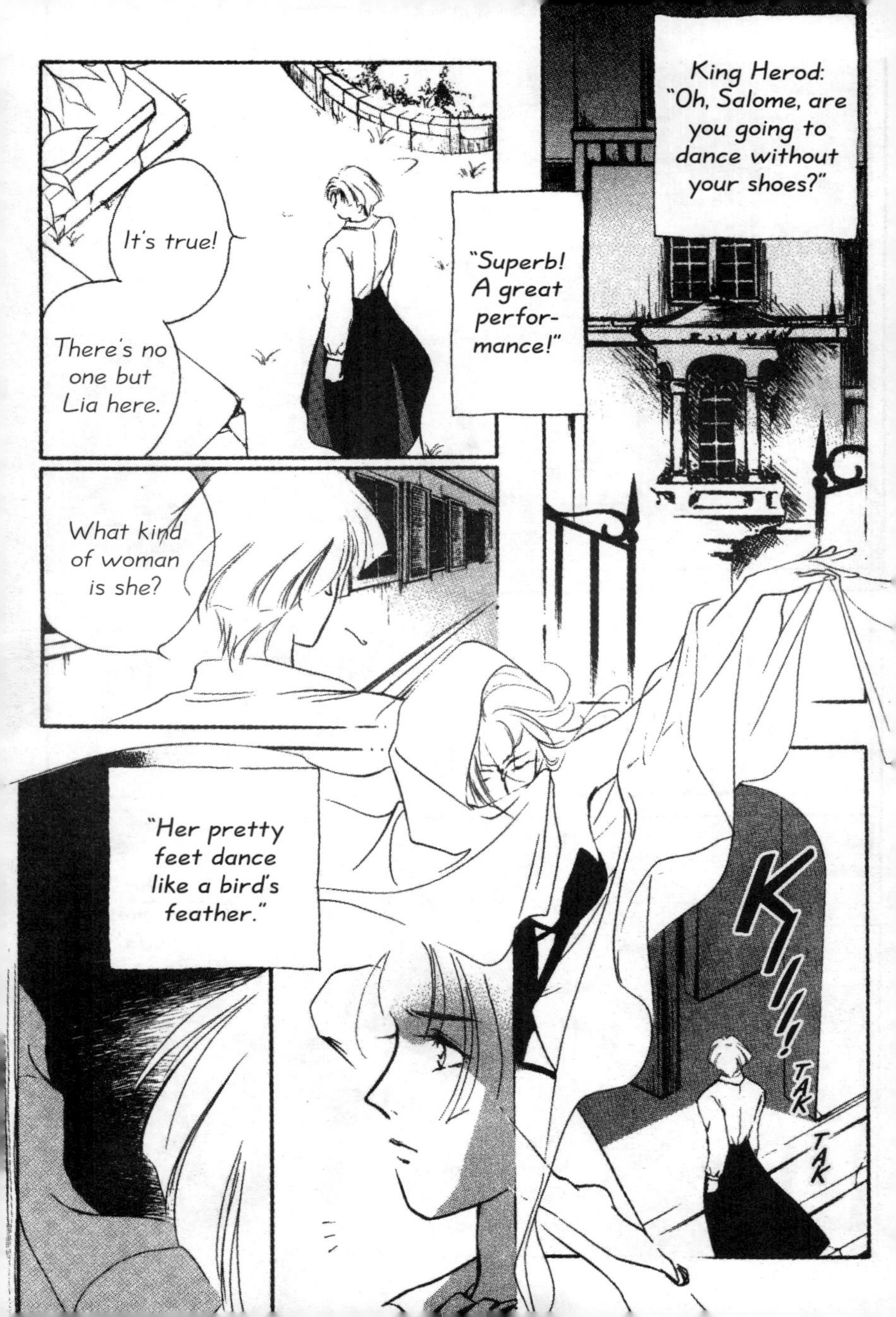
It's true!
There's no one but Lia here.
"Superb! A great perfor-mance!"
King Herod: "Oh, Salome, are you going to dance without your shoes?"
What kind of woman is she?
"Her pretty feet dance like a bird's feather."
KIII!
TAK TAK

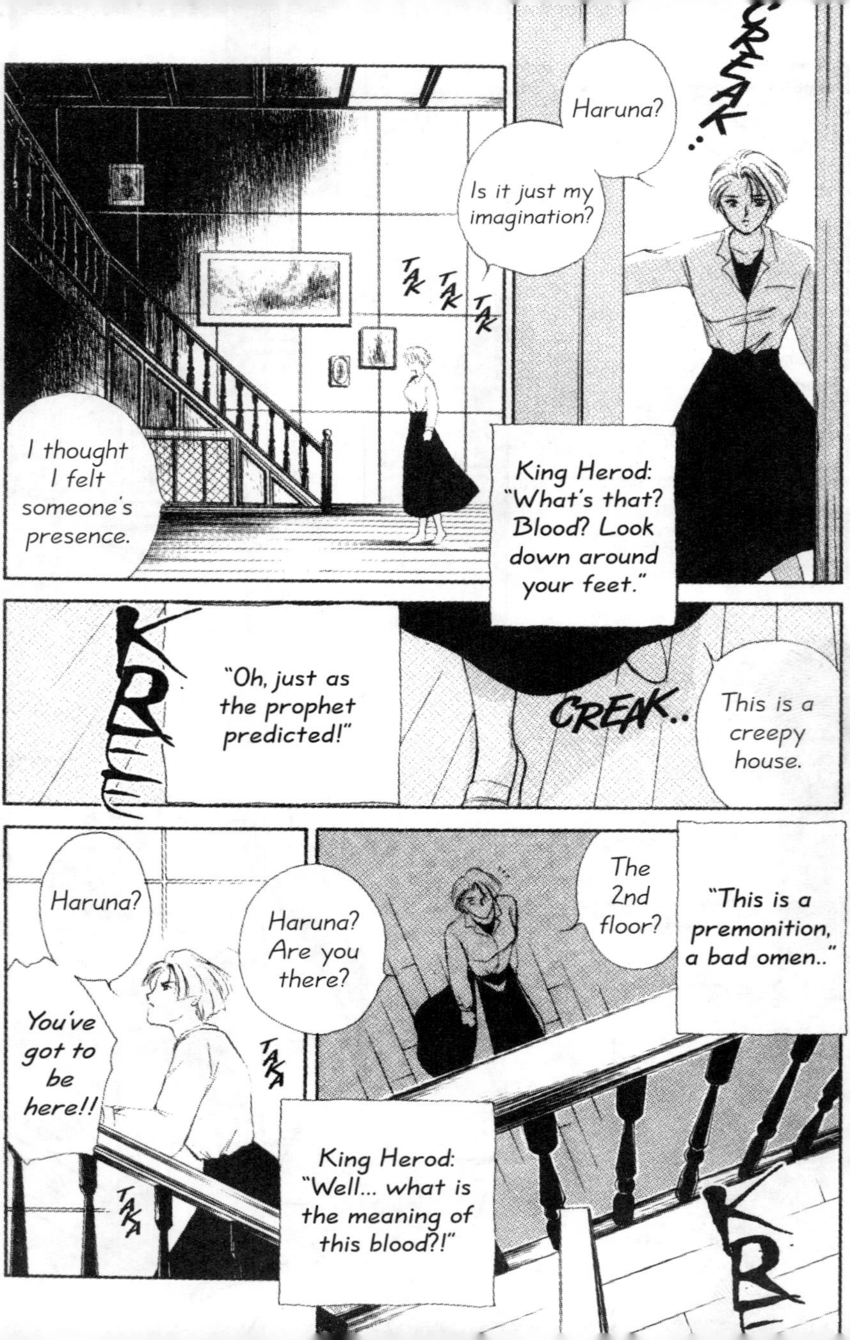
CREAK...
Haruna?
Is it just my imagination?
TAK TAK TAK
I thought I felt someone's presence.
King Herod: "What's that? Blood? Look down around your feet."
This is a creepy house.
CREAK..
"Oh, just as the prophet predicted!"
KRIII
"This is a premonition, a bad omen.."
The 2nd floor?
Haruna? Are you there?
Haruna?
You've got to be here!!
TAKA
TAKA
King Herod: "Well... what is the meaning of this blood?!"
KR

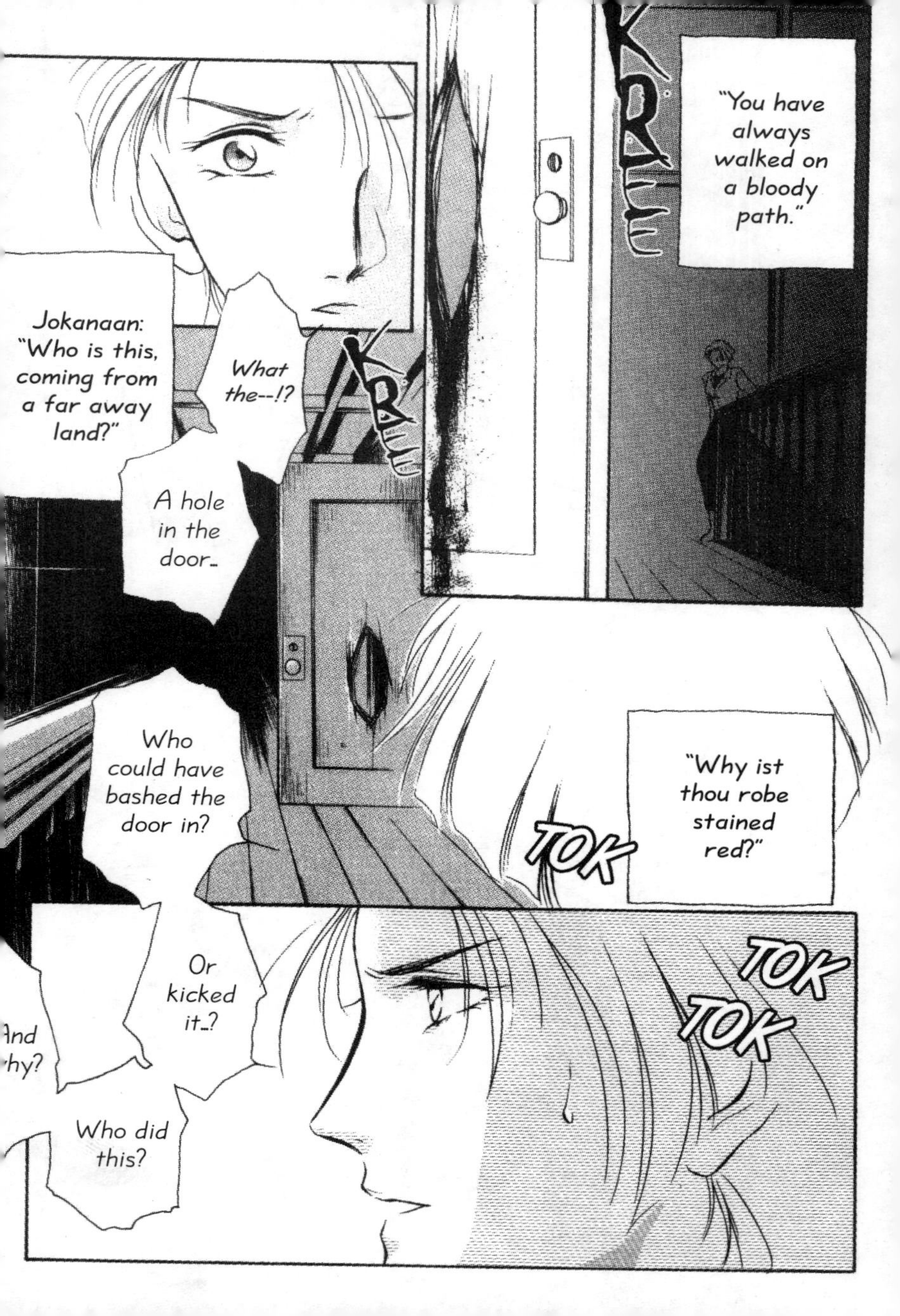
"You have always walked on a bloody path."
KREE
Jokanaan: "Who is this, coming from a far away land?"
What the--!?
KREE
A hole in the door..
"Why ist thou robe stained red?"
TOK
Who could have bashed the door in?
TOK TOK
Or kicked it..?
Who did this?

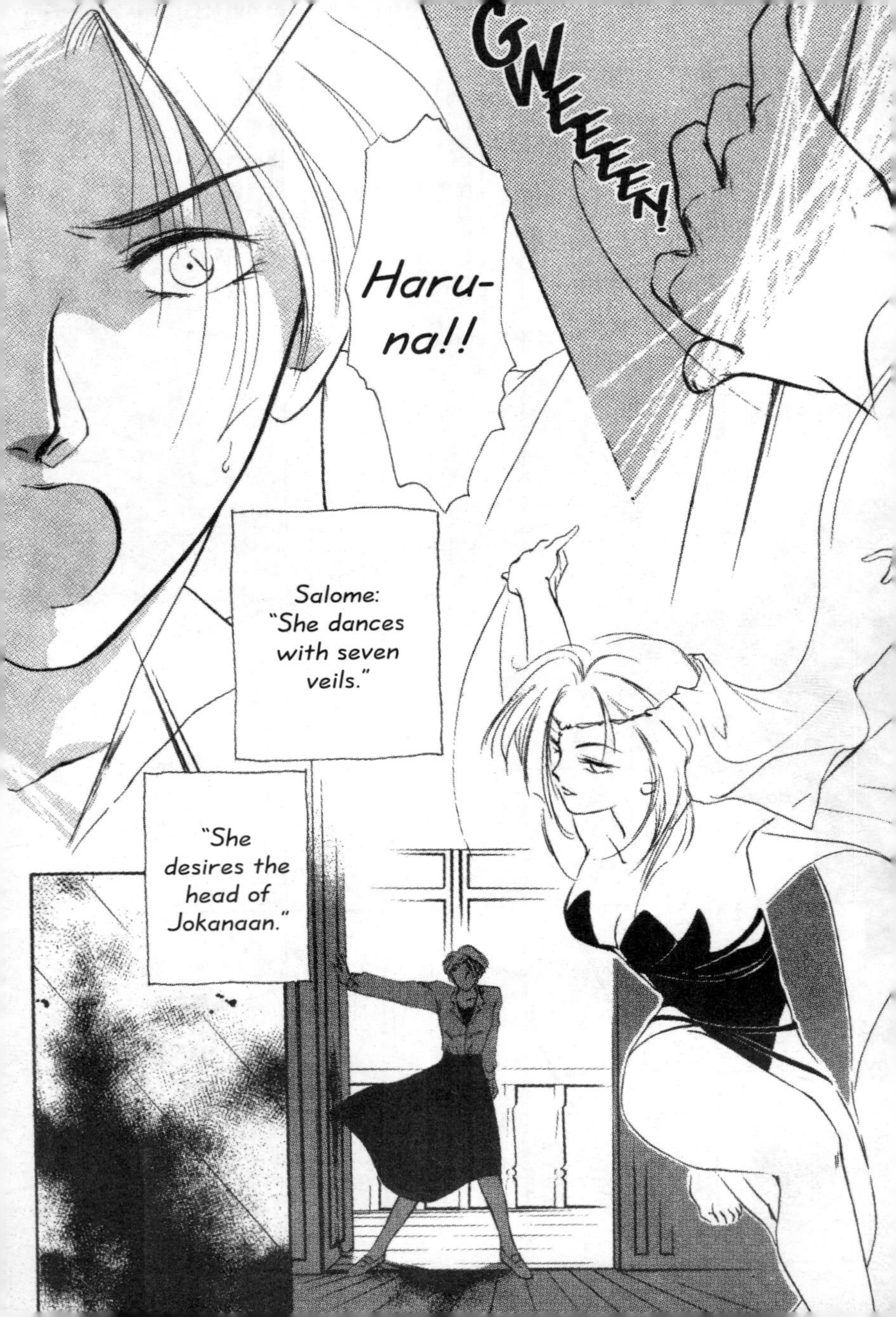
GWEEEEEN!
Haru-
na!!
Salome:
"She dances
with seven
veils."
"She
desires the
head of
Jokanaan."

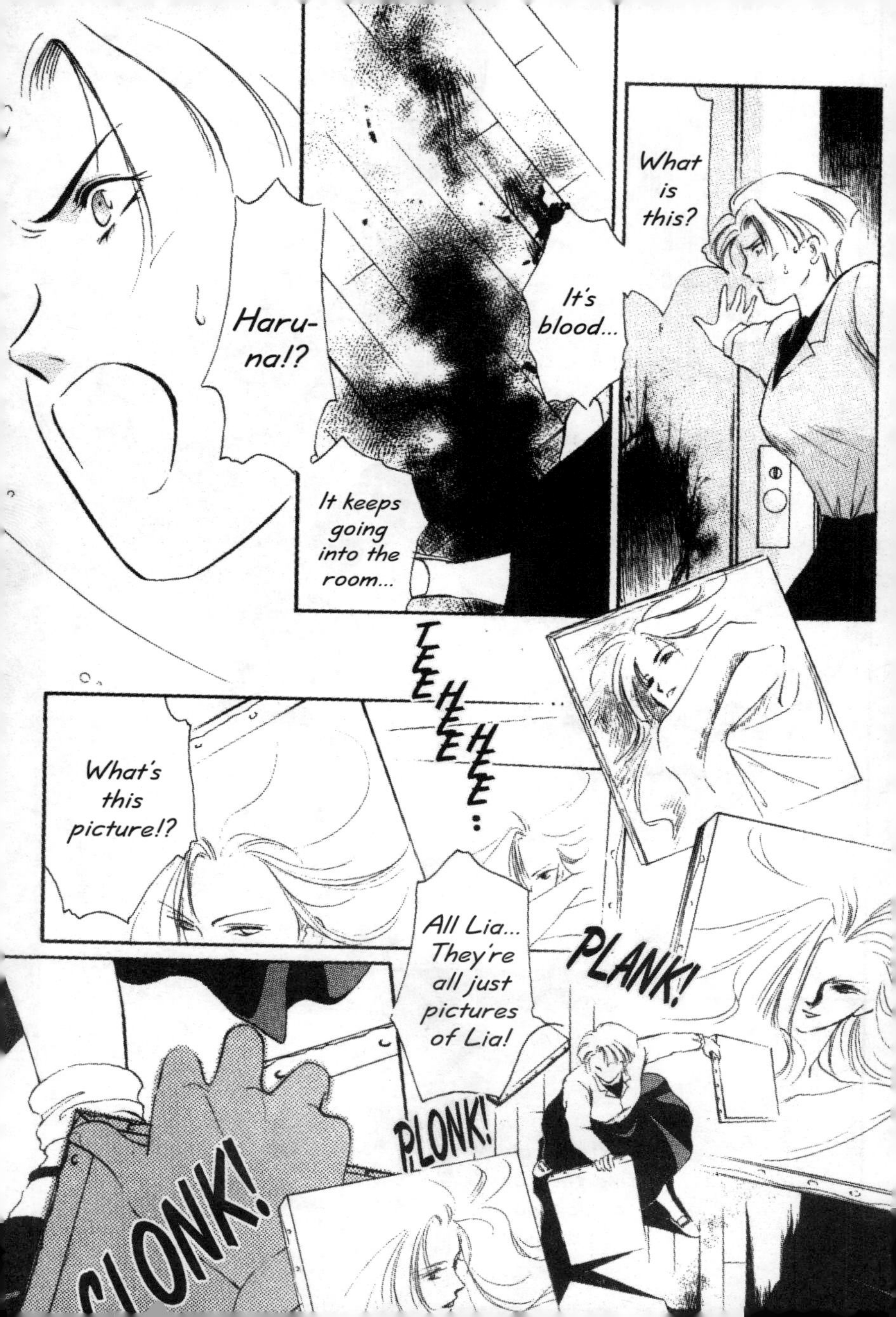
What is this?
It's blood...
It keeps going into the room...
Haruna!?
TEEHEEHEEHEE...
What's this picture!?
All Lia... They're all just pictures of Lia!
PLANK!
PLONK!
CLONK!

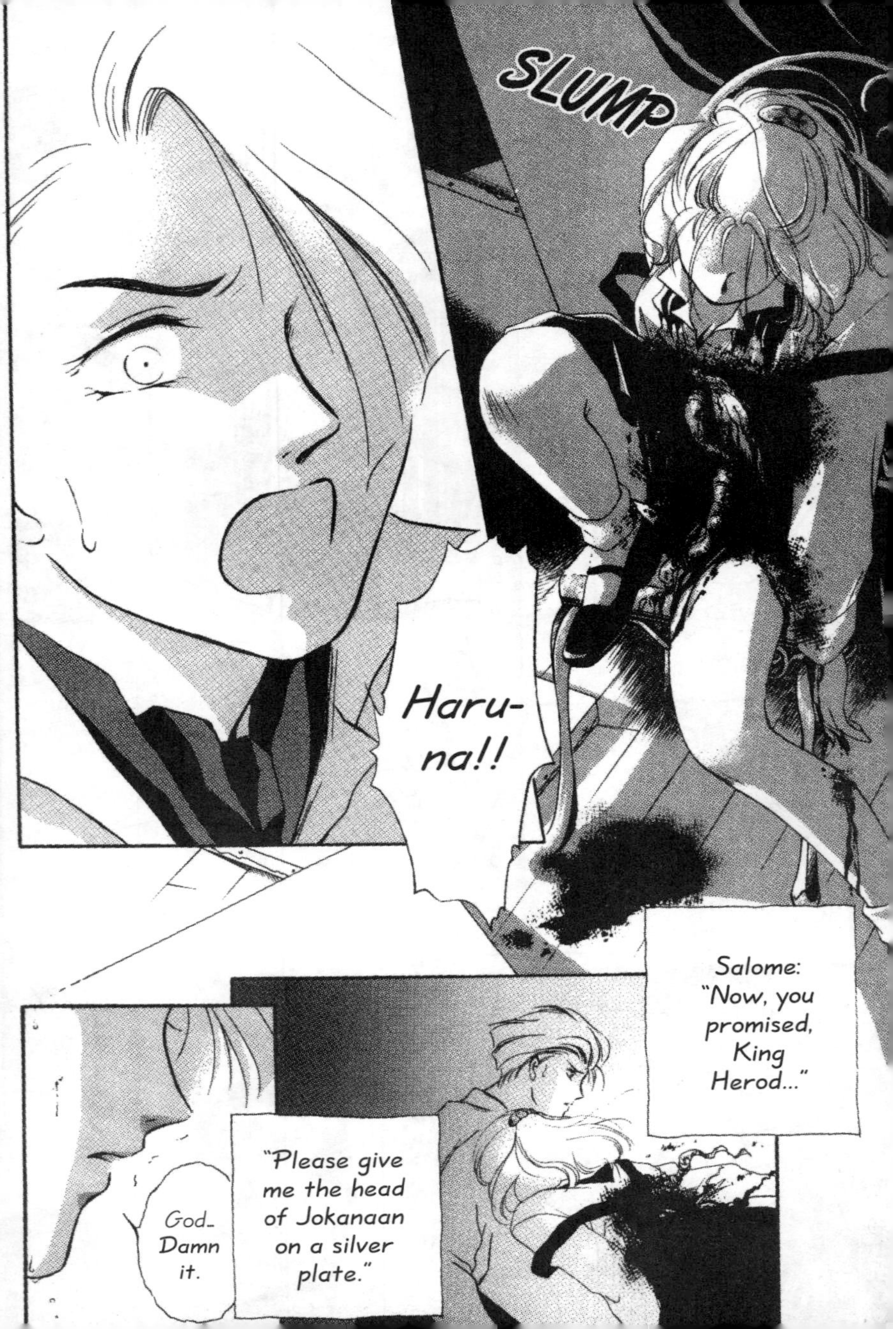
SLUMP
Haru-na!!
Salome: "Now, you promised, King Herod..."
"Please give me the head of Jokanaan on a silver plate."
God- Damn it.

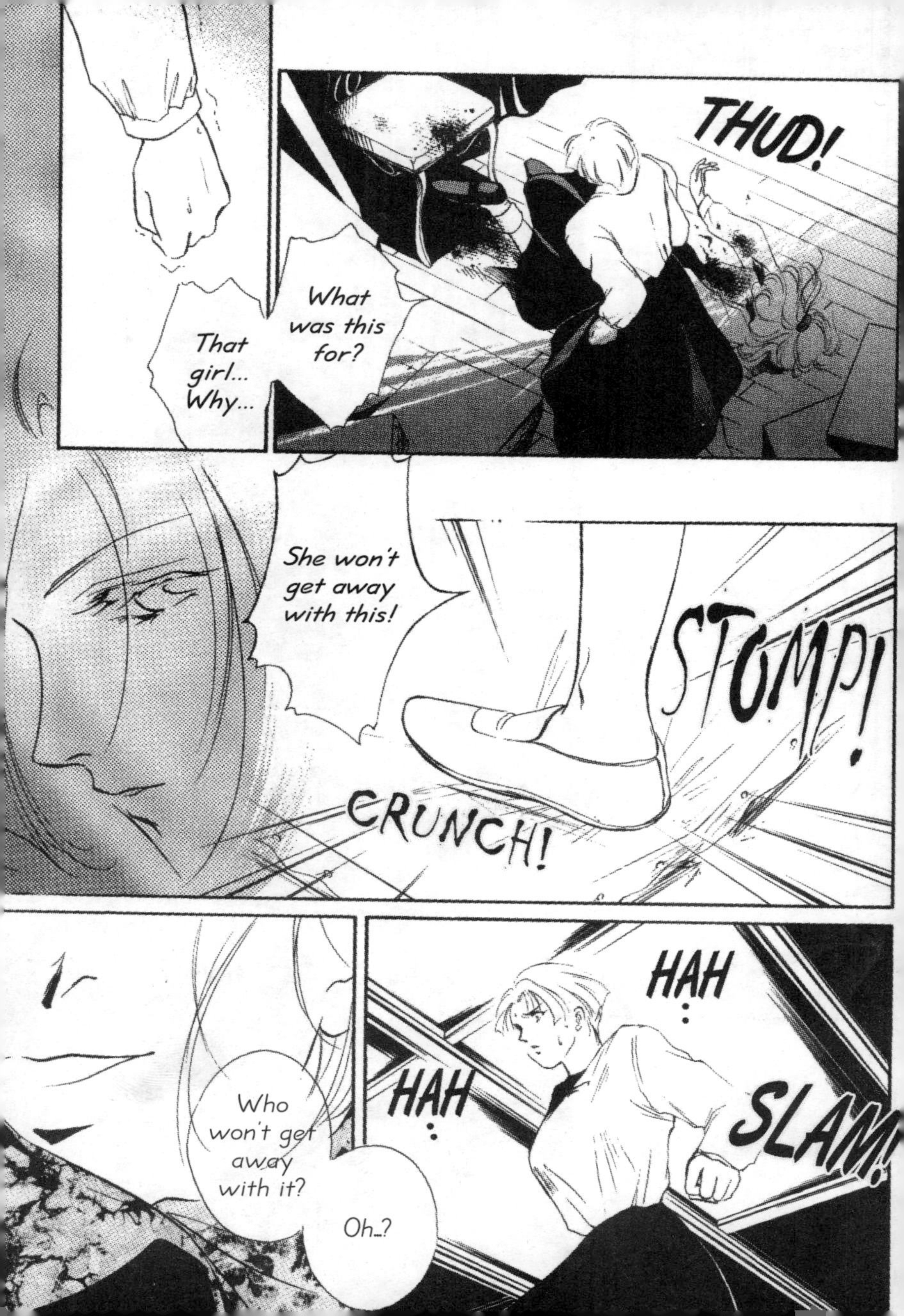
THUD!
What was this for?
That girl... Why...
She won't get away with this!
STOMP!
CRUNCH!
HAH
HAH
SLAM!
Who won't get away with it?
Oh...?

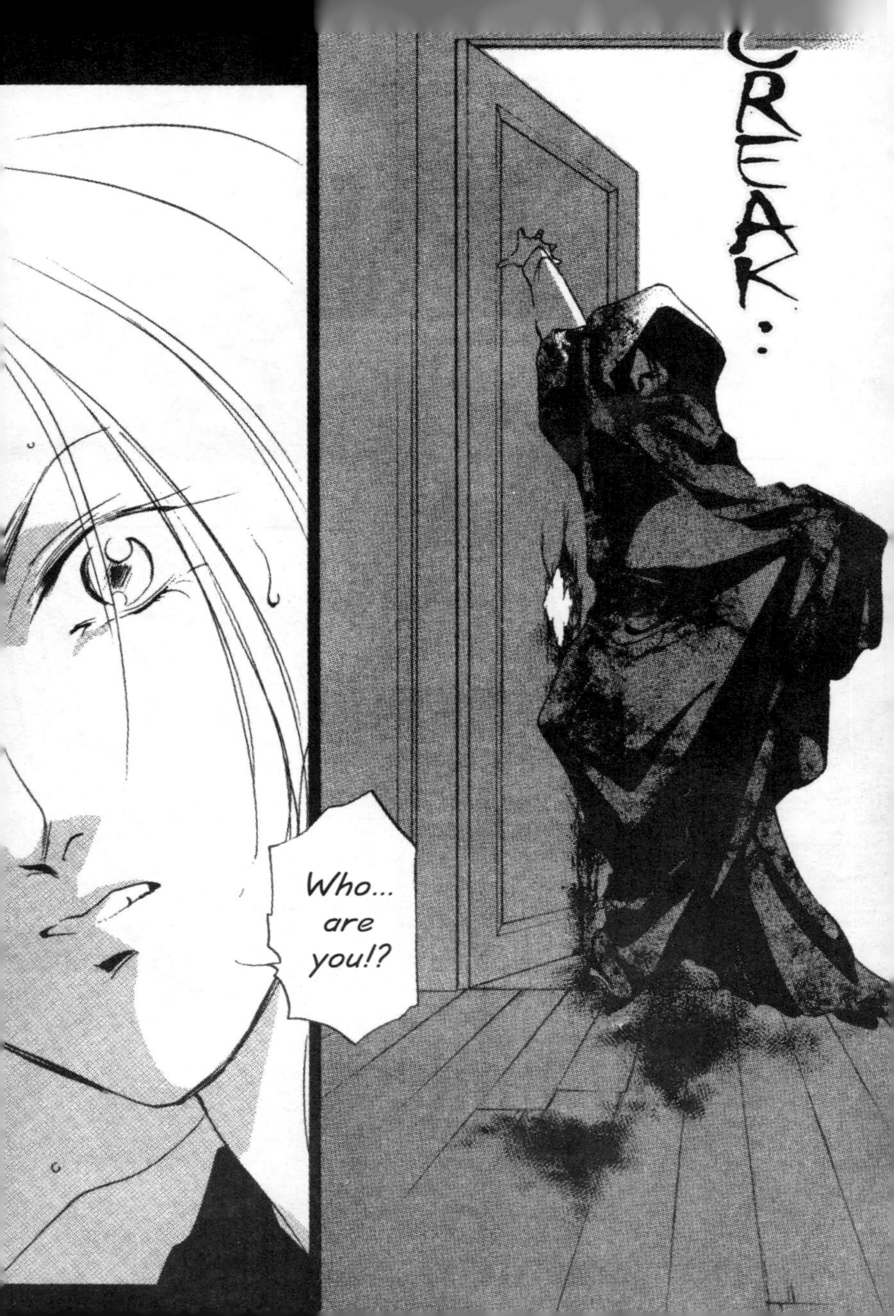
CREAK..
Who... are you!?

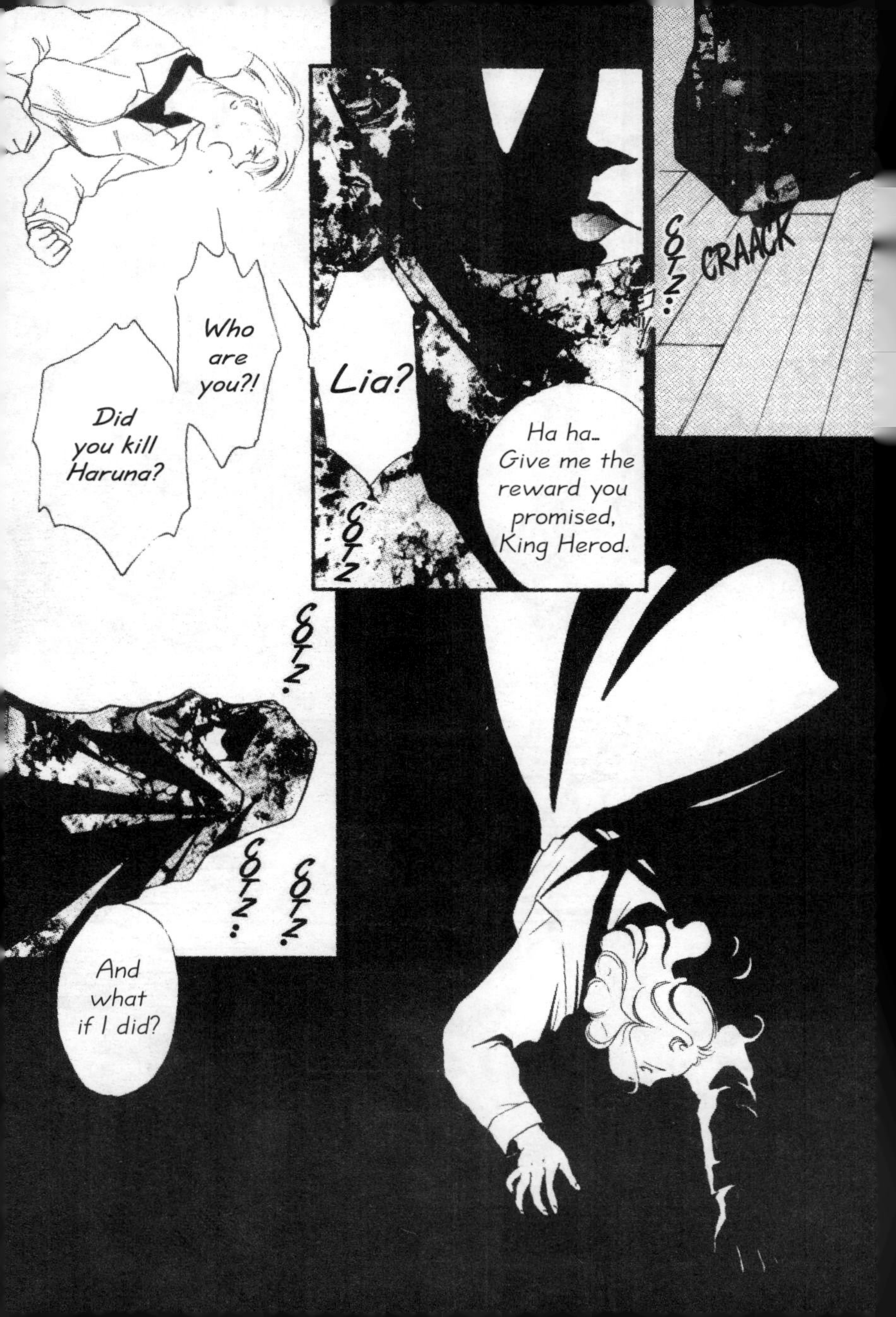
Who are you?!
Did you kill Haruna?
Lia?
COTZ
Ha ha.. Give me the reward you promised, King Herod.
COTZ..
CRAACK
COTZ.
COTZ..
COTZ.
And what if I did?

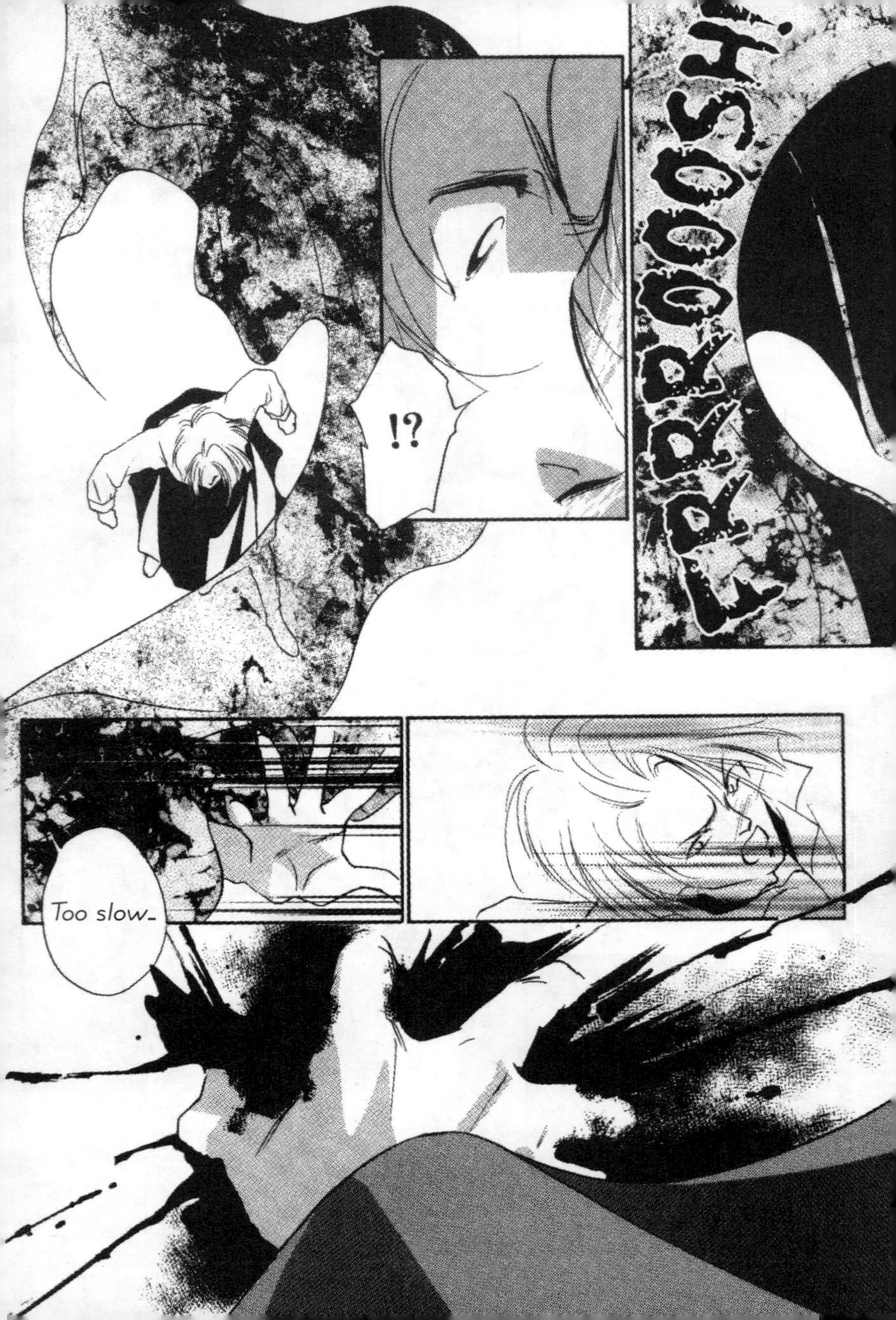
FRRROOOSH!
!?
Too slow...

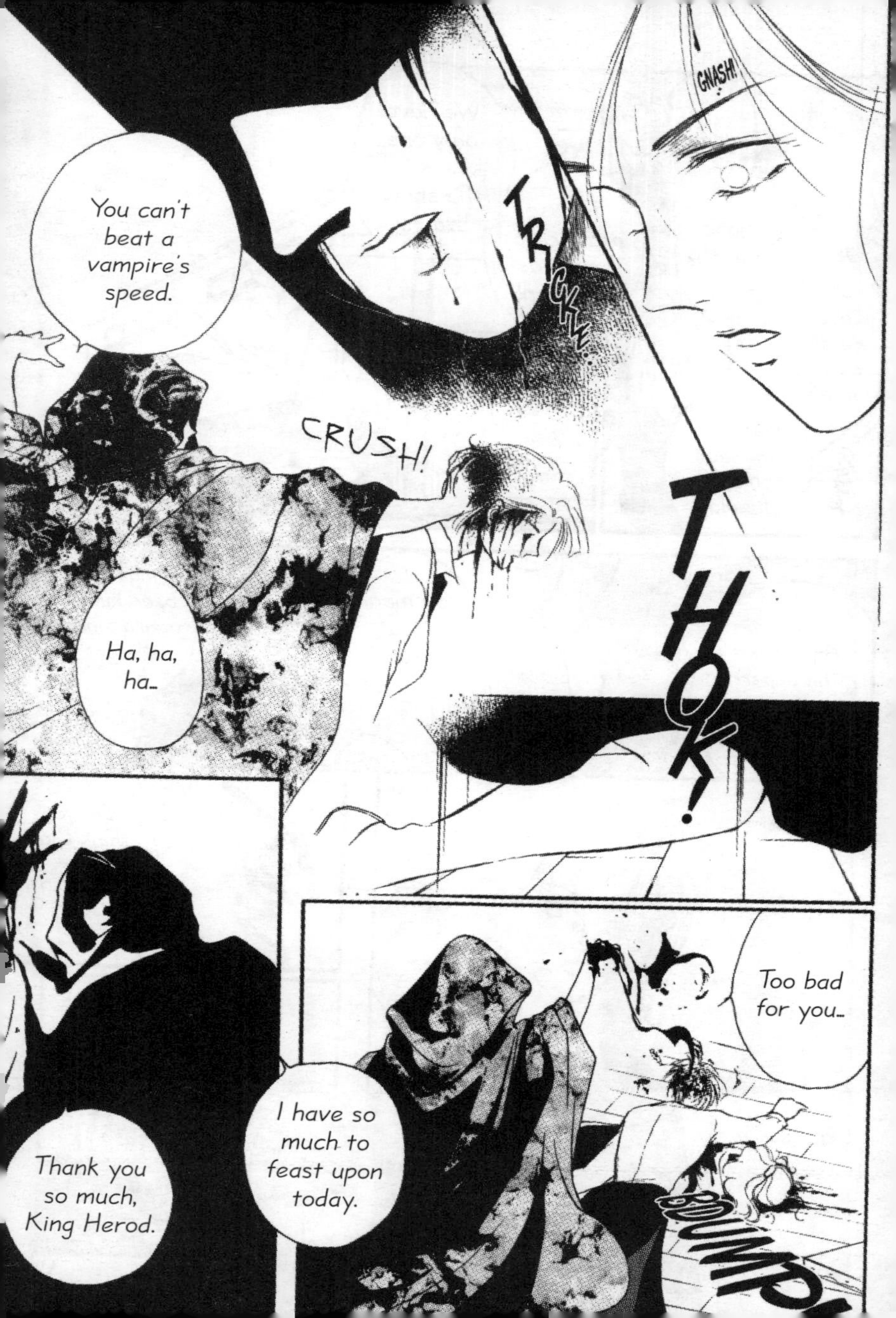
GNASH!
TRICKLE...
You can't beat a vampire's speed.
CRUSH!
Ha, ha, ha..
THOK!
Too bad for you..
BOUMP!
I have so much to feast upon today.
Thank you so much, King Herod.

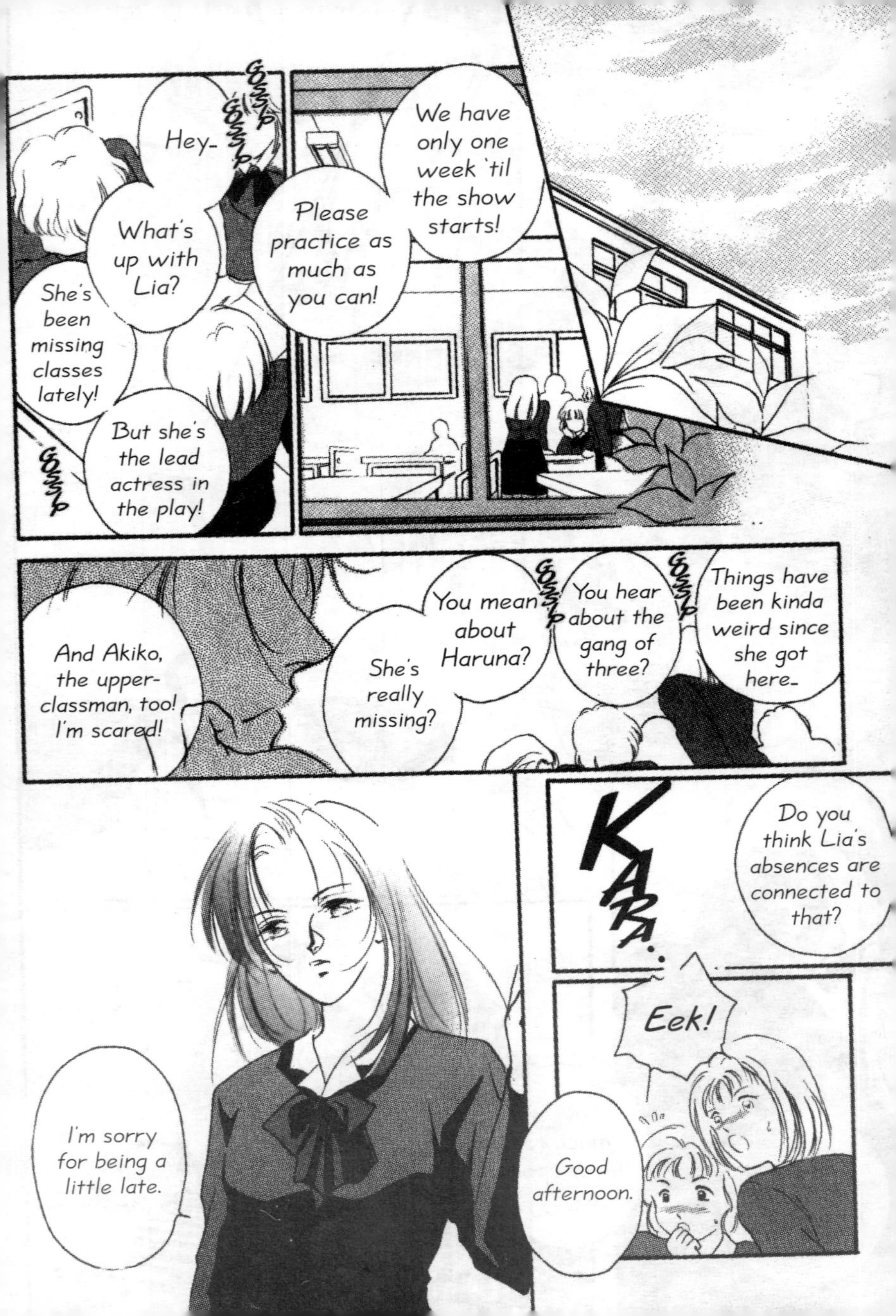
We have only one week 'til the show starts!
Please practice as much as you can!
GOSSIP GOSSIP
Hey...
What's up with Lia?
She's been missing classes lately!
But she's the lead actress in the play!
GOSSIP
Things have been kinda weird since she got here...
GOSSIP
You hear about the gang of three?
GOSSIP
You mean about Haruna?
She's really missing?
And Akiko, the upper-classman, too! I'm scared!
Do you think Lia's absences are connected to that?
KARA...
Eek!
Good afternoon.
I'm sorry for being a little late.

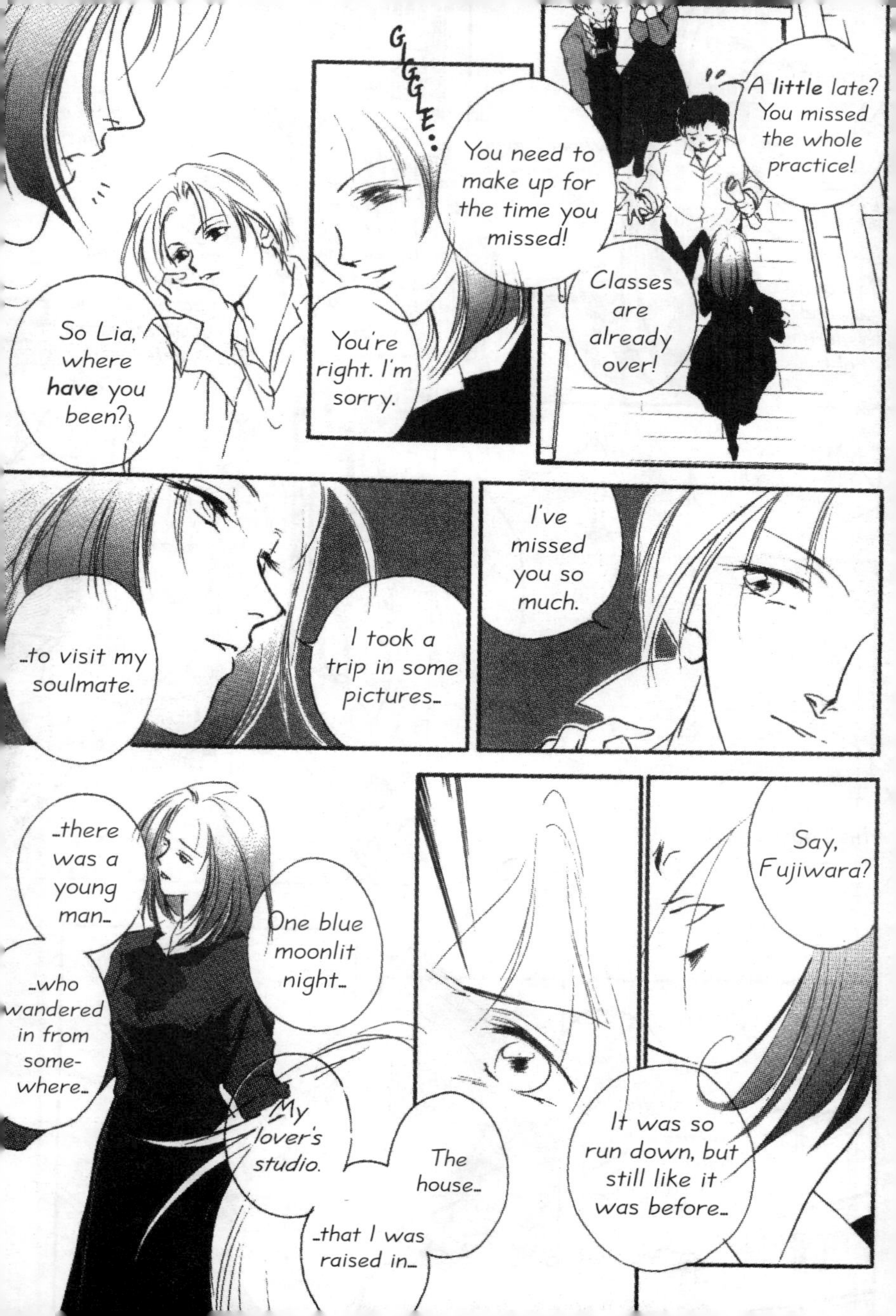

A little late? You missed the whole practice!
Classes are already over!
You need to make up for the time you missed!
GIGGLE...
You're right. I'm sorry.
So Lia, where have you been?
I've missed you so much.
I took a trip in some pictures...
...to visit my soulmate.
Say, Fujiwara?
It was so run down, but still like it was before...
The house...
...that I was raised in...
My lover's studio.
One blue moonlit night...
...there was a young man...
...who wandered in from somewhere...

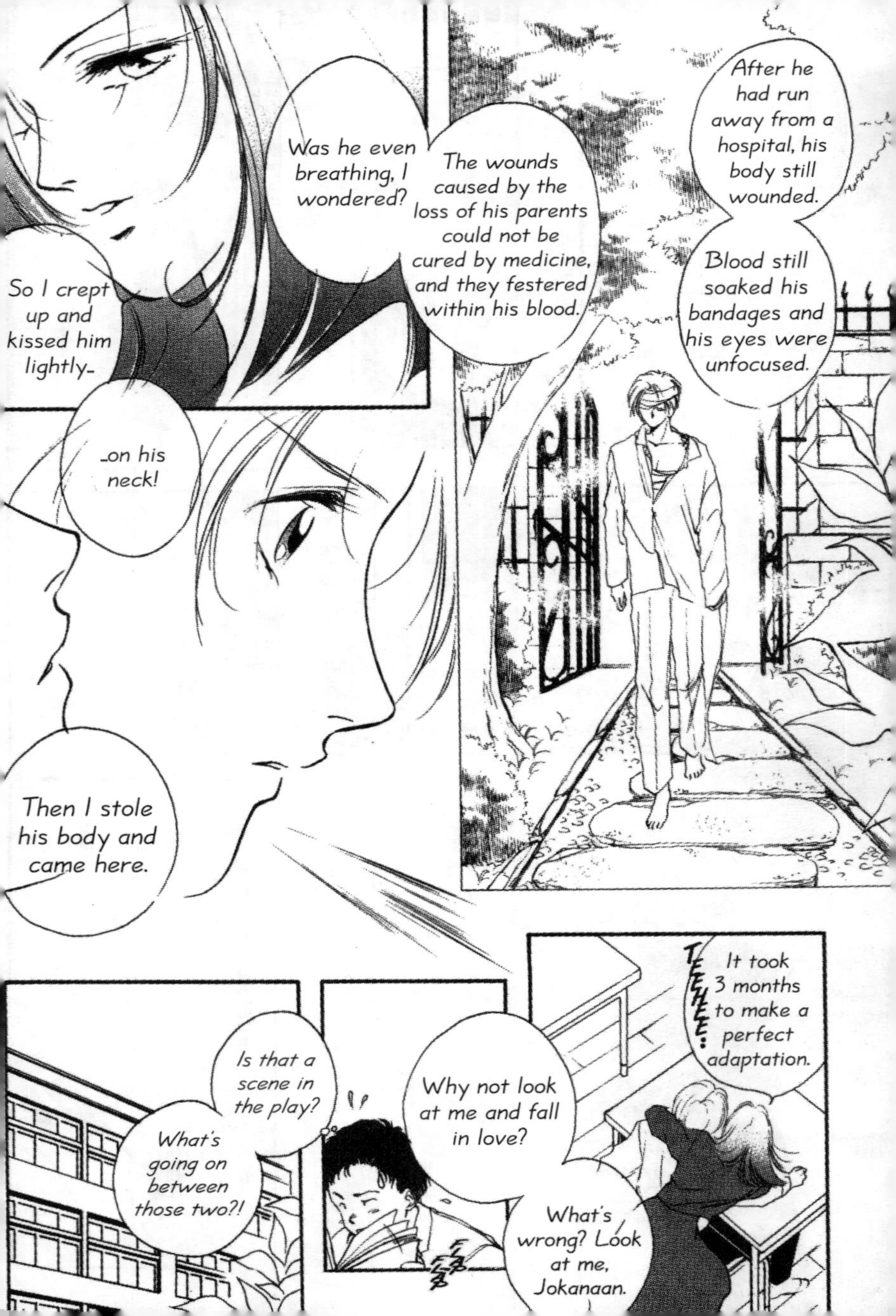
After he had run away from a hospital, his body still wounded.
Blood still soaked his bandages and his eyes were unfocused.
The wounds caused by the loss of his parents could not be cured by medicine, and they festered within his blood.
Was he even breathing, I wondered?
So I crept up and kissed him lightly...
...on his neck!
Then I stole his body and came here.
It took 3 months to make a perfect adaptation.
TEEHEE...
Why not look at me and fall in love?
What's wrong? Look at me, Jokanaan.
FLIP FLIP
Is that a scene in the play?
What's going on between those two?!

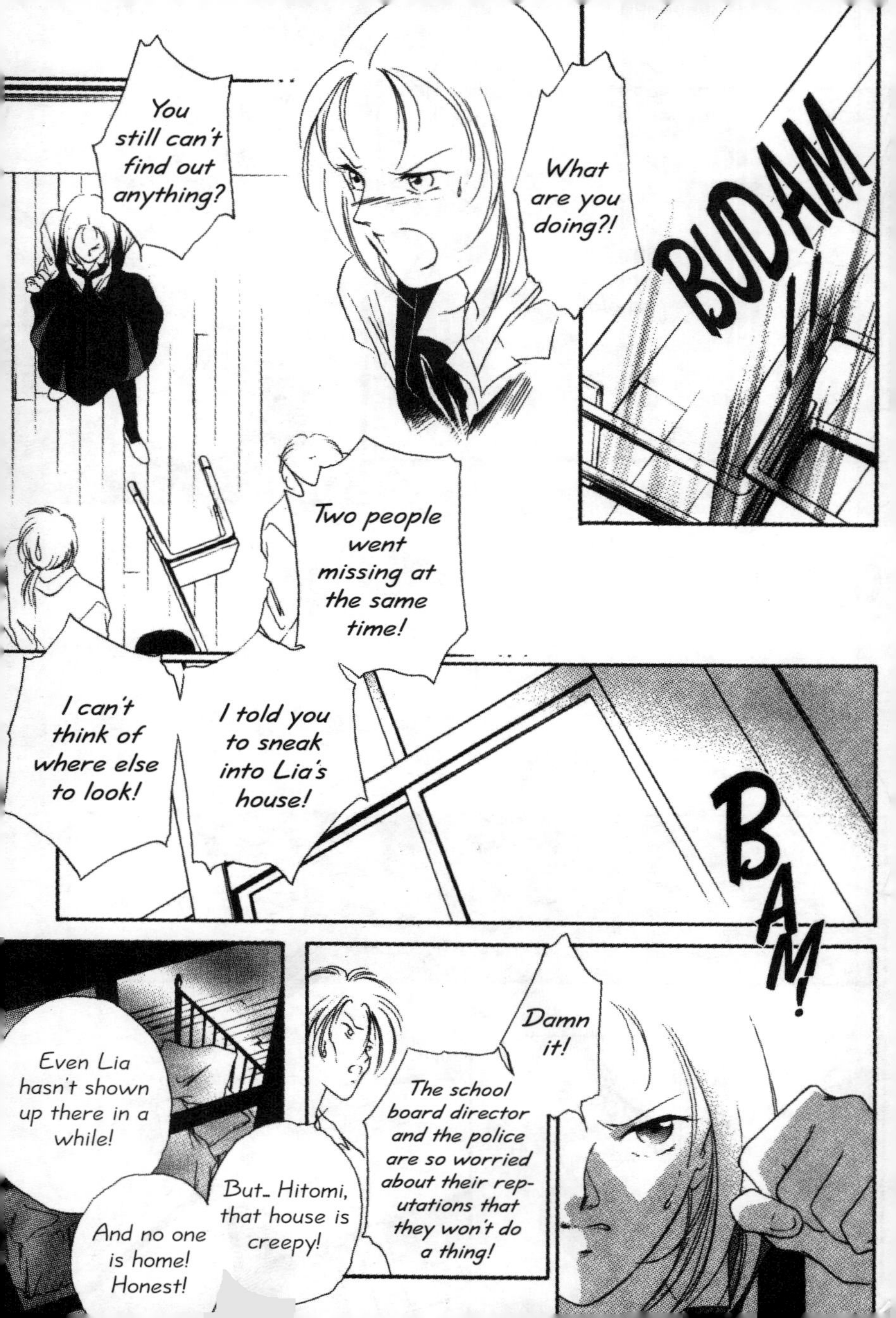

You still can't find out anything?
What are you doing?!
BUDAM!
Two people went missing at the same time!
I can't think of where else to look!
I told you to sneak into Lia's house!
BAM!
Even Lia hasn't shown up there in a while!
And no one is home! Honest!
But.. Hitomi, that house is creepy!
Damn it!
The school board director and the police are so worried about their reputations that they won't do a thing!

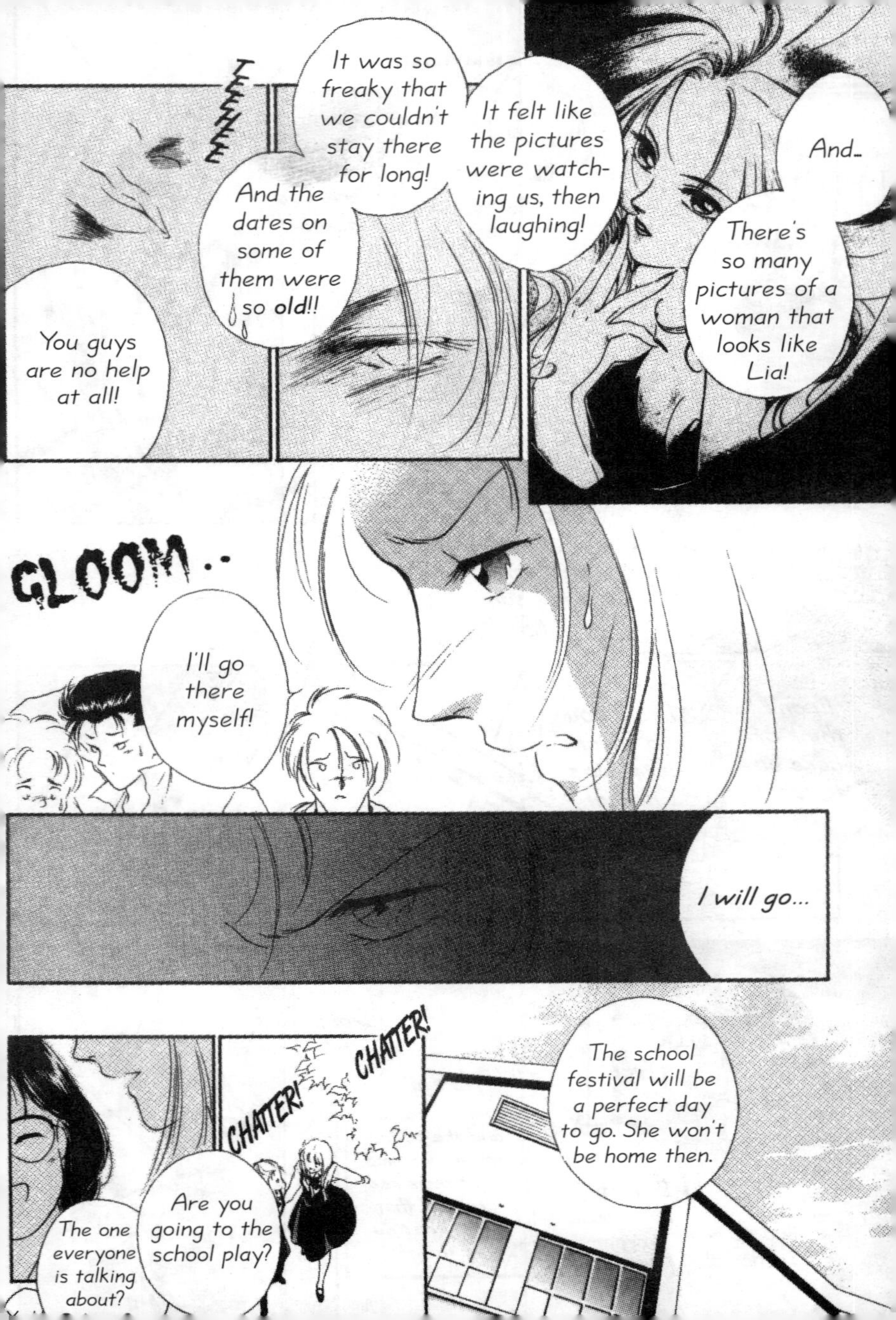
And..
There's so many pictures of a woman that looks like Lia!
It felt like the pictures were watching us, then laughing!
It was so freaky that we couldn't stay there for long!
And the dates on some of them were so **old**!!
TEEHEE
You guys are no help at all!
GLOOM..
I'll go there myself!
I will go...
The school festival will be a perfect day to go. She won't be home then.
CHATTER!
CHATTER!
Are you going to the school play?
The one everyone is talking about?

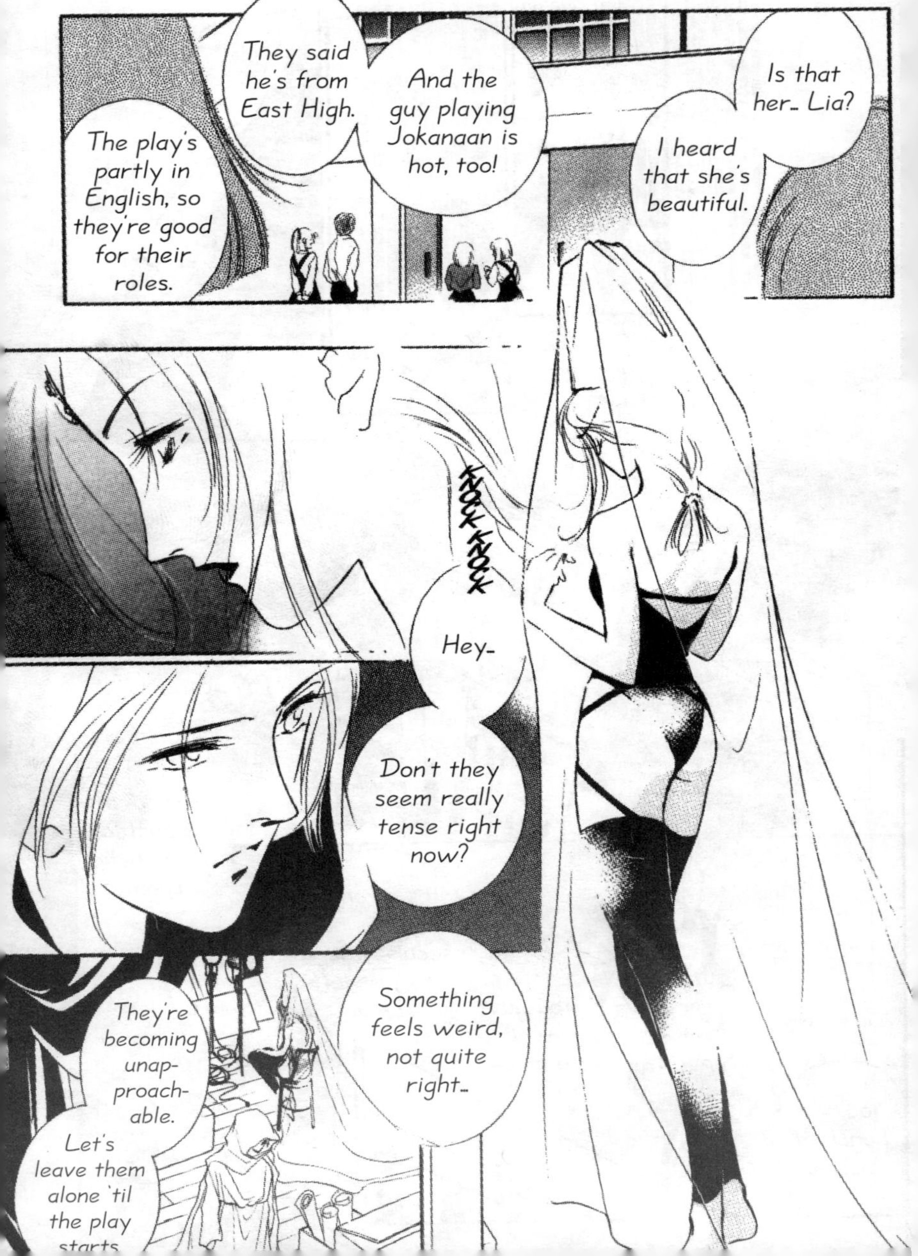

Is that her... Lia?
I heard that she's beautiful.
And the guy playing Jokanaan is hot, too!
They said he's from East High.
The play's partly in English, so they're good for their roles.
KNOCK KNOCK
Hey...
Don't they seem really tense right now?
Something feels weird, not quite right...
They're becoming unap-proach-able.
Let's leave them alone 'til the play starts

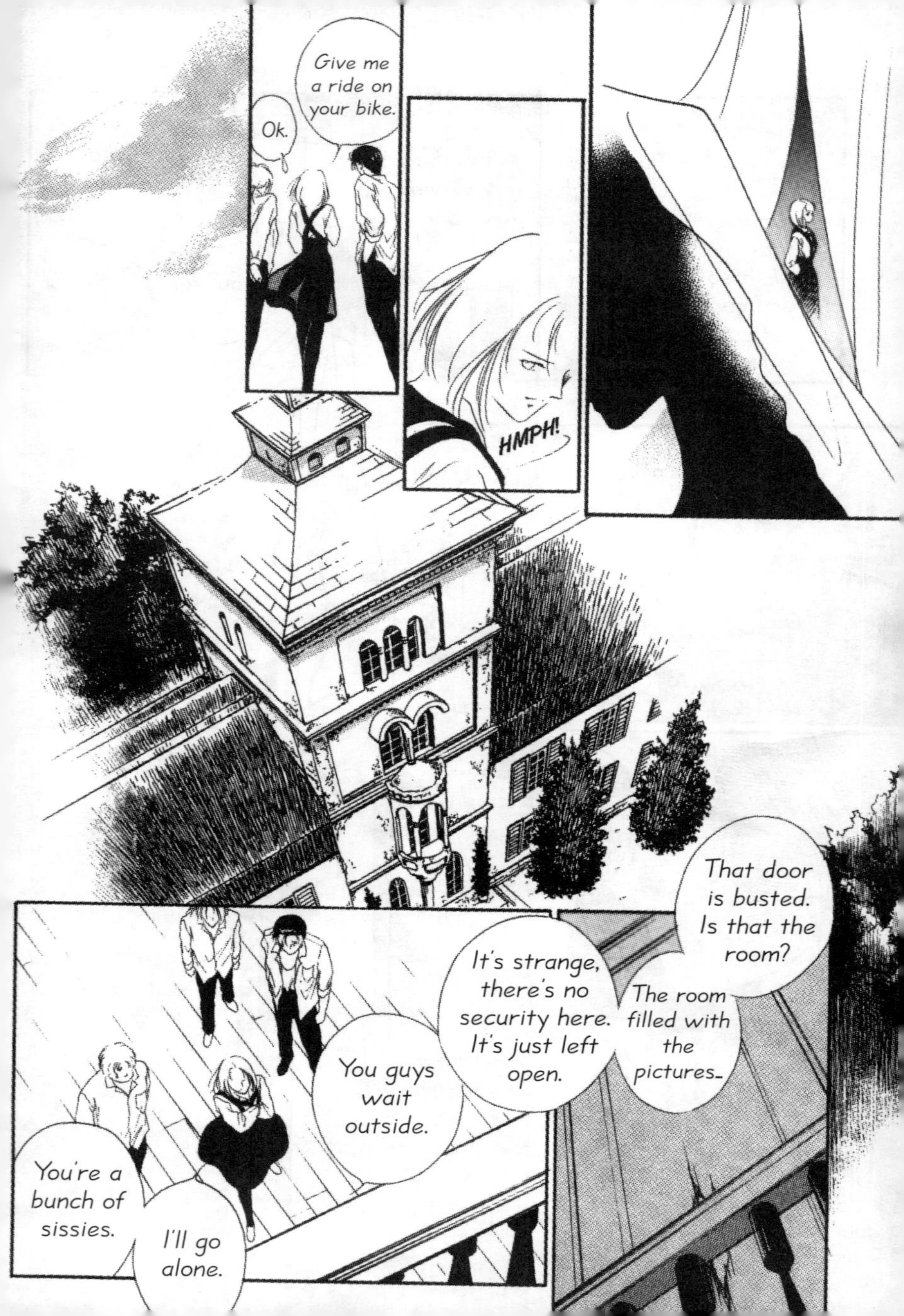
Give me a ride on your bike.
Ok.
HMPH!
You're a bunch of sissies.
I'll go alone.
You guys wait outside.
It's strange, there's no security here. It's just left open.
That door is busted. Is that the room?
The room filled with the pictures...

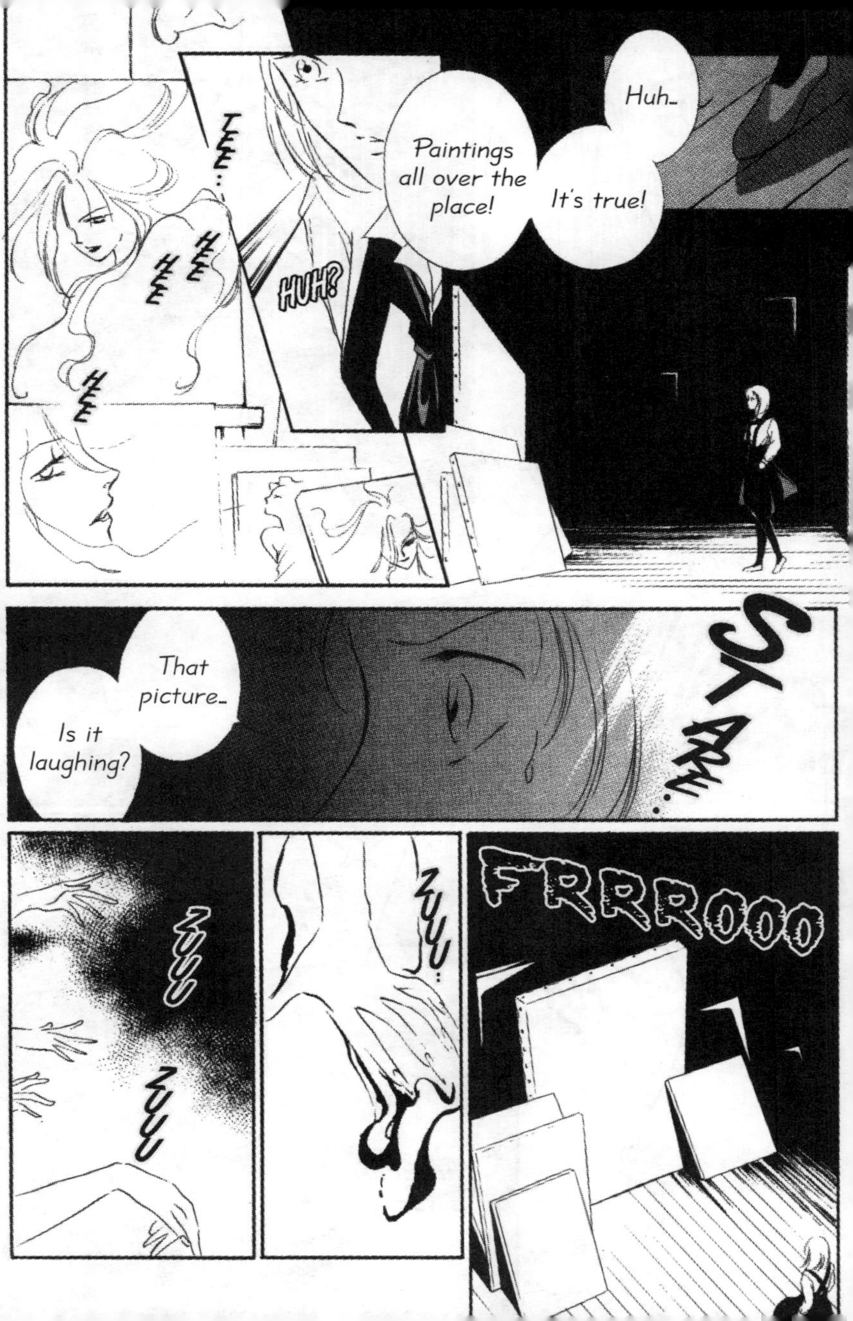
Huh..
It's true!
Paintings all over the place!
HUH?
TEE..
HEE HEE
HEE
That picture..
Is it laughing?
STARE..
FRRROOO
ZUUU..
ZUUU
ZUUU

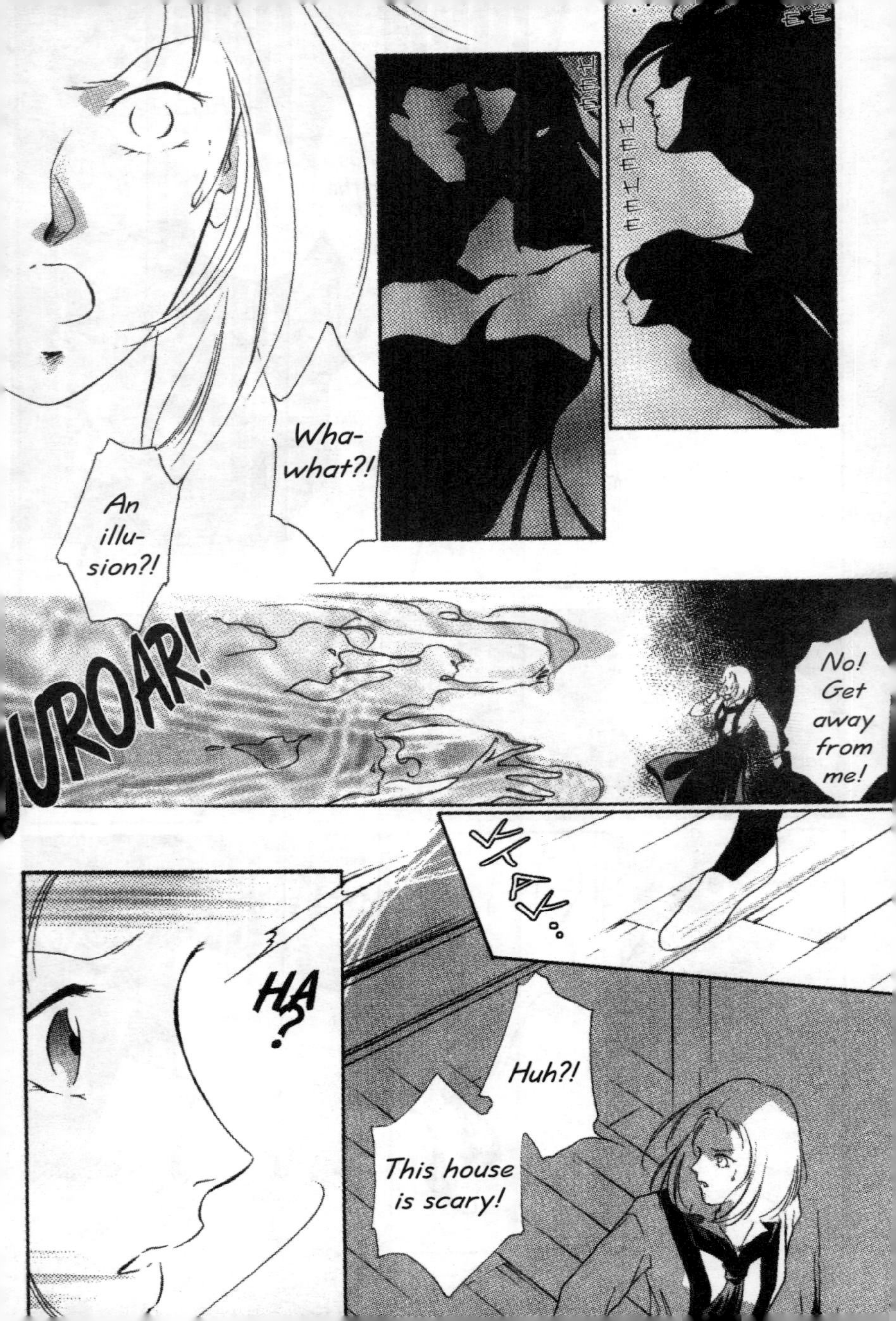
HEEHEE
Wha-what?!
An illusion?!
No! Get away from me!
UROAR!
HA?
Huh?!
This house is scary!

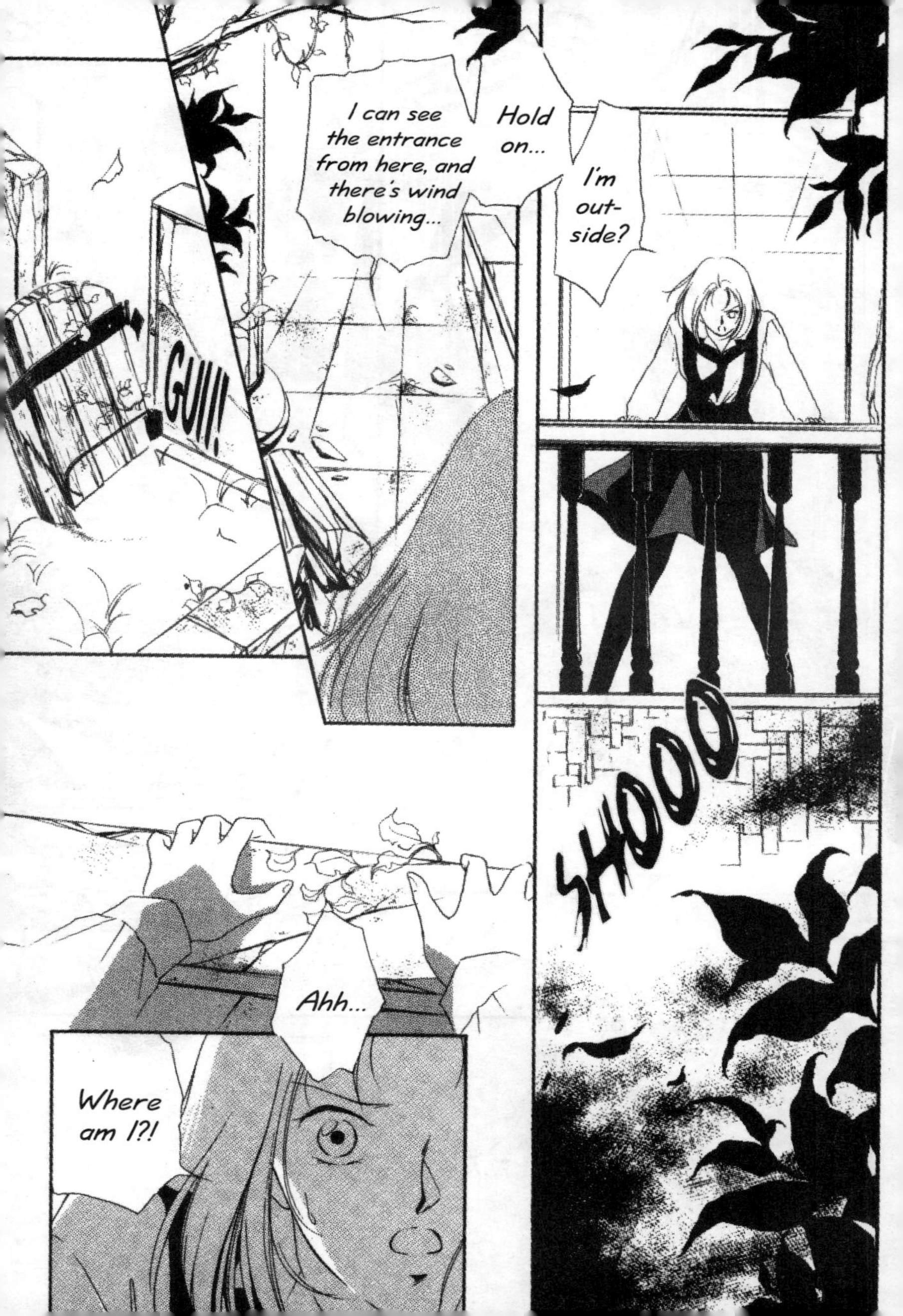
Hold on...
I'm out-side?
I can see the entrance from here, and there's wind blowing...
GUII!
SHOOOO
Ahh...
Where am I?!

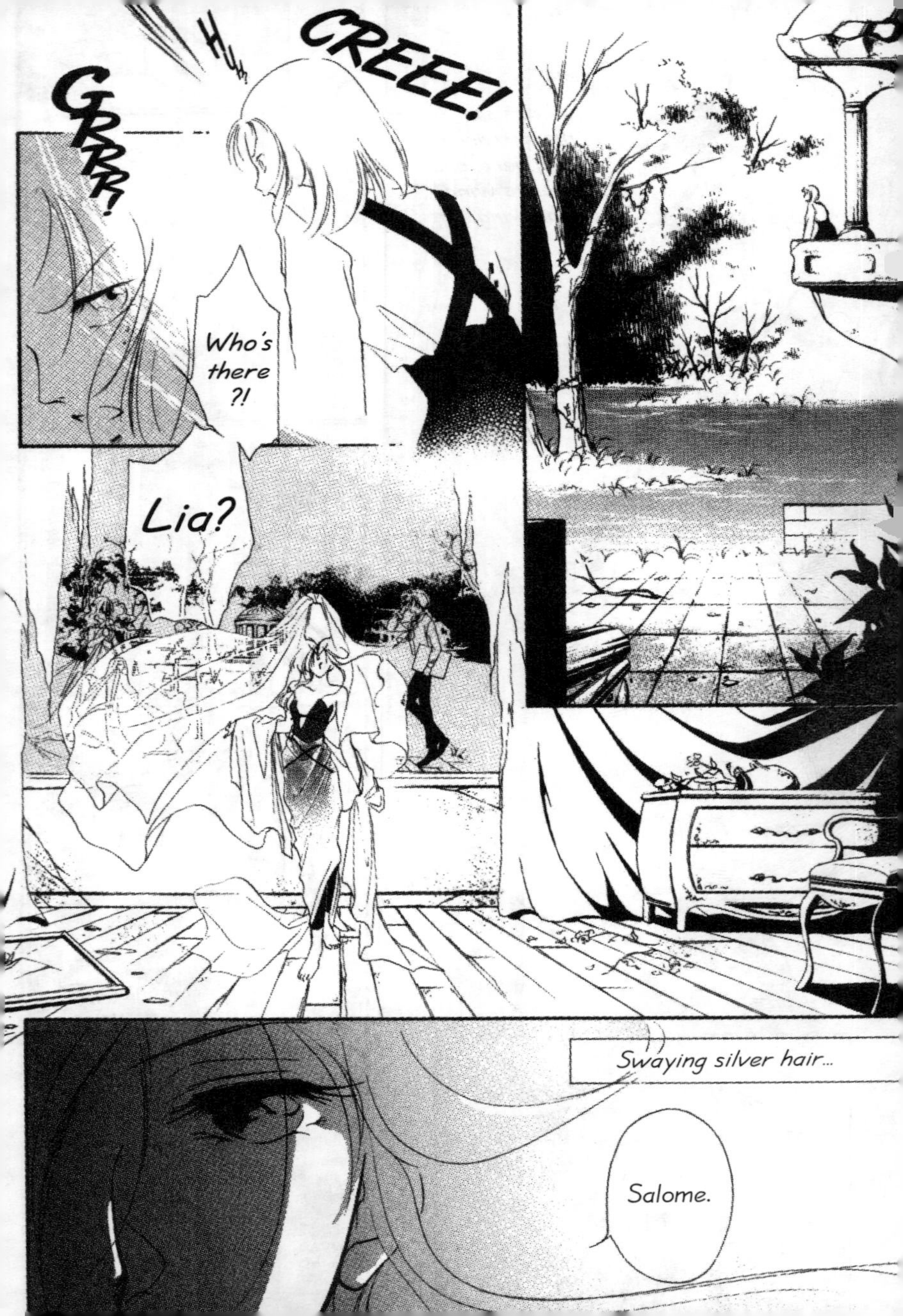
CREEEE!
HUH
GRRR!
Who's there ?!
Lia?
Swaying silver hair...
Salome.

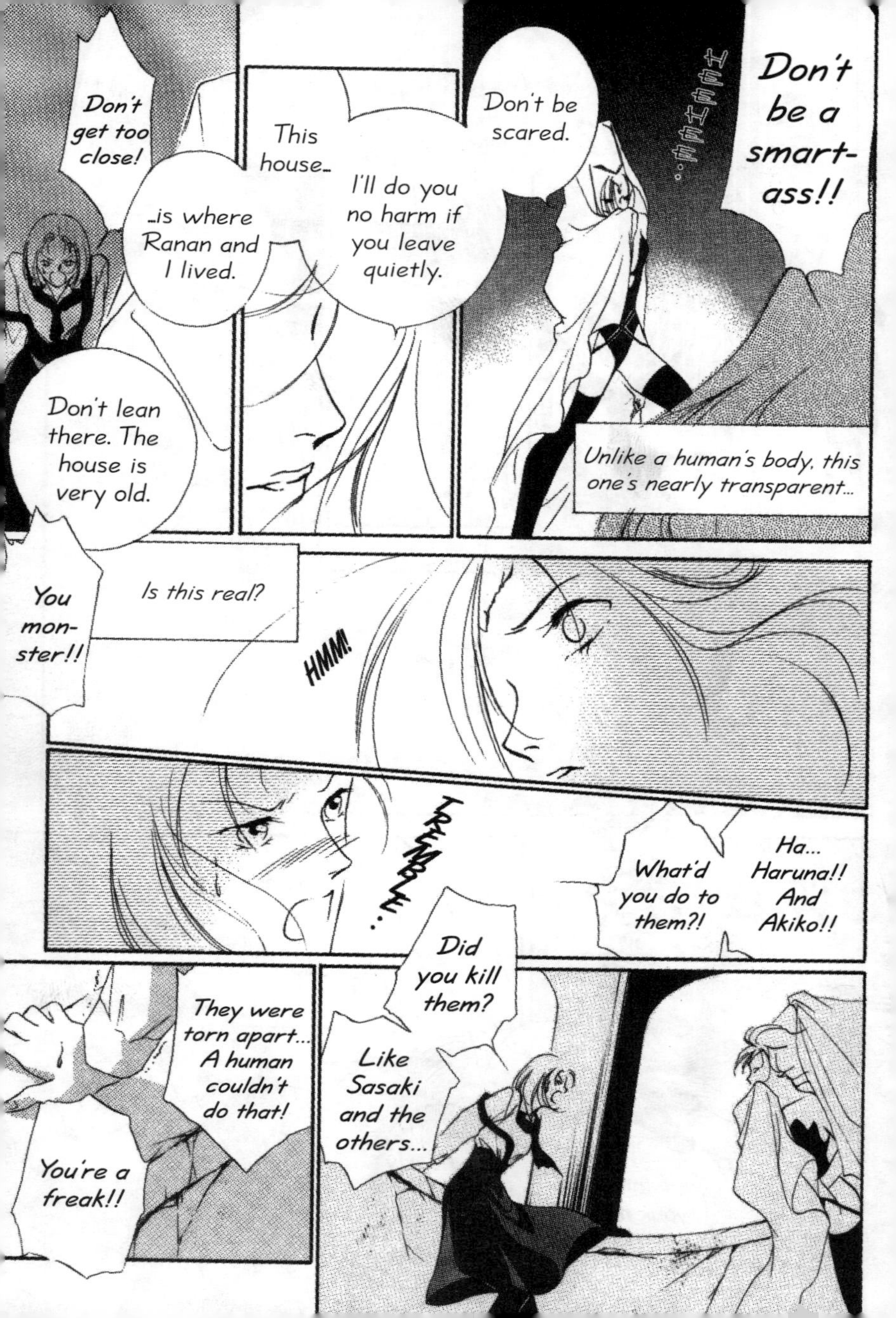

Don't be a smart-ass!!
HEEHEE...
Don't be scared.
Unlike a human's body, this one's nearly transparent...
This house...
I'll do you no harm if you leave quietly.
Don't get too close!
...is where Ranan and I lived.
Don't lean there. The house is very old.
You monster!!
Is this real?
HMM!
TREMBLE...
Ha... Haruna!! And Akiko!!
What'd you do to them?!
Did you kill them?
Like Sasaki and the others...
They were torn apart... A human couldn't do that!
You're a freak!!

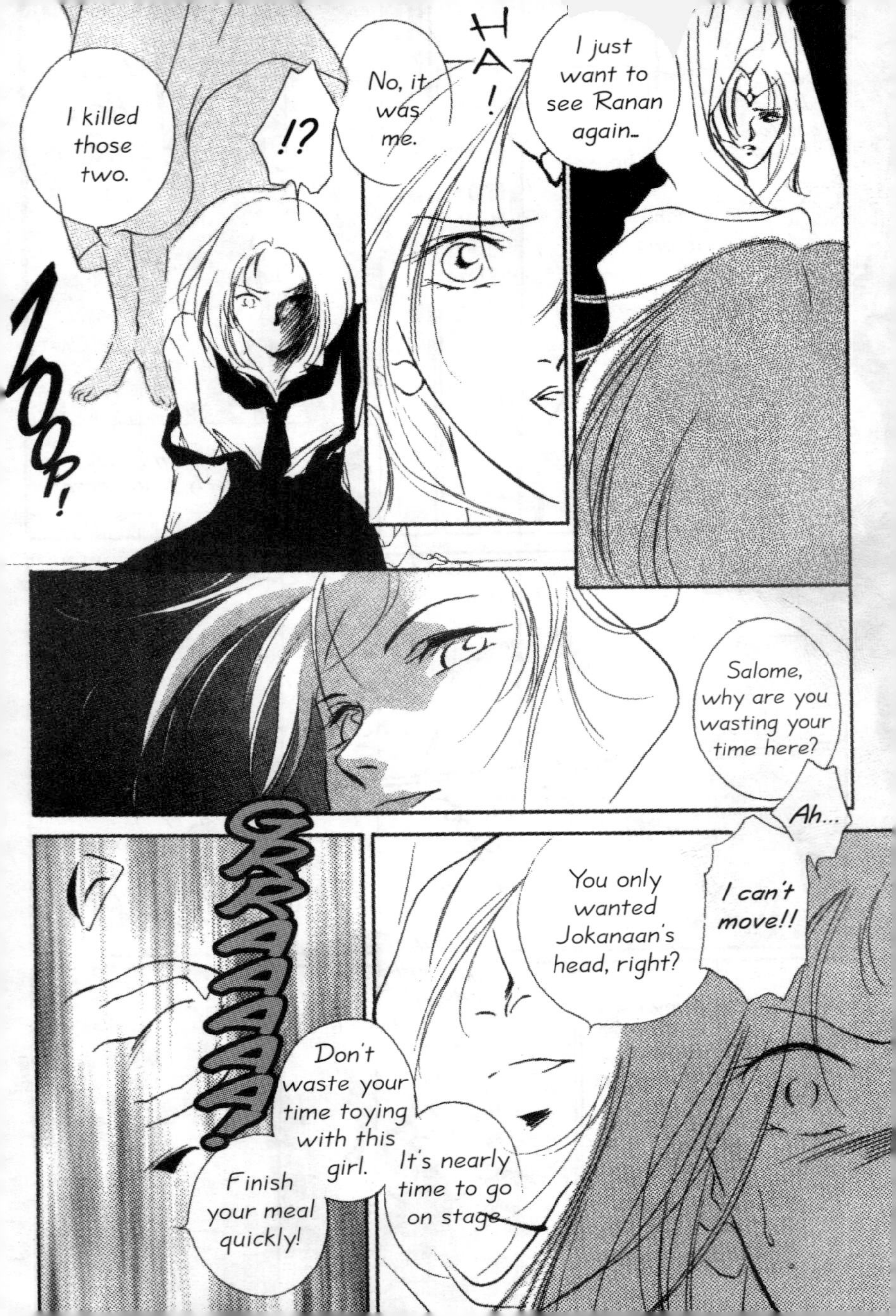
I just want to see Ranan again..
HA!
No, it was me.
!?
I killed those two.
WOOP!
Salome, why are you wasting your time here?
Ah...
I can't move!!
You only wanted Jokanaan's head, right?
Don't waste your time toying with this girl.
It's nearly time to go on stage..
Finish your meal quickly!

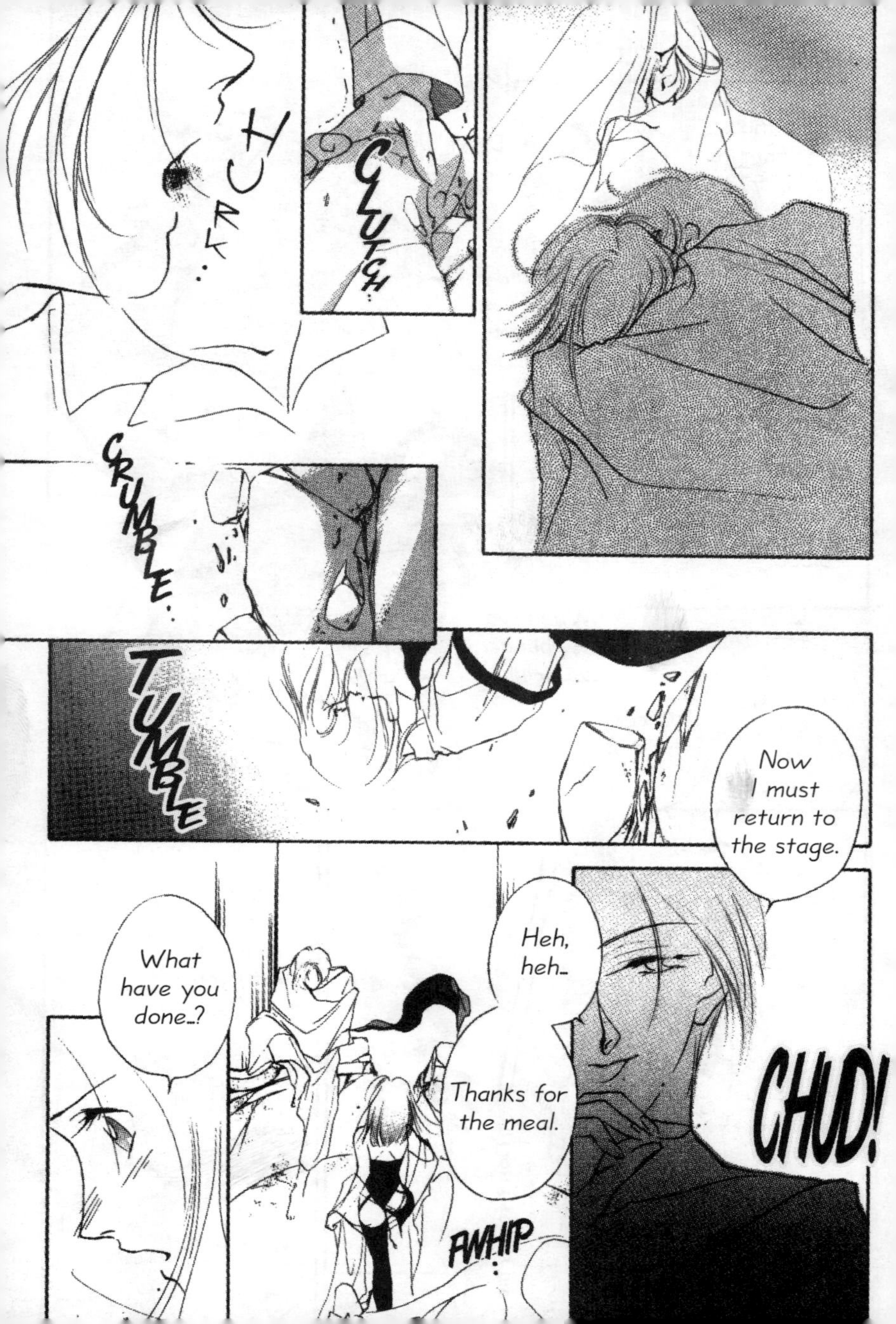
HURK..
CLUTCH..
CRUMBLE..
TUMBLE
Now I must return to the stage.
What have you done..?
Heh, heh..
Thanks for the meal.
CHUD!
FWHIP..

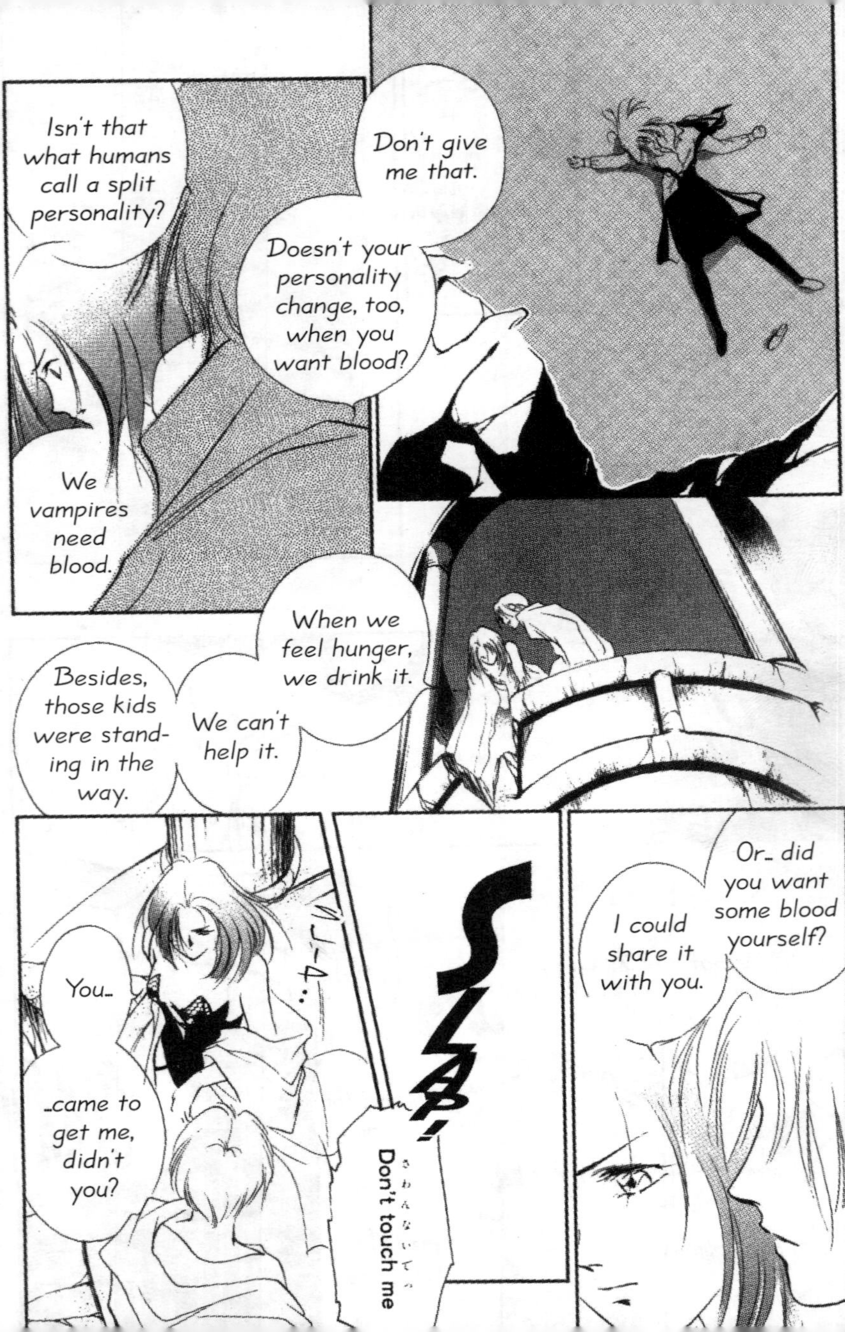
Don't give me that.
Doesn't your personality change, too, when you want blood?
Isn't that what humans call a split personality?
We vampires need blood.
When we feel hunger, we drink it.
We can't help it.
Besides, those kids were standing in the way.
Or... did you want some blood yourself?
I could share it with you.
SLAP!!
Don't touch me
You...
...came to get me, didn't you?

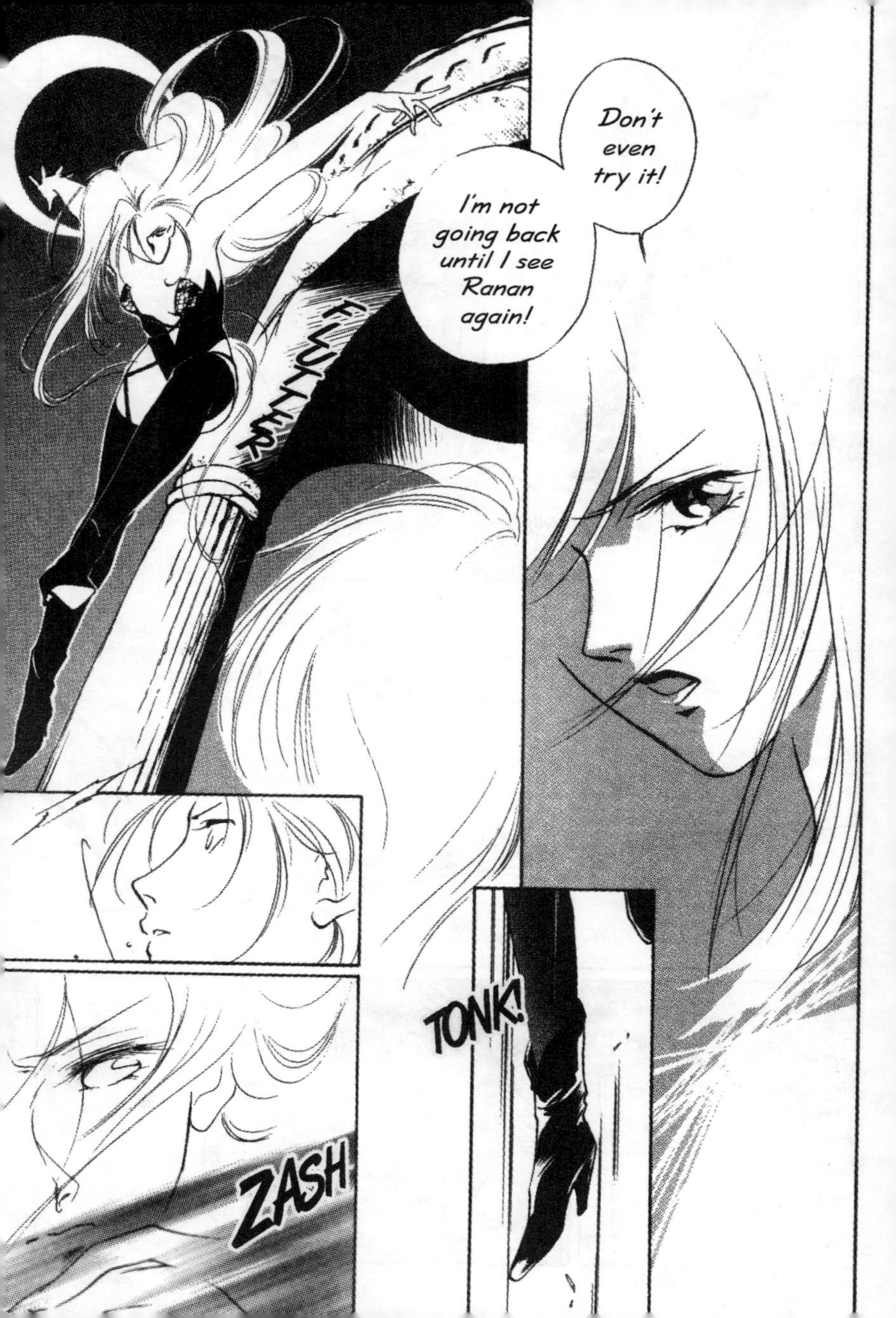

Don't even try it!
I'm not going back until I see Ranan again!
FLUTTER
TONK!
ZASH

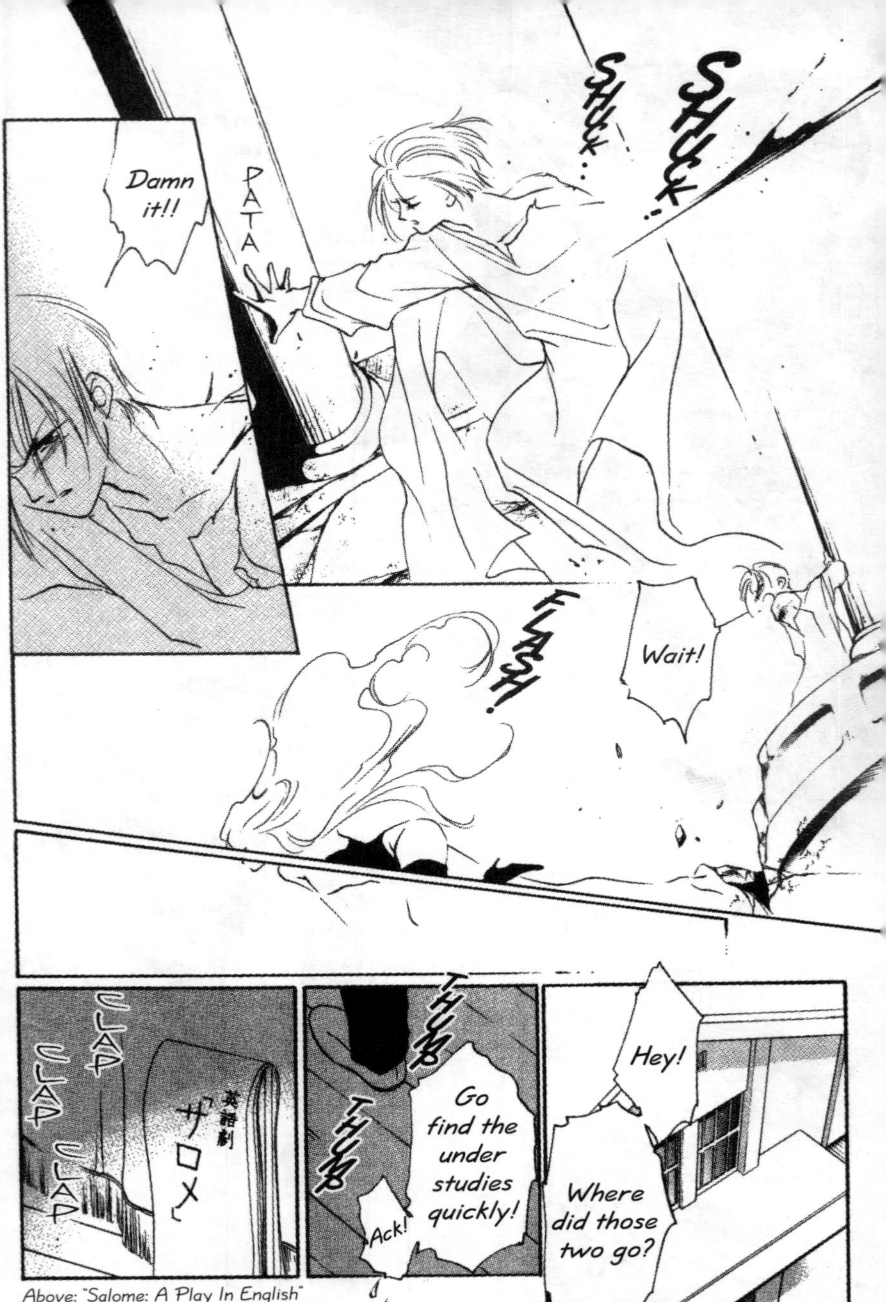
SHUCK..!
SHUCK...
PATA
Damn it!!
FLASH!
Wait!
Hey!
Where did those two go?
THUMP
THUMP
Go find the under studies quickly!
Ack!
CLAP
CLAP
CLAP
英語劇「サロメ」
Above: "Salome: A Play In English"

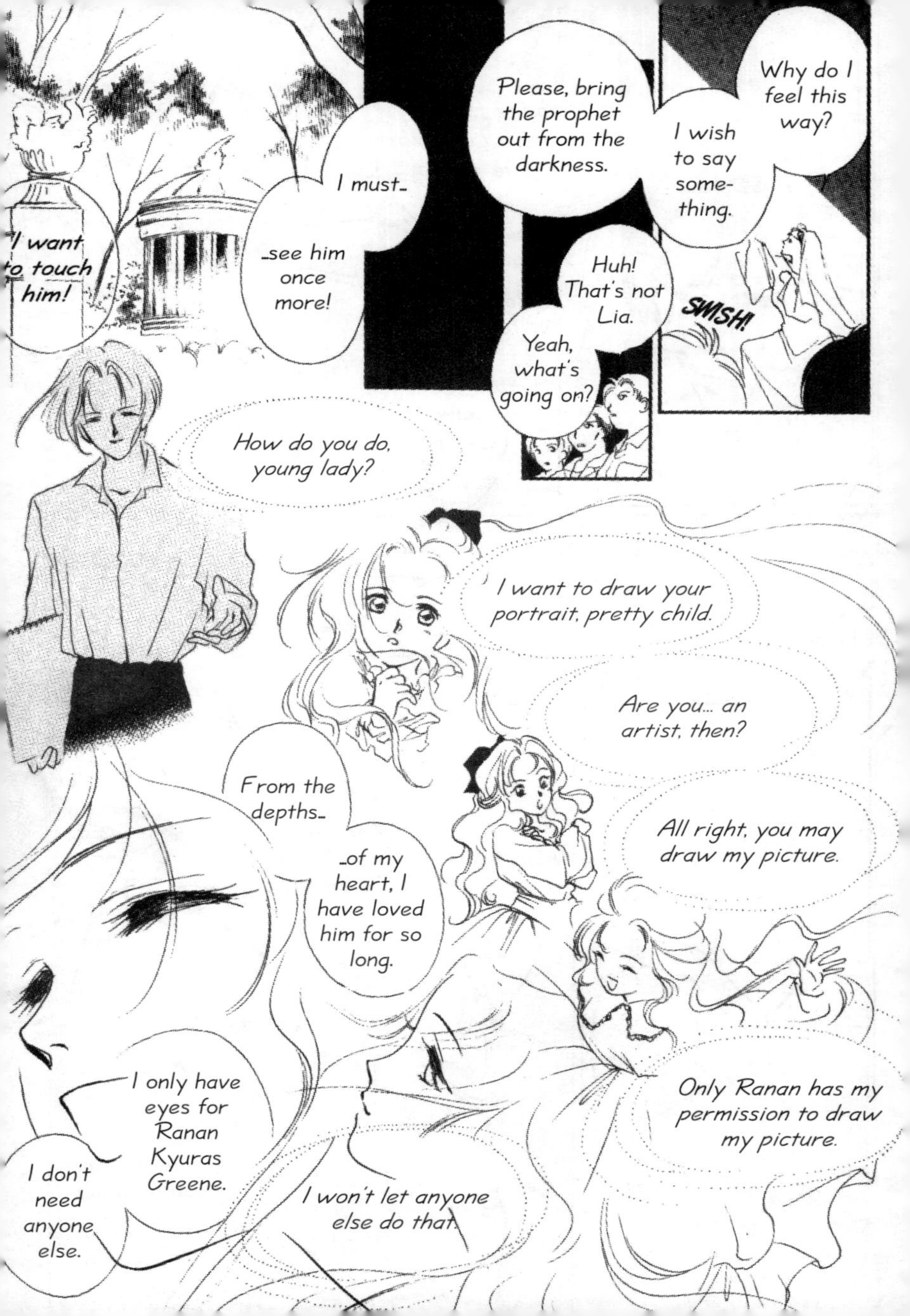
I want to touch him!
I must...
...see him once more!
Please, bring the prophet out from the darkness.
Why do I feel this way?
I wish to say something.
SWISH!
Huh! That's not Lia.
Yeah, what's going on?
How do you do, young lady?
I want to draw your portrait, pretty child.
Are you... an artist, then?
All right, you may draw my picture.
From the depths...
...of my heart, I have loved him for so long.
Only Ranan has my permission to draw my picture.
I only have eyes for Ranan Kyuras Greene.
I don't need anyone else.
I won't let anyone else do that.

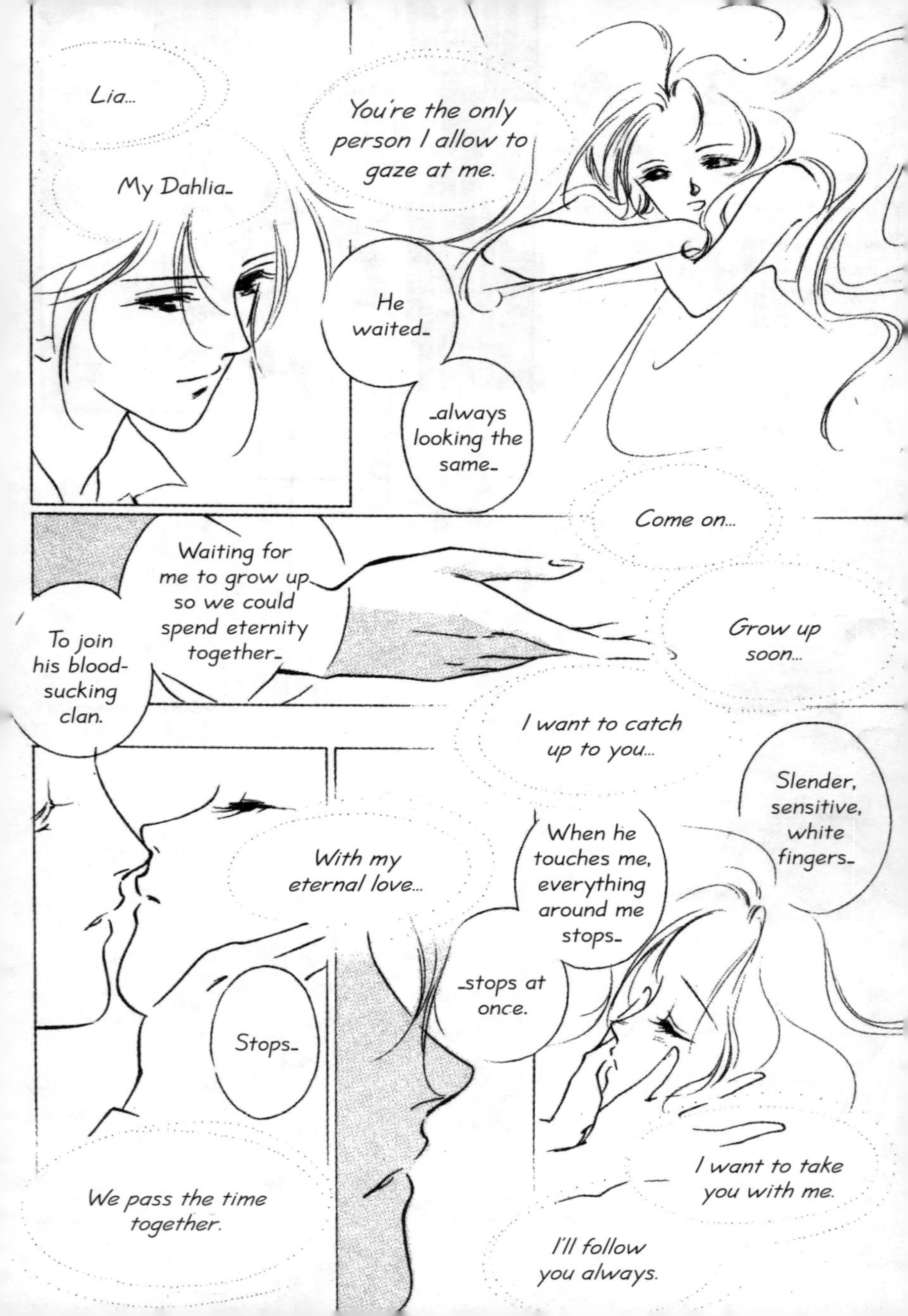
Lia...
My Dahlia...
You're the only person I allow to gaze at me.
He waited...
...always looking the same...
Come on...
Waiting for me to grow up so we could spend eternity together...
To join his blood-sucking clan.
Grow up soon...
I want to catch up to you...
Slender, sensitive, white fingers...
When he touches me, everything around me stops...
With my eternal love...
...stops at once.
Stops...
We pass the time together.
I want to take you with me.
I'll follow you always.

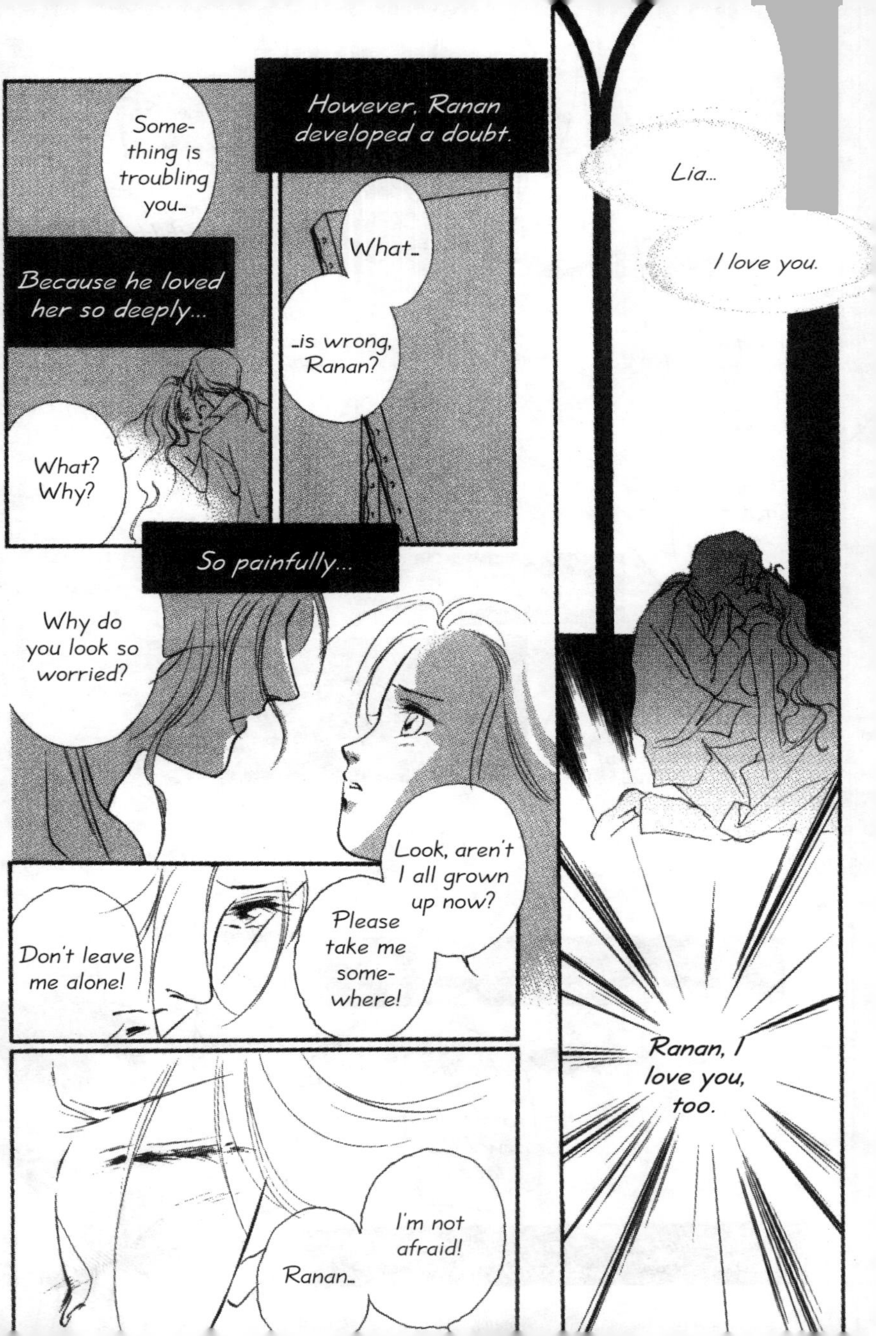

Lia...
I love you.
Ranan, I love you, too.
However, Ranan developed a doubt.
What..
..is wrong, Ranan?
Something is troubling you..
What? Why?
Because he loved her so deeply...
So painfully...
Why do you look so worried?
Look, aren't I all grown up now?
Please take me somewhere!
Don't leave me alone!
I'm not afraid!
Ranan..

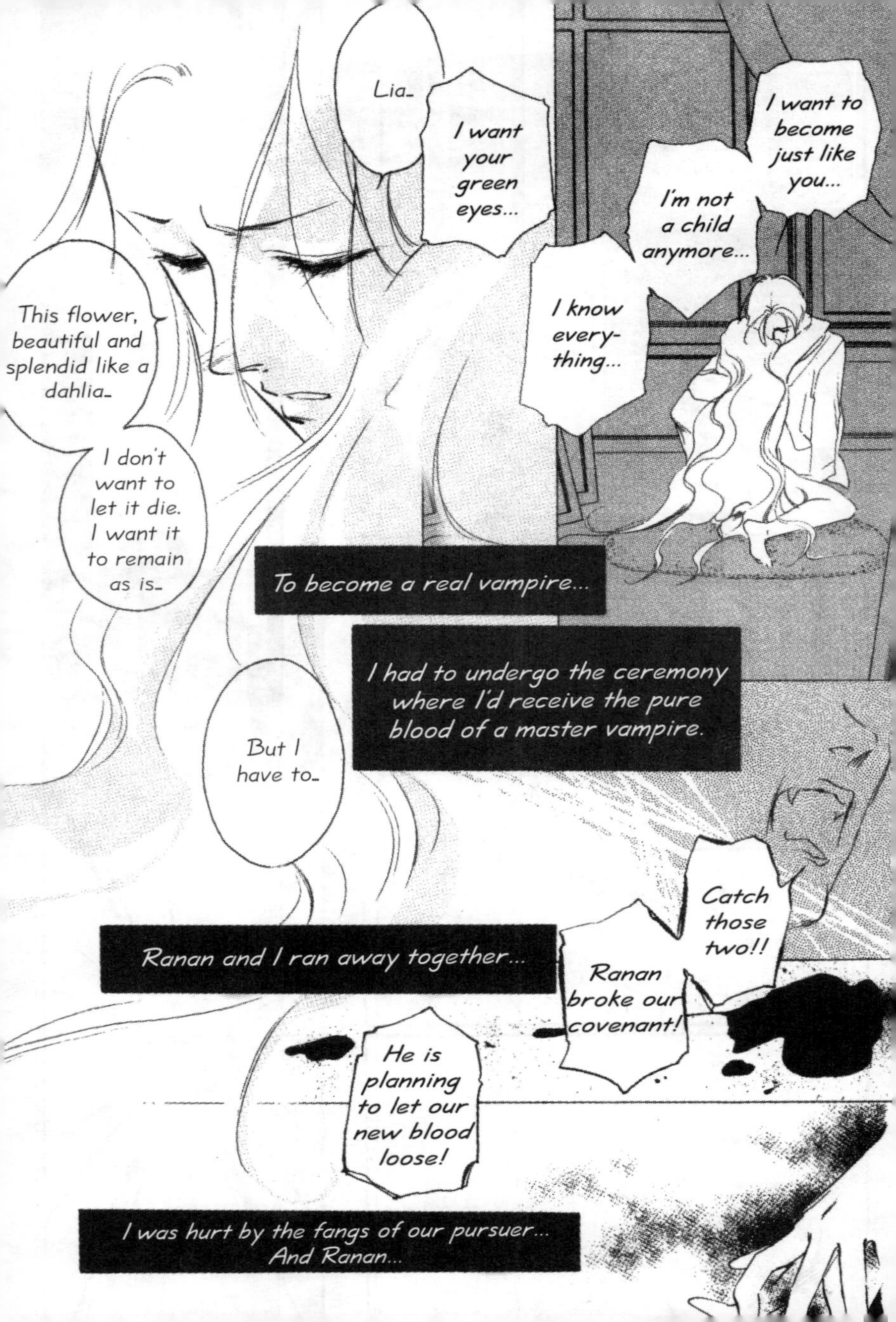
Lia...
I want your green eyes...
I want to become just like you...
I'm not a child anymore...
I know every-thing...
This flower, beautiful and splendid like a dahlia...
I don't want to let it die. I want it to remain as is...
To become a real vampire...
I had to undergo the ceremony where I'd receive the pure blood of a master vampire.
But I have to...
Catch those two!!
Ranan broke our covenant!
Ranan and I ran away together...
He is planning to let our new blood loose!
I was hurt by the fangs of our pursuer... And Ranan...

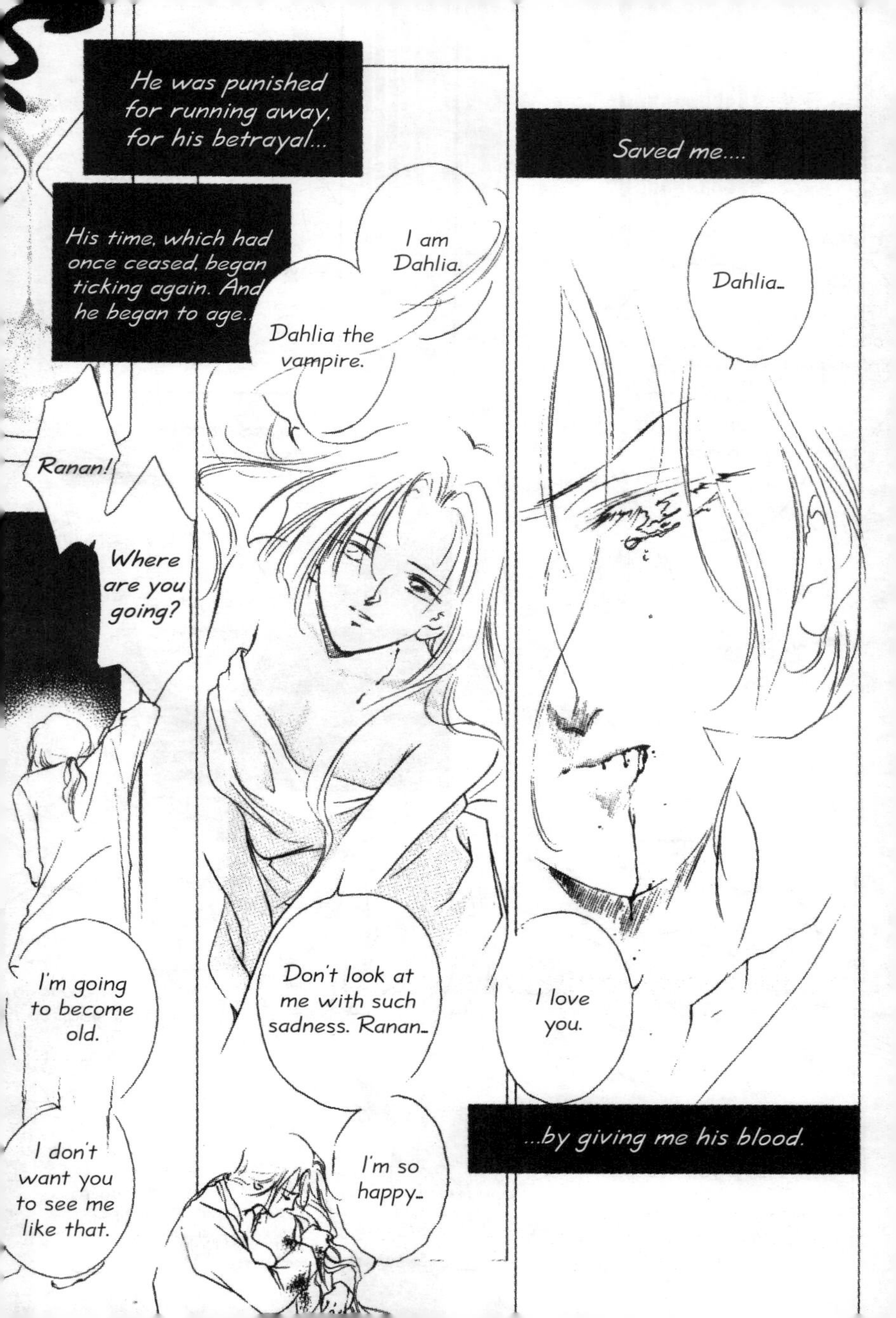
He was punished for running away, for his betrayal...
His time, which had once ceased, began ticking again. And he began to age...
I am Dahlia.
Dahlia the vampire.
Ranan!
Where are you going?
I'm going to become old.
I don't want you to see me like that.
Don't look at me with such sadness. Ranan...
I'm so happy...
Saved me....
Dahlia...
I love you.
...by giving me his blood.

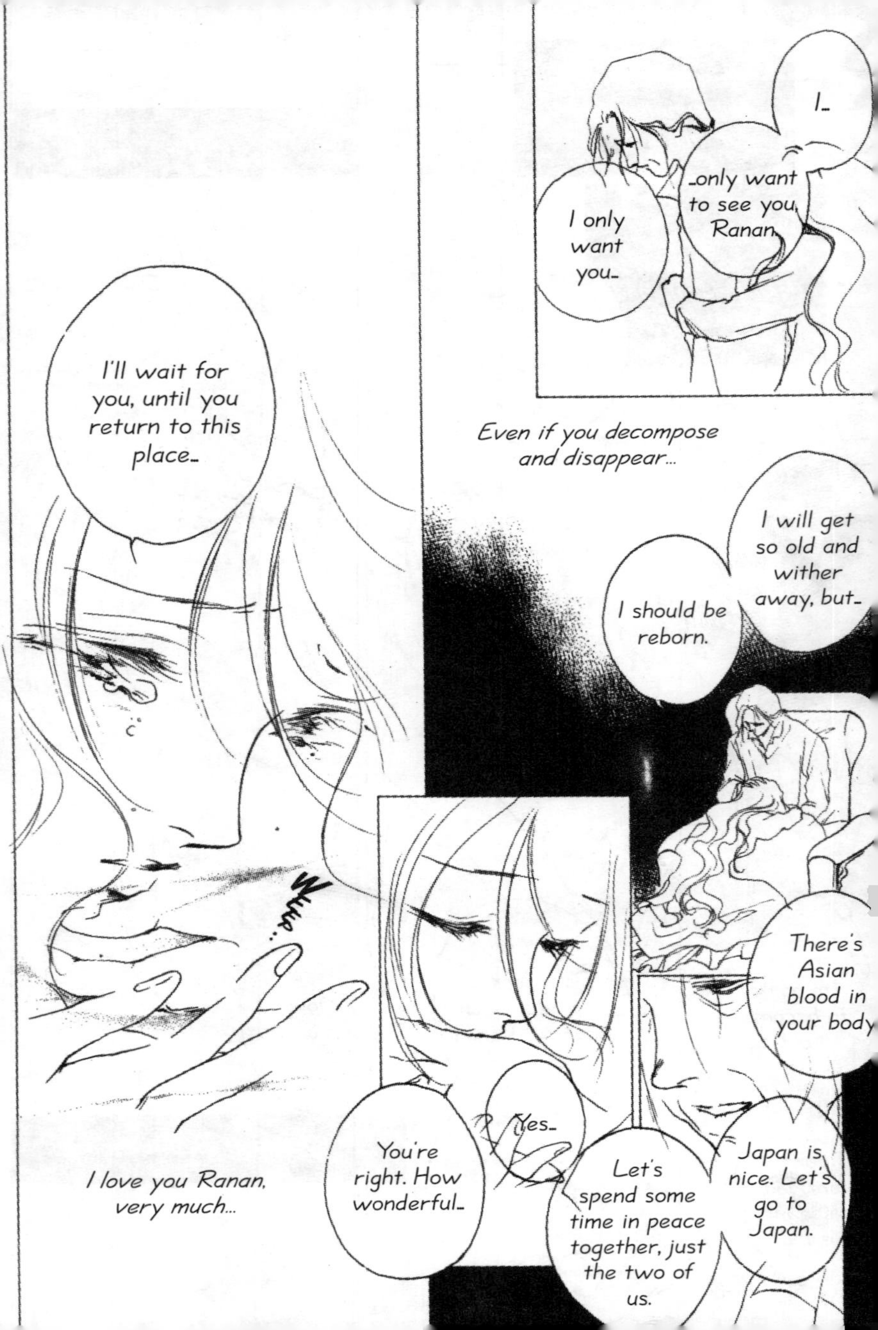
I...
...only want to see you, Ranan.
I only want you...
Even if you decompose and disappear...
I will get so old and wither away, but...
I should be reborn.
There's Asian blood in your body
Japan is nice. Let's go to Japan.
Let's spend some time in peace together, just the two of us.
Yes...
You're right. How wonderful...
I'll wait for you, until you return to this place...
I love you Ranan, very much...

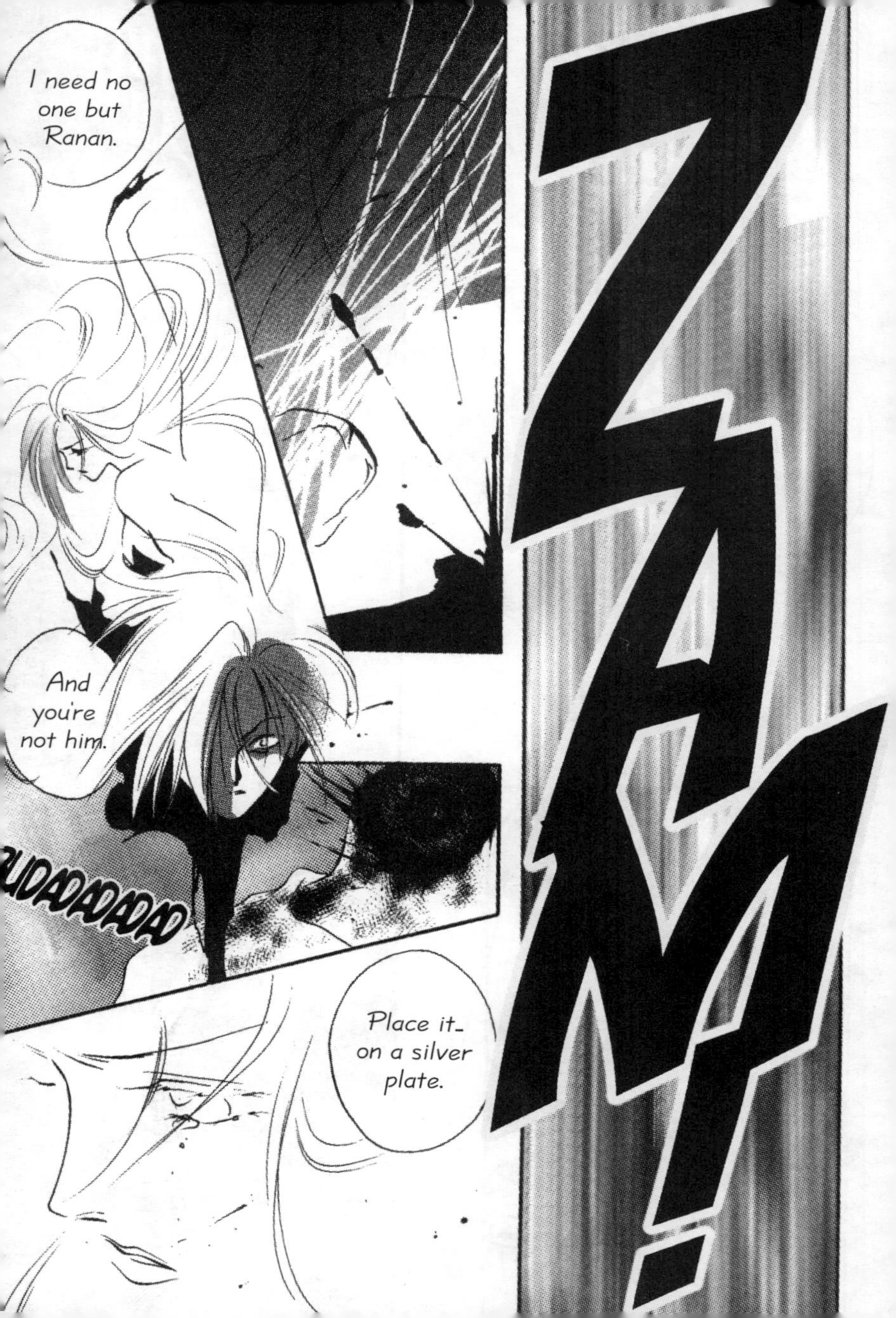
I need no one but Ranan.
And you're not him.
Place it on a silver plate.

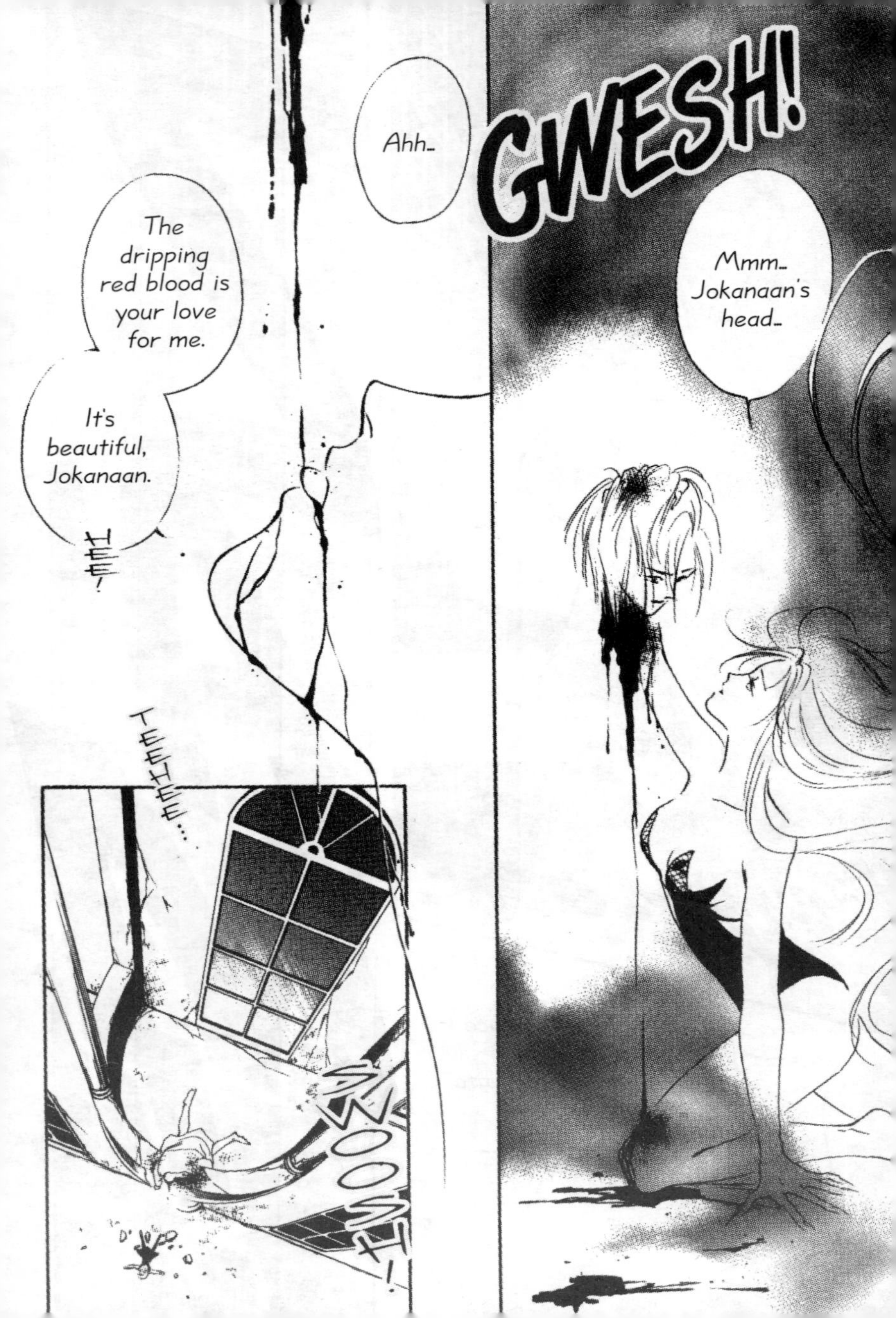
GWESH!
Mmm... Jokanaan's head...
Ahh...
The dripping red blood is your love for me.
It's beautiful, Jokanaan.
HEE!
TEEHEE...
SWOOSH!

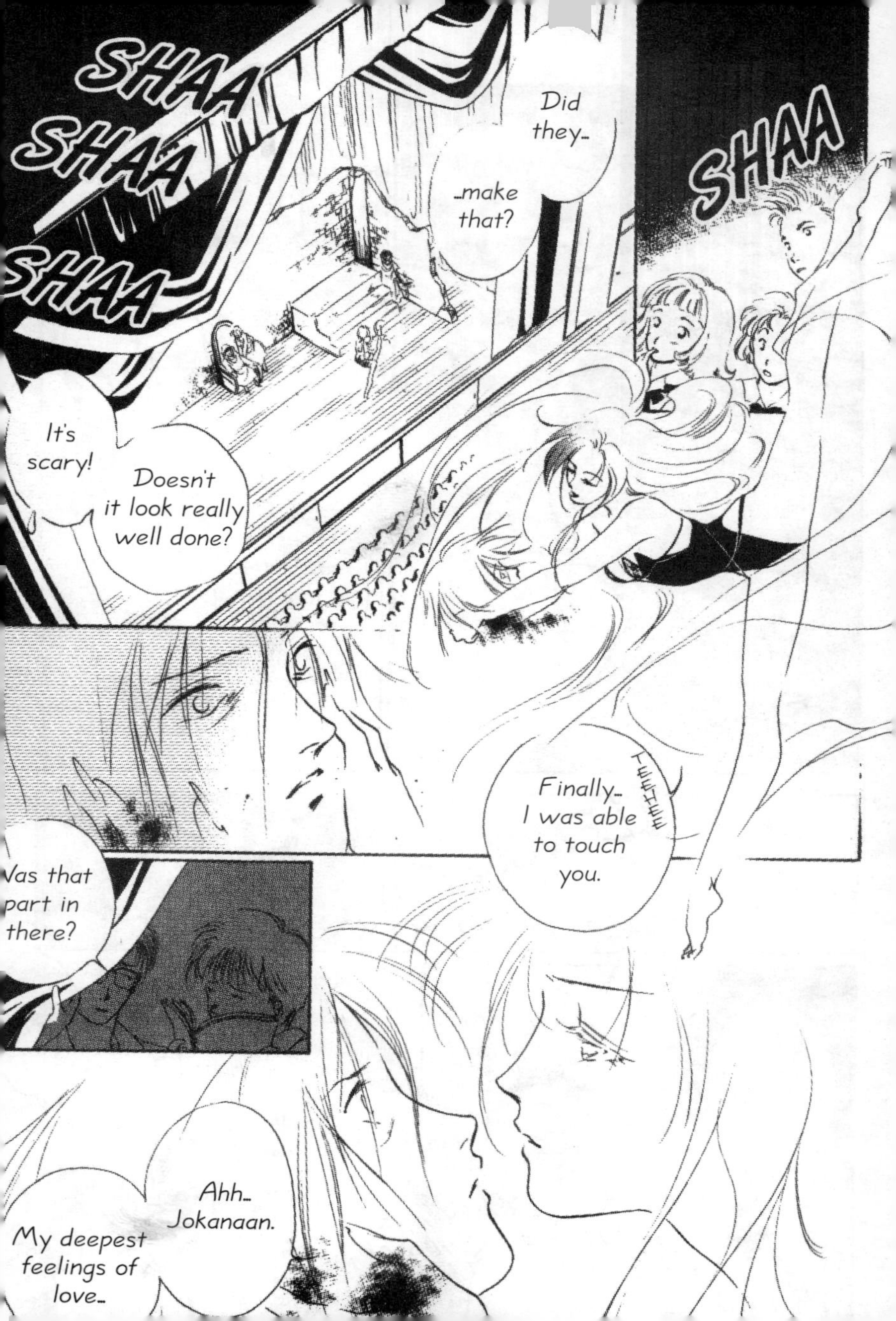
SHAA
SHAA
SHAA
SHAA
Did they...
...make that?
It's scary!
Doesn't it look really well done?
Finally... I was able to touch you.
TEEHEE
Vas that part in there?
Ahh... Jokanaan.
My deepest feelings of love...

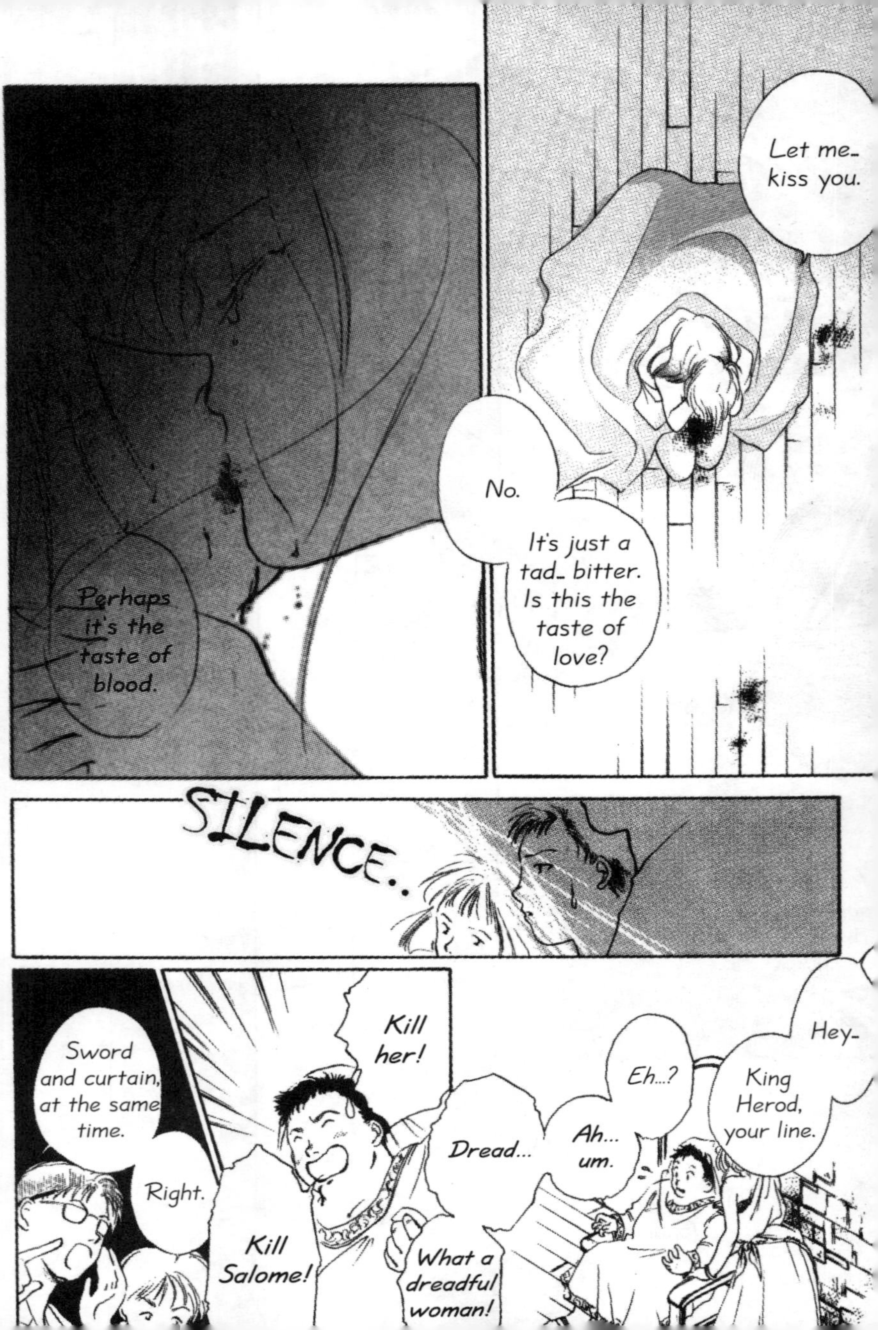
Let me– kiss you.
No.
It's just a tad– bitter. Is this the taste of love?
Perhaps it's the taste of blood.
SILENCE..
Hey–
King Herod, your line.
Eh...?
Ah... um.
Dread...
What a dreadful woman!
Kill her!
Kill Salome!
Sword and curtain, at the same time.
Right.

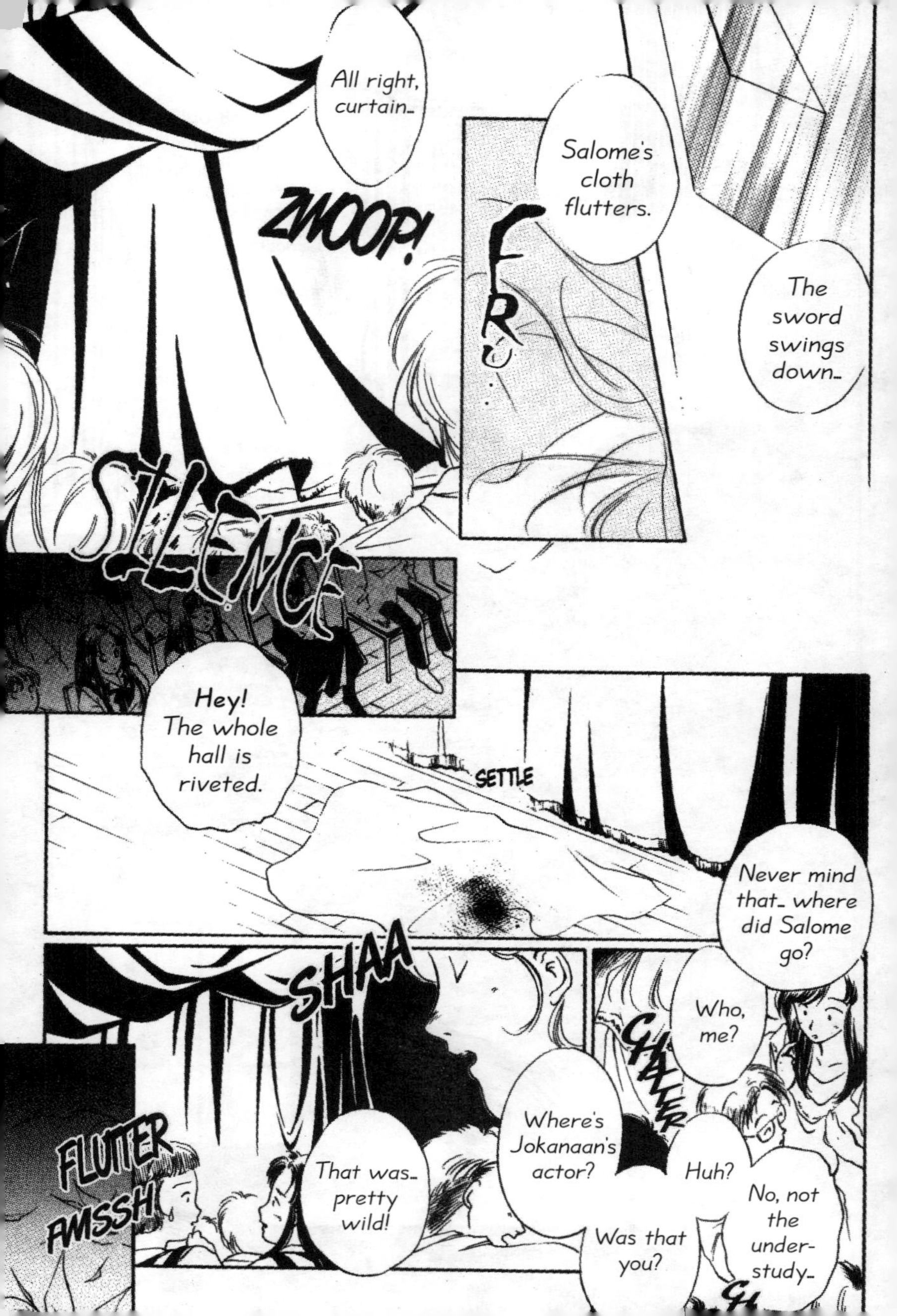

All right, curtain...
ZWOOP!
Salome's cloth flutters.
FR
The sword swings down...
SILENCE
Hey! The whole hall is riveted.
SETTLE
Never mind that... where did Salome go?
SHAA
Who, me?
Where's Jokanaan's actor?
Huh?
That was... pretty wild!
No, not the under-study...
Was that you?
FLUTTER
FMSSH

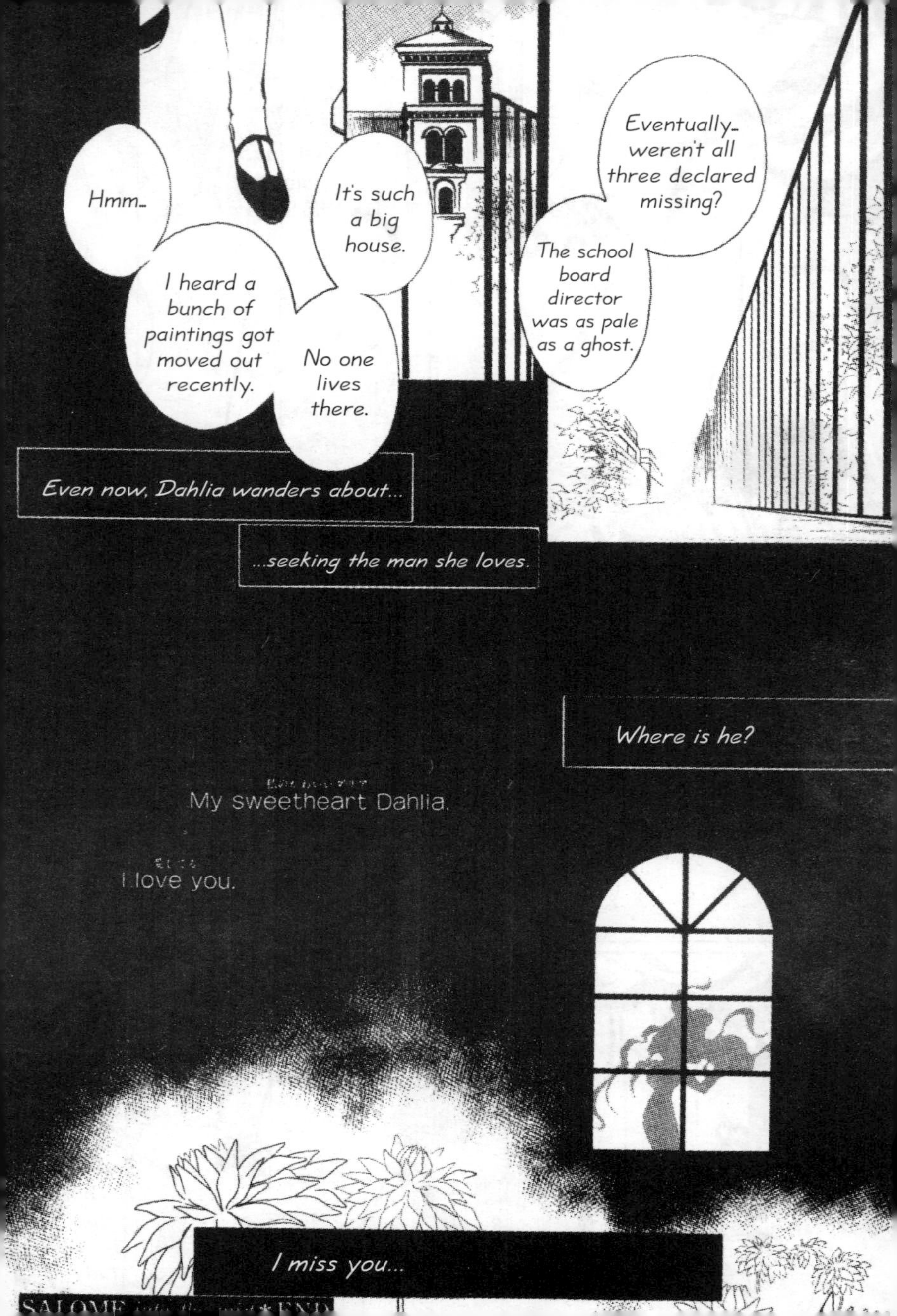
Eventually.. weren't all three declared missing?
The school board director was as pale as a ghost.
It's such a big house.
Hmm..
No one lives there.
I heard a bunch of paintings got moved out recently.
Even now, Dahlia wanders about...
...seeking the man she loves.
Where is he?
My sweetheart Dahlia.
I love you.
I miss you...
SALOME

第3幕 act.3

CHINA BLUE

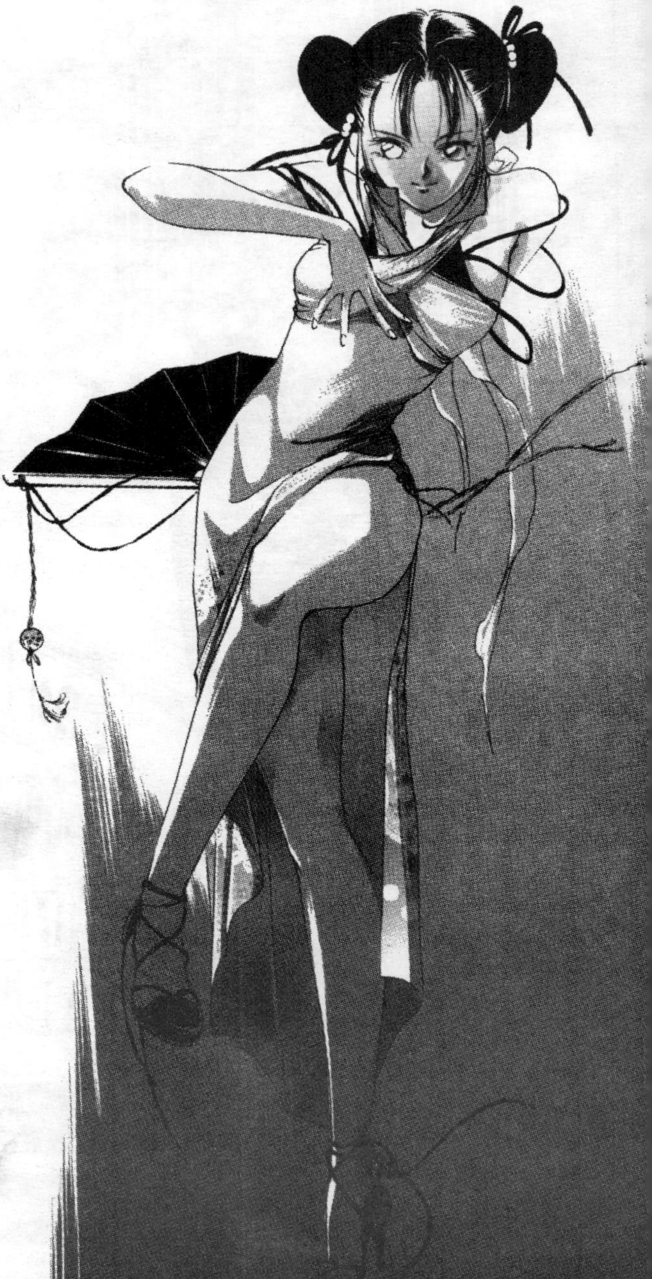

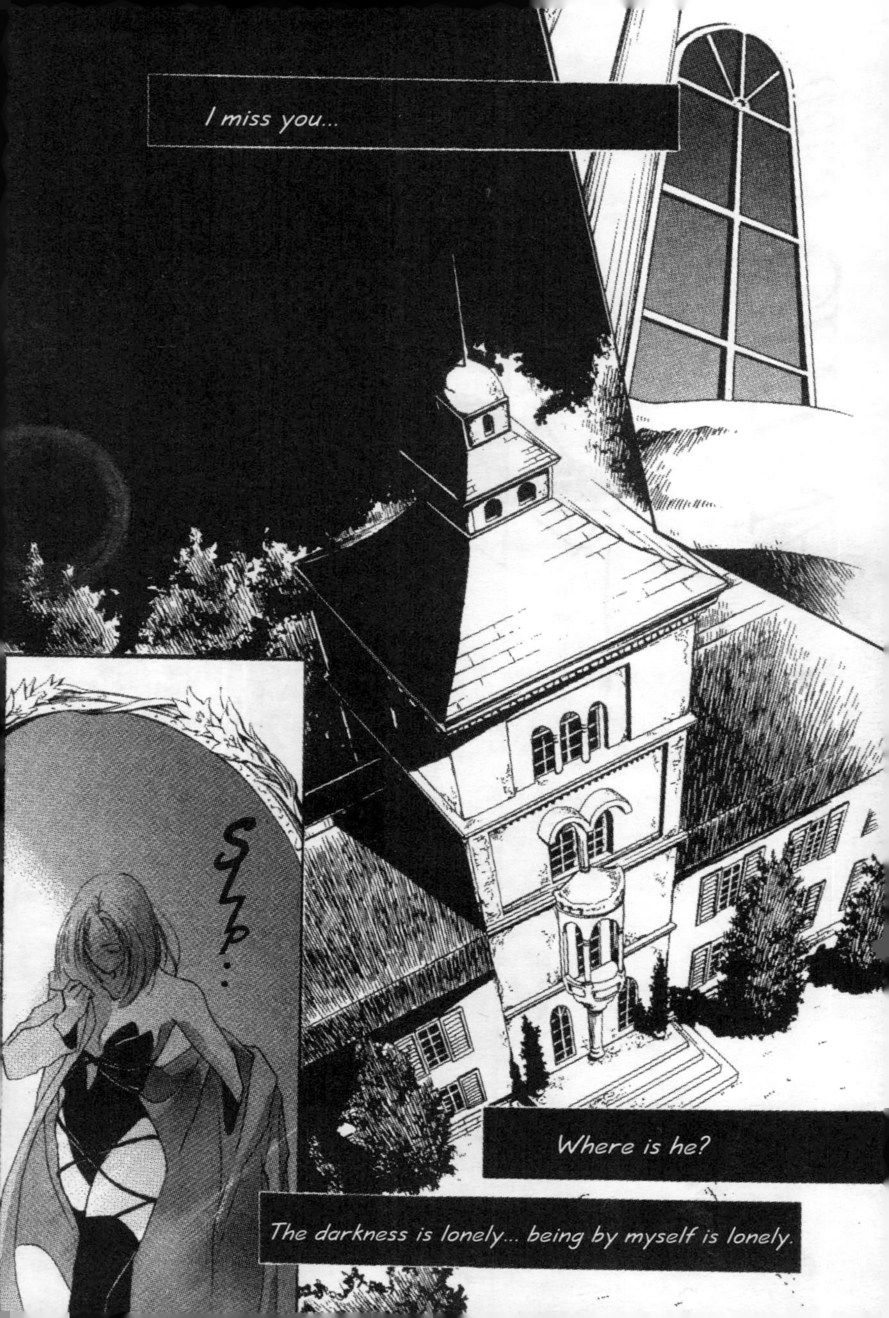
I miss you...
SLIP...
Where is he?
The darkness is lonely... being by myself is lonely.

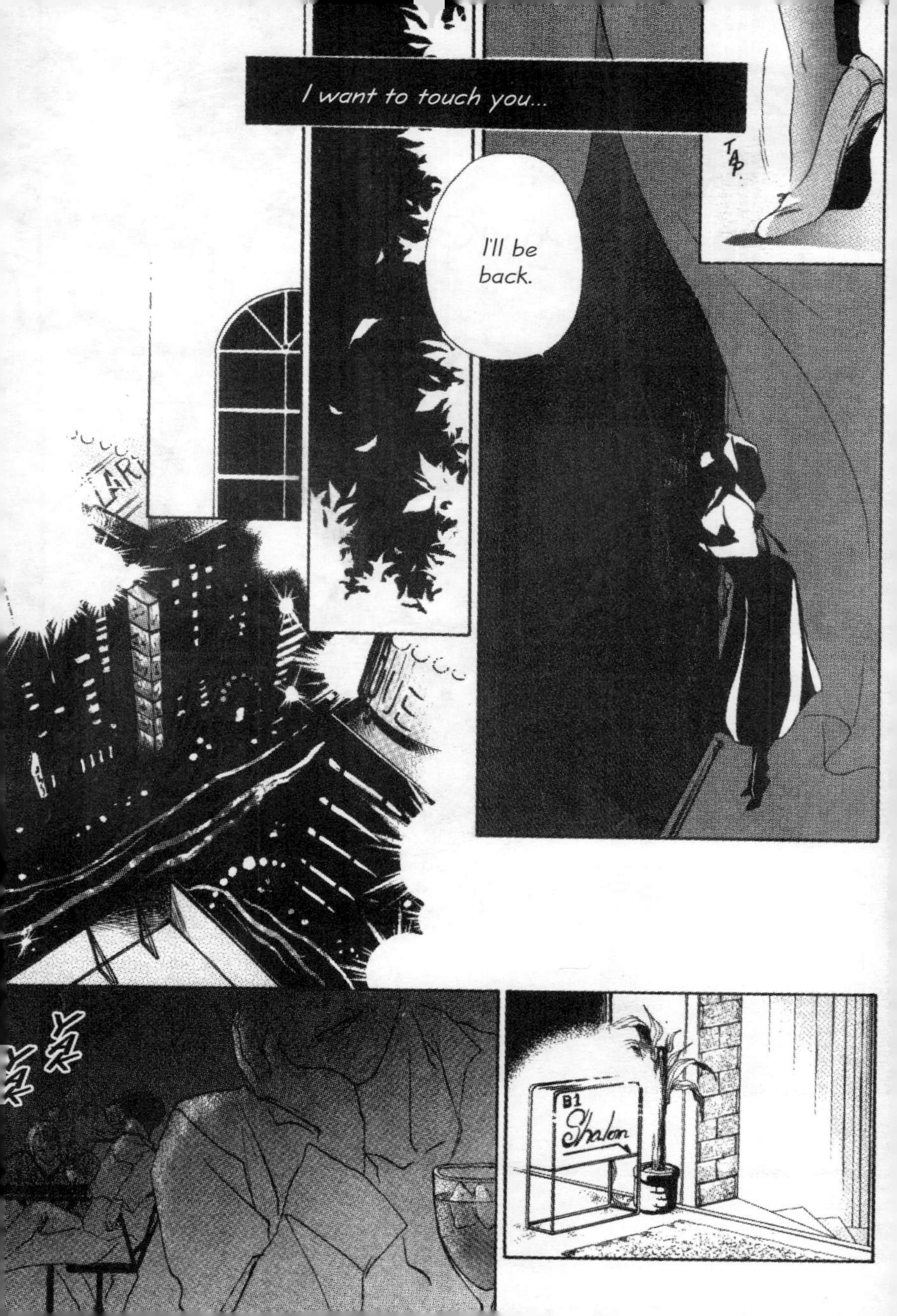

I want to touch you...
TAP.
I'll be back.
B1
Shalon

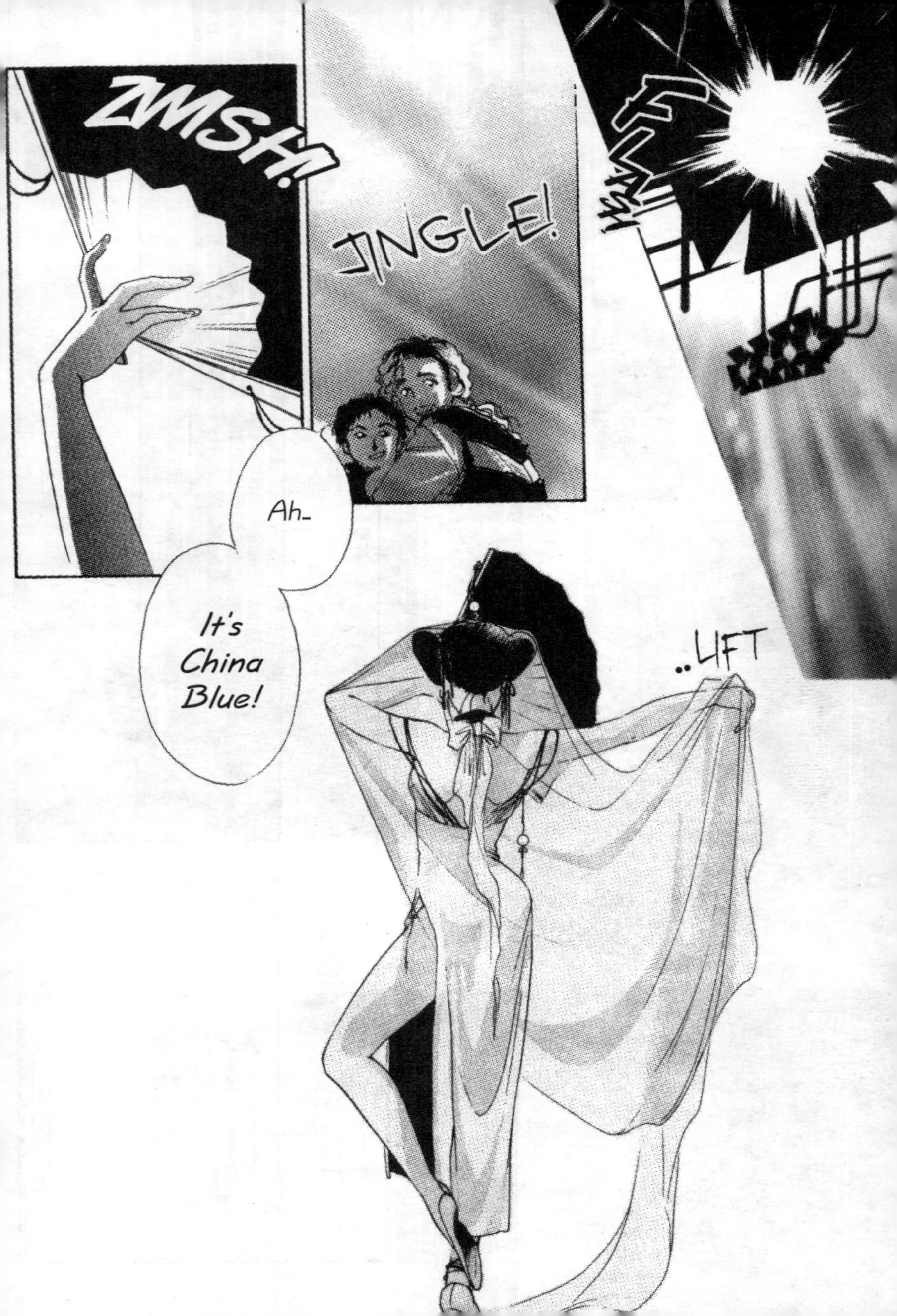
FLASH!
JINGLE!
ZWSH!
Ah...
It's China Blue!
..LIFT

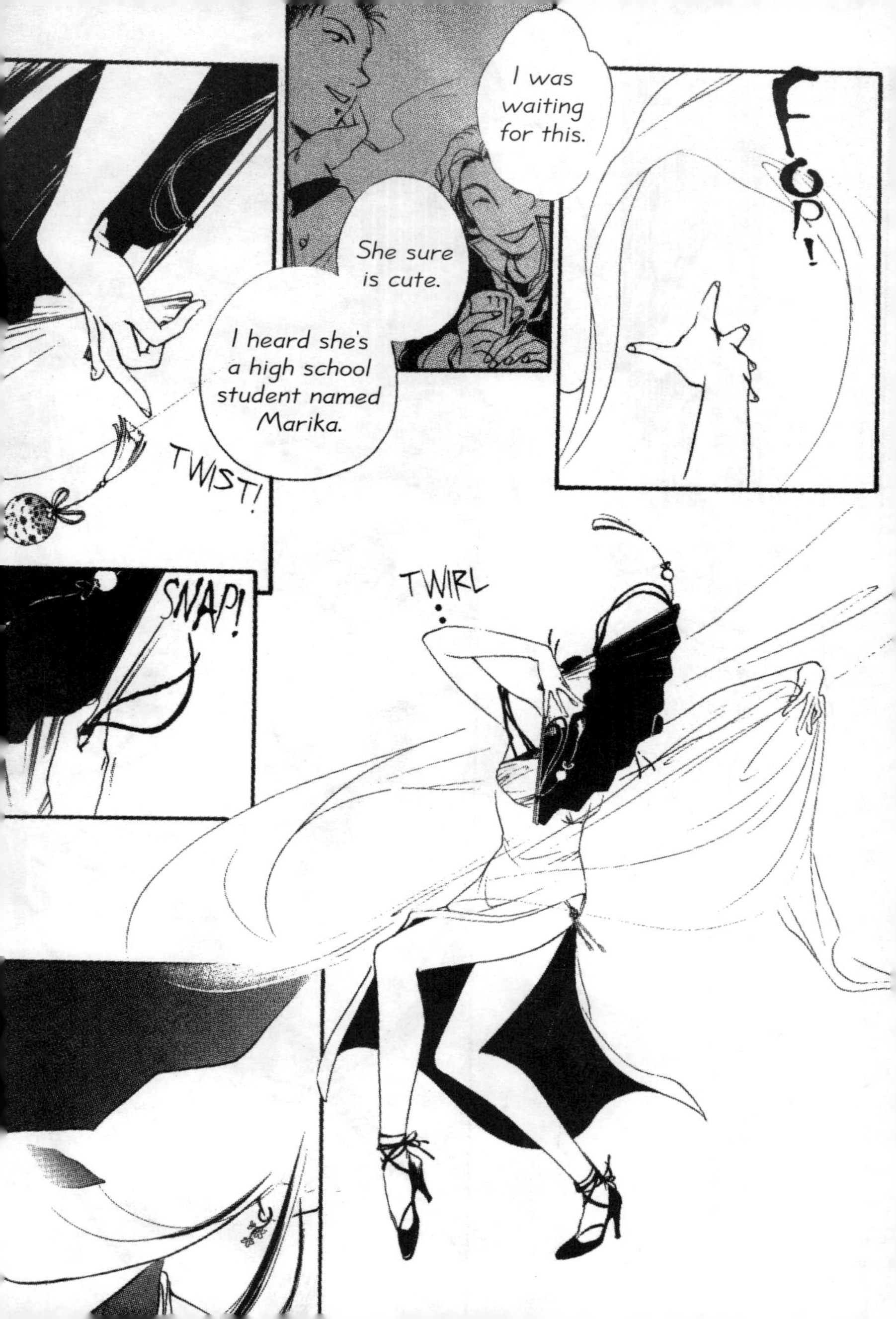

I was waiting for this.
She sure is cute.
I heard she's a high school student named Marika.
FOP!
TWIST!
SNAP!
TWIRL

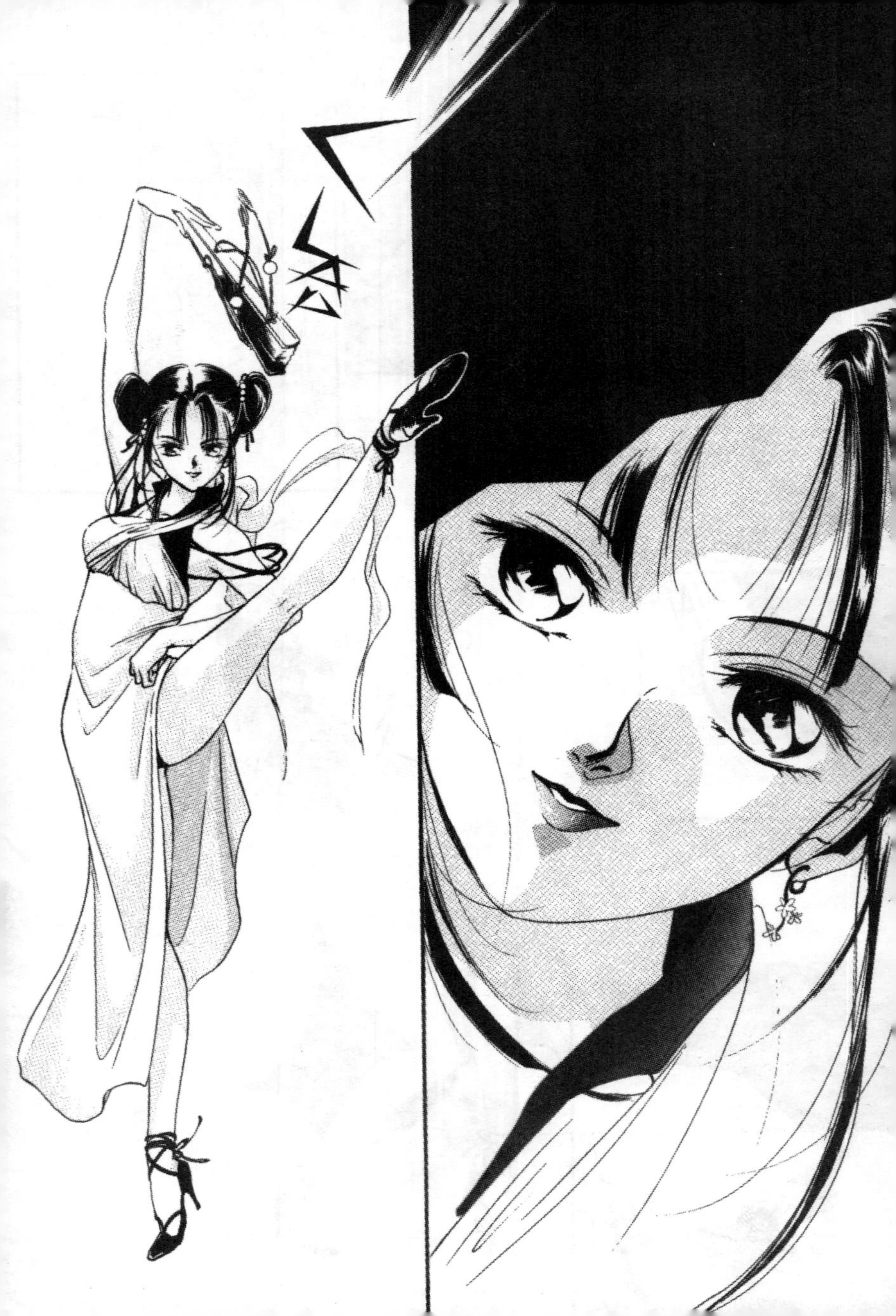

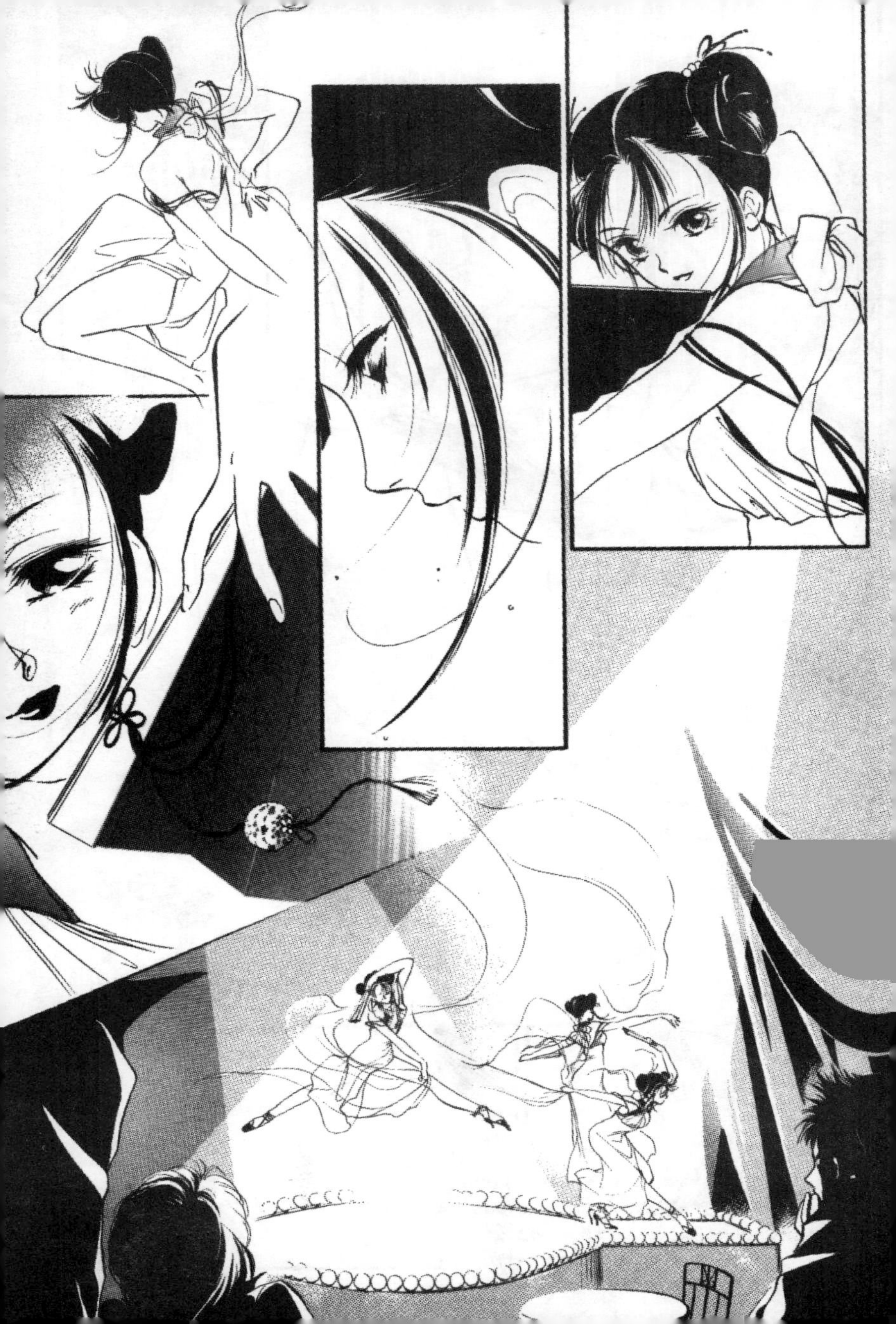

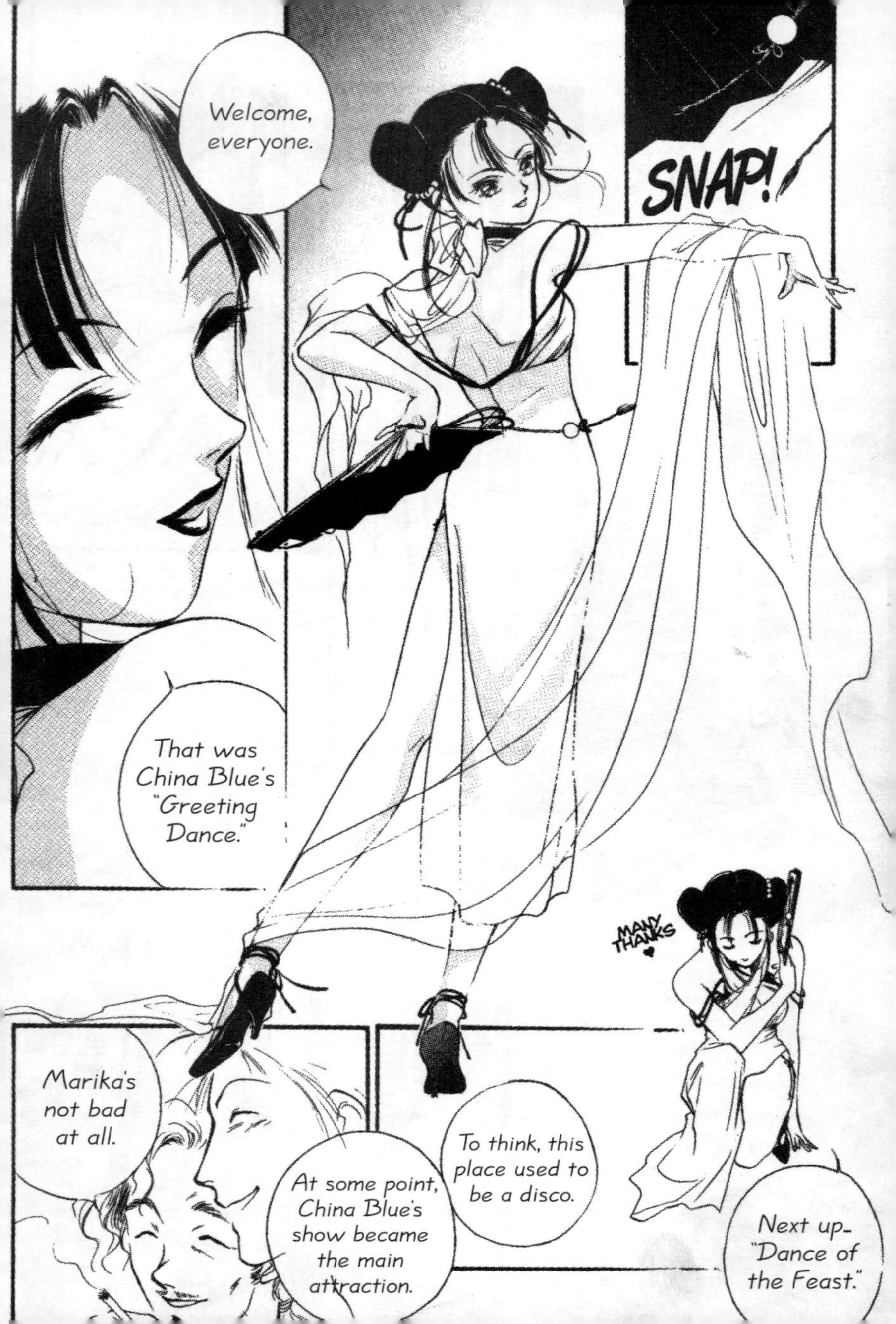
Welcome, everyone.
SNAP!
That was China Blue's "Greeting Dance."
MANY THANKS
Marika's not bad at all.
At some point, China Blue's show became the main attraction.
To think, this place used to be a disco.
Next up... "Dance of the Feast."

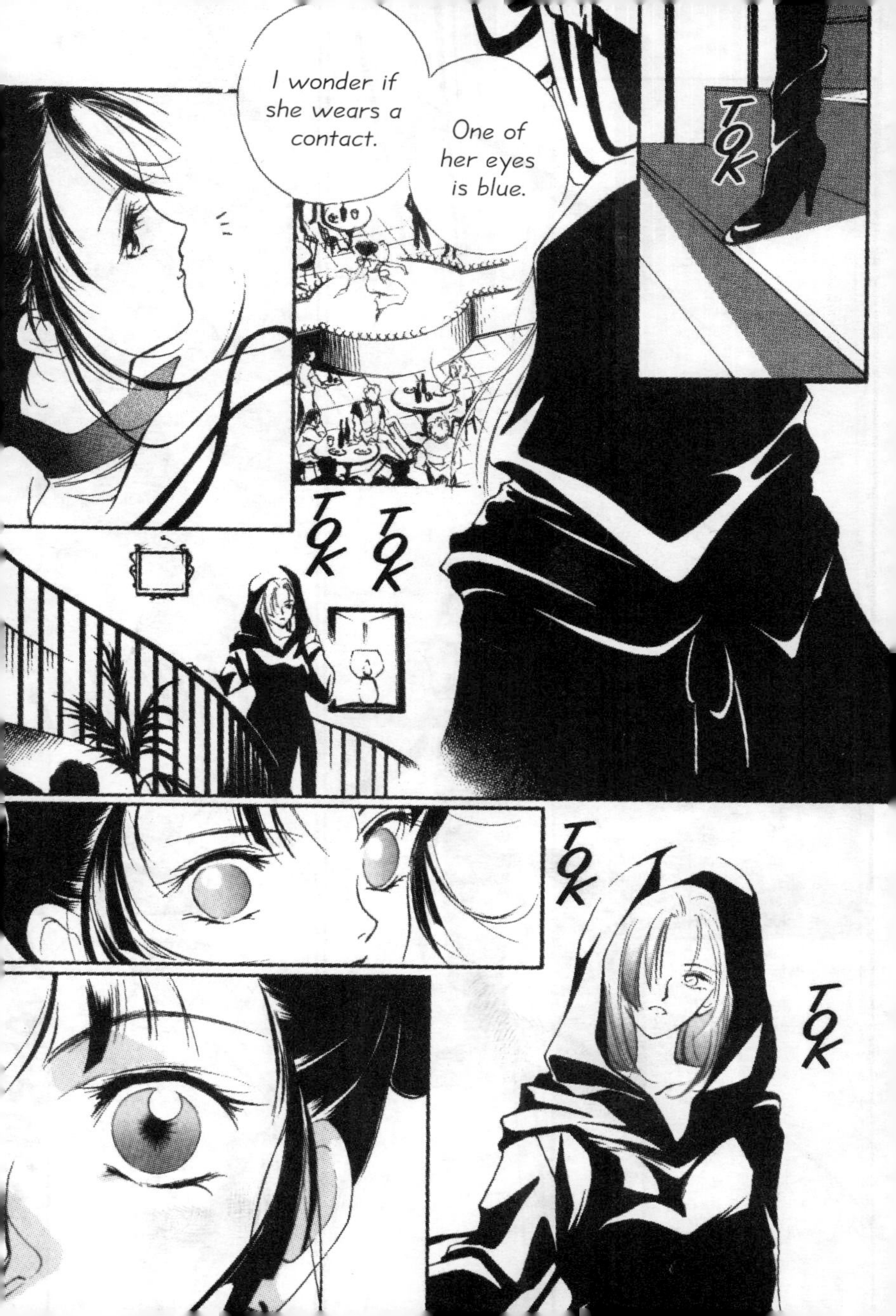

TOK
One of her eyes is blue.
I wonder if she wears a contact.
TOK TOK
TOK
TOK

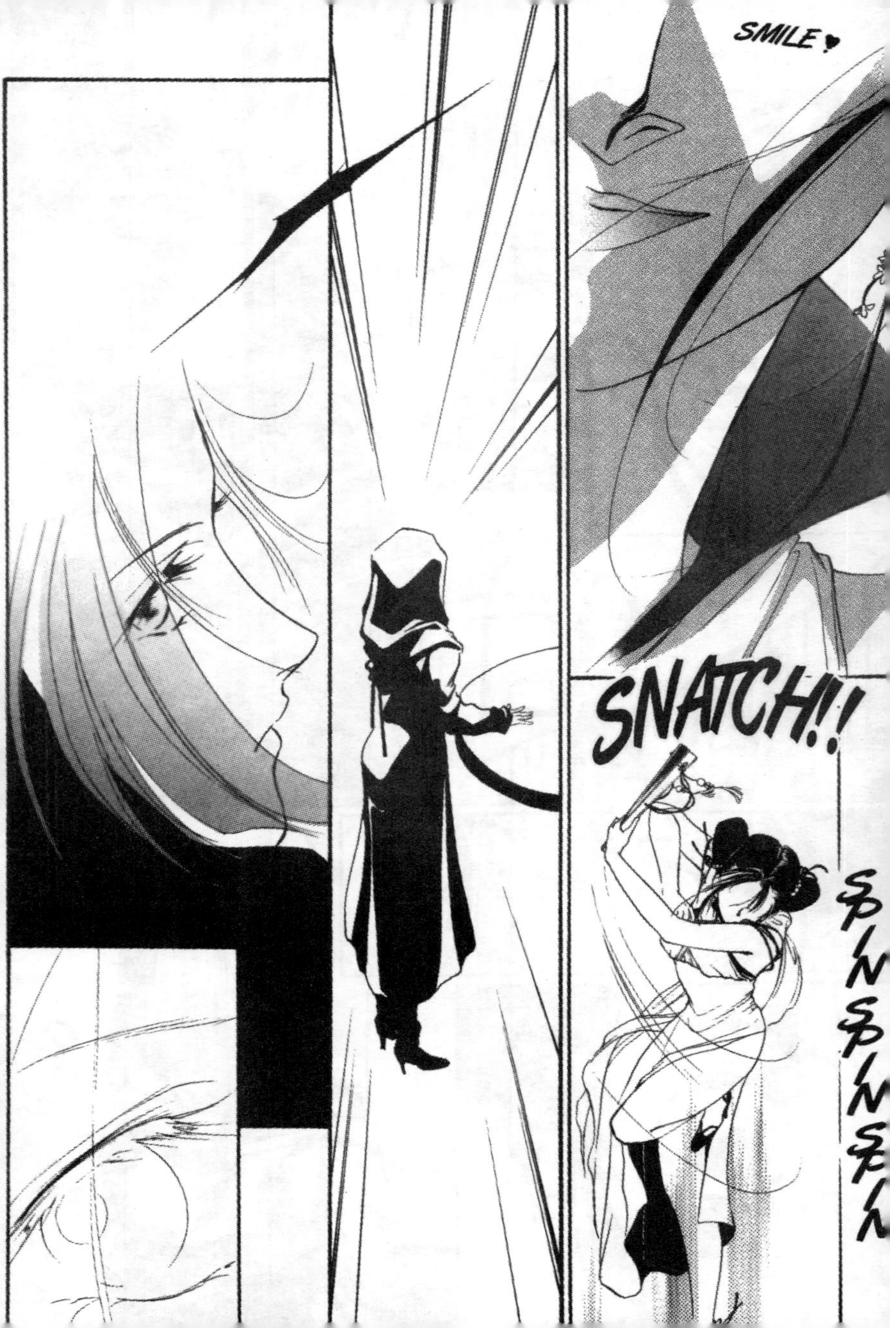
SMILE ♥
SNATCH!!
SPIN SPIN SPIN SPIN

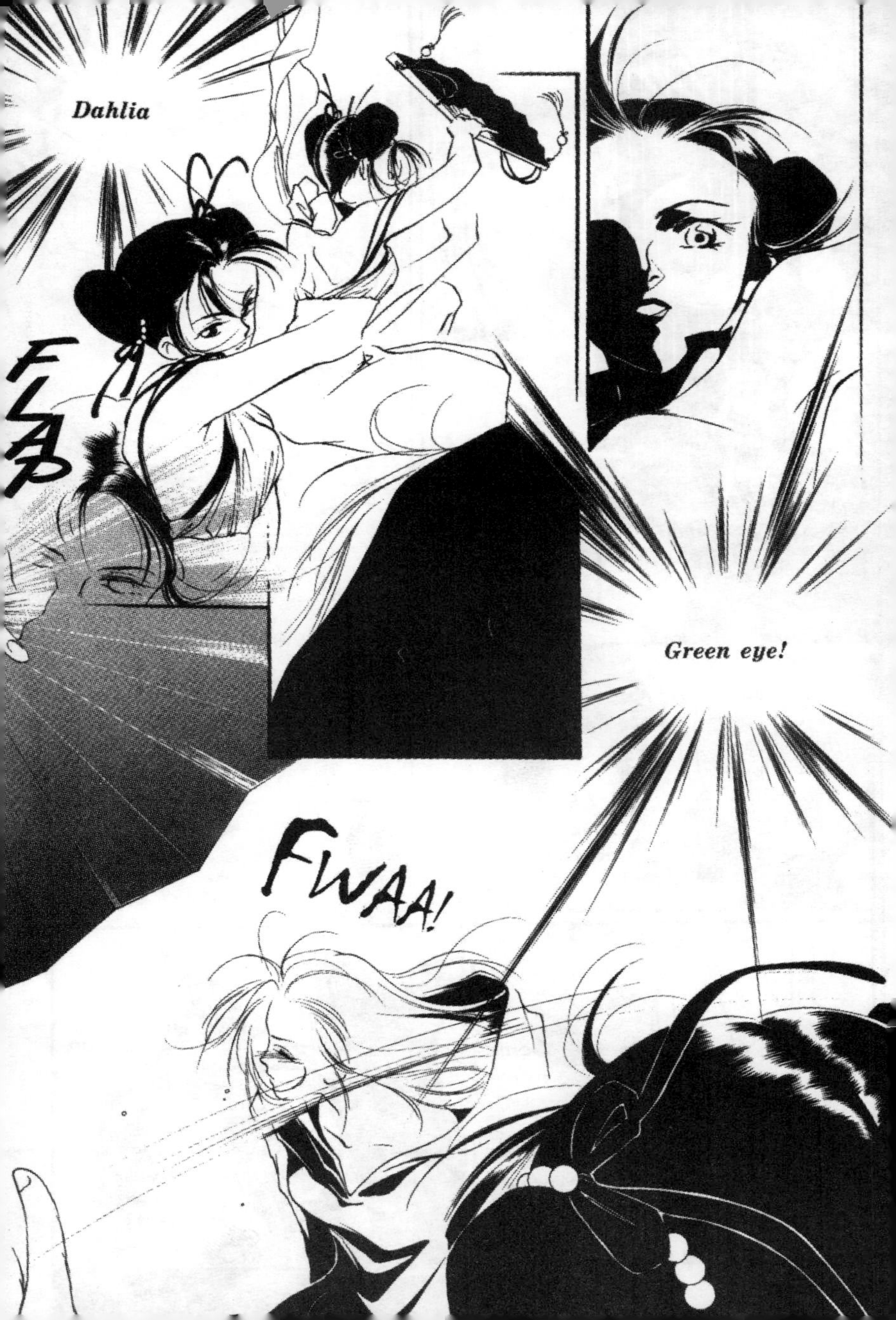
Dahlia
FLAP
Green eye!
FWAA!

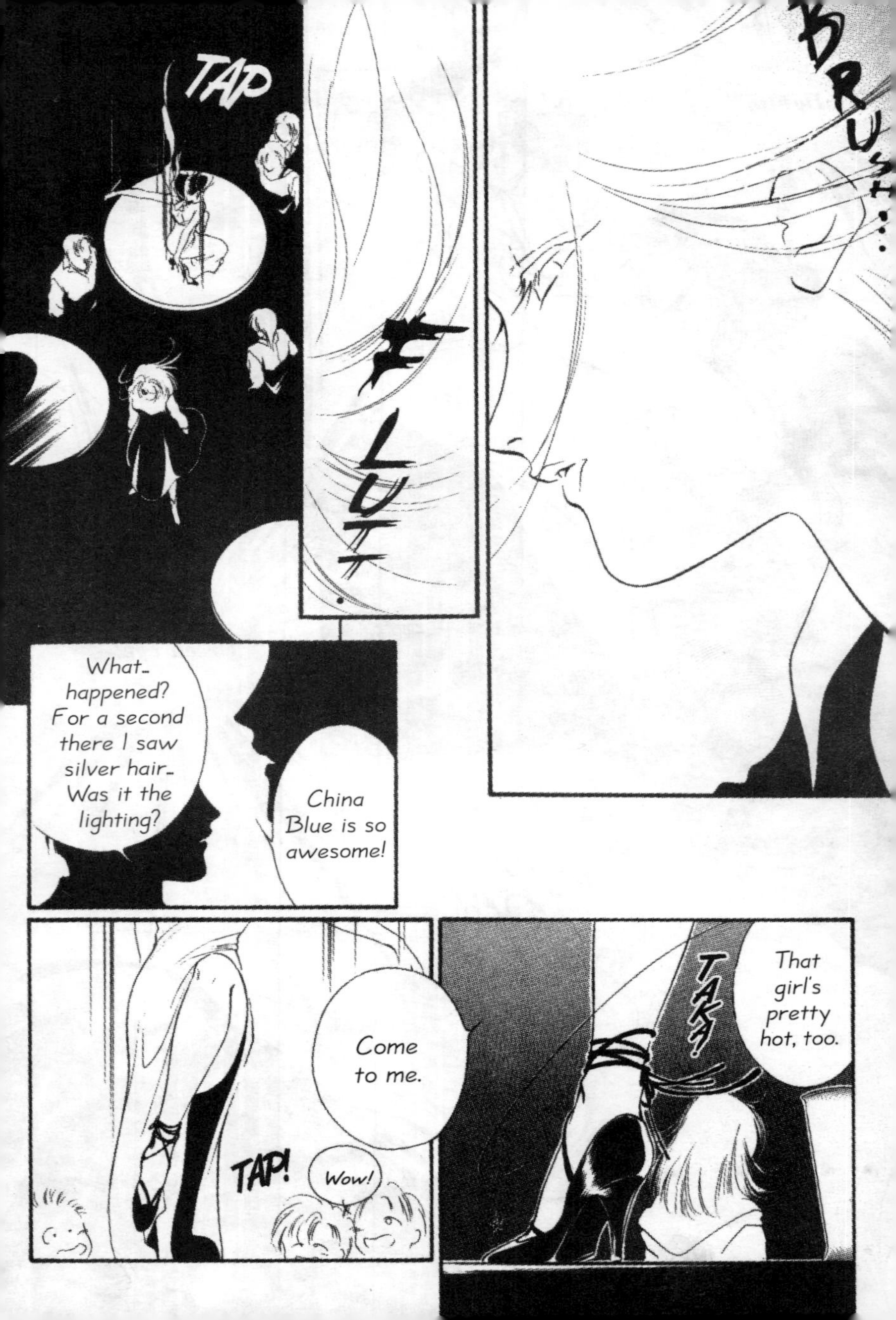
TAP
FLUTT.
BRUSH...
What.. happened? For a second there I saw silver hair.. Was it the lighting?
China Blue is so awesome!
Come to me.
TAP!
Wow!
TAKA!
That girl's pretty hot, too.

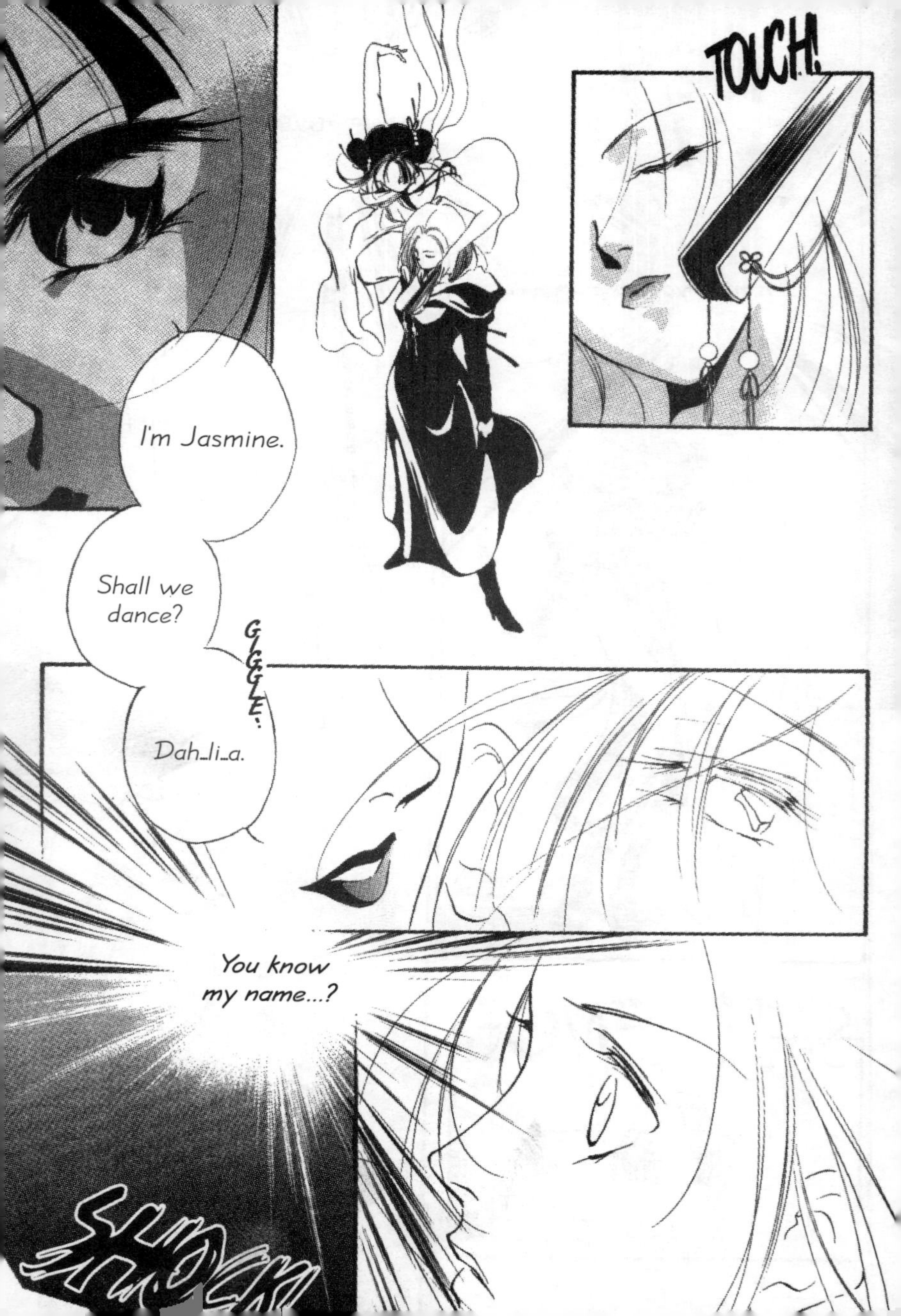

TOUCH!
I'm Jasmine.
Shall we dance?
GIGGLE..
Dah-li-a.
You know my name...?

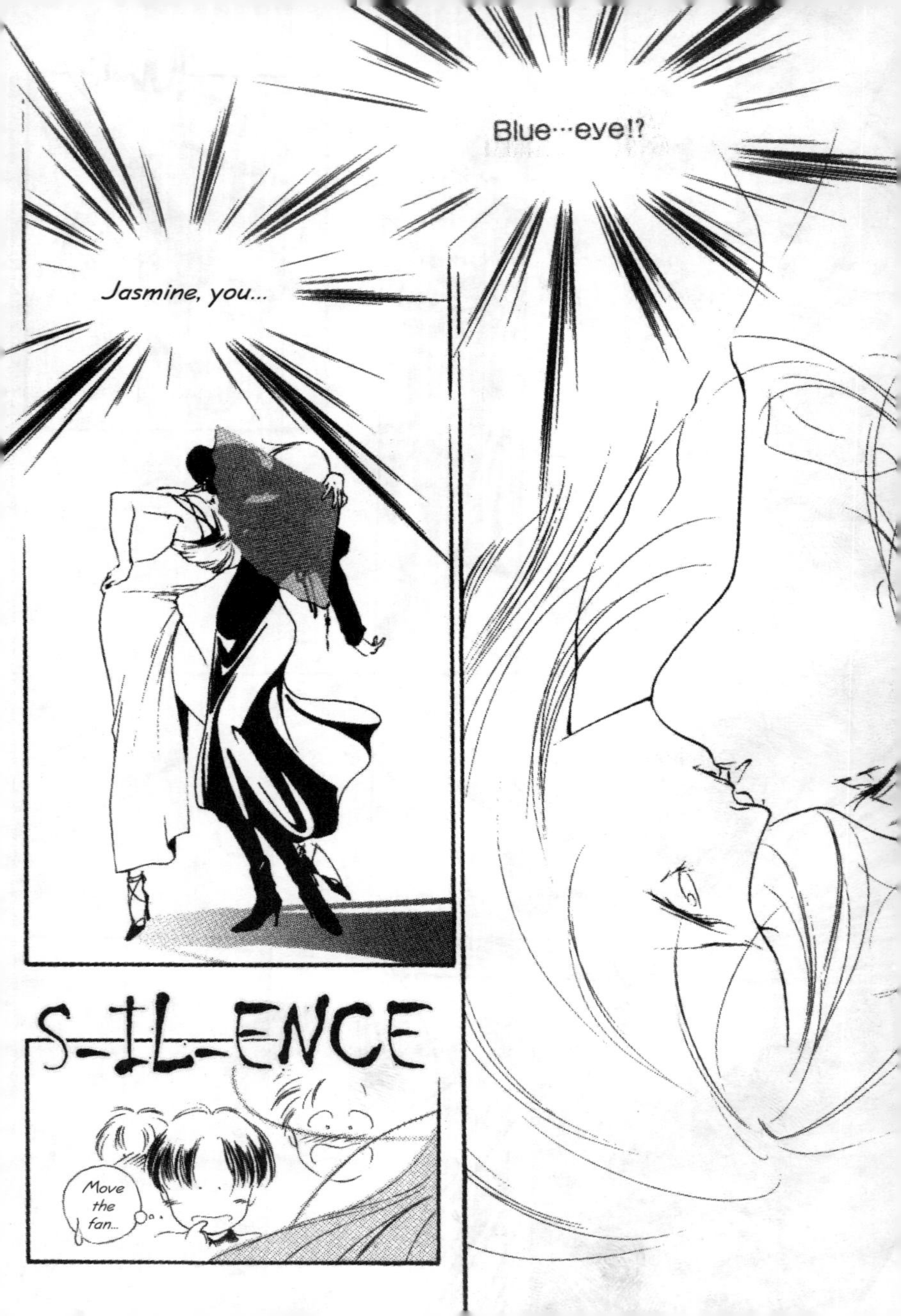
Blue···eye!?
Jasmine, you...
S-IL-ENCE
Move the fan...

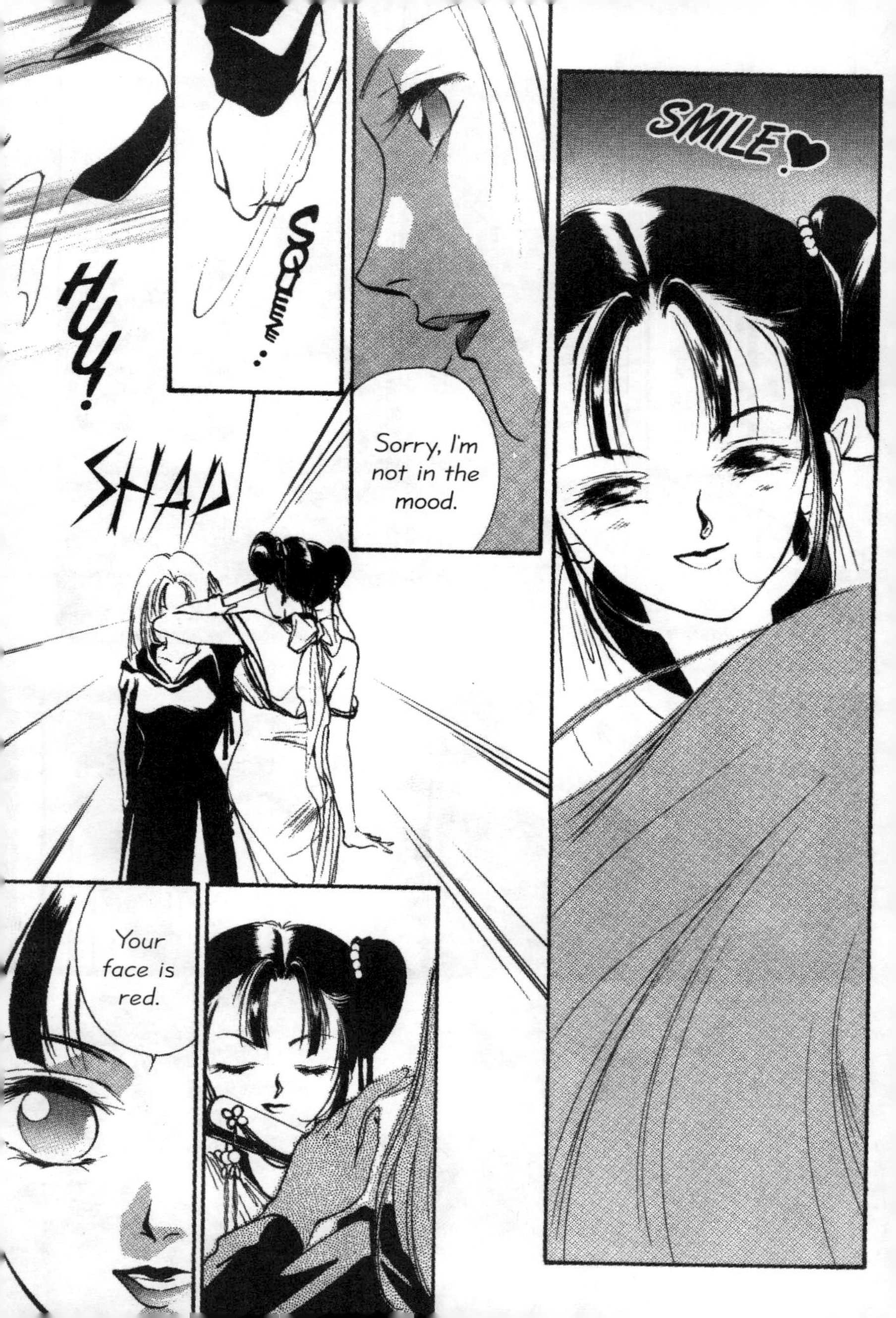
SMILE♥
Sorry, I'm not in the mood.
SQUEEE..
HUU!
SHAP
Your face is red.

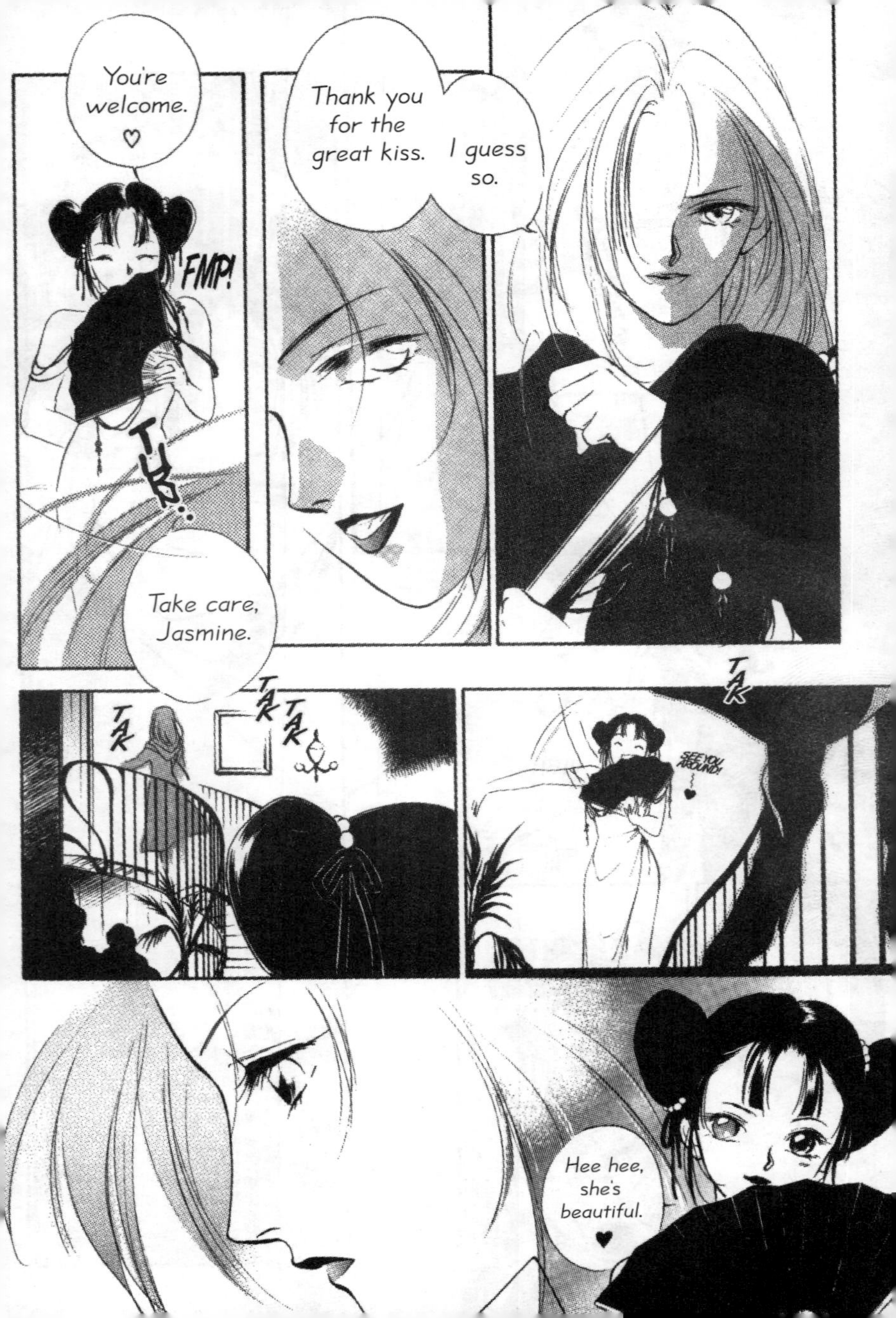
Thank you for the great kiss.
I guess so.
You're welcome. ♡
FMP!
Take care, Jasmine.
TAK
TAK TAK
TAK
SEE YOU AROUND! ♥
Hee hee, she's beautiful. ♥

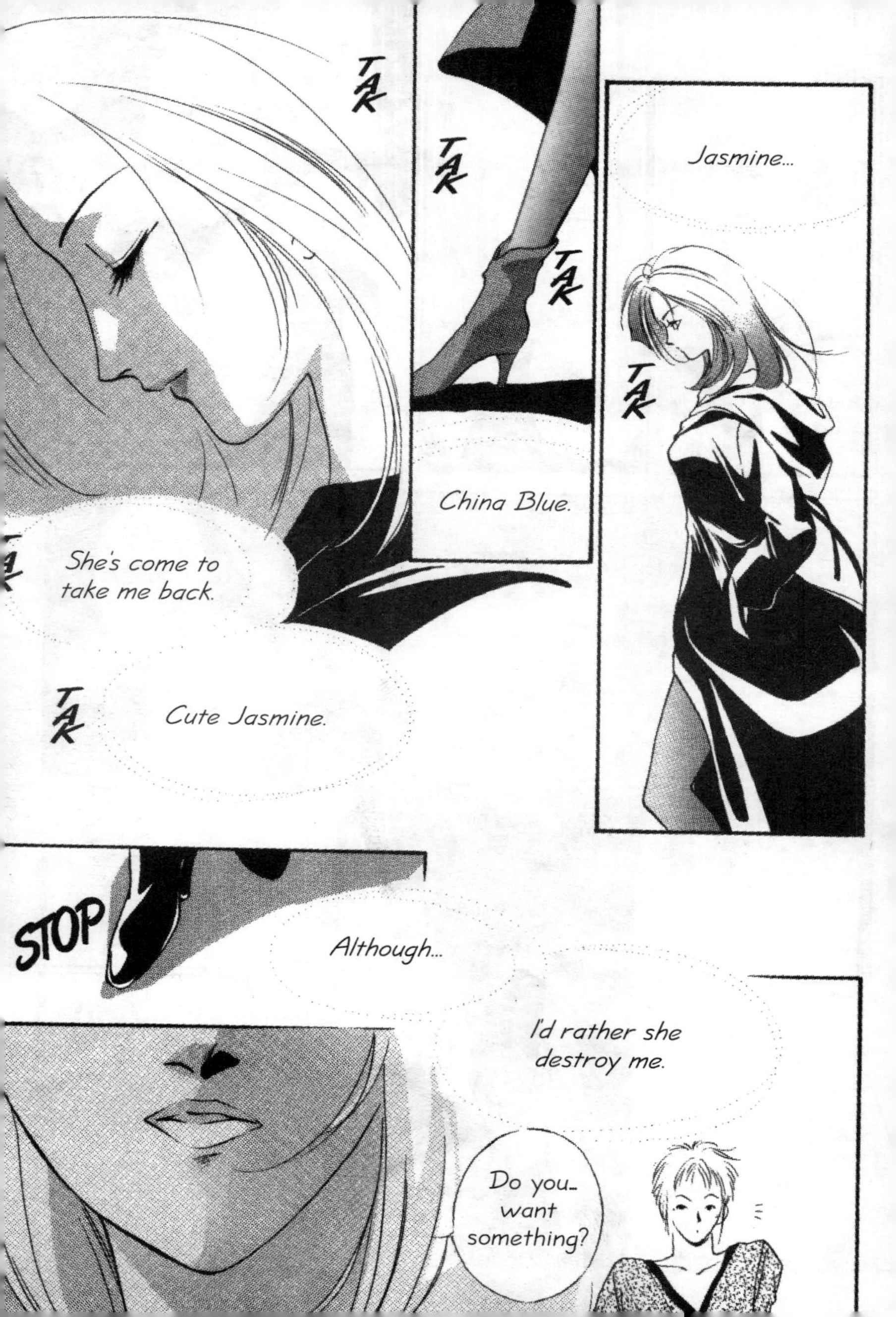

Jasmine...
TAK
TAK
TAK
China Blue.
TAK
She's come to take me back.
TAK
Cute Jasmine.
STOP
Although...
I'd rather she destroy me.
Do you... want something?

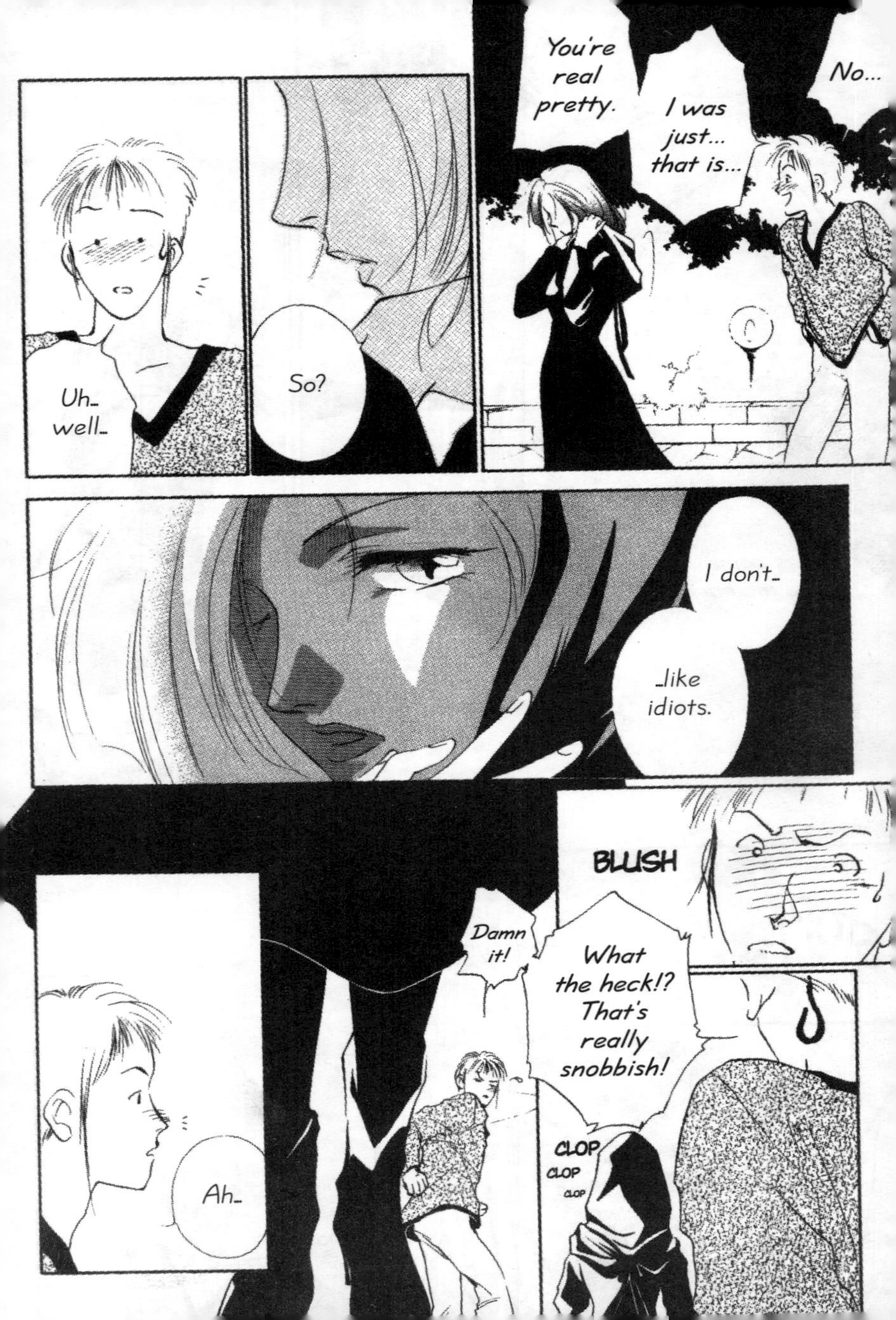
Uh-
well-
So?
You're real pretty.
No...
I was just... that is...
I don't-
-like idiots.
Ah-
BLUSH
Damn it!
What the heck!? That's really snobbish!
CLOP
CLOP
CLOP

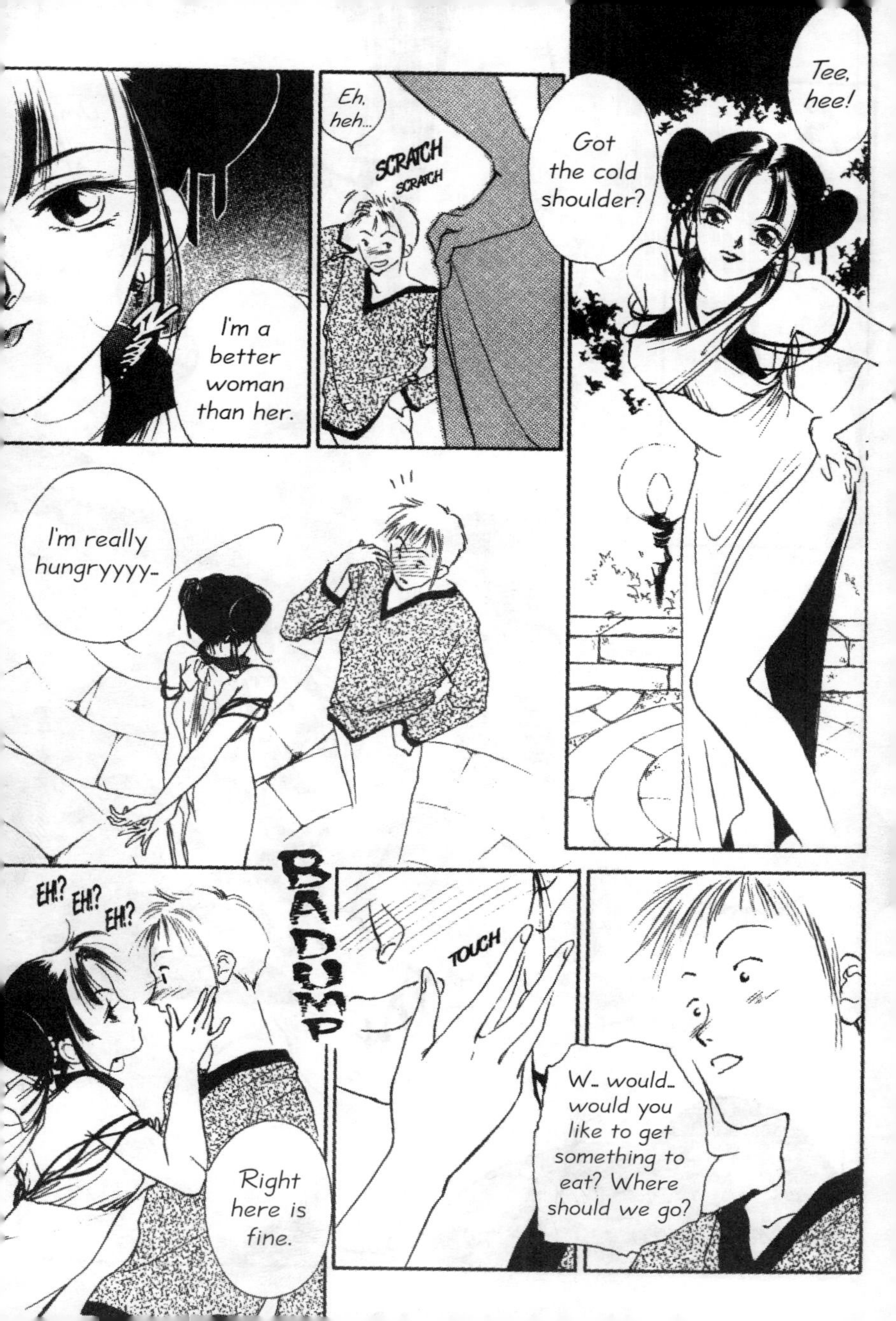
Tee, hee!
Got the cold shoulder?
Eh, heh...
SCRATCH
SCRATCH
I'm a better woman than her.
I'm really hungryyyy-
W... would... would you like to get something to eat? Where should we go?
TOUCH
BADUMP
EH!? EH!? EH!?
Right here is fine.

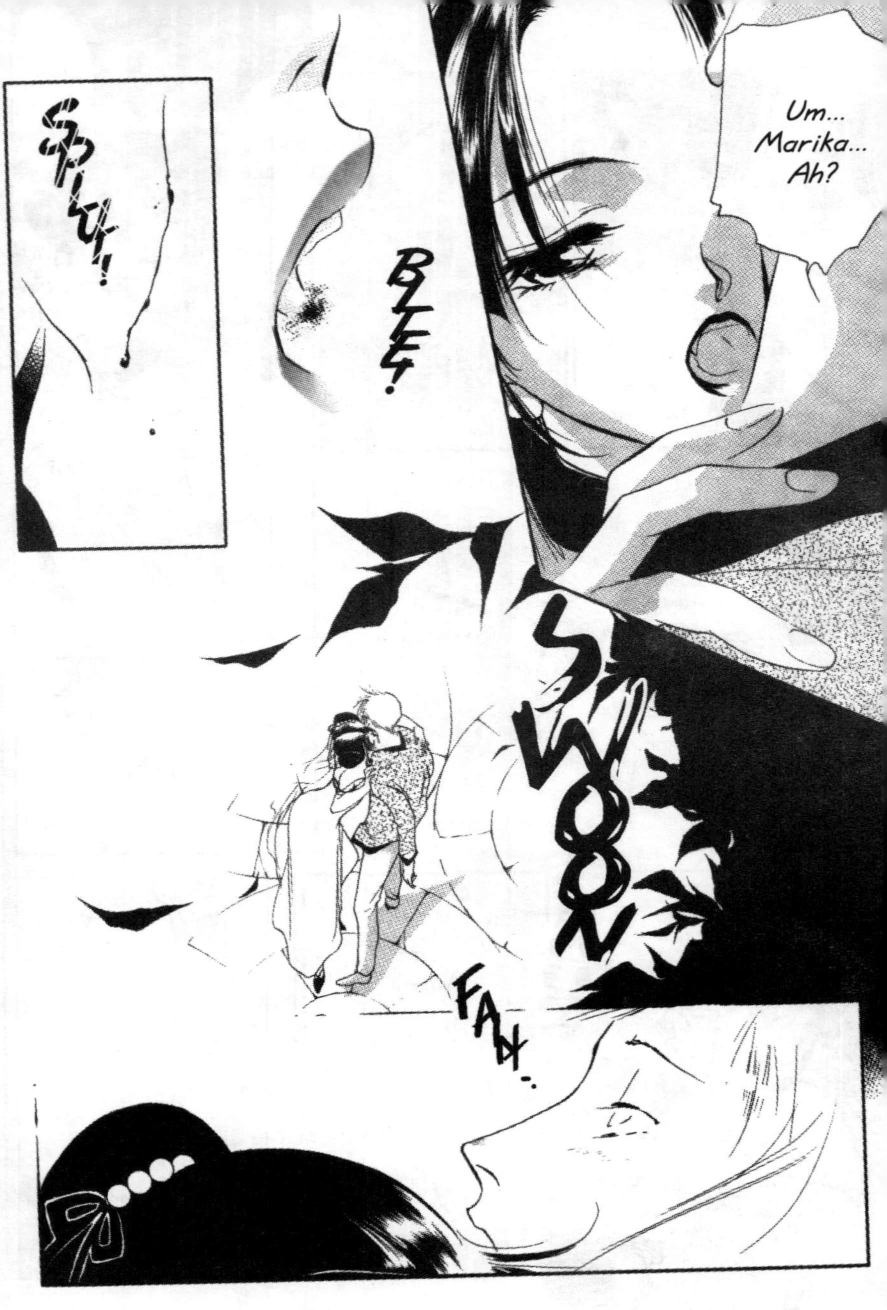

Um...
Marika...
Ah?
SPLUK!
BLEE!
SWOON
FAH..

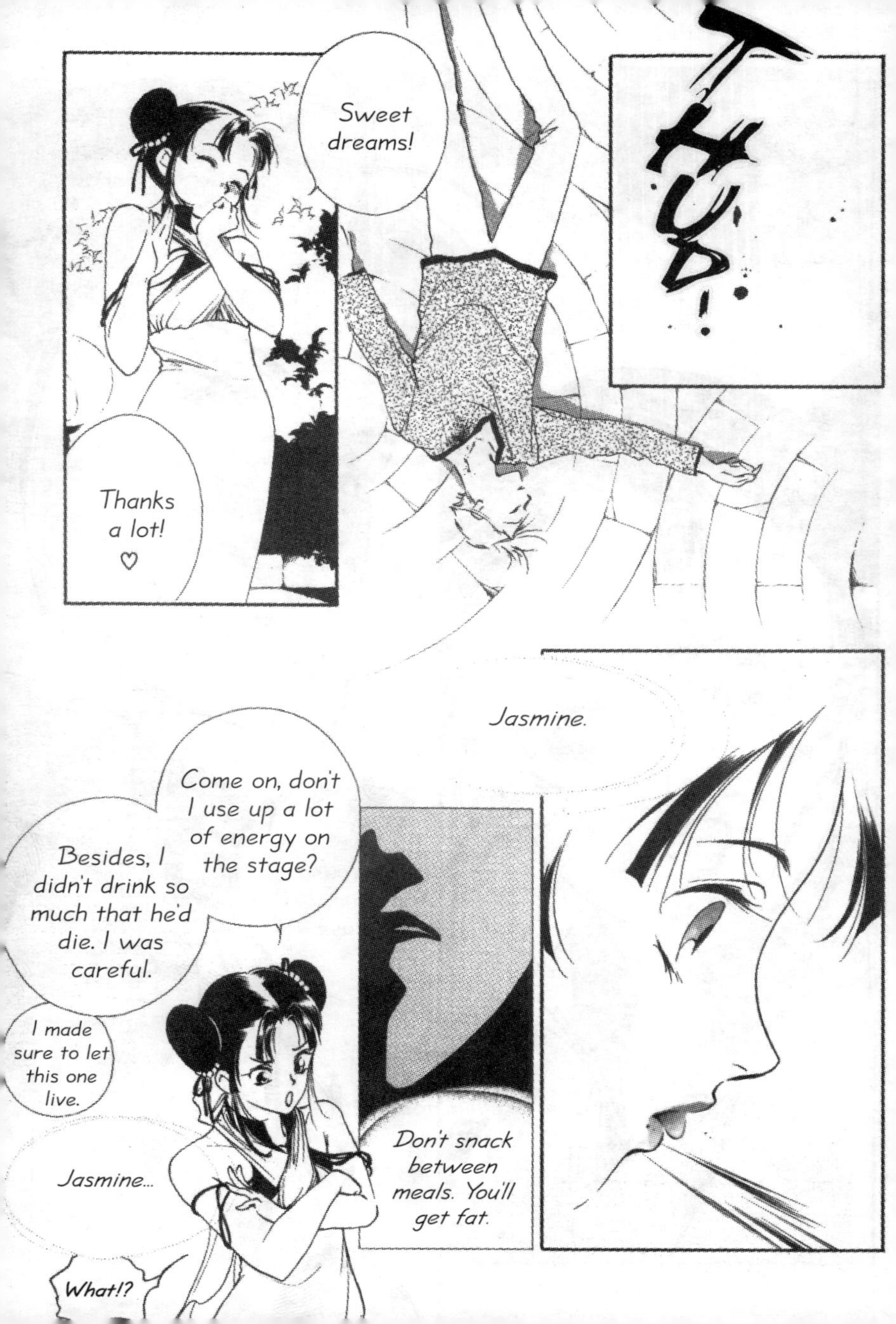
THUD!
Sweet dreams!
Thanks a lot! ♡
Jasmine.
Don't snack between meals. You'll get fat.
Come on, don't I use up a lot of energy on the stage?
Besides, I didn't drink so much that he'd die. I was careful.
I made sure to let this one live.
Jasmine...
What!?

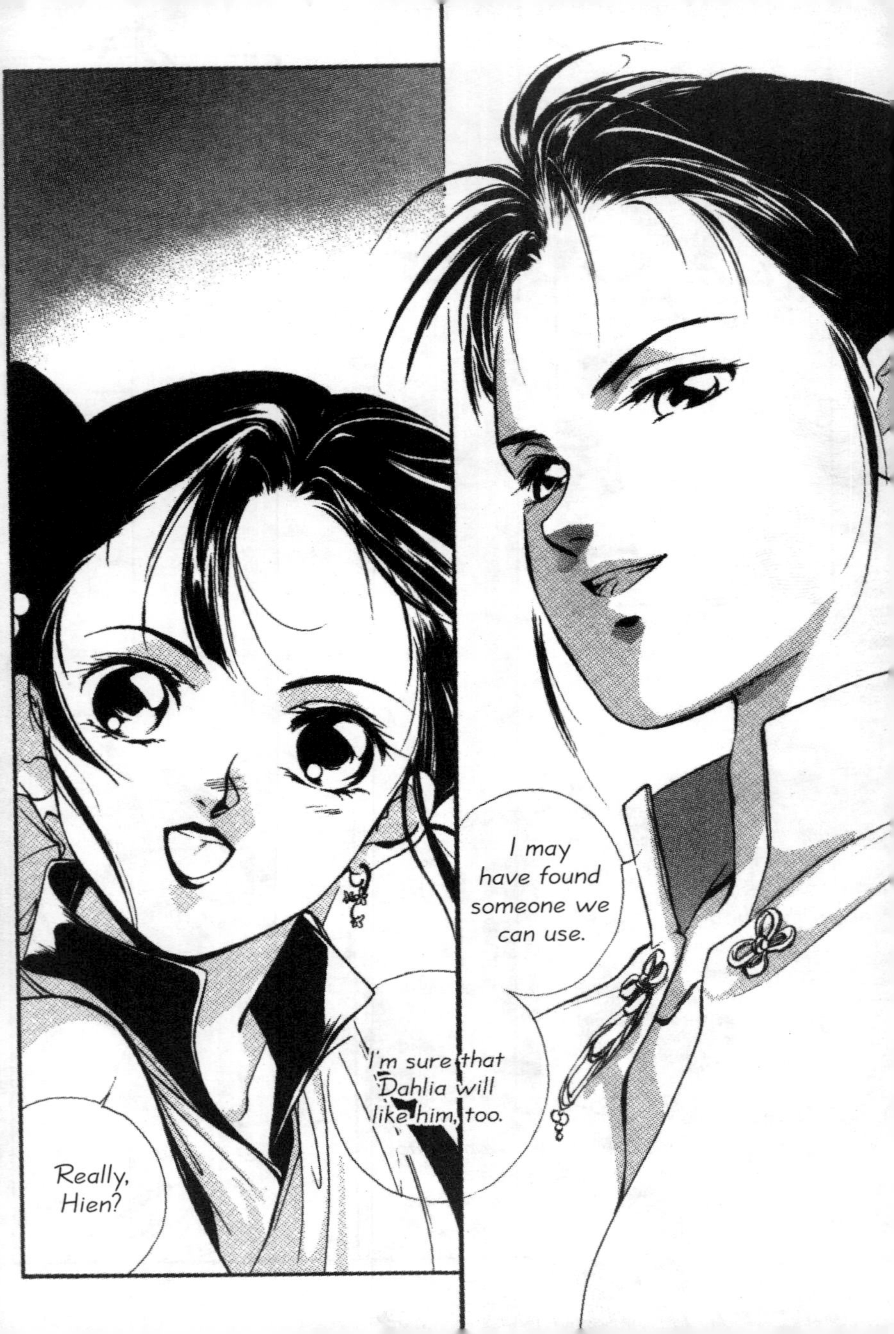
I may have found someone we can use.
I'm sure that Dahlia will like him, too.
Really, Hien?

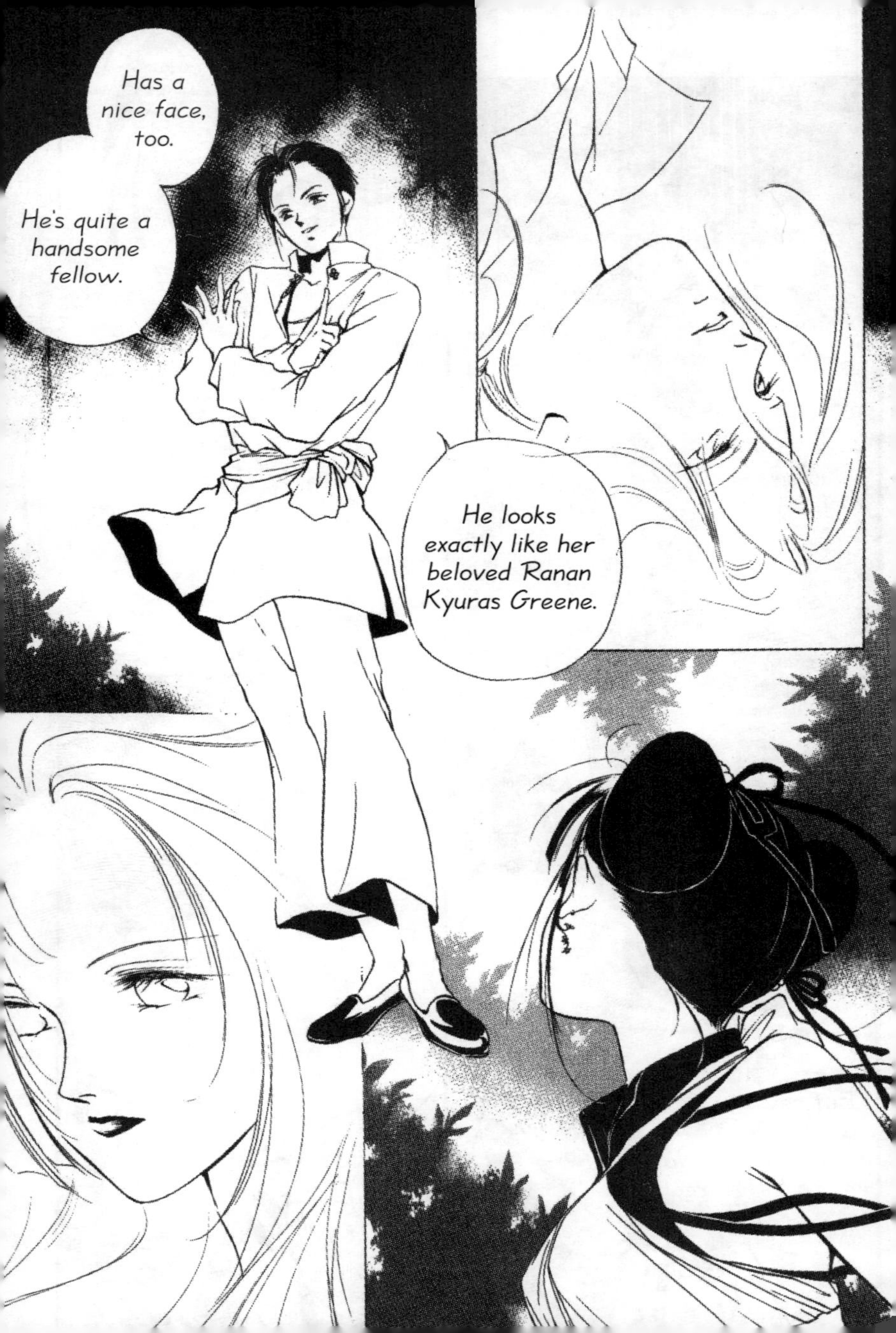
Has a nice face, too.
He's quite a handsome fellow.
He looks exactly like her beloved Ranan Kyuras Greene.

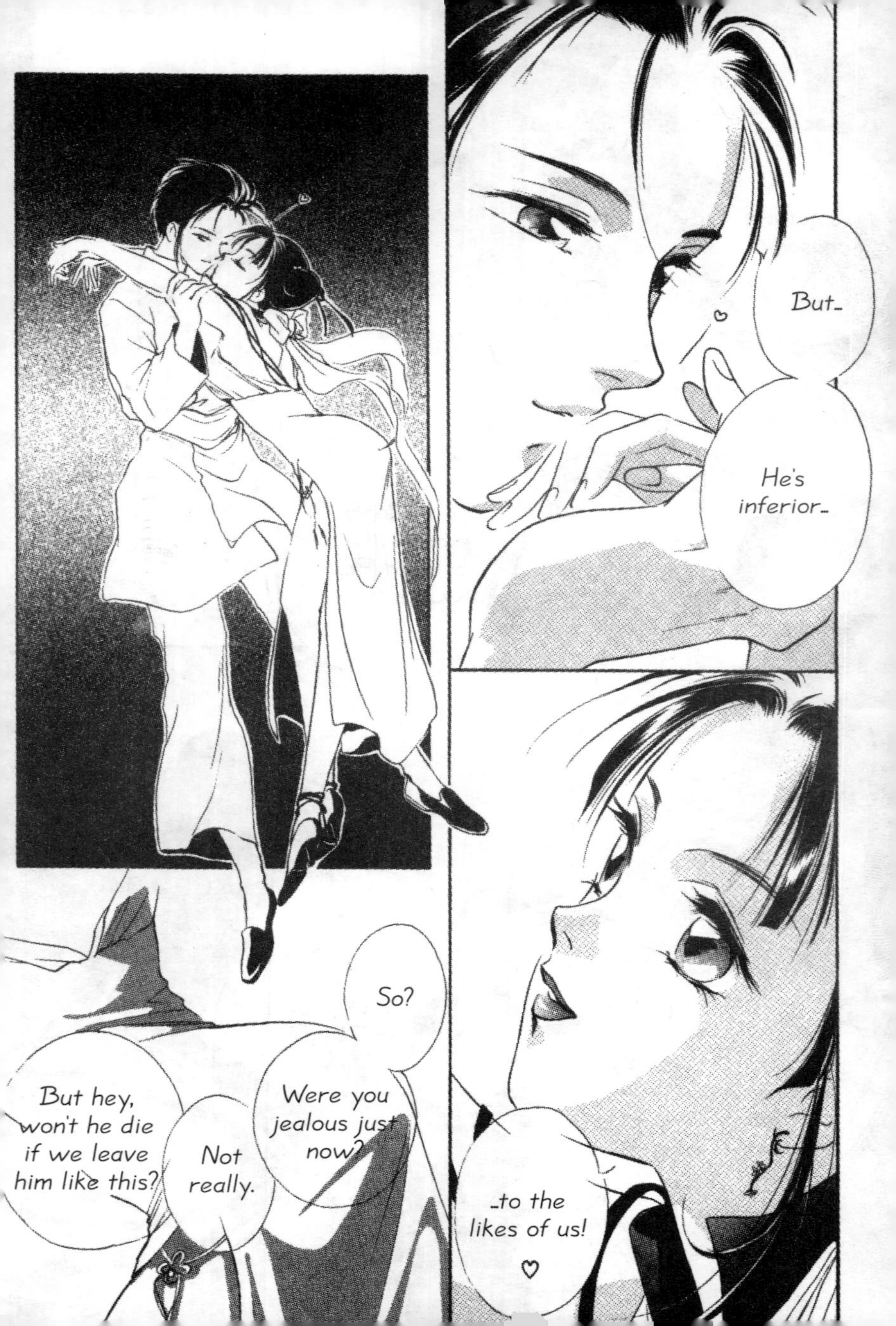

But..
He's inferior..
..to the likes of us! ♡
So?
Were you jealous just now?
Not really.
But hey, won't he die if we leave him like this?

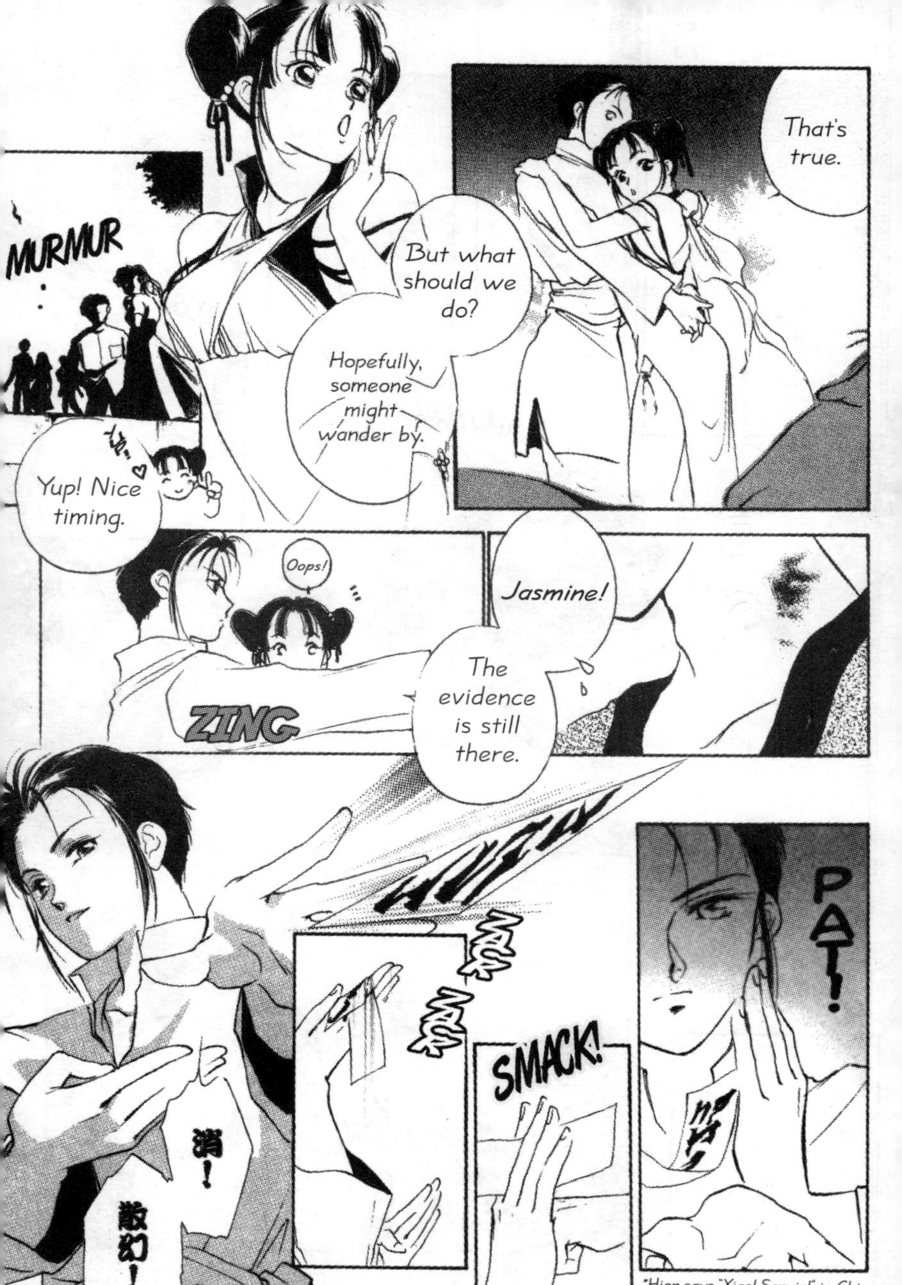
That's true.
But what should we do?
Hopefully, someone might wander by.
MURMUR
Yup! Nice timing.
Jasmine!
The evidence is still there.
Oops!
ZING
PAT!
SMACK!
消！
散幻！

*Hien says "Xiao! Sanyin!" in Chinese. It means, "Disappear! Scatter the evidence!"

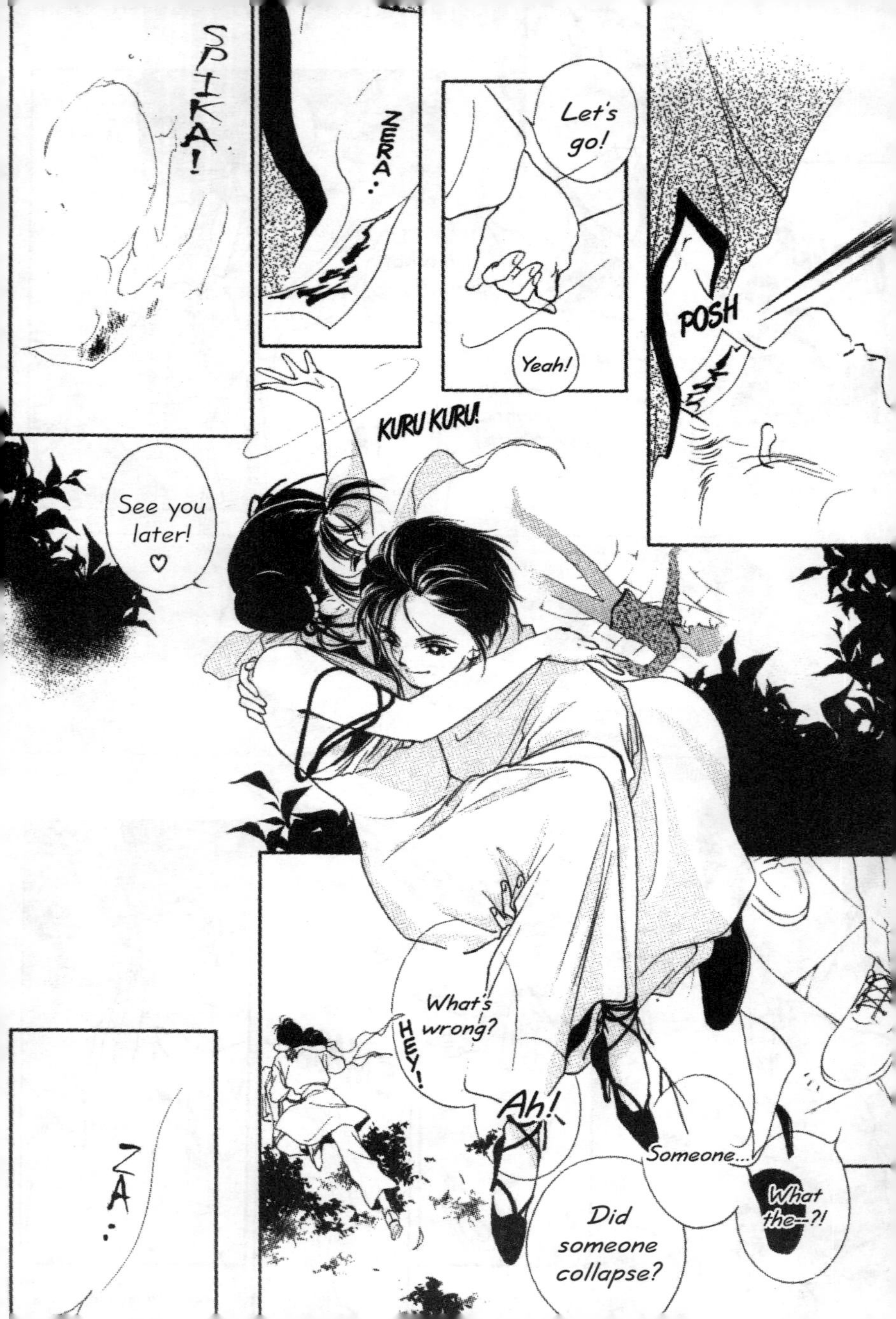

POSH
Let's go!
Yeah!
ZERA..
SPIKA!
KURU KURU!
See you later! ♡
What the--?!
Someone...
Did someone collapse?
Ah!
HEY!
What's wrong?
ZA..

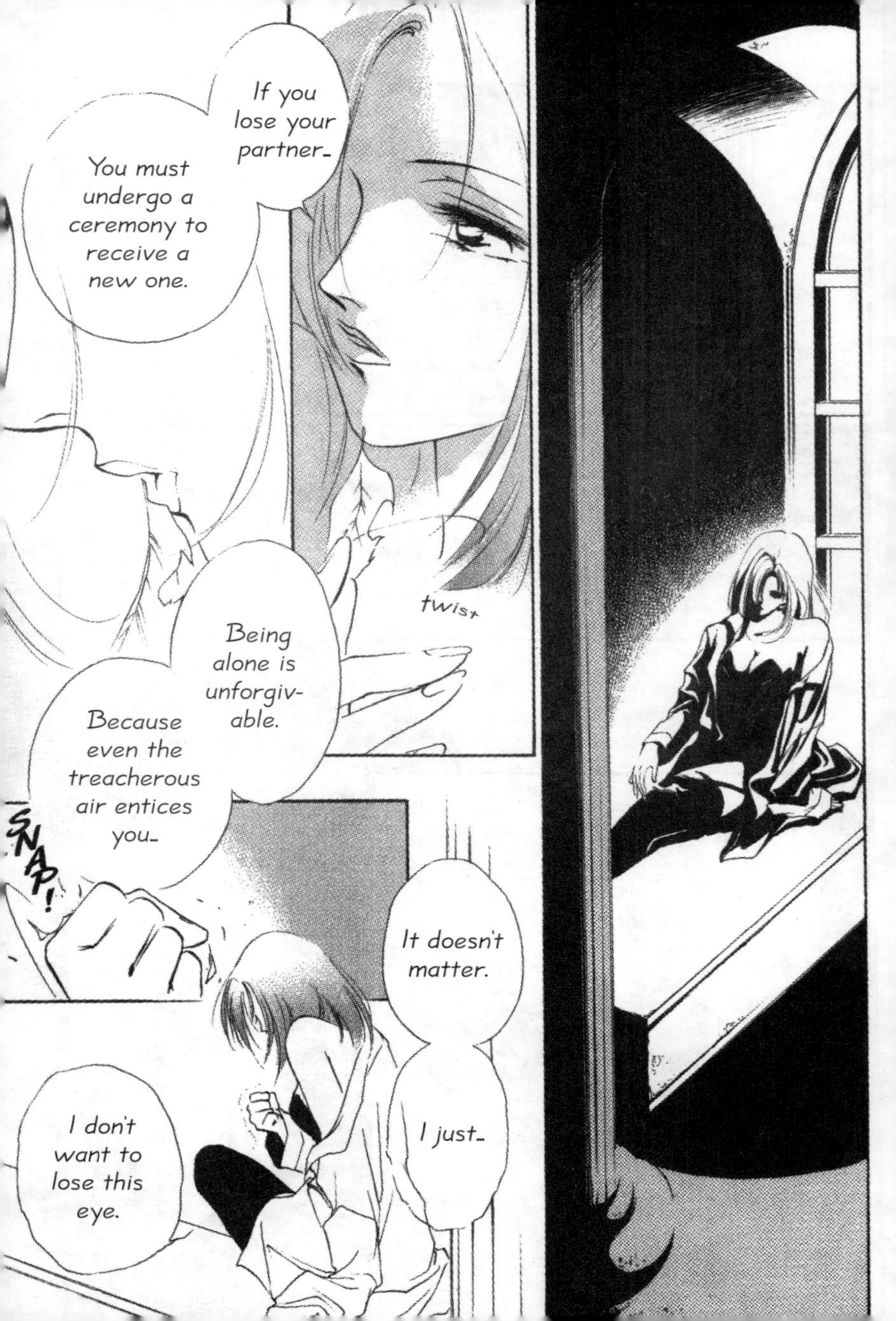
If you lose your partner..
You must undergo a ceremony to receive a new one.
twist
Being alone is unforgiv-able.
Because even the treacherous air entices you..
SNAP!
It doesn't matter.
I just..
I don't want to lose this eye.

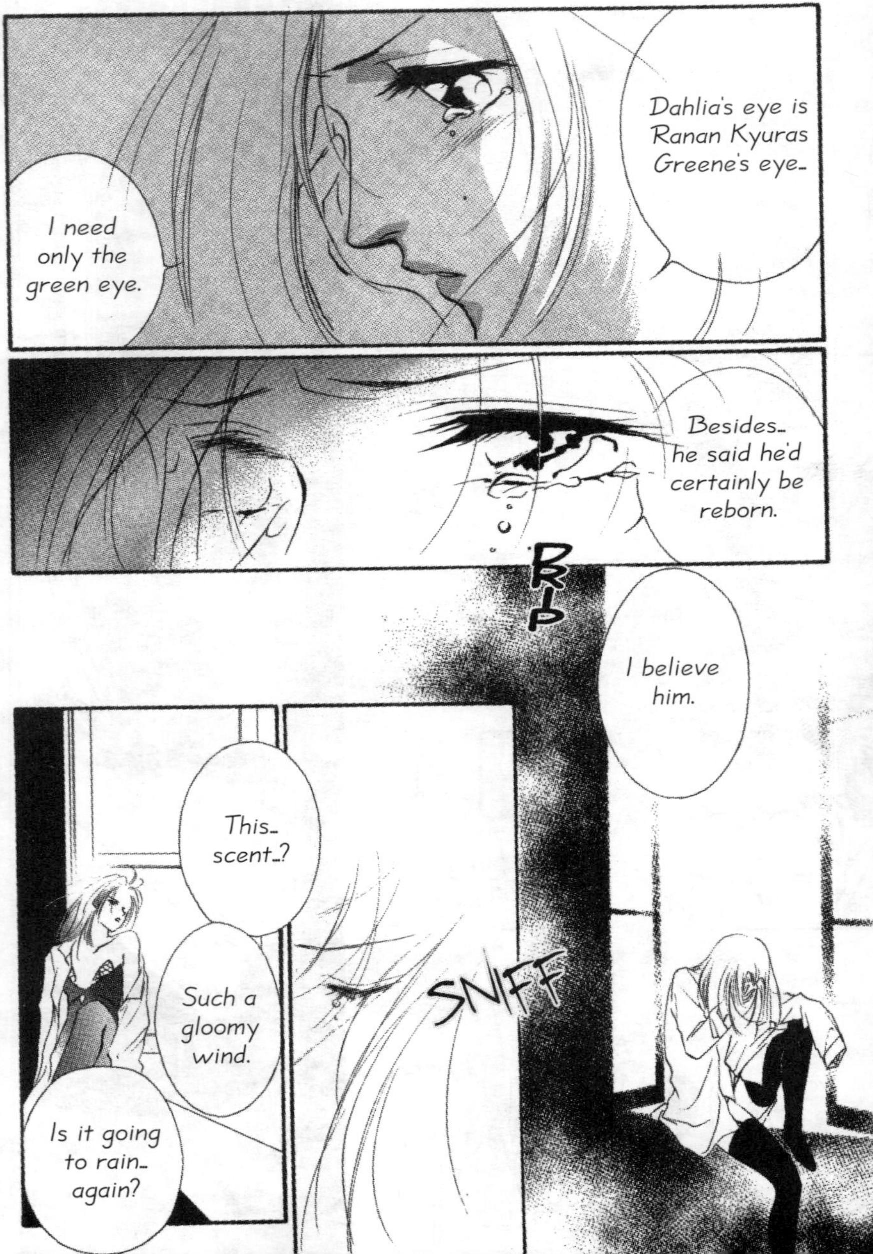

Dahlia's eye is Ranan Kyuras Greene's eye..
I need only the green eye.
Besides.. he said he'd certainly be reborn.
RIP
I believe him.
SNIFF
This.. scent..?
Such a gloomy wind.
Is it going to rain.. again?

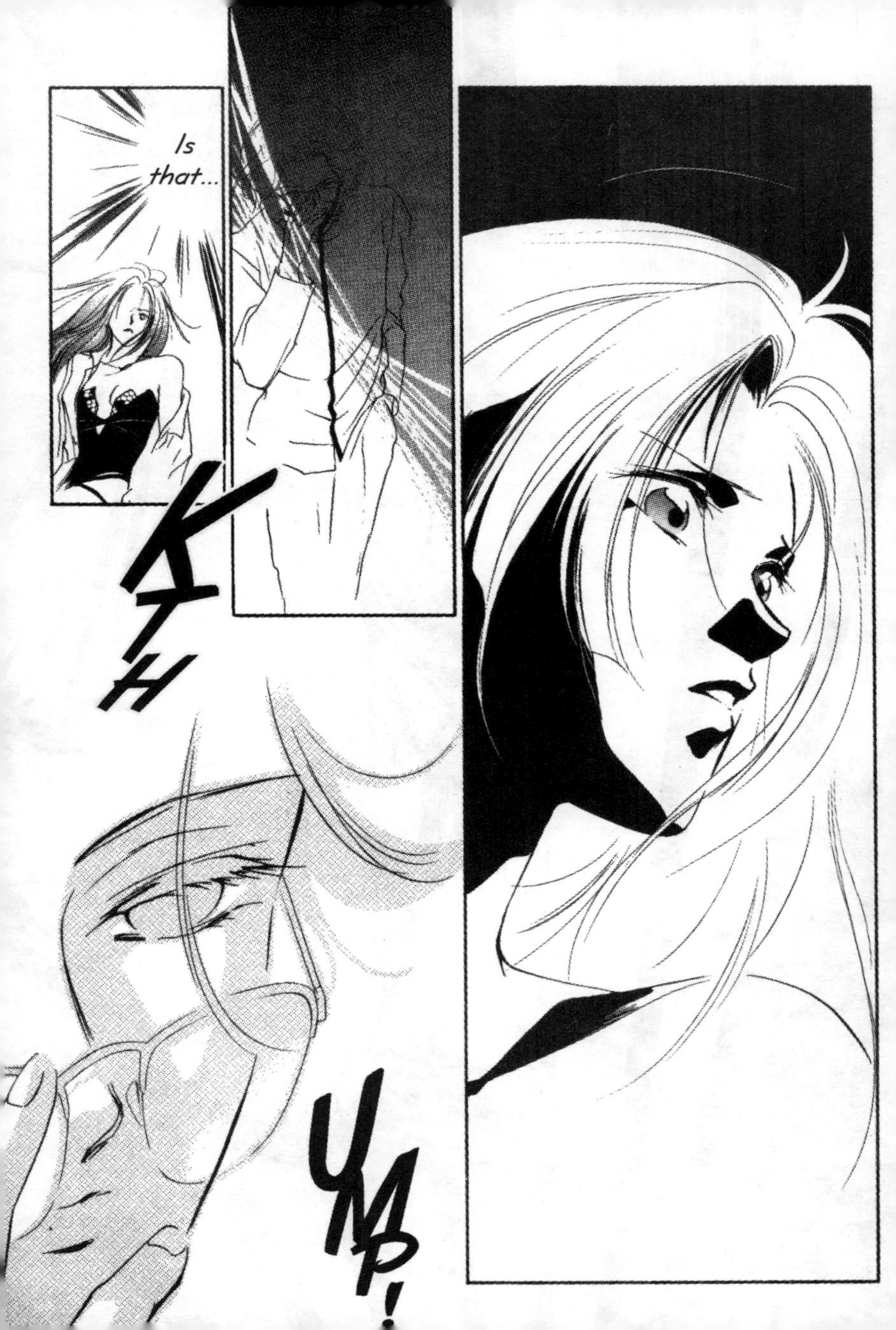
Is that...
KTHH
UMP!

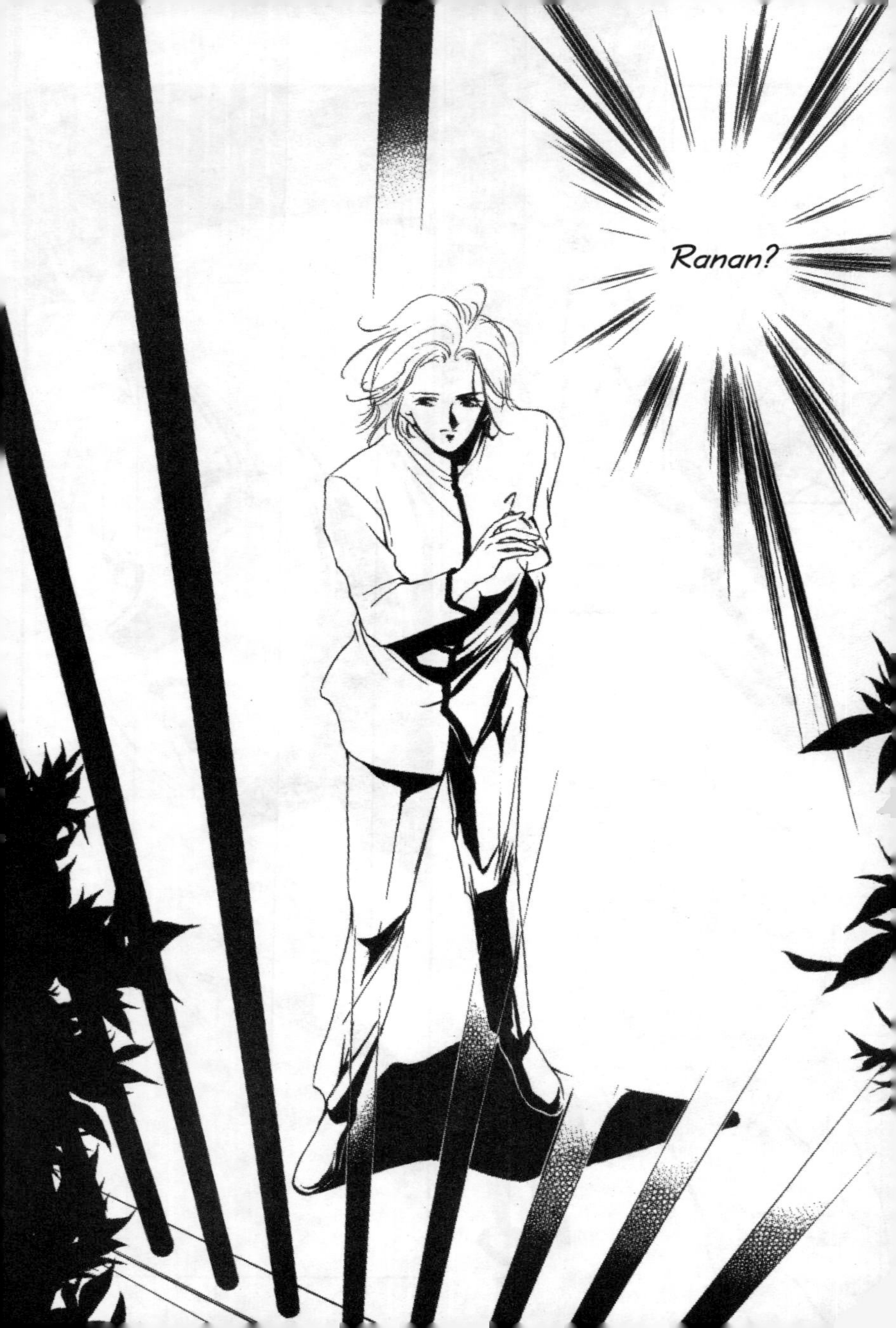
Ranan?

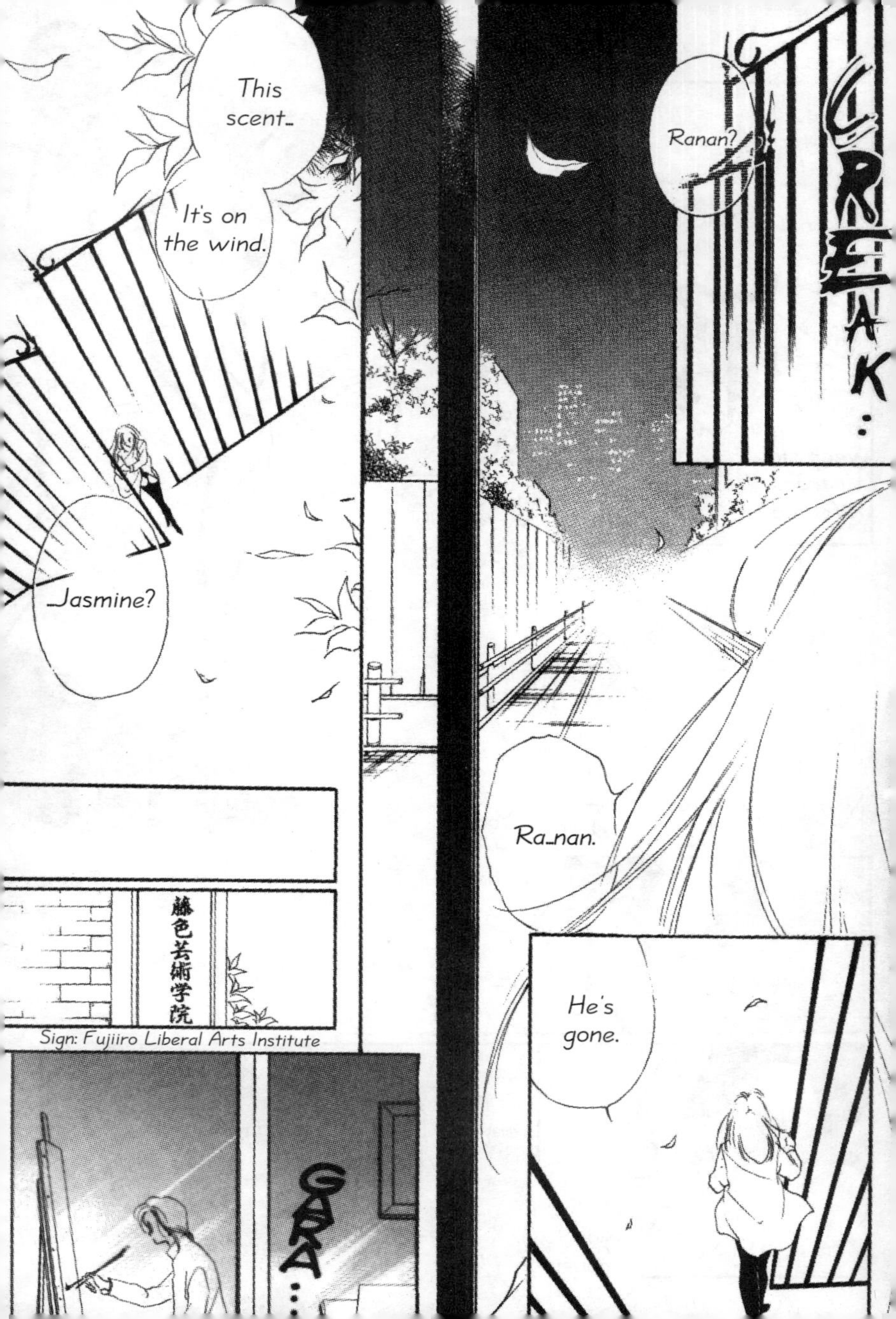
Ranan?
CREAK…
Ra…nan.
He's gone.
This scent…
It's on the wind.
Jasmine?
藤色芸術学院
Sign: Fujiiro Liberal Arts Institute
GABA…

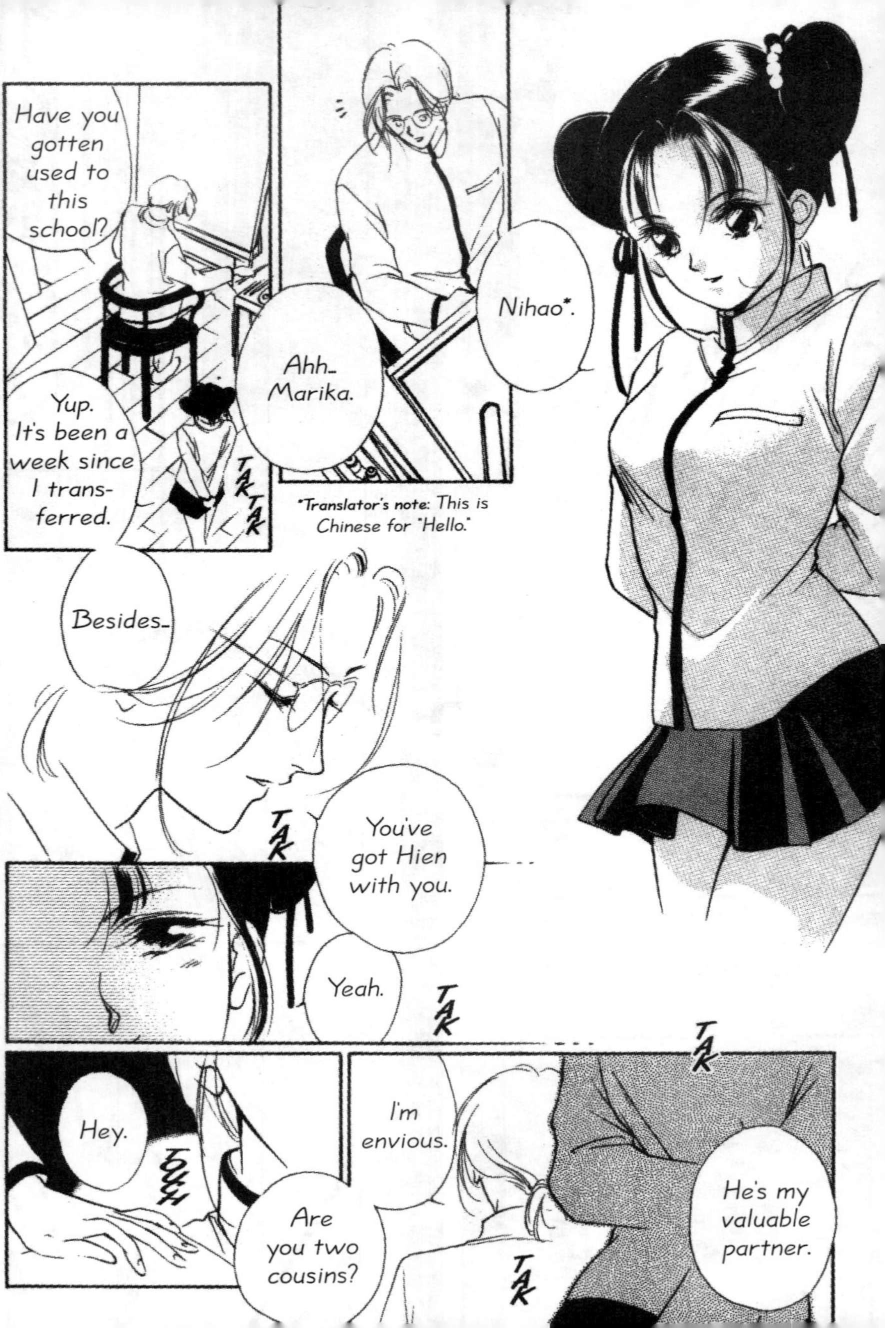
Have you gotten used to this school?
Yup. It's been a week since I transferred.
TAK TAK
Ahh... Marika.
Nihao*.
*Translator's note: This is Chinese for "Hello."
Besides...
TAK
You've got Hien with you.
Yeah.
TAK
TAK
Hey.
TOUCH
I'm envious.
Are you two cousins?
TAK
He's my valuable partner.

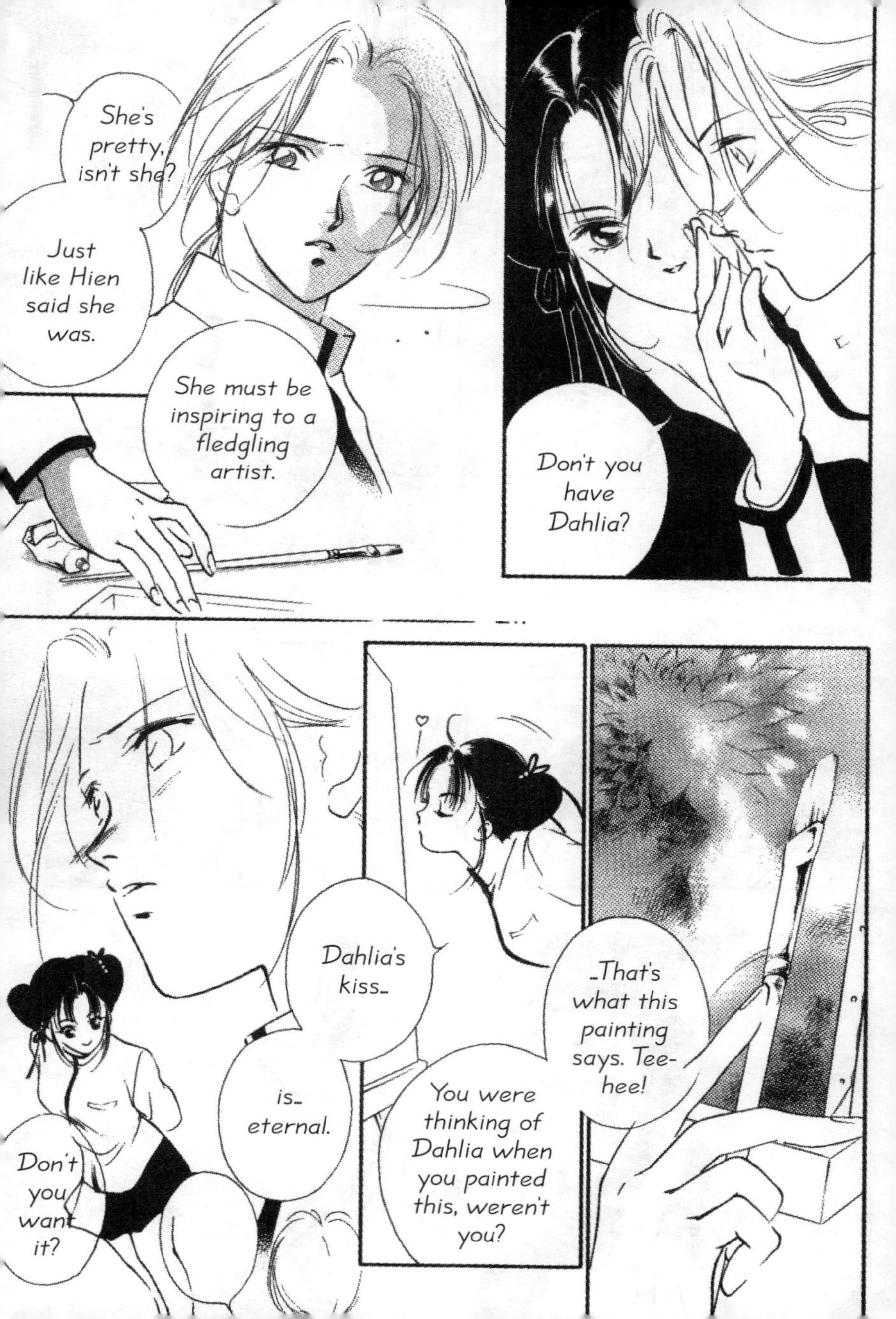
She's pretty, isn't she?
Just like Hien said she was.
She must be inspiring to a fledgling artist.
Don't you have Dahlia?
Dahlia's kiss...
is... eternal.
Don't you want it?
...That's what this painting says. Tee-hee!
You were thinking of Dahlia when you painted this, weren't you?

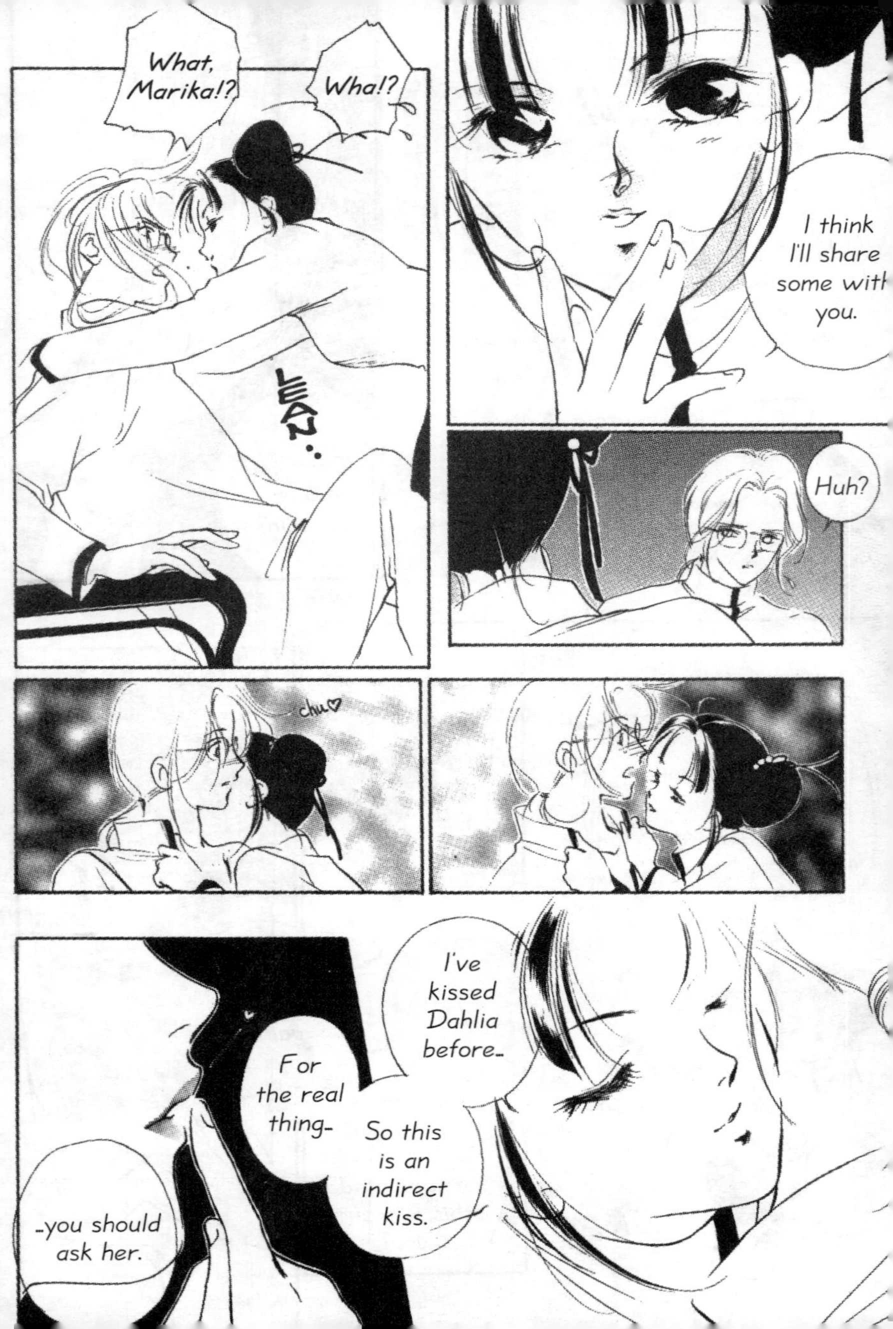
I think I'll share some with you.
Huh?
LEAN..
What, Marika!?
Wha!?
chu♡
So this is an indirect kiss.
I've kissed Dahlia before..
For the real thing..
..you should ask her.

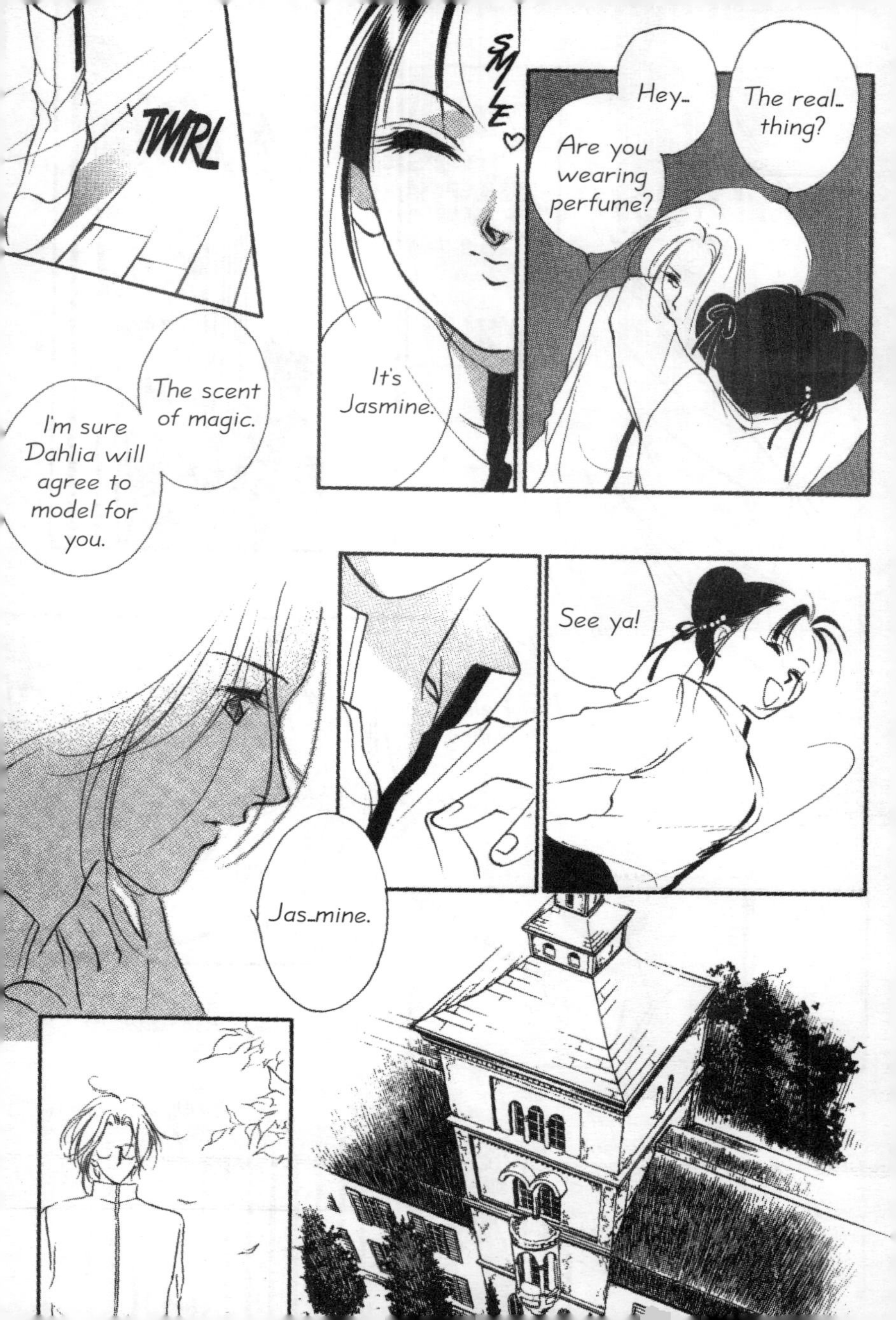

TWIRL
SMILE
Hey...
Are you wearing perfume?
The real... thing?
It's Jasmine.
The scent of magic.
I'm sure Dahlia will agree to model for you.
See ya!
Jas...mine.

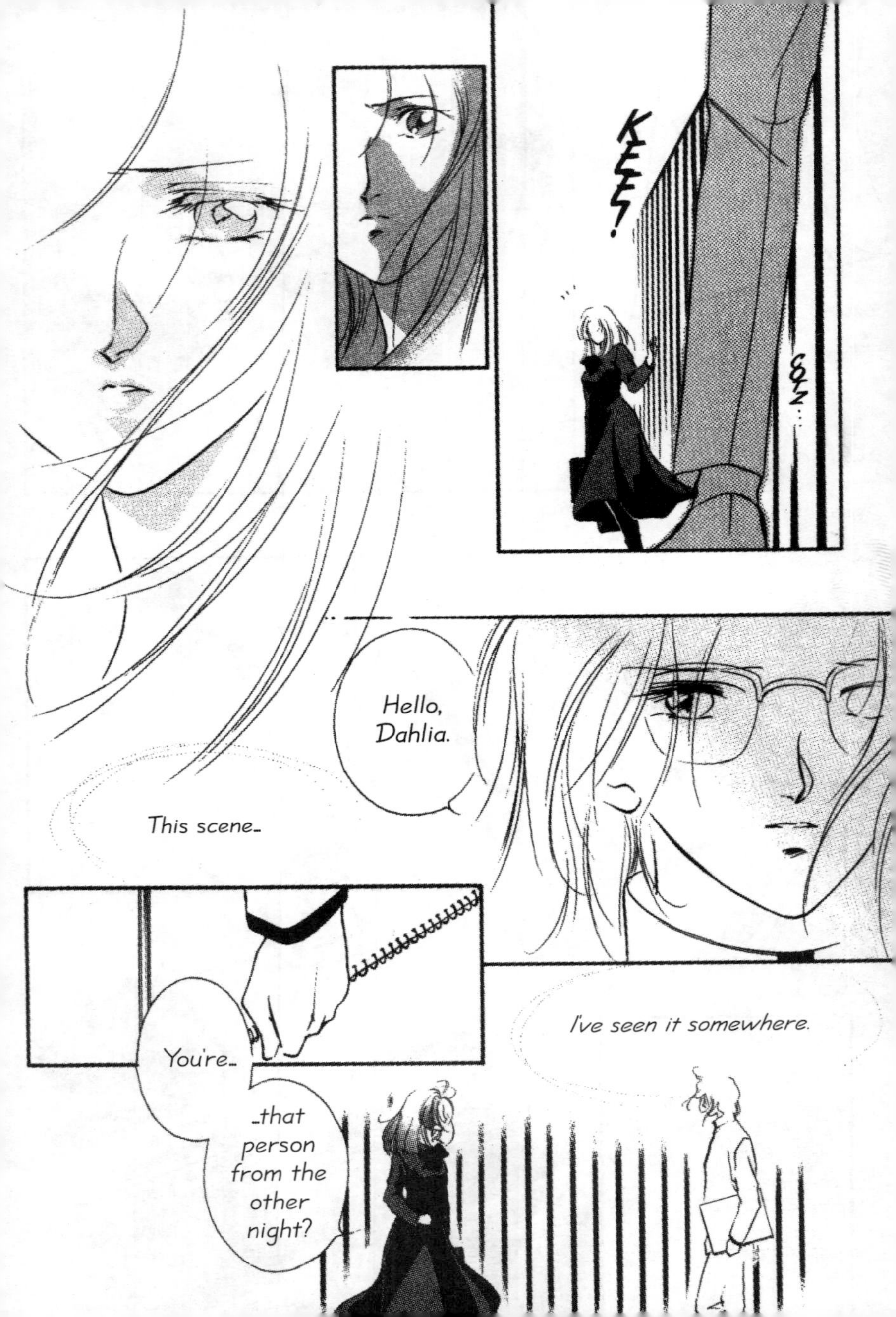
KEES!
Hello, Dahlia.
This scene...
I've seen it somewhere.
You're...
...that person from the other night?

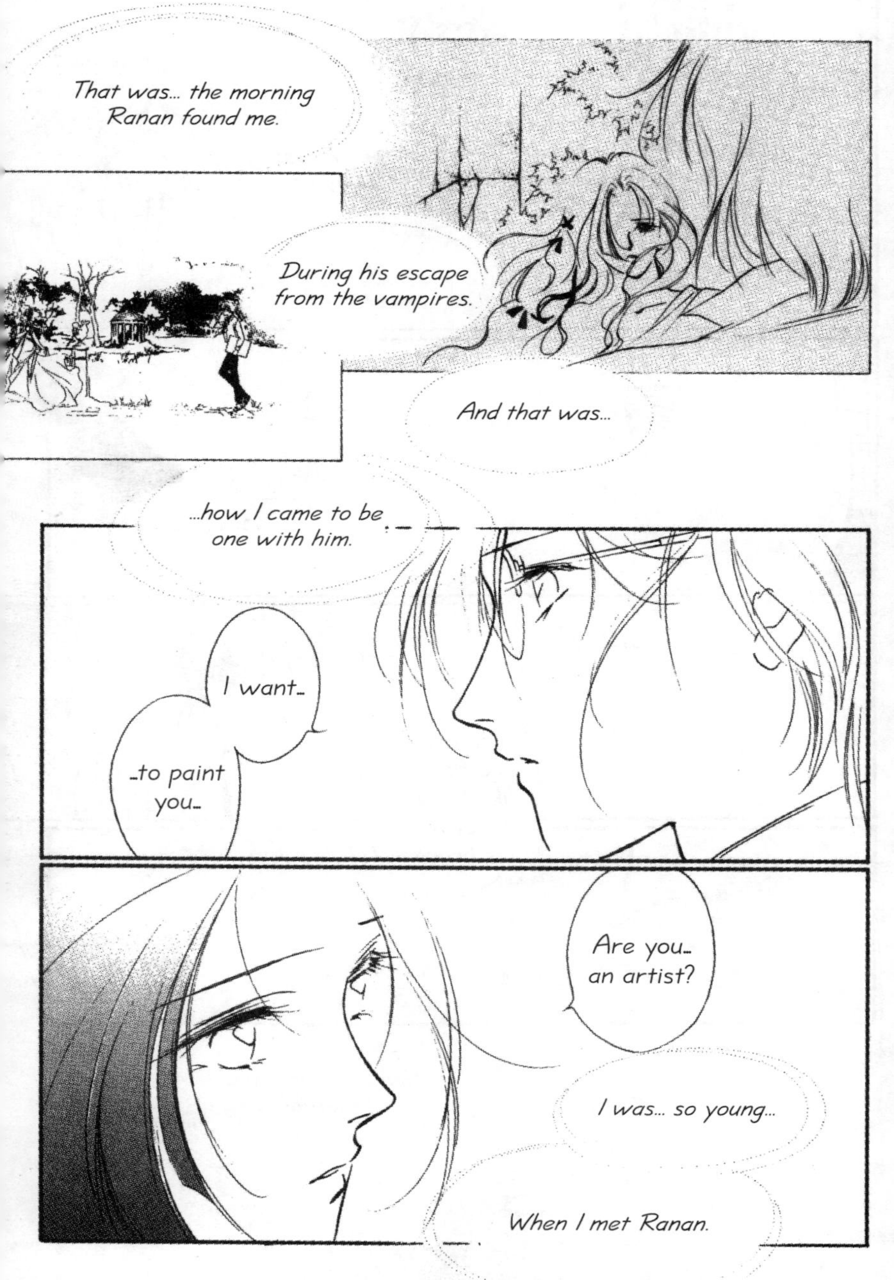
That was... the morning Ranan found me.
During his escape from the vampires.
And that was...
...how I came to be one with him.
I want...
...to paint you...
Are you... an artist?
I was... so young...
When I met Ranan.

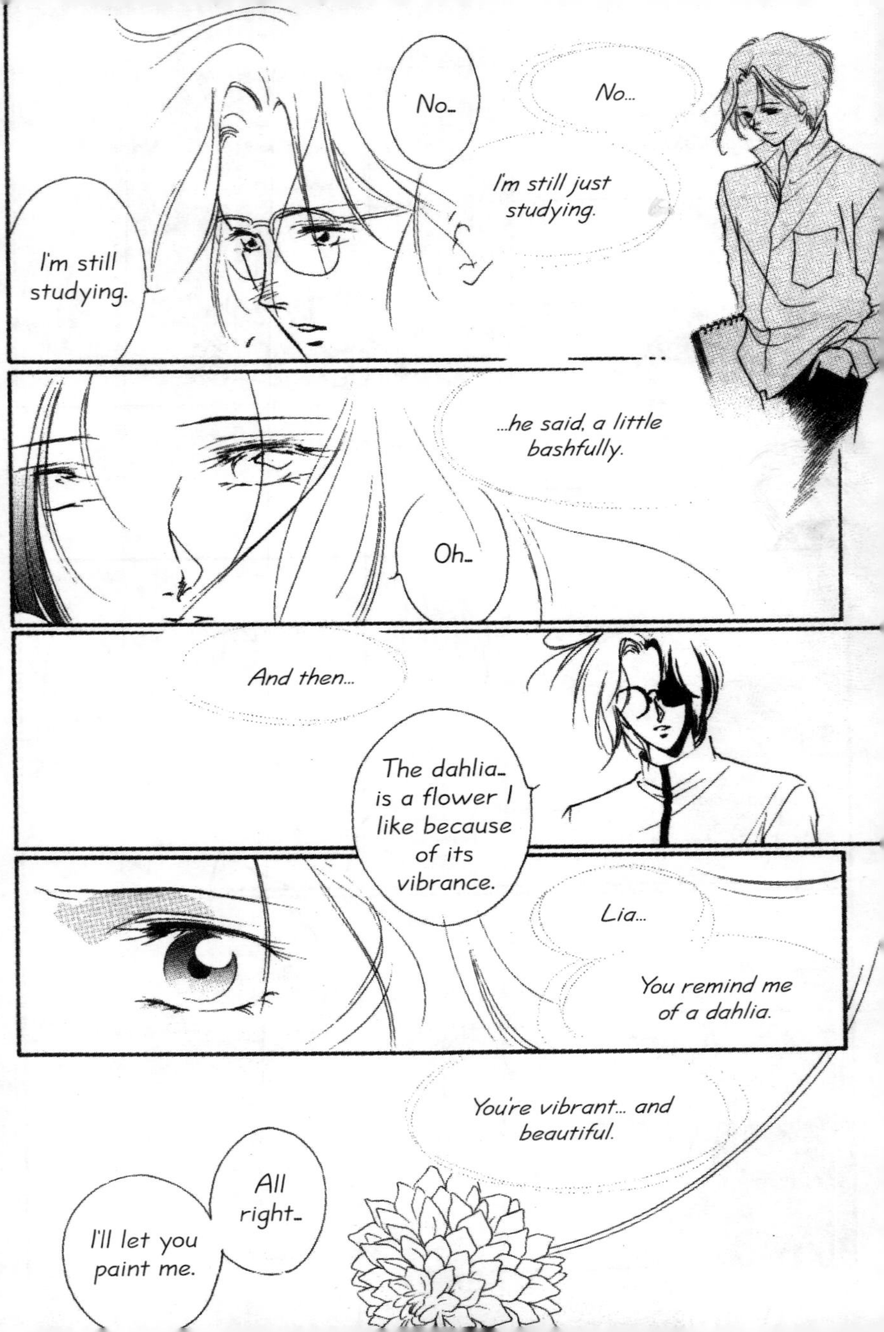
No...
No...
I'm still just studying.
I'm still studying.
...he said, a little bashfully.
Oh...
And then...
The dahlia... is a flower I like because of its vibrance.
Lia...
You remind me of a dahlia.
You're vibrant... and beautiful.
All right...
I'll let you paint me.

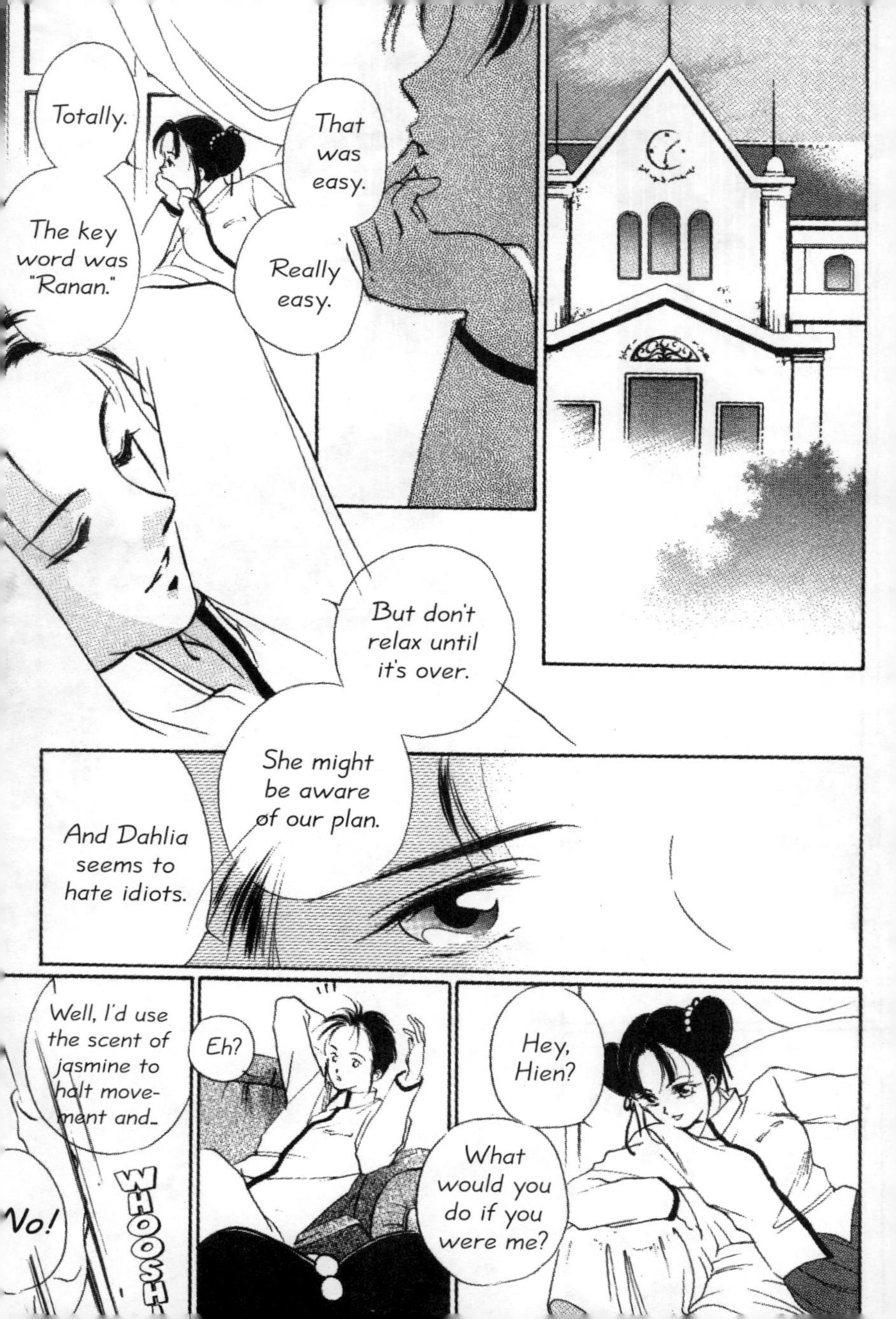
Totally.
The key word was "Ranan."
That was easy.
Really easy.
But don't relax until it's over.
She might be aware of our plan.
And Dahlia seems to hate idiots.
Hey, Hien?
What would you do if you were me?
Eh?
Well, I'd use the scent of jasmine to halt movement and...
WHOOSH
No!

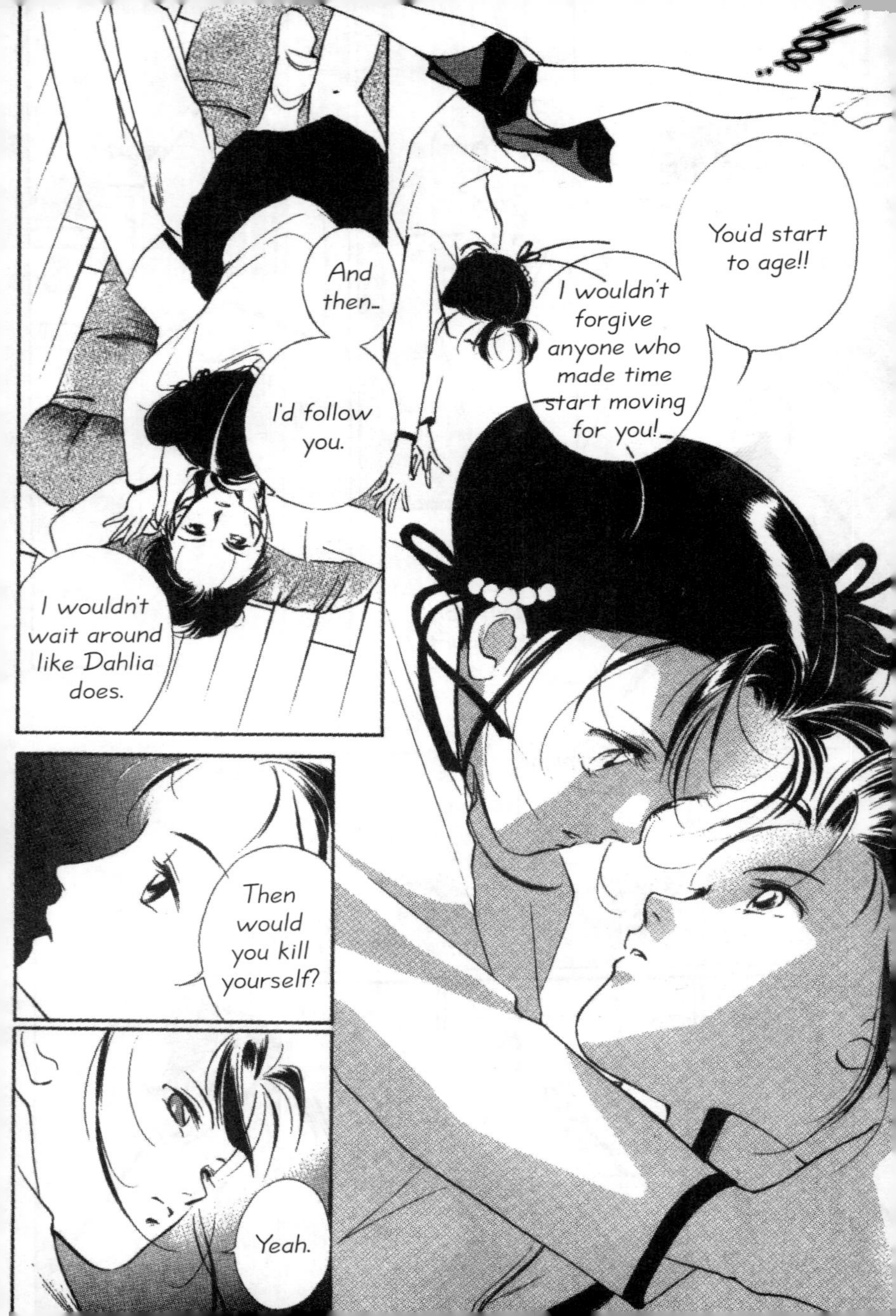
Hoo..
You'd start to age!!
I wouldn't forgive anyone who made time start moving for you!..
And then..
I'd follow you.
I wouldn't wait around like Dahlia does.
Then would you kill yourself?
Yeah.

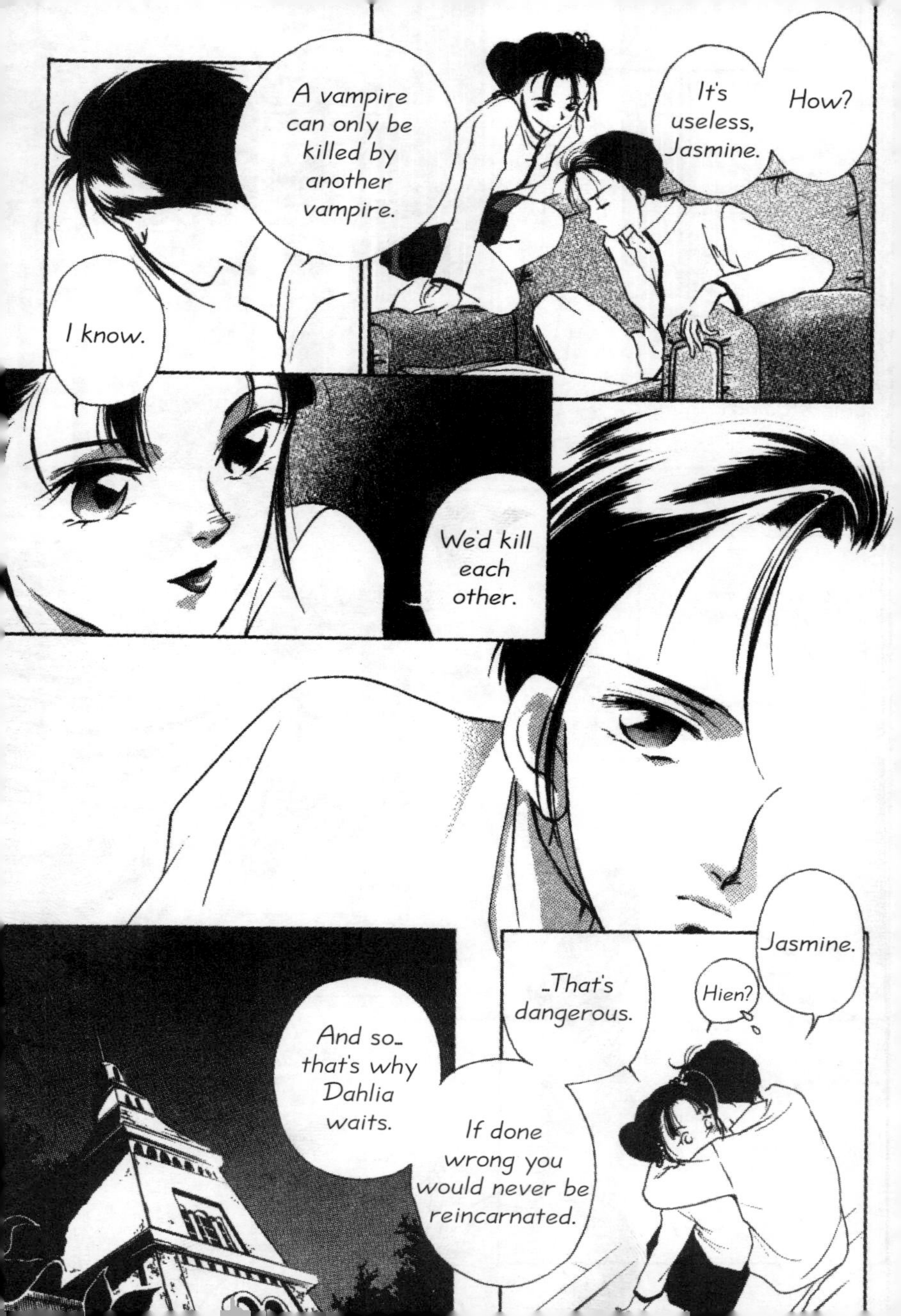
How?
It's useless, Jasmine.
A vampire can only be killed by another vampire.
I know.
We'd kill each other.
Jasmine.
Hien?
...That's dangerous.
If done wrong you would never be reincarnated.
And so... that's why Dahlia waits.

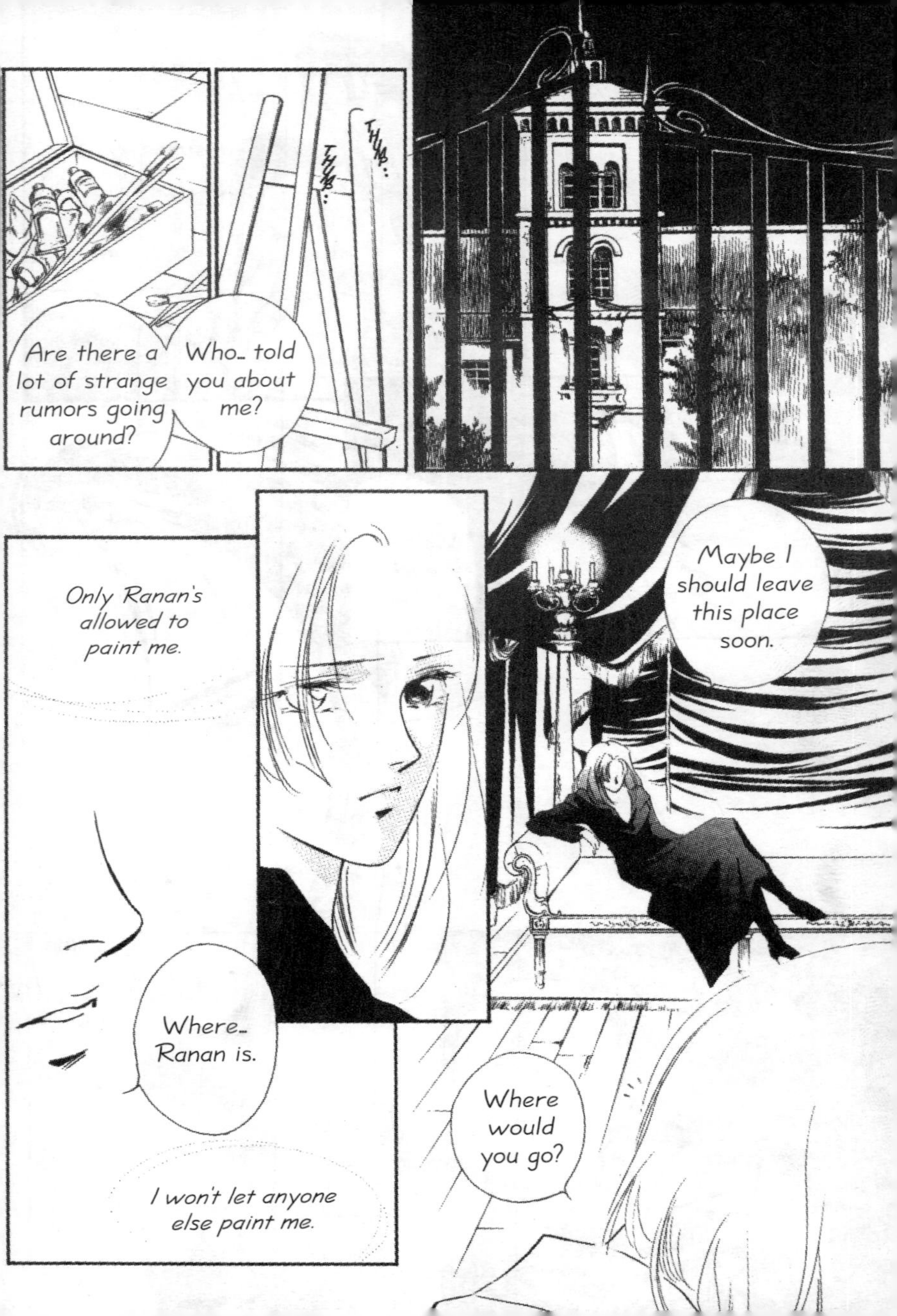

Are there a lot of strange rumors going around?
Who.. told you about me?
Maybe I should leave this place soon.
Where would you go?
Where.. Ranan is.
Only Ranan's allowed to paint me.
I won't let anyone else paint me.

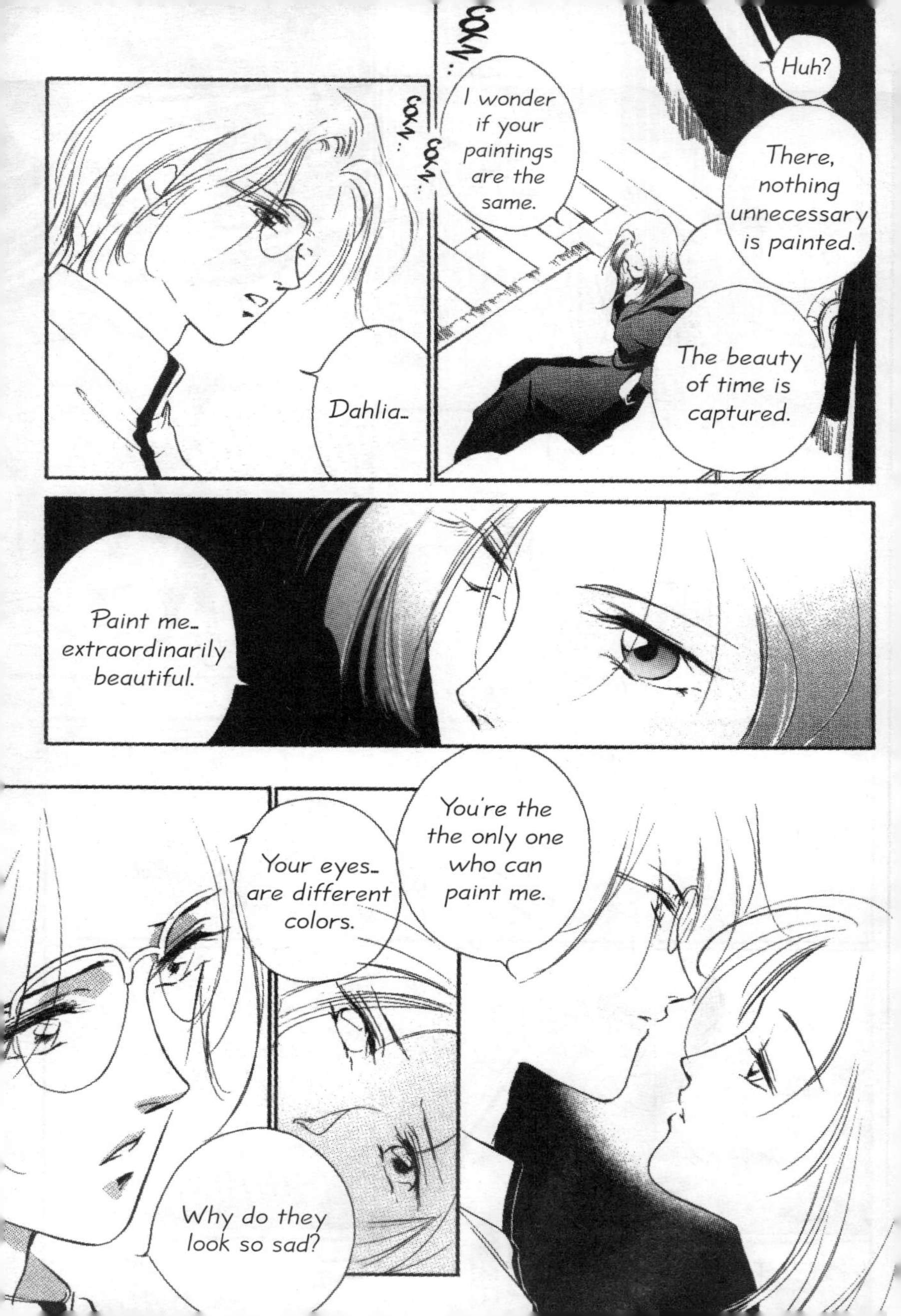
Huh?
There, nothing unnecessary is painted.
The beauty of time is captured.
I wonder if your paintings are the same.
COKN...
COKN...
COKN...
Dahlia...
Paint me... extraordinarily beautiful.
You're the the only one who can paint me.
Your eyes... are different colors.
Why do they look so sad?

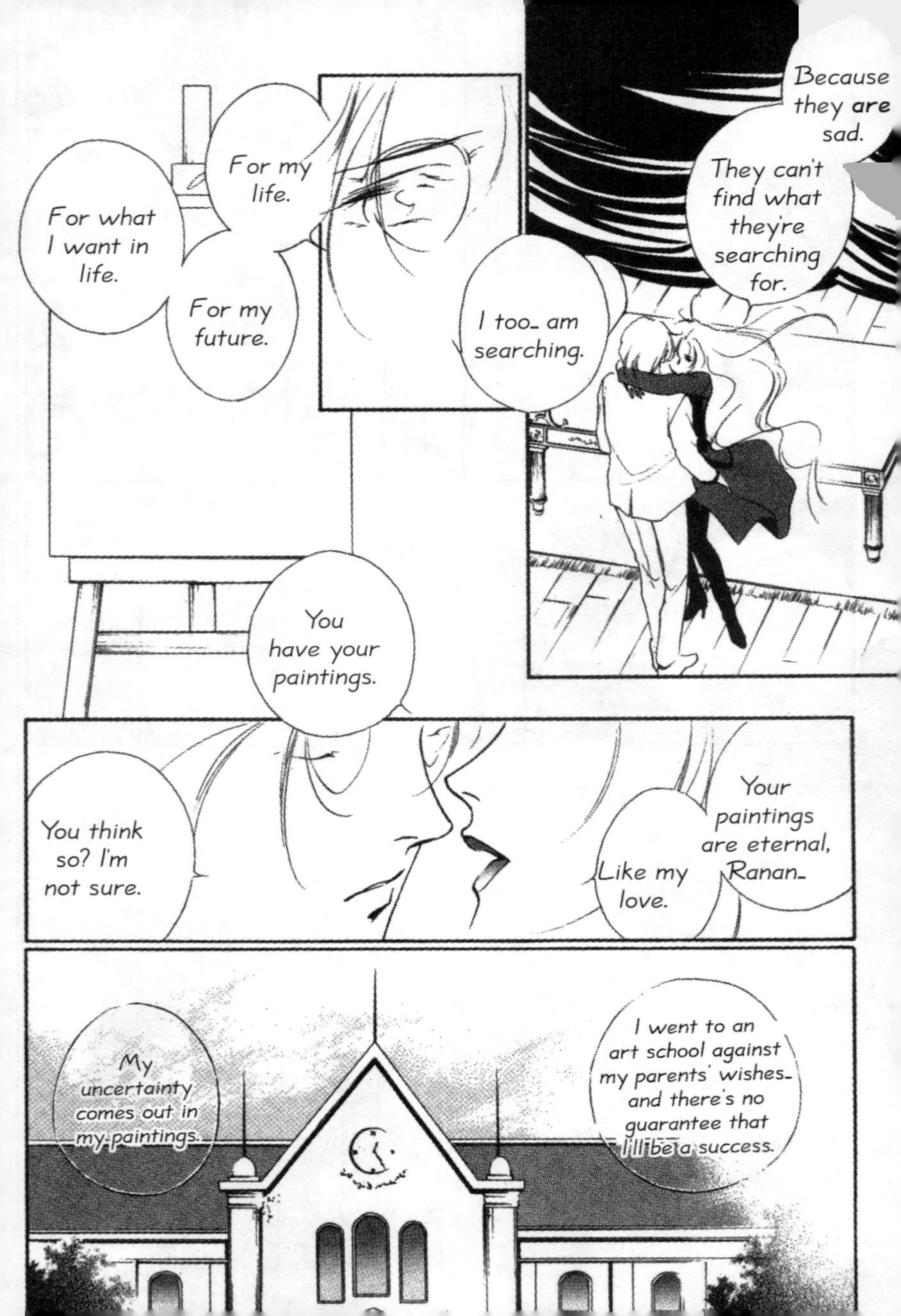
Because they are sad.
They can't find what they're searching for.
I too... am searching.
For my life.
For what I want in life.
For my future.
You have your paintings.
Your paintings are eternal, Ranan...
Like my love.
You think so? I'm not sure.
I went to an art school against my parents' wishes... and there's no guarantee that I'll be a success.
My uncertainty comes out in my paintings...

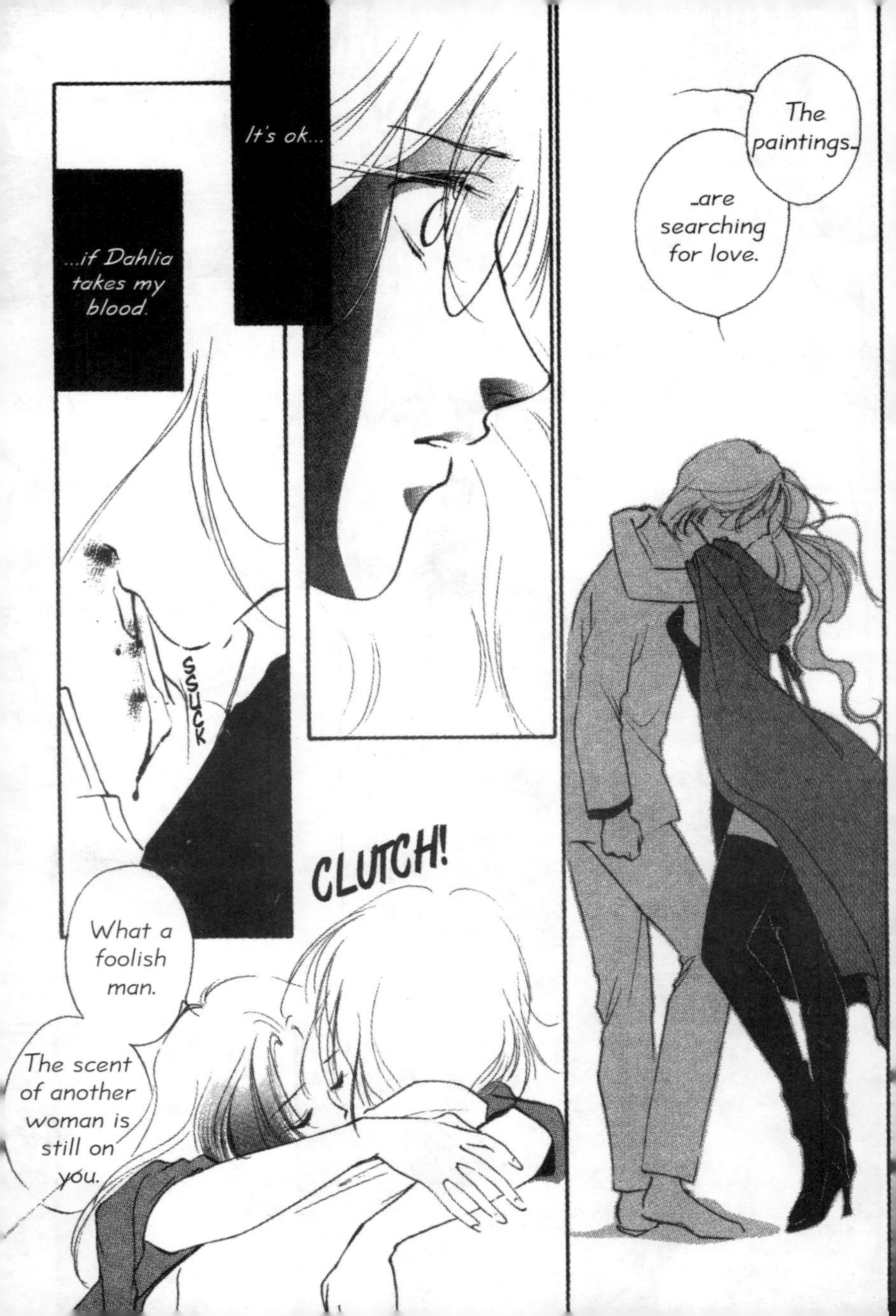
The paintings...
...are searching for love.
It's ok...
...if Dahlia takes my blood.
SSUCK
CLUTCH!
What a foolish man.
The scent of another woman is still on you.

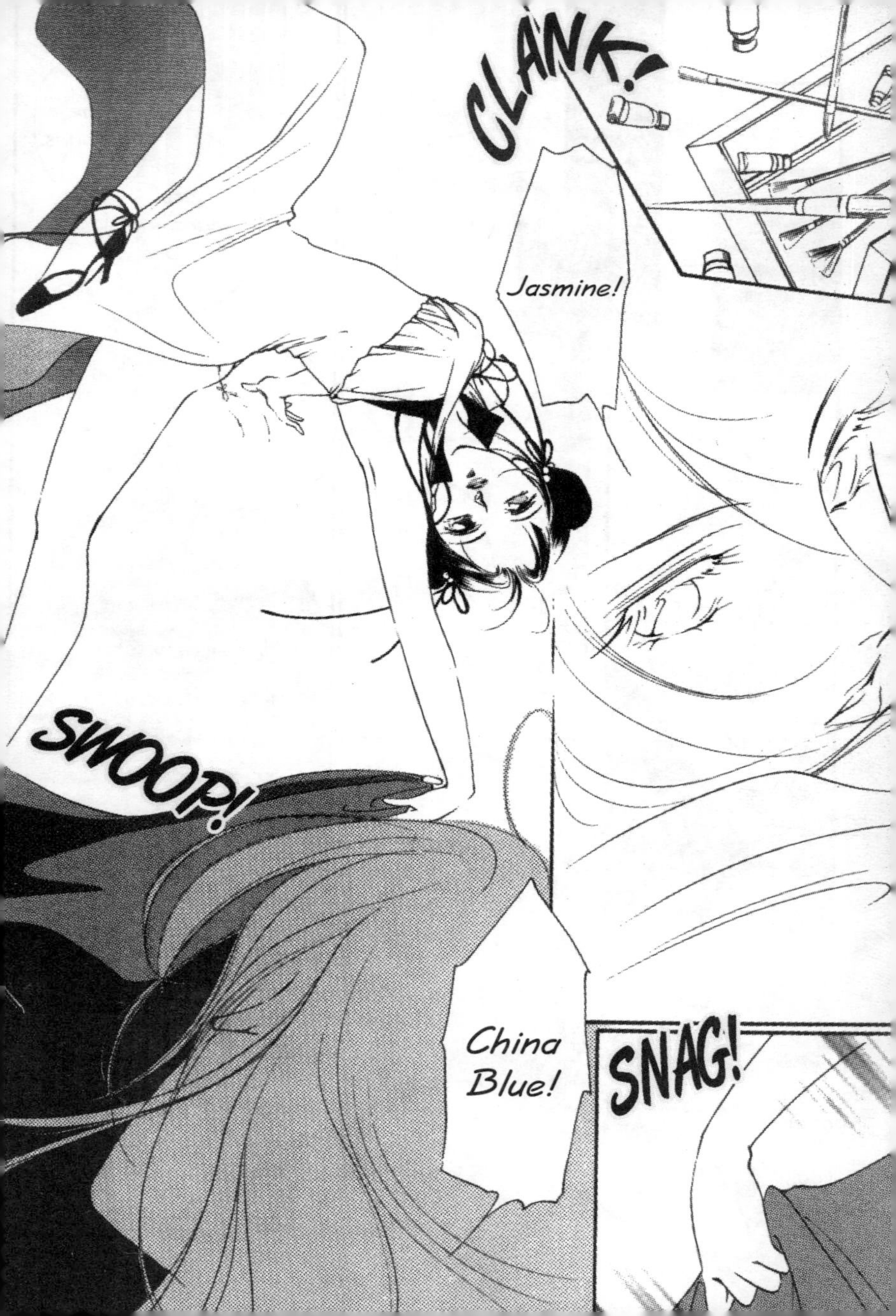
CLANK!
Jasmine!
SWOOP!
China Blue!
SNAG!

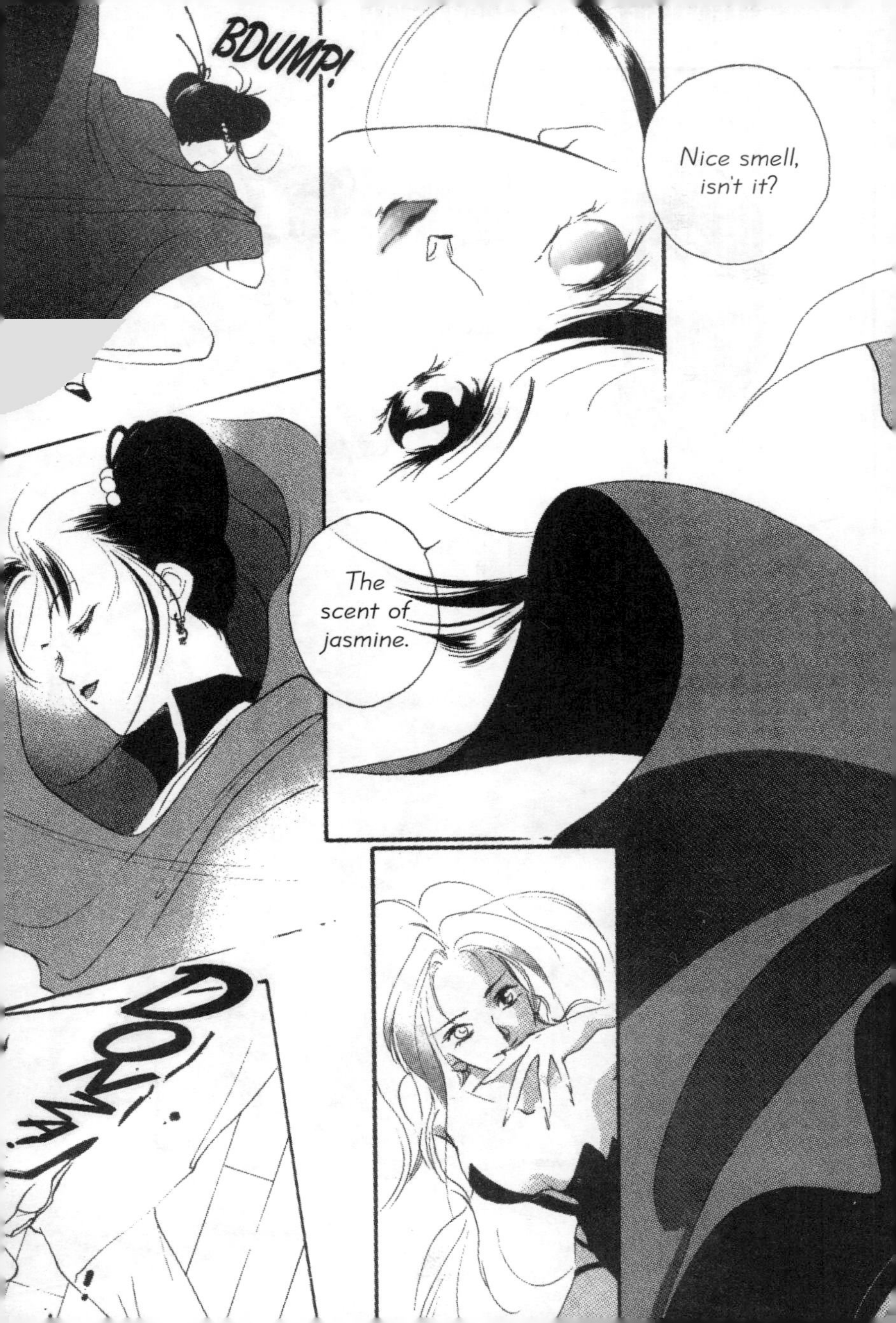

BDUMP!
Nice smell, isn't it?
The scent of jasmine.
DOWN!

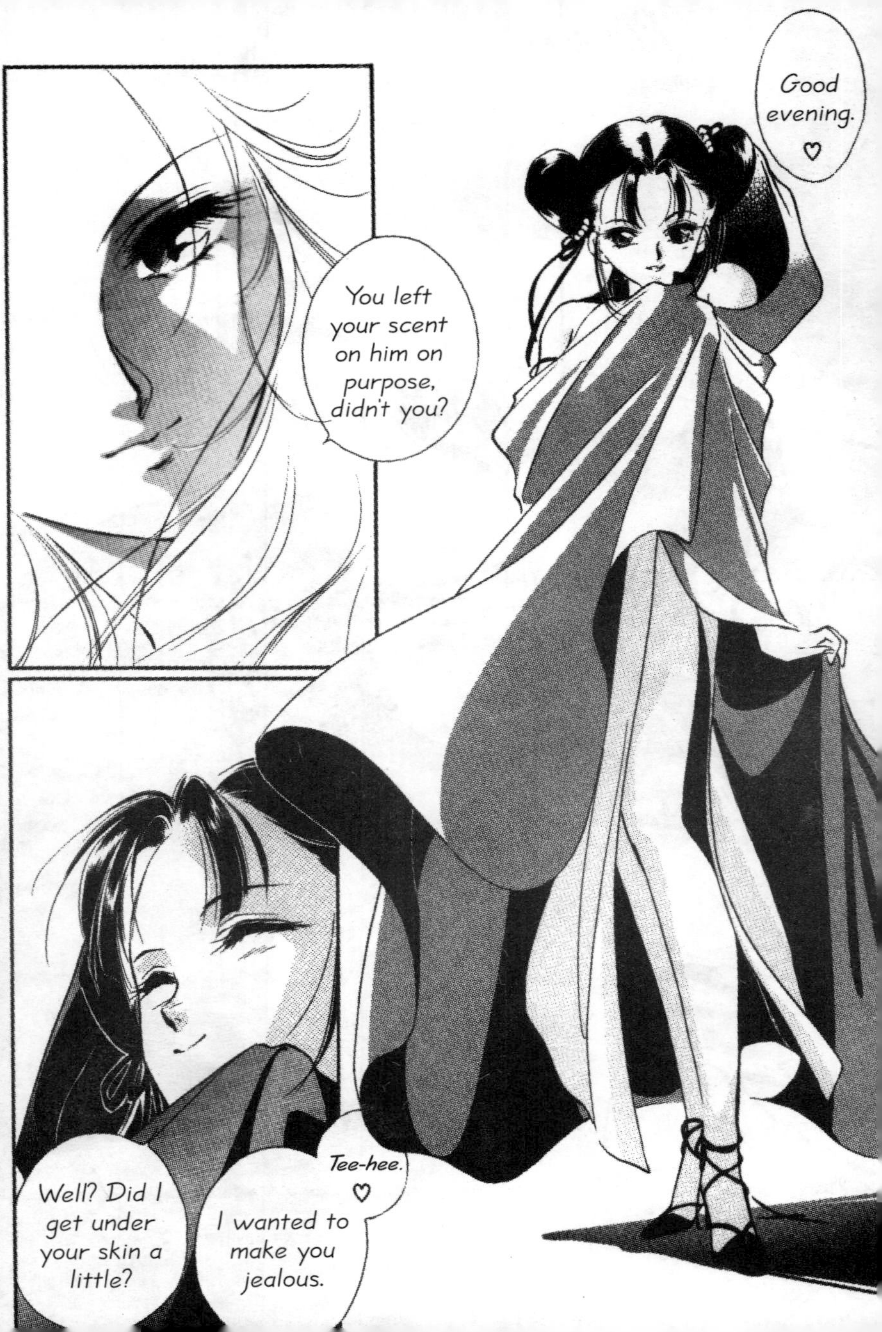
Good evening. ♡
You left your scent on him on purpose, didn't you?
Tee-hee. ♡
I wanted to make you jealous.
Well? Did I get under your skin a little?

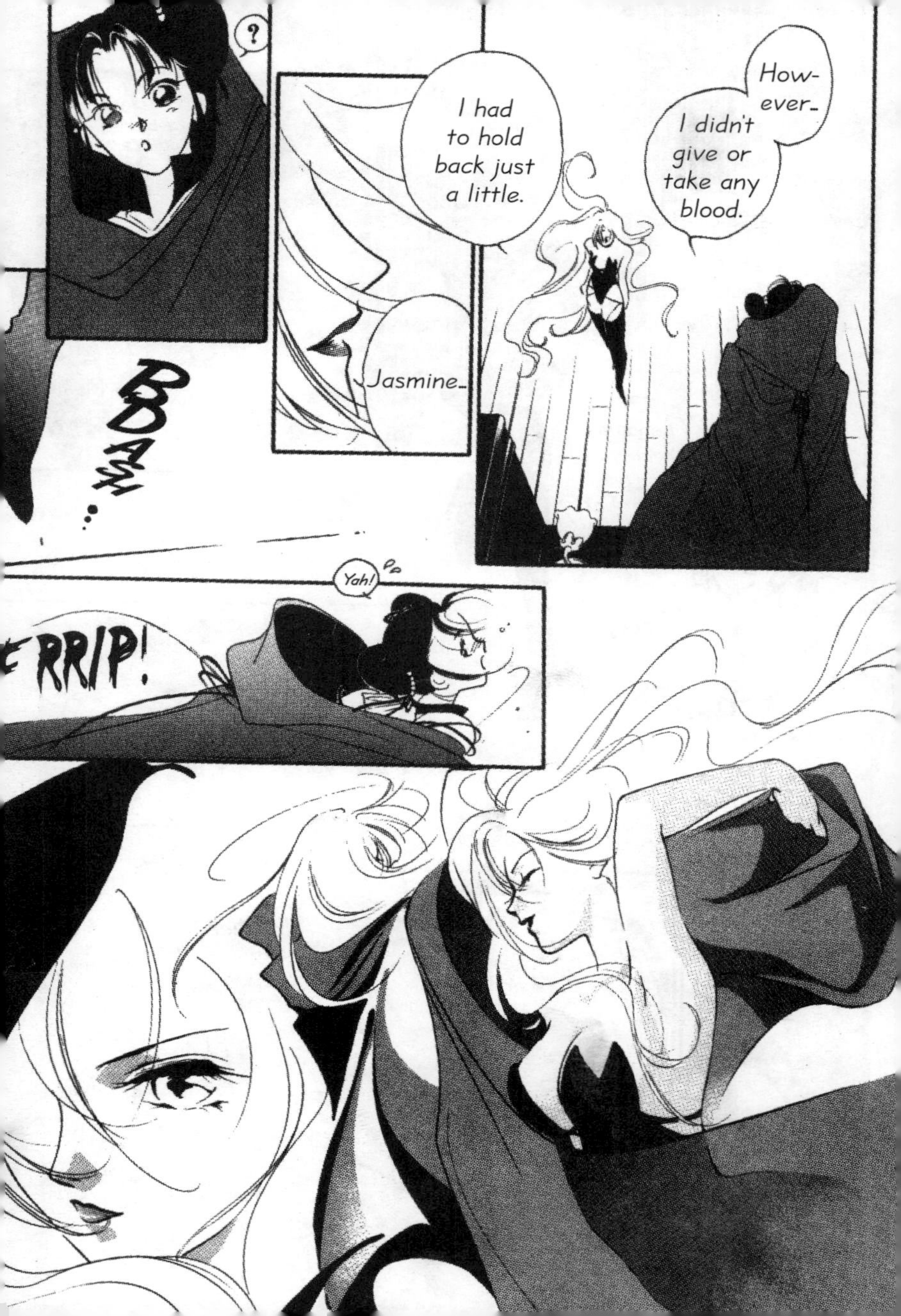

How-ever...
I didn't give or take any blood.
I had to hold back just a little.
Jasmine...
?
BBASH
Yah!
RRIP!

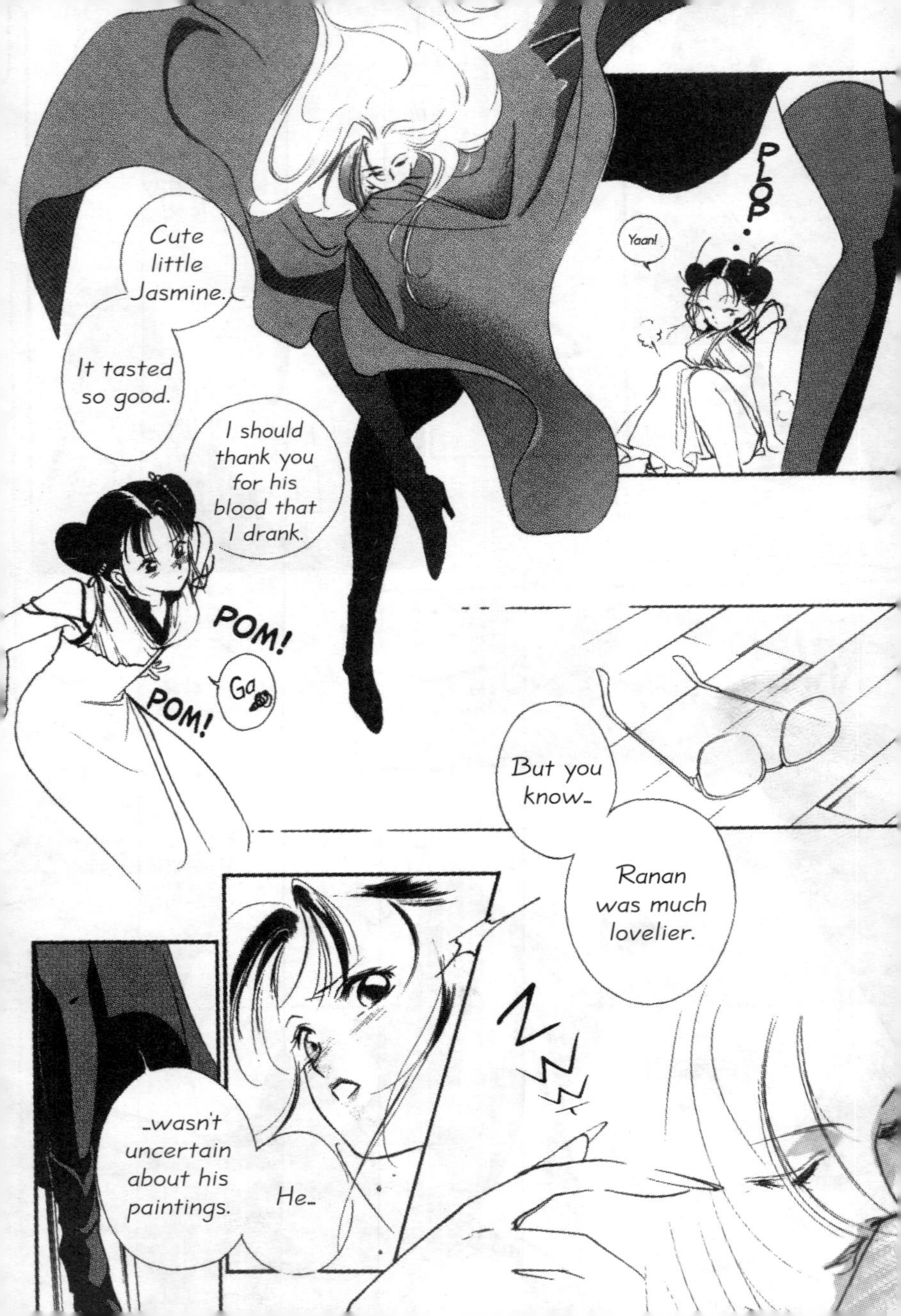
Cute little Jasmine.
It tasted so good.
I should thank you for his blood that I drank.
PLOP..
Yaan!
POM!
Ga
POM!
But you know..
Ranan was much lovelier.
He..
..wasn't uncertain about his paintings.

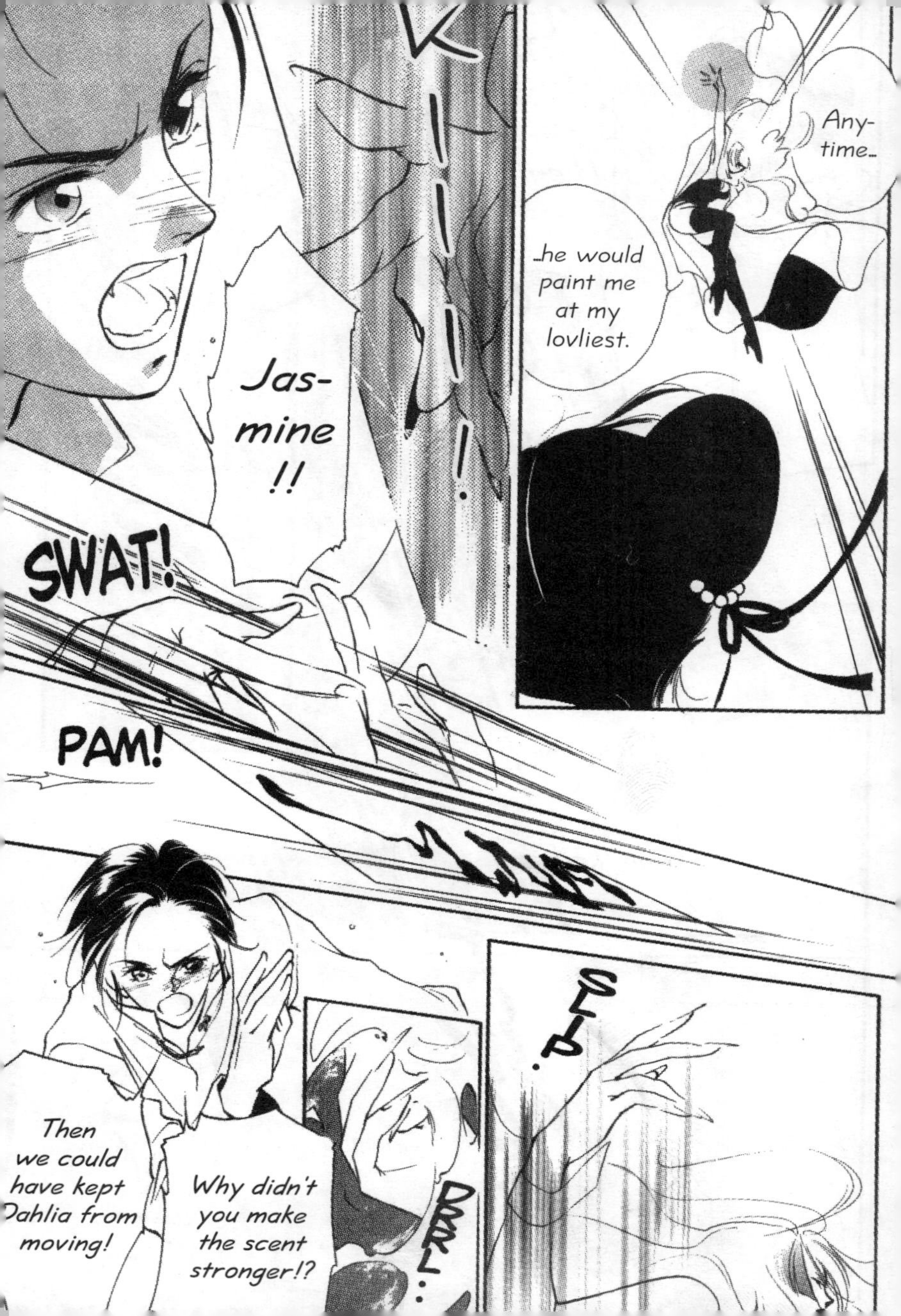

Any-time...
...he would paint me at my lovliest.
Jas-mine!!
SWAT!
PAM!
SLIP.
DRRL..
Why didn't you make the scent stronger!?
Then we could have kept Dahlia from moving!

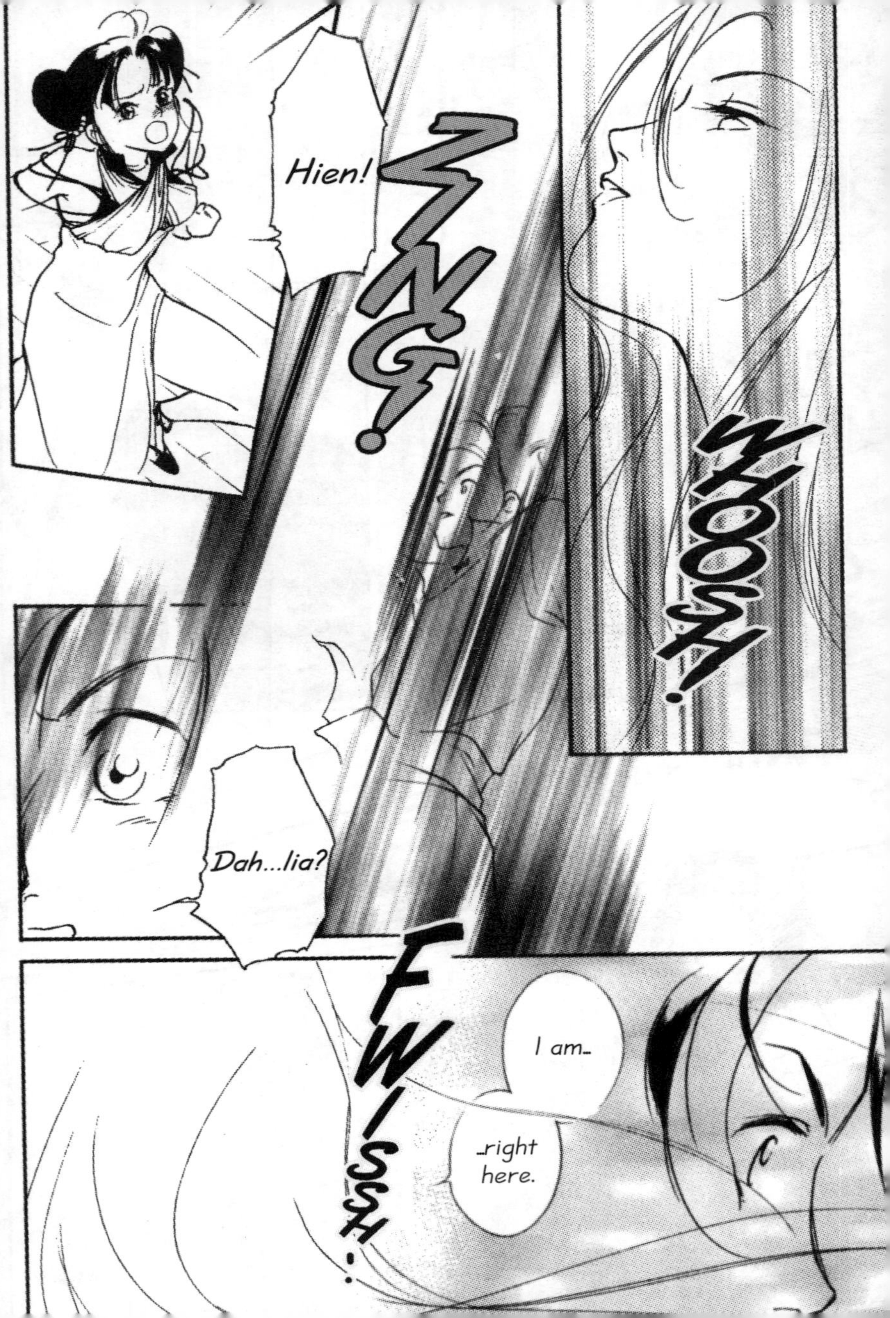
WHOOSH!
Hien!
Dah...lia?
FWISSH..
I am...
...right here.

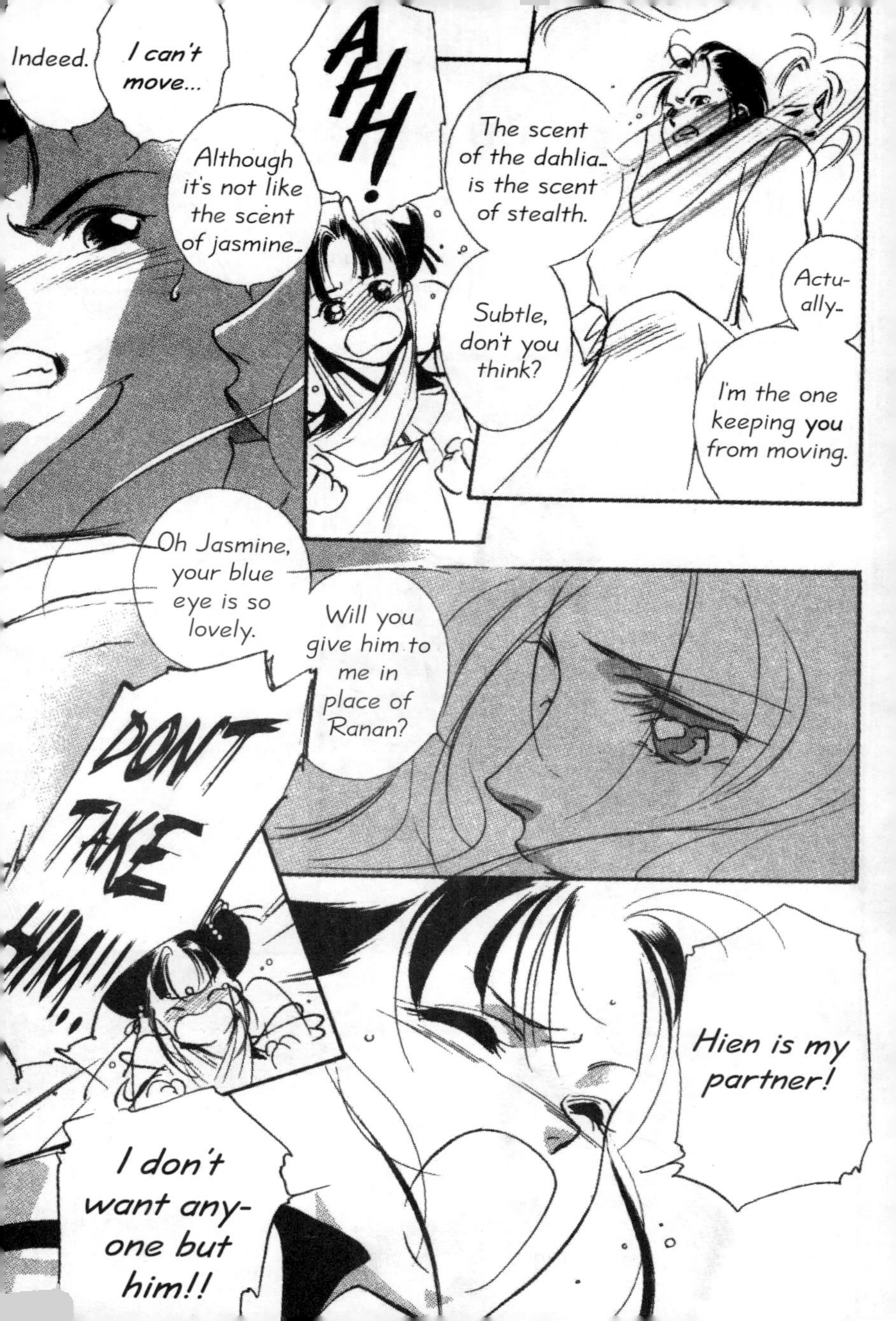

The scent of the dahlia... is the scent of stealth.
Subtle, don't you think?
Actu-ally...
I'm the one keeping **you** from moving.
AHH!
Although it's not like the scent of jasmine...
I can't move...
Indeed.
Oh Jasmine, your blue eye is so lovely.
Will you give him to me in place of Ranan?
DON'T TAKE HIM!!...
Hien is my partner!
I don't want any-one but him!!

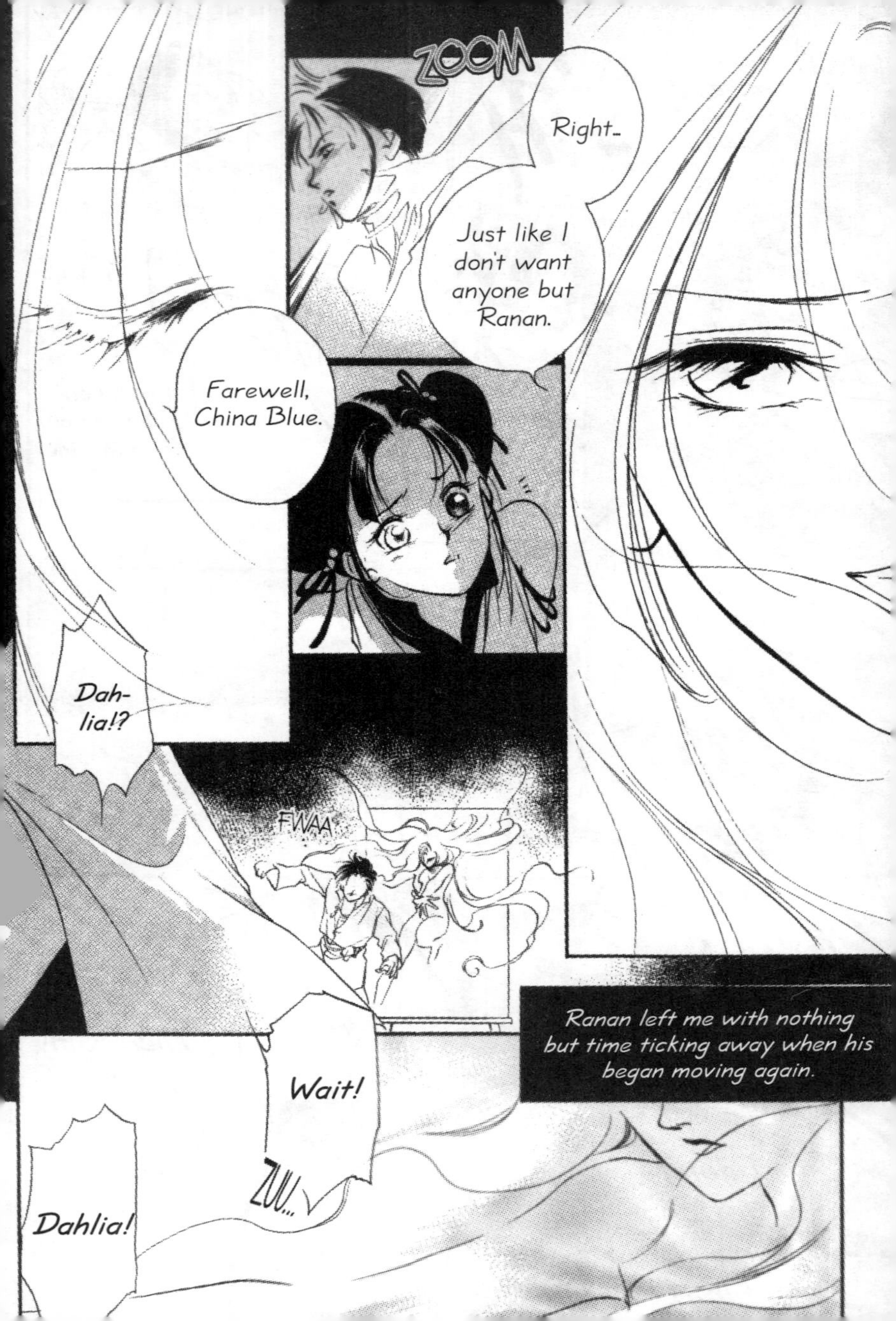
ZOOM
Right..
Just like I don't want anyone but Ranan.
Farewell, China Blue.
Dah-lia!?
FWAA
Ranan left me with nothing but time ticking away when his began moving again.
Wait!
ZUU...
Dahlia!

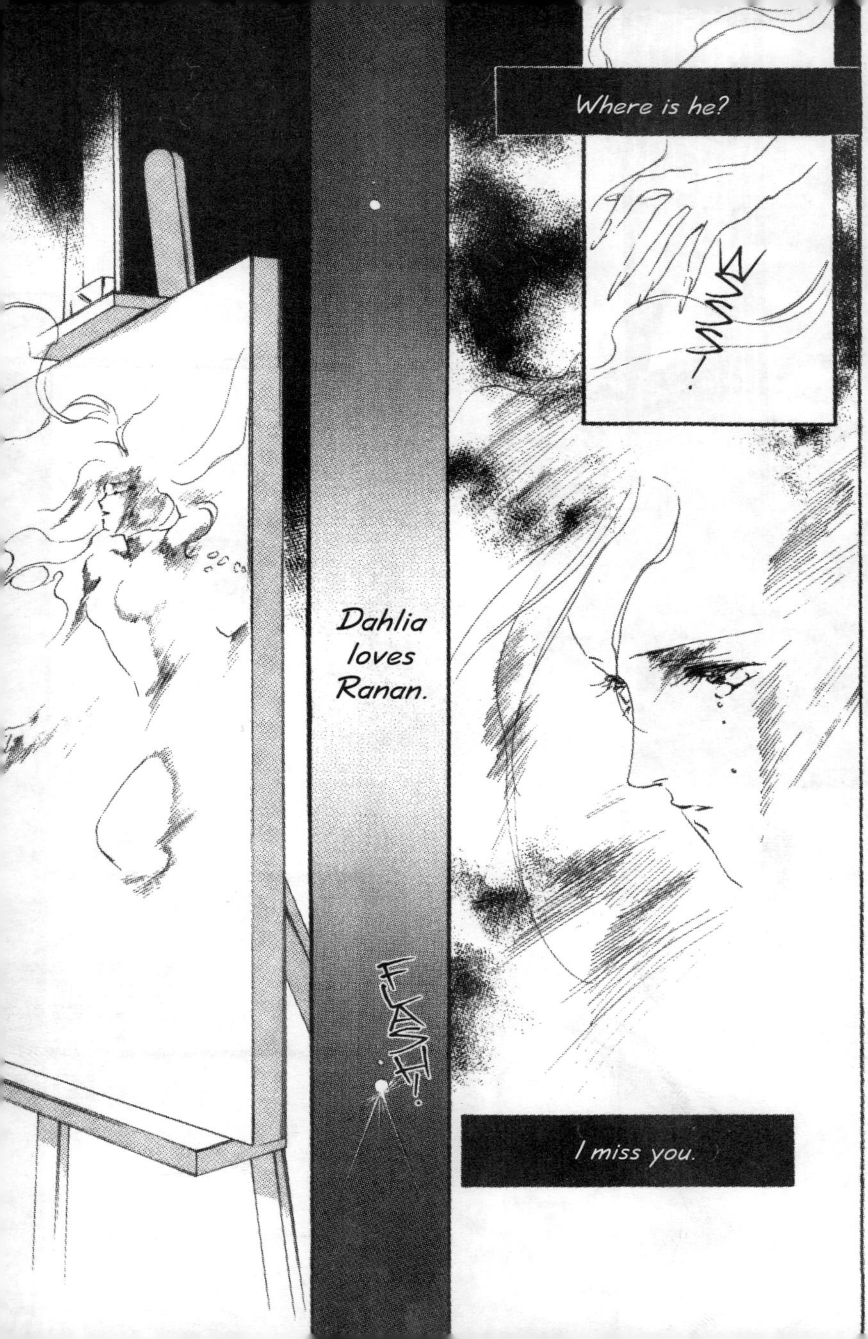

Where is he?
WSSS!
I miss you.
Dahlia loves Ranan.
FLASH!

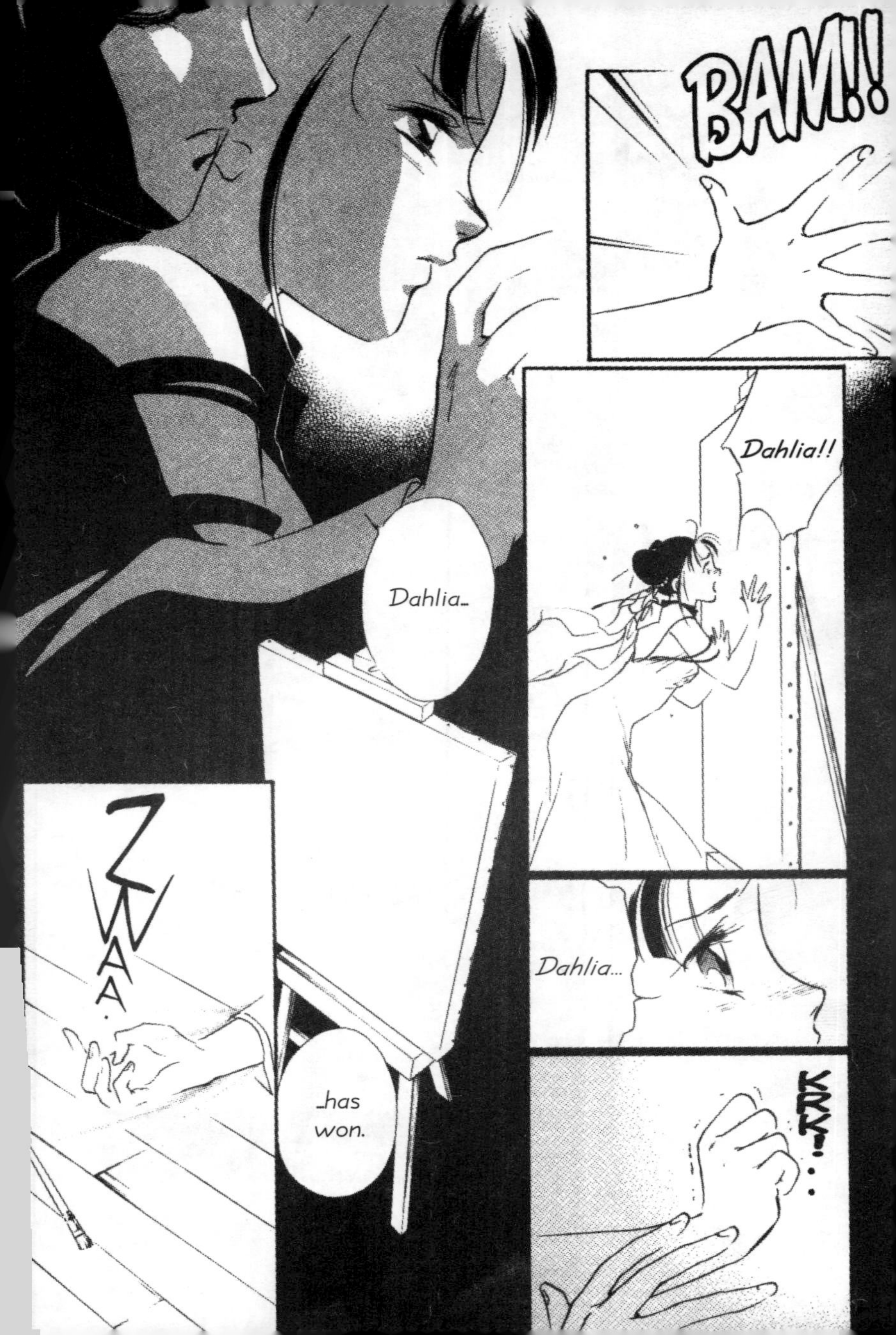
BAM!!
Dahlia!!
Dahlia...
Dahlia...
..has won.
ZWAA.
KRK!..

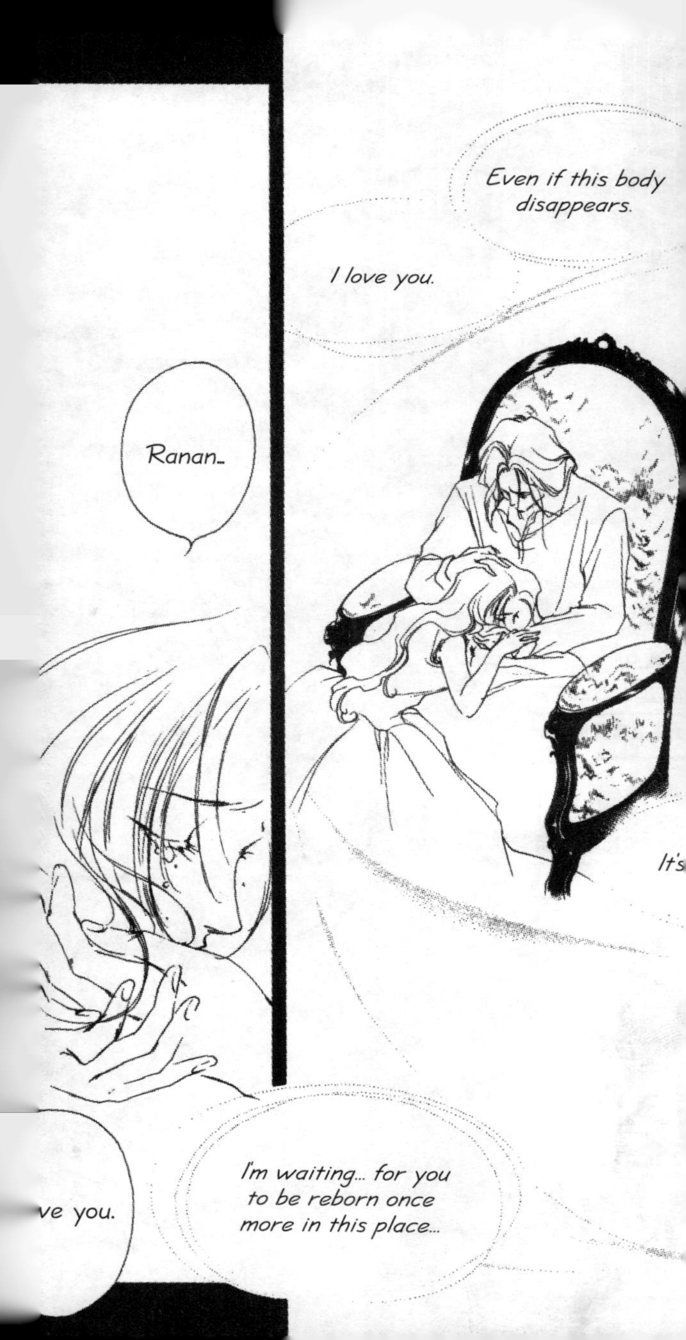
Even if this body disappears.
I love you.
Ranan...
It's
ve you.
I'm waiting... for you to be reborn once more in this place...

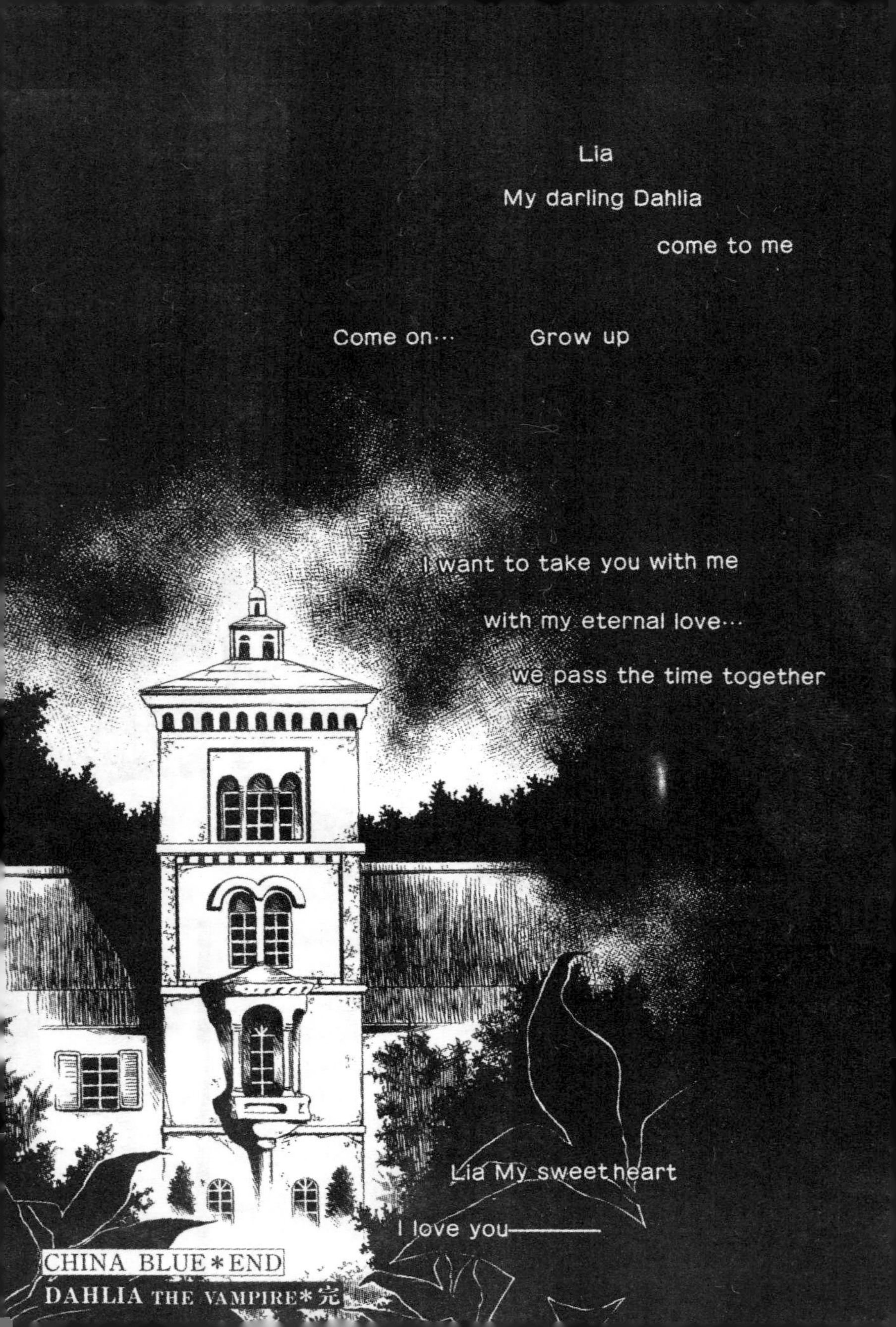

Lia
My darling Dahlia
come to me
Come on··· Grow up
I want to take you with me
with my eternal love···
we pass the time together
Lia My sweetheart
I love you———
CHINA BLUE＊END
DAHLIA THE VAMPIRE＊完

Dahlia Club

ダリア
クラブ

By Narumi Kakinouch

I tried dealing with a vampire girl a bit more ~~erotic~~ mature than Miyu or Yui... So how did it go over?

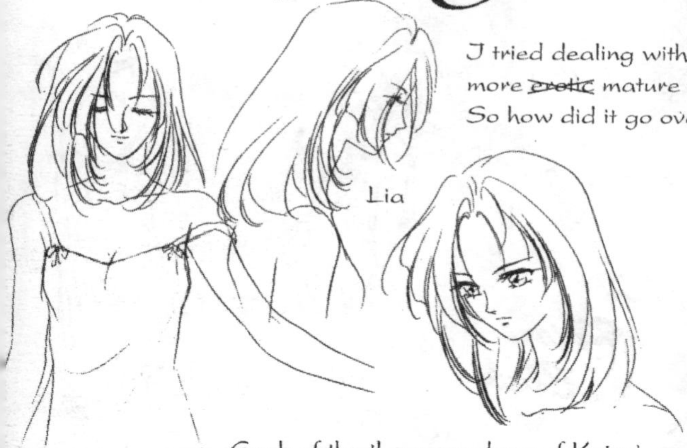
Lia

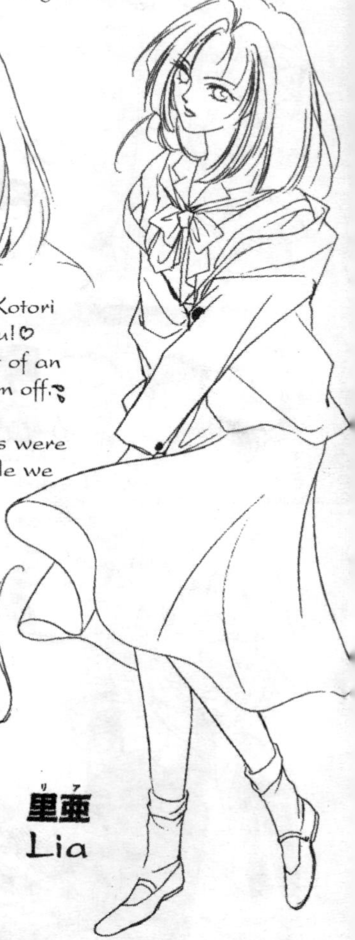

Each of the three members of Kotori Club drew for me, one after the other. Thank you! ♡
We tried giving the character designs somewhat of an anime feel. Heheh... Sorry for killing most of them off.
But hey, the only one Dahlia needs is Ranan...
This was "Dahlia the Vampire," in which the girls were much more vital than the boys. But honestly, while we were developing the story, I was thinking it's rather sad.

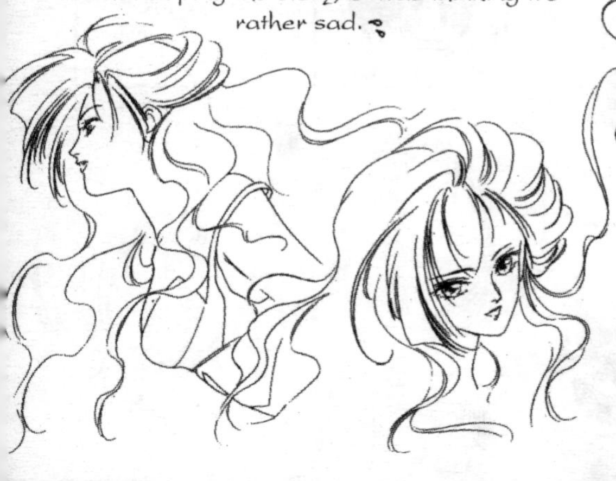

里亜（リア）
Lia

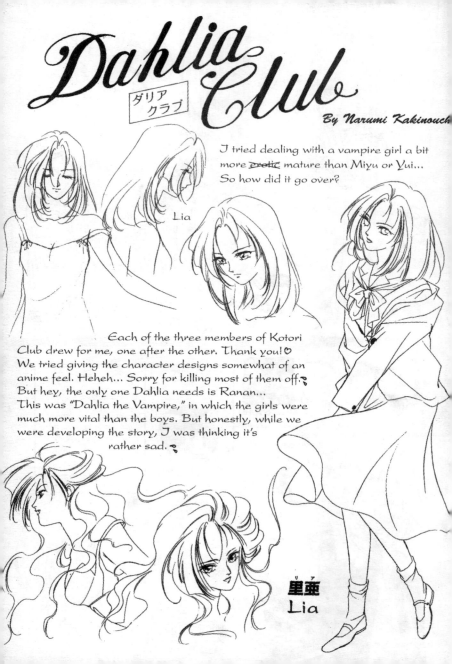

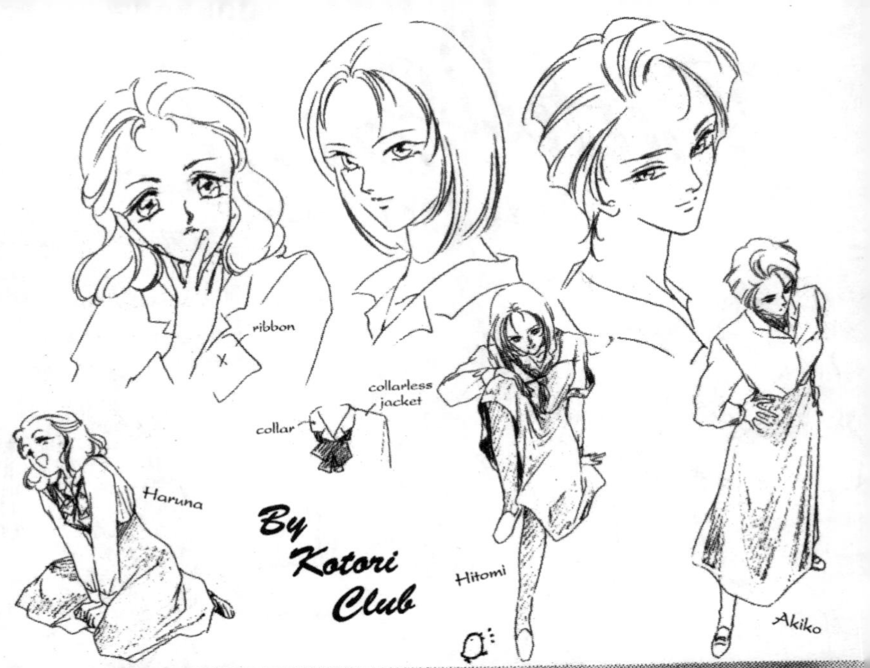
ribbon
collarless jacket
collar
Haruna
By Kotori Club
Hitomi
Akiko

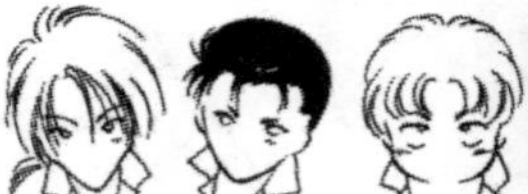

AFTERWORD

Originally, trying to draw on Mrs. Kakinouchi's level was pretty difficult. (I was afraid of reactions from readers, too...). Somehow or other, this ended at some point, but I think it was a very good experience. It was fun drawing Hitomi, but to be honest, it was more fun drawing the three guys who tag along with her.

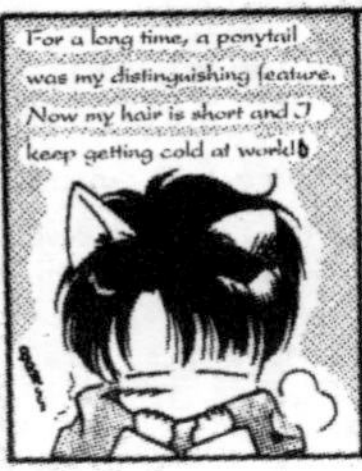
For a long time, a ponytail was my distinguishing feature. Now my hair is short and I keep getting cold at work!

Akiko Hosoya

Born December 14th.
Blood type A.
She loves speed lines and sketching. At the moment, she is the longest running of the assistants.

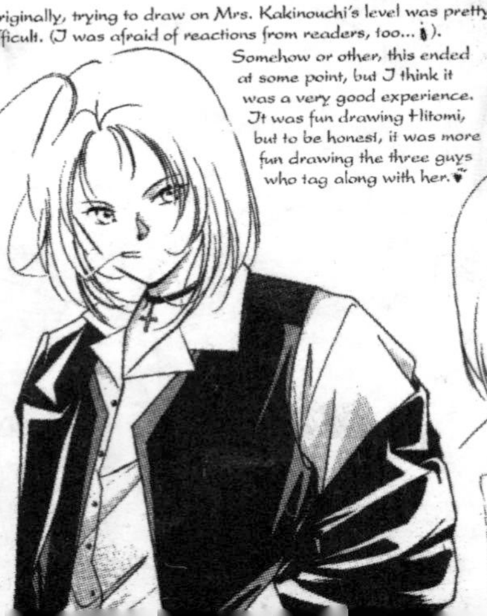

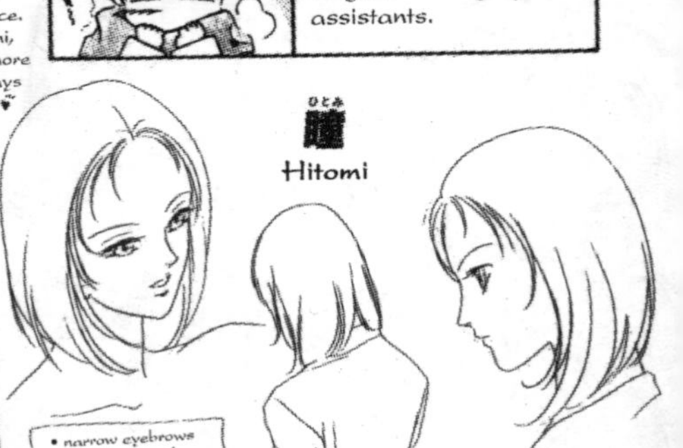
ひとみ
瞳
Hitomi

- narrow eyebrows
- slightly almond-shaped eyes
- leader of the three girls
- slim nose ridge

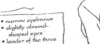

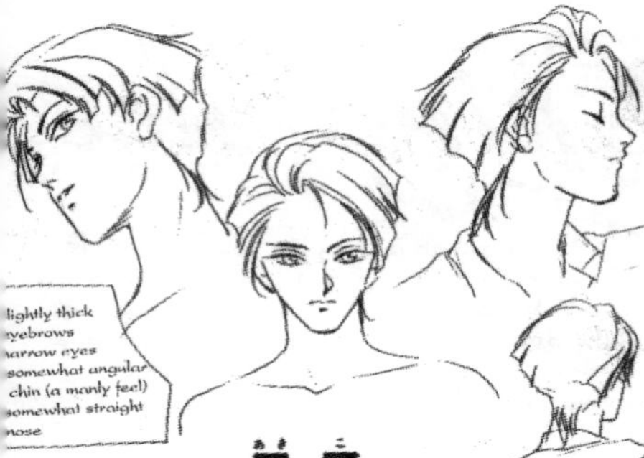
lightly thick eyebrows
narrow eyes
somewhat angular chin (a manly feel)
somewhat straight nose

By the way, sometimes within the book, Mrs. Kakinouchi drew Akiko. Now where would that be?

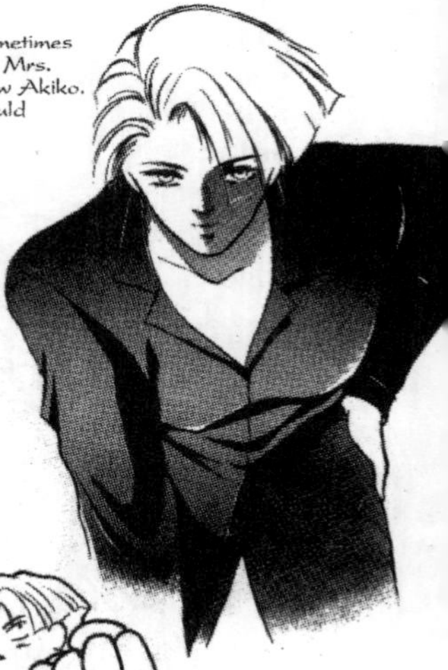

晃子
Akiko

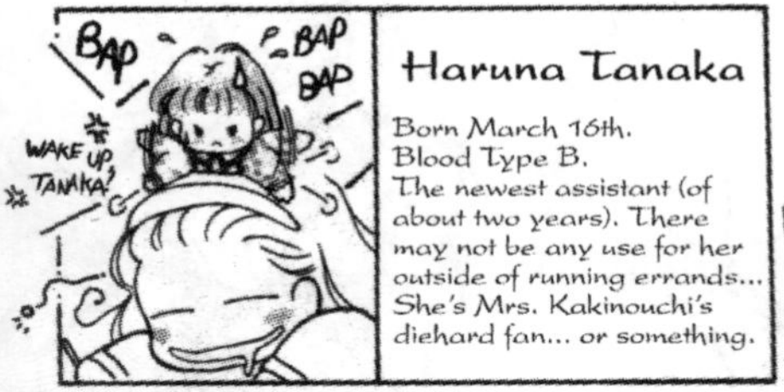
BAP
BAP
BAP
WAKE UP, TANAKA!

Haruna Tanaka

Born March 16th.
Blood Type B.
The newest assistant (of about two years). There may not be any use for her outside of running errands... She's Mrs. Kakinouchi's diehard fan... or something.

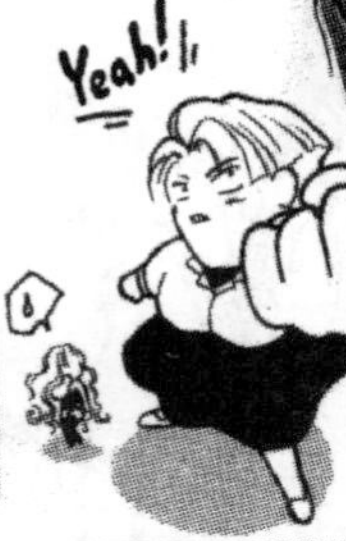
Yeah!

If Akiko didn't seem manly all, that's my fault. I'm rec ering her... It's too bad she She was very close to her frien That's rare among Mrs. Kakinou female characters, so I'd like to her appear again in another story

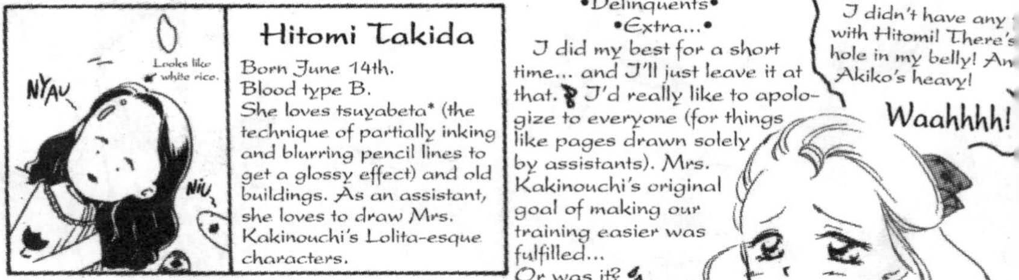
Looks like white rice.
NYAU
NIU

Hitomi Takida

Born June 14th.
Blood type B.
She loves tsuyabeta* (the technique of partially inking and blurring pencil lines to get a glossy effect) and old buildings. As an assistant, she loves to draw Mrs. Kakinouchi's Lolita-esque characters.

•Background•
•Delinquents•
•Extra...•

I did my best for a short time... and I'll just leave it at that. I'd really like to apologize to everyone (for things like pages drawn solely by assistants). Mrs. Kakinouchi's original goal of making our training easier was fulfilled...
Or was it?

I didn't have any with Hitomi! There's hole in my belly! An Akiko's heavy!

春菜
Haruna

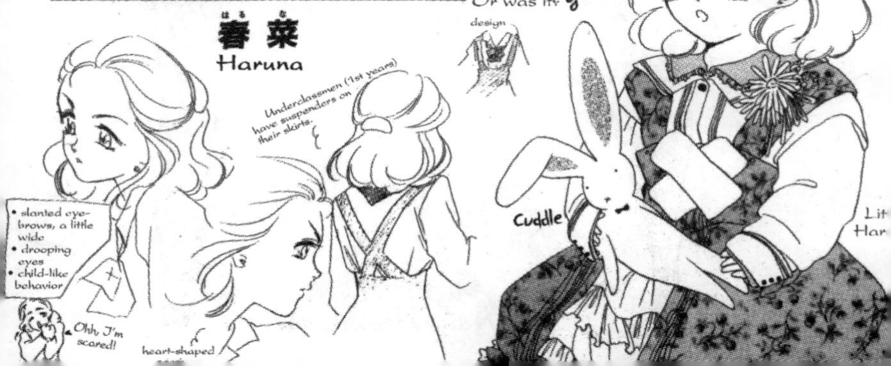
Underclassmen (1st years) have suspenders on their skirts.
• slanted eyebrows, a little wide
• drooping eyes
• child-like behavior
Ohh, I'm scared!
heart-shaped
design
Waahhhh!
Cuddle
Lit
Har

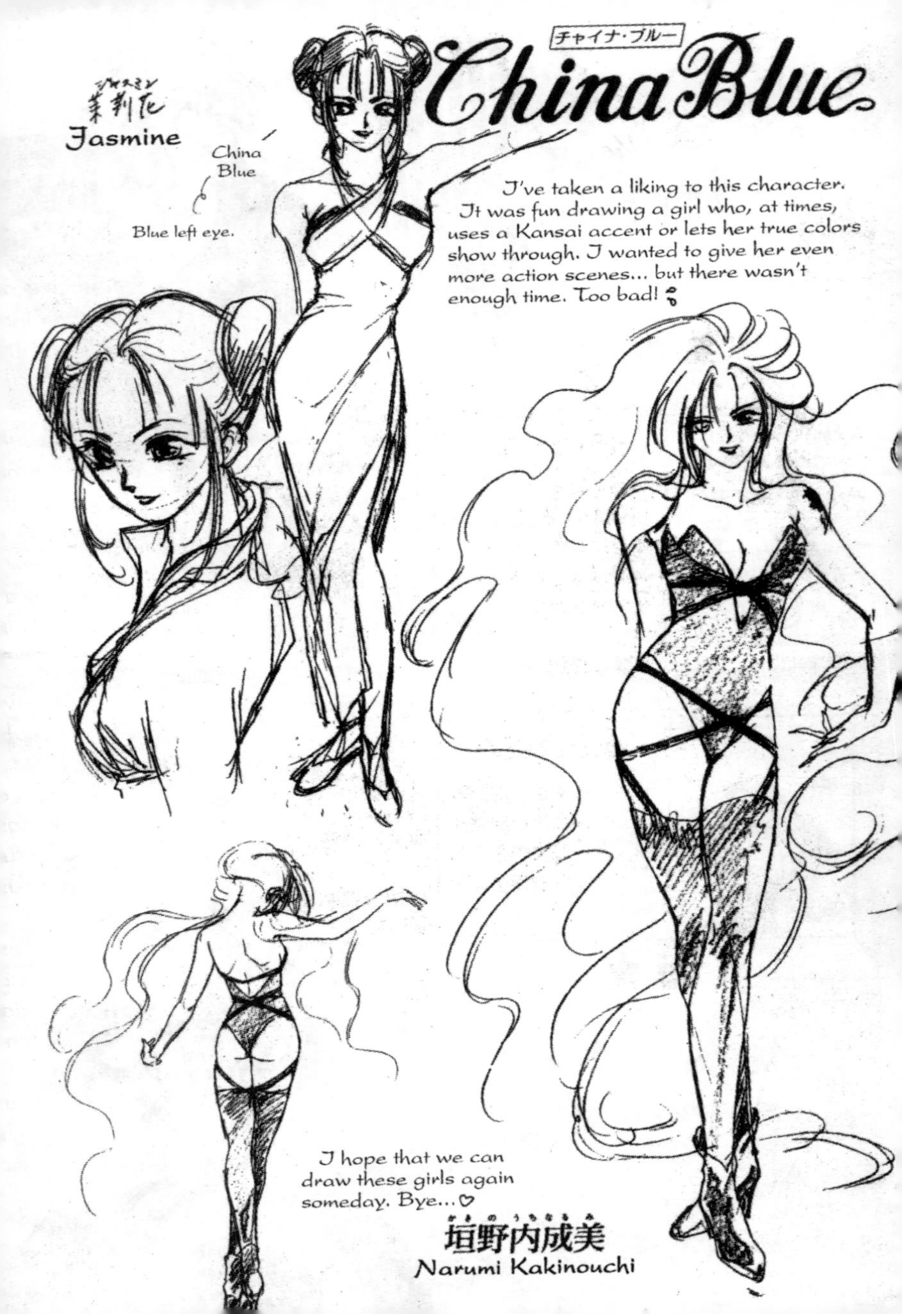

チャイナ・ブルー
China Blue
ジャスミン
茉莉花
Jasmine
China Blue
Blue left eye.
I've taken a liking to this character. It was fun drawing a girl who, at times, uses a Kansai accent or lets her true colors show through. I wanted to give her even more action scenes... but there wasn't enough time. Too bad!
I hope that we can draw these girls again someday. Bye...♡
垣野内成美
Narumi Kakinouchi

Dahlia

"The girl who kisses in the dark."

Interview with Ryuuichi Hiroki (film director):

I won't make some haughty claim that this is an original piece of wor among Dracula stories. "Dahlia" is not a story about blood everywhere c someone using a cross. She doesn't hate garlic either. She has simply bee drawn into the world of the Vampire. As a vampire she is immortal, and it this fate of immortality that has drawn her in. But Dahlia doesn't even reall perceive her own immortality...

Normally, a girl isn't a girl forever. Eventually she grows into an adu woman. Maybe that time is defined by when she first opens her eyes to th experience of love, or maybe it's when she first loses love. Certainly th happens in its own time and season, before she or anyone around her has chance to notice.

I think back to when I was first exposed to love, certainly still as a boy c the time. The pain, excitement, and sadness of that experience are inscribed i my memory. Dahlia takes those feelings that ev eryone goes through as a boy or a girl and sea them within herself. It's the pain of being in love.

It's because Dahlia, as a vampire, must remain girl forever. As a girl, only Dahlia's surrounding change over time. I can't help but think how painf it must be to have to remember things forever c she does.

Certainly, there are no such things as vampire who live forever (though perhaps it's more allurin to think otherwise). So because it's a fantasy worl they can be portrayed at their most beautiful, pair ful, sad, and (conversely) realistic within manga.

However, as a film director, I have to use re people (actors) to express ideas through imagery. the power within that imagery can just be used t capture her immortal memory, I have a feeling th a new heroine, Dahlia, will once more be born.

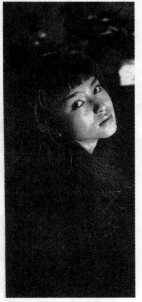

Dahlia's model: Mai Hosho
(Photographer: Sadao Ohkawa)

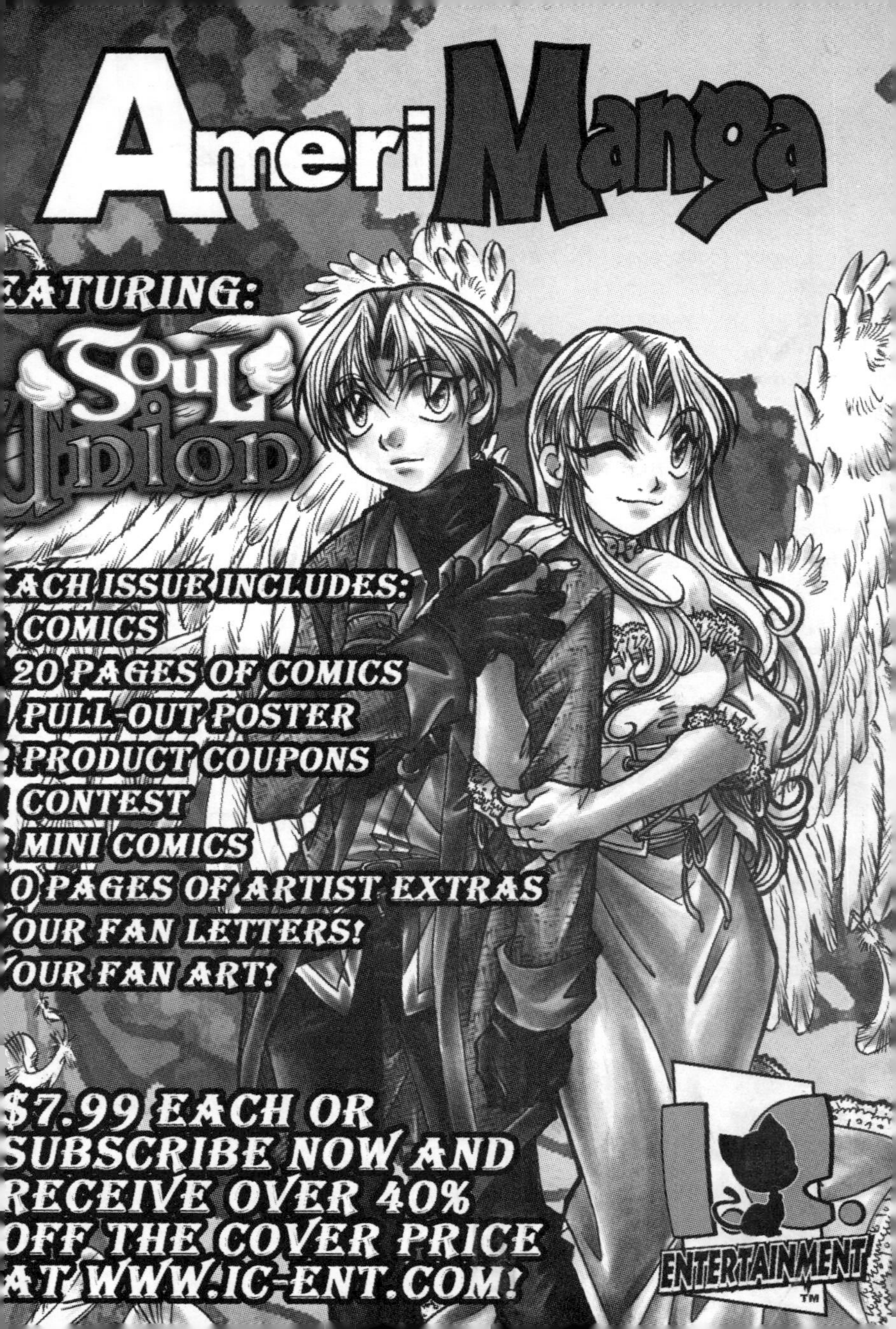

AmeriManga
EATURING:
SOUL
NION
ACH ISSUE INCLUDES:
COMICS
20 PAGES OF COMICS
PULL-OUT POSTER
PRODUCT COUPONS
CONTEST
MINI COMICS
0 PAGES OF ARTIST EXTRAS
OUR FAN LETTERS!
OUR FAN ART!
$7.99 EACH OR
SUBSCRIBE NOW AND
RECEIVE OVER 40%
OFF THE COVER PRICE
AT WWW.IC-ENT.COM!
ENTERTAINMENT

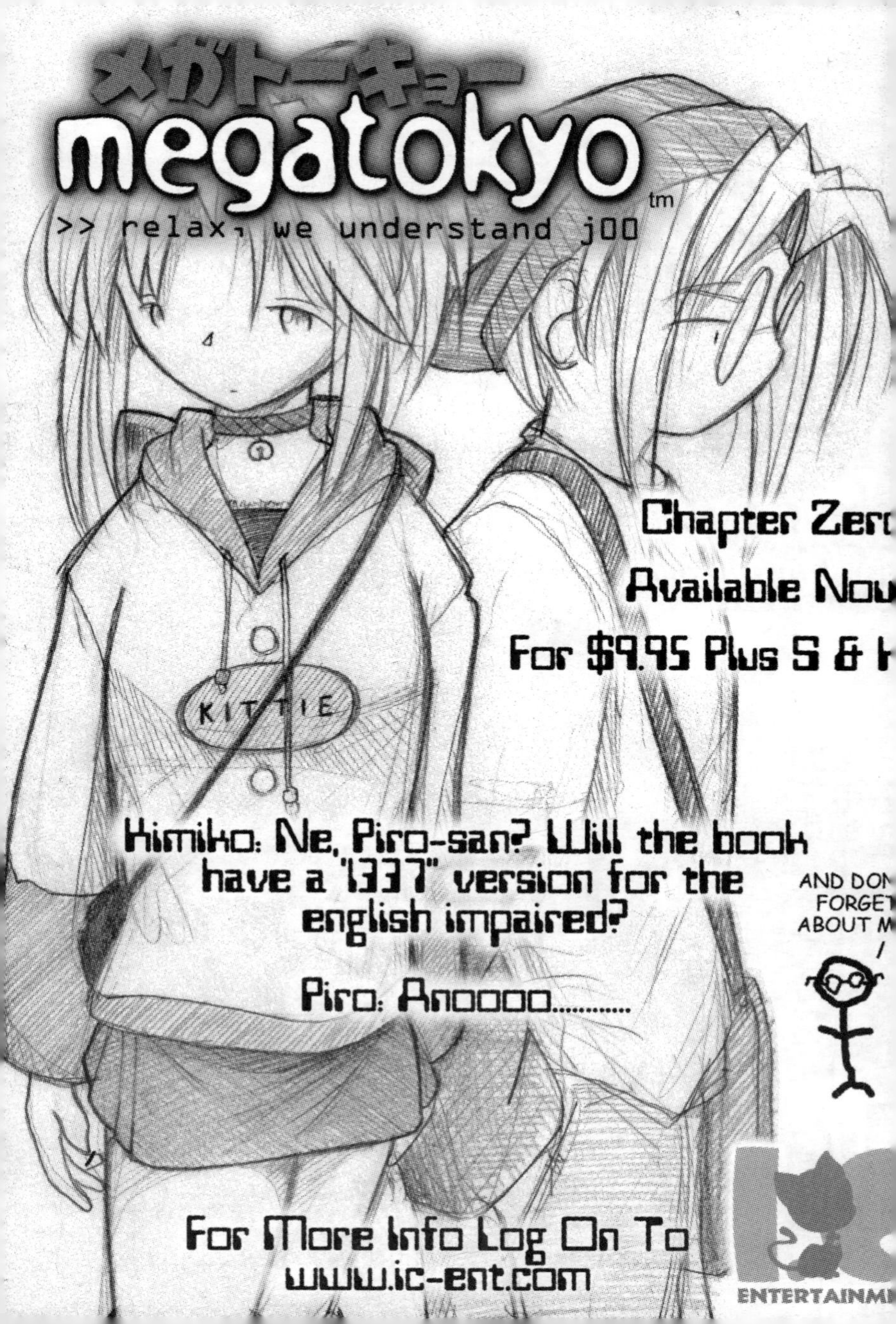

メガトーキョー
megatokyo
tm
>> relax, we understand j00
Chapter Zer
Available No
For $9.95 Plus S &
KITTIE
Kimiko: Ne, Piro-san? Will the book have a "1337" version for the english impaired?
Piro: Anoooo............
AND DON
FORGET
ABOUT M
For More Info Log On To
www.ic-ent.com
ENTERTAINM

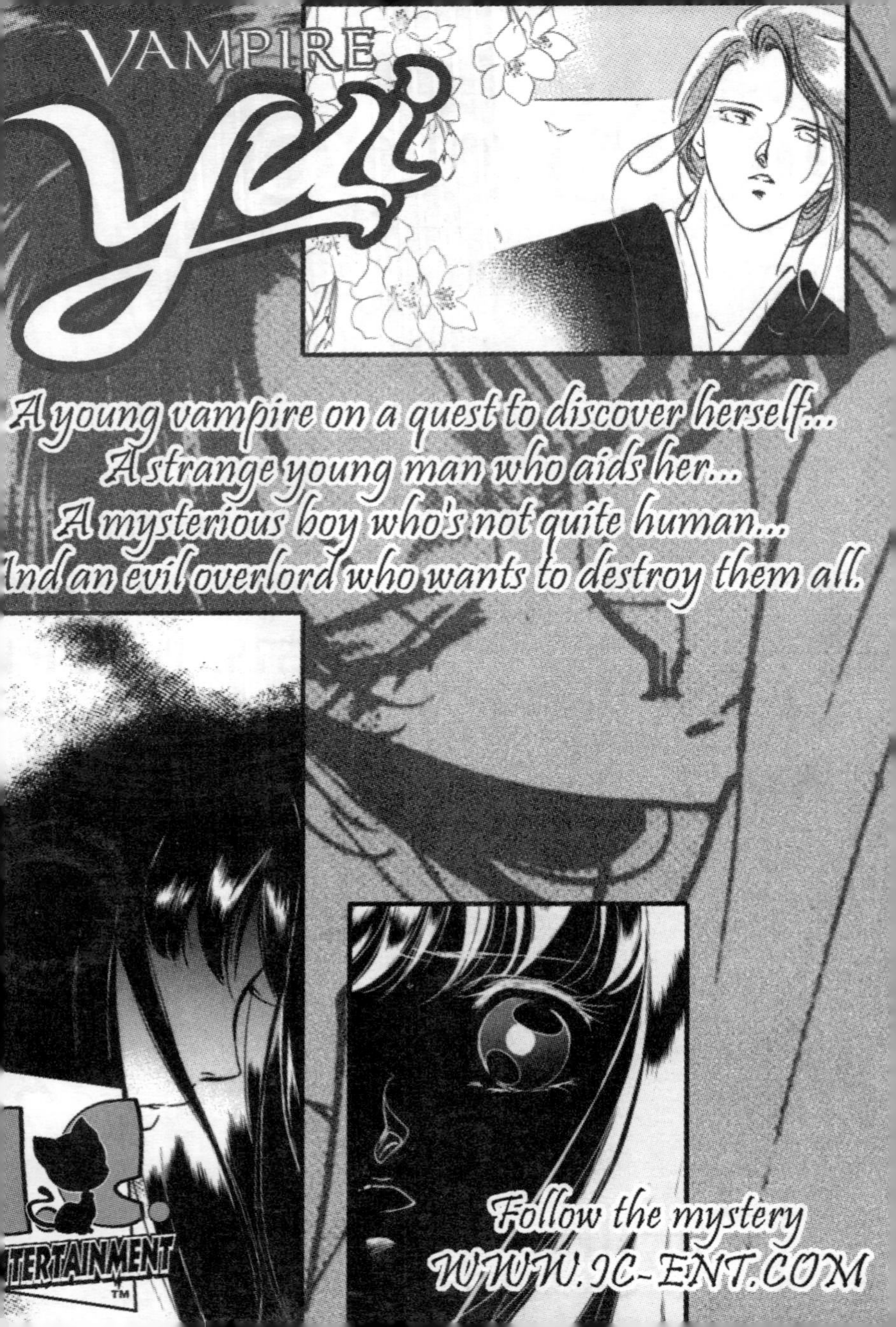
VAMPIRE
Yui
A young vampire on a quest to discover herself...
A strange young man who aids her...
A mysterious boy who's not quite human...
Ind an evil overlord who wants to destroy them all.
TERTAINMENT
TM
Follow the mystery
WWW.IC-ENT.COM